LANDSCAPES *of* MOVEMENT

Trails, Paths, and Roads in Anthropological Perspective

Penn Museum International Research Conferences
Holly Pittman, Series Editor, Conference Publications

Volume 1: Proceedings of "Landscapes of Movement:
Trails, Paths, and Roads in Anthropological Perspective"
Philadelphia, May 29–June 2, 2006

LANDSCAPES
of MOVEMENT
Trails, Paths, and Roads
in Anthropological Perspective

EDITED BY

James E. Snead
Clark L. Erickson
J. Andrew Darling

University of Pennsylvania Museum of Archaeology and Anthropology
Philadelphia

Contents

Figures

Tables

Penn Museum International Research Conferences

Foreword

For more than a century, a core mission of the University of Pennsylvania Museum of Archaeology and Anthropology has been to foster research that leads to new understandings about human culture. For much of the 20th century, this research took the form of worldwide expeditions that brought back both raw data and artifacts whose analysis continues to shed light on early complex societies of the New and Old worlds. The civilizations of pharonic Egypt, Mesopotamia, Iran, Greece, Rome, Mexico, Peru, and Native Americans are represented in galleries that display only the most remarkable of Penn Museum's vast holdings of artifacts. These collections have long provided primary evidence for many distinct research programs engaging scholars from around the world.

As we moved into a new century, indeed a new millennium, Penn Museum sought to reinvigorate its commitment to research focused on questions of human societies. In 2005, working with then Williams Director Richard M. Leventhal, Michael J. Kowalski, Chairman of the Board of Overseers of Penn Museum, gave a generous gift to the Museum to seed a new program of high-level conferences designed to engage themes central to the Museum's core research mission. According to Leventhal's vision, generating new knowledge and frameworks for understanding requires more than raw data and collections. More than ever, it depends on collaboration among communities of scholars investigating problems using distinct lines of evidence and different modes of analysis. Recognizing the importance of collaborative and multidisciplinary endeavors in the social sciences, Penn Museum used the gift to launch a program of International Research Conferences that each brought together ten to fifteen scholars who have reached a critical point in their consideration of a shared problem.

During the three years until the spring of 2008, it was my privilege to identify, develop, run, and now to oversee the publication of eight such conferences. The dozen or so papers for each conference were submitted to all participants one month in advance of the meeting. The fact that the papers were circulated beforehand meant that no time was lost introducing new material to the group. Rather, after each paper was briefly summarized by its author, an intense and extended critique followed that allowed for sustained consideration of the contribution that both the data and the argument made to the larger questions. The discussions of individual papers were followed by a day discussing crosscutting issues and concluded with an overarching synthesis of ideas.

Landscapes of Movement: Trails, Paths, and Roads in Anthropological Perspective was the first conference of the series, held in the spring of 2006. It is also the first to see publication. Over the next two years, more volumes will appear that consider such diverse topics as the Rise of the Maya State; Diplomatics of the Persian Language; the Evolution of Mind, Brain, and Culture; Mapping the Modern State of Mongolia; Gender Justice in the Islamic World; Kingship and Cosmos in Egypt and Mesopotamia; and Human Adaptation to Environmental Change. In each of these conferences, through intense face-to-face deliberations for three or four days and nights in a setting detached from the daily demands of their professional life, more than one hundred scholars were able to come to a more integrated grasp of their endeavor. The publication of the results of each of these conferences allows their new knowledge and understanding to be shared broadly and to contribute to the uniquely human enterprise of self understanding.

HOLLY PITTMAN
Series Editor
Deputy Director for Academic Programs,
Penn Museum, 2005–2008
Curator, Near East Section

Preface

When you set out for Ithaka
Ask that your way be long.

— C. P. Kafavy, "Ithaka" (translation)

This volume represents the results of the inaugural Penn Museum International Resesarch Conference, "Landscapes of Movement: Trails, Paths, and Roads in Anthropological Perspective." Organized by James E. Snead, Clark L. Erickson, and J. Andrew Darling, this conference took place at the Penn Museum May 29–June 2, 2006. Invited participants ranged from recent Ph.D.s to long-established scholars, all of whom shared a professional interest and personal preoccupation with the anthropology of moving through the landscape. The session that unfolded was genuinely collaborative in the way that can only be established by the continuity that begins at breakfast and ends with late-night conversations on the porch.

Our discussion began from the shared premise that trails, paths, and roads are the manifestation of human movement through the landscape and are central to an understanding of that movement at multiple scales. The study of these features connects with many intellectual domains, engaging history, geography, environmental studies, and, in particular, anthropology and its subfields. In the process we are developing a better understanding of infrastructure, social, political, and economic organization, cultural expressions of patterned movement, and the ways that trails, paths, and roads materialize traditional knowledge and engineering, world view, memory, and identity.

This volume emphasizes a critical balance between empirically based research and nuanced cultural understanding through context, ethnography, and history, collectively representing a new direction in the study of landscapes and human society. Our case studies range from simple to complex societies, prehistoric to contemporary, physical to metaphorical, and everyday to sacred. The authors are particularly concerned with the forms, functions, scale, boundaries, and meanings of movement within landscapes.

Specific themes addressed include labor energetics, technology, terrain characteristics, landscape features, facilities, access, interaction, ownership, and stewardship of networks of movement. Diverse scales of movement are also addressed, ranging from travel between home and fields to long-distance journeying. Some of the studies emphasize particular contexts, while others are synthetic and comparative. All reflect the heightened awareness produced by three days of living and working together, honing scholarship, and developing shared principles.

The editors would like to acknowledge, first, Michael J. Kowalski who provided funding. Richard Leventhal, then director of the Penn Museum, guided our plans from an early stage, and not only served as a congenial host but participated in many of the sessions and brought his own experience to bear on the topic. His successor, Richard Hodges, has maintained this commitment. Holly Pittman, coordinator of the International Research Conferences, pulled everything together with skill and grace, and supervised the complex arrangements needed to bring a dozen participants from all corners of the country. Robert Preucel sat in on a regular basis and proved a reliable sounding board. Louise Krasniewicz opened her home for a lively reception and is gratefully acknowledged. Superb technical assistance was provided by anthropology students Kristen Gardella and Leo Benitez. Walda Metcalf, former Director of Publications at the Penn Museum, coordinated the initial pre-publication process with a friendly, experienced hand, and two anonymous reviewers contributed useful critiques. This role was subsequently taken on by Jim Mathieu, who ably guided the volume to completion. The myriad production details were attended to by Jennifer Quick, who stepped in at a difficult moment and whose labors are greatly appreciated.

Thanks are also due to the participants, many of whom had signed on to the project when it was a more modest conference session and stayed with us while the final format was being developed. Discussant Tim Earle was a constant source of encouragement, as was Payson Sheets, both of whom had served on a panel discussing the archaeology of paths, trails, and roads some years ago and were enthusiastic supporters of a new generation of research and synthesis.

We decided to begin with a chapter written by the editors that provides a broad overview of issues associated with landscapes of movement with a particular focus on archaeology. This subject is notably balkanized, and this chapter is designed to summarize regional approaches, methodology, and theoretical strategies, as well as to outline the landscape perspective that is taken up in more detail by many of the following chapters. Each participant explored distinct theoretical terrain within this shared framework, providing a rich context for further thought and fieldwork.

A set of chapters on the American West begins with Chapter 2, "*Kukhepya:* Searching for Hopi Trails," by T. J. Ferguson, G. Lennis Berlin, and Leigh J. Kuwanwisiwma. Engaging empirical aspects of these trails and their role as cultural heritage, this work introduces many of the themes of the volume. In Chapter 3, "Trails of Tradition: Movement, Meaning, and Place," James Snead explores the landscape paradigm as it applies to the late precolumbian Pueblo trails, stairs, and entryways of New Mexico's Pajarito Plateau. In contrast, J. Andrew Darling describes larger-scale regional trails in Chapter 4, "O'odham Trails and the Archaeology of Space." Darling's focus on the ethnographic context of song and travel in the southern Southwest is complemented by Catherine S. Fowler's ethnohistoric approach to Mojave trails in Chapter 5, "Reconstructing Southern Paiute–Chemehuevi Trails in the Mojave Desert of Southern Nevada and California: Ethnographic Perspectives from the 1930s." A continued theme of cultural movement permeates Chapter 6, "From Path to Myth: Journeys and the Naturalization of Territorial Identity along the Missouri River," by María Nieves Zedeño, Kacy Hollenback, and Calvin Grinnell.

In Chapter 7, Angela Keller shifts attention away from North America and toward "complex" society, with "A Road by Any Other Name: Trails, Paths, and Roads in Maya Language and Thought." The deep ethnohistoric context available for the study of Maya roads contrasts with the more explicitly empirical study of Costa Rican paths discussed by Payson Sheets in Chapter 8, "When the Construction of Meaning Preceded the Meaning of Construction: From Footpaths to Monumental Entrances in Ancient Costa Rica." His proposal that diachronic study of these features allows us to examine aspects of sociopolitical complexity is also a theme of Chapter 9, "Emergent Landscapes of Movement in Early Bronze Age Northern Mesopotamia," by Jason Ur. The trackways associated with settlements and agricultural hinterlands that Ur describes provide an empirical case for many of the approaches developed in this volume. It forms a useful comparison with work in the Bolivian Amazon by Clark Erickson in Chapter 10, "Agency, Causeways, Canals, and the Landscapes of Everyday Life in the Bolivian Amazon," and by Clark Erickson and John Walker in Chapter 11, "Precolumbian Causeways and Canals as Landesque Capital." Both evaluate the complex built environment of seasonally inundated wetlands, first from the theoretical perspective of agency and then in terms of the aggregate effect of such an engineered landscape of movement on issues of settlement, agriculture, water management, and inherited control of land improvements.

The concluding section begins with Chapter 11, "Routes through the Landscape: A Comparative Approach," by Timothy Earle. Earle takes up themes outlined in his 1991 chapter on cross-cultural approaches to paths, trails, and roads, drawing from the studies published here. The information on which his arguments are based is presented in the appendices, a body of data designed to stimulate further discussion that brings the volume to a close.

1

Making Human Space:
The Archaeology of Trails, Paths, and Roads

JAMES E. SNEAD, CLARK L. ERICKSON,
AND J. ANDREW DARLING

Foi paths are the graphic effect of intentional,
creative movement across the earth. They transform the ground,
partition the earth and create human space . . .

— James Weiner, *The Empty Place: Poetry, Space,
and Being among the Foi of Papua New Guinea*

Trails, paths, and roads are essential structures of the human landscape. They weave together the disparate elements of daily lives, bridging distance and obstacles to connect us to each other. James Weiner's description of the paths made by the Foi people of New Guinea captures the complex relationships between space, place, and movement that these features articulate (1991). Trails, paths, roads, ways, tracks, trackways, and related phenomena represent *landscapes of movement,* a context for "getting there" that evolves through action and design, incorporating everything from the traces of daily strolls to the mailbox to continent-spanning superhighways. In the process their physical structures engage such diverse fields as engineering, knowledge systems, aesthetics, historical memory, and cosmology.

Despite their fundamental nature in structuring and reflecting human

---

Epigraph. 1991:38.

life, substantive treatments of these features are rare in the anthropological literature. "Few of these show on my maps," wrote T. T. Waterman in
his ethnogeography of the Yurok country of northern California, "because
I did not travel the trails myself" (1920:222). Ethnographies may explore
the varied semantic fields associated with such features—the metaphor
of the "path," in particular, is widely employed cross-culturally (cf. Evans
1999; Koskinen 1963; Toren 1999; Abercrombie 1998; Keller, Chapter 7, this
volume)—but rarely is such conceptual material complemented by a concern for the physical features themselves.

These circumstances have also characterized archaeological approaches
to trails, paths, and roads, but a handful of recent publications have demonstrated the potential for this research to contribute to broader discussions
of the human past. In the New World, John Hyslop's *The Inka Road System*
(1984; see also Hyslop 1991) used the dramatic archaeological evidence of
Inka roads to highlight the value of long-term regional archaeological research, a systematic survey field program, and careful use of historical and
ethnographic documents to build a detailed understanding of such critical infrastructure. Of even greater influence was *Ancient Road Networks and
Settlement Hierarchies in the New World,* which included diverse studies from
throughout the Americas (Trombold 1991a). This volume made the case
that trails, paths, and roads could be treated as built environment, amenable
to description, classification, analysis, and interpretation in much the same
way artifacts or architecture are treated in traditional archaeology. New
theoretical ground was also broken, as some authors sought ways to bring
trails, paths, and roads into larger explanatory structures of archaeological
theory, particularly in the context of cultural evolution (Earle 1991; Hassig
1991).

Even the successful application of archaeological strategies regarding
trails, paths, and roads as outlined by the Hyslop and Trombold volumes
highlighted the considerable challenges that further work would have to
overcome. Questions of definition and scale are particularly daunting. Our
traditional emphasis on sites and monuments is a poor fit for features that
cannot be reduced to points on a map or bounded spaces. By their nature,
trails, paths, and roads often have no beginning or end. The complex web-
like characteristics of local and regional scale networks of landscapes of
movement are difficult to map and bound as data. The discontinuous, seg-
mentary nature of archaeological landscapes of movement also confuses

and confounds. Even the most flexible research strategy breaks down when confronted with features that span continents and centuries.

Structures of archaeological knowledge present additional limitations on the study of trails, paths, and roads. Despite the universality of these features most research has been conducted in isolation, with rare cross-citation. Potentially productive insights and concepts thus either languish or are continually re-invented.

In the face of these daunting challenges, the rising influence of landscape theory in archaeology has provided the opportunity for a revolution in the study of trails, paths, and roads. The concept of landscape bridges methodological barriers and regional differences, creating a flexible analytical framework in which previously overlooked archaeological data can be seamlessly integrated into a broader discussion (e.g., Anschuetz, Wilshusen, and Scheick 2001; Ashmore 2003; Ashmore and Knapp 1999; Bender 1993; Bender and Winer 2001; David and Wilson 2002; Feld and Basso 1996; Hirsch and O'Hanlon 1995; Low and Lawrence-Zuniga 2002; Rodman 1992; Tilley 1994, 2003; Ucko and Layton 1999; Wilkinson 2003). The lens of landscape focuses our attention on issues of pattern, scale, context, and association, all critical components of movement, without mandating a particular structure for each category. In a landscape sense, both the path to the corner and the superhighway are *meaningful,* each a part of the broader context.

Taking a new look at trails, paths, and roads is thus a logical outgrowth of the paradigm shift towards the archaeology of landscape. Movement is a central component of many of the influential landscape studies of the past two decades (e.g., Barrett 1999a, 1999b; Thomas 1996), although the topic is seldom treated in detail. Peter Fowler, however, argues that movement is essential to the "dynamism" of landscape itself (1998:25), a primary theme both of Heather Miller's "landscapes of transportation" (2006:28) and Pierce Lewis's "landscapes of mobility" (1996).

We contend that the next step in building the framework for landscapes of movement is the thorough establishment of context, with all the intricate cultural and material details that this implies. One particular strength of the landscape approach to the study of trails, paths, and roads is that it sidesteps questions of their definitions. Landscapes of movement imply a focus on pattern, scale, context, and association incorporating the fabric of the features themselves. These articulations ultimately provide a much stronger source for inference and interpretation, making the question of whether something is a "trail," "path," or "road" largely irrelevant.

GLOBAL PERSPECTIVES: A BRIEF REVIEW

A brief review of the more recent archaeological literature on trails, paths, and roads highlights the considerable value in this work, both in terms of the aggregate data available and on the different approaches adopted (for overviews, see Morriss 2005; Scarre 1996). The older literature remains useful reading, both in terms of the evidence itself and in the structures of knowledge that produced it (Addison 1980; Brew 1950; Ayres 1940; Myer 1929; McClintock 1910; Timperley and Brill 1965).

Formal study of landscapes of movement has the longest history in the greater Mediterranean region, where generations of scholars have documented networks of roads associated with the Roman Empire (Chevallier 1976; Staccioli 2004; Vermeulen and Antrop 2001). These studies are traditionally topographic in nature, identifying routes and contexts of Roman roads in intricate detail. This research is most advanced in the former imperial core, and researchers working in Italy have synthesized archaeological and textual data from many of the famous imperial *viae* (for example, the Via Appia, Della Portella 2004; the Via Severiana, Fogagnolo and Valenti 2005; the Via Claudia Augusta, Galliazo 2002), as well as secondary routes in the Italian countryside (Fredricksen and Ward-Perkins 1957; Kahane, Threipland, and Ward-Perkins 1968). Some recent research focuses on technical aspects of road building (Capedri 2003) and on roads associated with particular types of activity, such as quarrying (Vanhove 1996). On the whole interpretative treatment of the Roman road network at large scale remains documentary and conservative, a situation echoed by research on their Etruscan predecessors (Barker and Rasmussen 1998:172; Potter 1979: 79–81) (for exceptions, see Laurence 1999; Bell, Wilson, and Wickham 2002; Vermuelen and Antrop 2001).

Road studies are also numerous from the former Roman provinces. The Northern European literature is extensive, including general syntheses (Crawford 1953; Davies 2002; Margary 1967) and studies of particular routes and regions (e.g., Dowdle 1987; Fowler 2000; Matthews 2002; Vermeulen and Antrop 2001). Anatolia and the Levant are other areas where significant attention has been paid to Roman roads, both the inter-regional routes (e.g., Fischer, Isaac, and Roll 1996; French 1981, 1996; Graf 1995, 1997; Kennedy and Riley 1990; MacDonald 1996; Savage, Zamora, and Keller 2002; Van Liere and Lauffray 1954) and connectors (e.g., Ben-David 2002; Borstad 2000; Comfort, Abadie-Reynal, and Ergeç 2000; Comfort and Ergeç 2001; Isaac and Roll 1982; Kennedy 1997; Roll 2002; Strobel 1997).

Research on landscapes of movement for earlier Mediterranean periods has been less systematic. A body of research on road systems dating as early as the Aegean Bronze Age does exist (i.e., Jansen 2001; Lavery 1990, 1995; Mylonas 1966). Field documentation of Classical Greek roads, part of a generations-long topographical program (Pikoulas 1999; Pritchett 1980; Young 1956), is rapidly expanding, with several recent dissertations that address the subject (Bynum 1995; Lolos 1998; Marchand 2002).

A similar situation exists for the pre-Roman Near East, where reconnaissance and studies based on texts or artifact style are the rule (Birmingham 1961; Dearman 1997; Dorsey 1991; Garstang 1943; Kloner and Ben-David 2003; McDonald 1988; Sevin 1988). The Achaemenid road system, famous in its day (Briant 1996), has stimulated relatively little archaeological research, although the situation is changing (Graf 1994; French 1998; Tal 2005) and new excavations at a road station possibly used by Achaemenid elites promise interesting results (Potts et al. 2007). Relatively few systematic studies of landscapes of movement at a large scale have been conducted in the region, making the recent contributions of Jason Ur (2003, 2004; Chapter 9, this volume) and Tony Wilkinson (1993, 2003) on Bronze Age roads in Syria and Mesopotamia particularly valuable (Borstad 2000; Blakely and Sauer 1985). The Egyptian case is distinct, since in many cases the Pharaonic, Ptolemaic, and Roman period road networks coincide (Gates 2005a, 2005b; Jackson 2002; Sidebotham and Zitterkopf 1995; Sidebotham, Zitterkopf, and Riley 1991; Wright 2003). Studies more explicitly focused on the Pharaonic period and earlier also exist (Darnell 2002; Darnell and Darnell 2002; Fenwick 2004; Hester, Hobler, and Russell 1970).

Information on the trails, paths and roads of prehistoric Europe is based on rigorous field archaeology. Studies of "barrow roads" in the Netherlands (Bakker 1976; Jager 1985) and on cursus features in Britain (Barrett 1994:137; Barrett, Bradley, and Green 1990; Johnston 1999) have documented the close association between particular forms of movement and monumental architecture. Evidence preserved in relict upland landscapes in Britain (Fleming 1988, 1998; Fowler 2000) and south-central France (Fowler 1998) reflects patterns of local travel over long periods of time. Similar inferences have been derived from studies of preserved trackways in wetland environments (Casparie 1987; Coles and Coles 1986; Raftery 1990; Thomas and Rackham 1996).

Archaeological study of landscapes of movement elsewhere in Eurasia remains embryonic (Chakrabarti 2005; Hiebert 1999; Miller 2006; UNESCO 2004). Work is expanding in several areas, however, including road networks associated with the Khmer polity in Southeast Asia (Bruguier 2000; Coe 2003:152: Hendrickson 2007, 2008; Im 2004). Despite significant ethnohistoric evidence (e.g., Falola 1991), roads and paths in West Africa have yet to be the subject of archaeological research. Descriptions of deeply incised trails associated with the Ife earthworks (Darling 1984:12), references to the "royal roads" built by the Asante kings of Kumase (McLeod 1981: 20), and formal stairways in the Mandara Mountains of Cameroon and Nigeria (Sterner 2003) indicate considerable opportunity for archaeological fieldwork, as do scattered notations in the southern Africa literature (e.g., Dierks 1992; Kinahan 1986).

The medieval and historic periods represent a final area of concern for Old World research on trails, paths, and roads. Associated studies include broad regional overviews (Guest 2005; Hindle 1993, 1998; Ferreira Priegue 1988) as well as detailed landscape studies (Fleming 1998) and examinations of specific features (Gibson 2007; Pasztor et al. 2000). Relatively little archaeological attention has been directed toward the growth of regional transportation networks in Europe during more recent centuries, but this is changing (e.g., Quartermaine, Trinder, and Turner 2003).

Turning to the New World, research on landscapes of movement in Latin America has largely been associated with precolumbian states and empires. Hyslop's groundbreaking research on the Inka roads was preceded by others (Kosok 1965; Regal 1936; Stothert-Stockman 1967; Strube 1963; Ubbeloedde Doering 1966; Von Hagen 1979). In more recent decades, there have been numerous detailed studies that either fill in gaps in coverage of the main imperial network (Castro et al. 2004; Gutiérrez 2005; Gutiérrez and Jaimes 2000; Hocquenghem 1994; Hyslop 1990; Hyslop and Rivera 1985; Niemeyer and Rivera 1983; Raffino 1993; Sanhueza Tohá 2004; Stehberg, Carvajal, and Seguel 1996; Stehberg and Cabeza 1991; Stehberg and Carvajal 1986; Espinoza 2002), discuss roads in the context of the complex landscape of the Inka capital of Cuzco (Bauer 1998), or examine specific local or provincial routes (Coello R. 2000; Kendall 2000; Lynch 1993, 1996; Protzen 1993). Studies of Pre-Inka road systems for the Wari (Isbell and Vranich 2004; McEwan 1987; Schreiber 1984, 1991, 1992) and Moche (Beck 1979, 1991), and other cultures (Wallace 1991) show that Andean peoples have a long history of roadbuilding. Most studies emphasize economic and political aspects of trails, paths, and roads; but a substantial body of literature emphasizes ritual movement in the Andean context (Aveni 1990; Bauer 1998; Bauer and Dearborn 1995; Clarkson 1990; Dearborn and Bauer 1996; Hawkins 1969, 1974; Mejia Xesspe 1939; Morrison 1978; Zuidema 1964), in addition to a growing body of literature on roads of the colonial Andes (Amodio, Navarrete, and Rodriguez 1997; Moreno and Gonzales 1995; Abercrombie 1998).

Interest in indigenous landscapes of movement beyond the central Andes has recently expanded, including preliminary studies on precolumbian trails, paths, and roads in the Atacama desert of Chile (Briones, Nuñez, and Standen 2005; Clarkson and Briones 2002, 2001; Valenzuela 2004; Bowman 1924), Colombia (Botero Páez, Vélez Escobar, and Guingue Valencia 2000; Cardale de Schrimpff 1996, 2000a, 2000b; Groot de Mahecha 2000; Herrera and Cardale del Schrimpff 2000; Oyuela-Caycedo 1990; Vidal and Zucchi 2000), and lowland Ecuador (Lippi 2000). New research in the Amazon Basin (Bengtsson and Avilés 2000; Erickson 2000c, 2001; Heckenberger 2005, 2008; Heckenberger et al. 2007) has significantly transformed our views of roads, paths, and trails in this difficult terrain (also see Silverman and Isbell 2008).

In Mesoamerica and the Intermediate Area, formal research on landscapes of movement remains relatively sparse, despite the significant archaeological remains present and despite early attention to this question (e.g., Saville 1930; Villa-Rojas 1936) and provocative ideas developed by research based on ethnography and indigenous documents (Bolles and Folan 2001; Castillo 1969; Genotte 2001; Jett 1994; Keller 2006; Reina A. 1998). The literature is most comprehensive on the subject of Maya *sakbeh* (summarized in Shaw 2001), with a particular emphasis on those features connecting different areas within or adjacent to major centers (i.e., Charlton 1991; Chase and Chase 2001; Cobos and Winemiller 2001; Folan 1991; Folan et al. 2001; Keller 2006), plus examination of *sakbeob* (pl. of *sakbeh*) on a more regional level (Kurjack and Andrews 1976; Reid 1995; Shaw 2008). Rare examples from highland Mesoamerica beyond the Maya region indicate potential opportunities (Gorenstein and Pollard 1991; Hirth 1991; Trombold 1991c). Fieldwork conducted by Payson Sheets in Costa Rica (McKee, Sever, and Sheets 1994; Sheets and Sever 1991; Sheets, Chapter 8, this volume) also points the way towards new studies of precolumbian roads in this region, as do examinations of historic period roads (Ng 2007; Ng and Cackler 2006).

Early fieldwork on landscapes of movement in western North America emphasized secondary data such as trade goods (e.g., Davis 1963; Sample 1950) and some field reconnaissance (Britt 1973; Colton 1964; Eiseman 1959; Harner 1957; Hindes 1959; Howard 1959; Ives 1946; Johnson and Johnson 1957; Rogers 1966). Intensive fieldwork followed, greatly enriching our understanding of local context (Becker and Altschul 2008; Pigniolo, Underwood, and Cleland 1997; Von Werlhof 1988; Waters 1982). In a similar fashion early fieldwork on paths and trails in the Great Plains and Northern Rockies (Malouf 1962) stimulated continuing study, producing among other things an entire issue of *Archaeology in Montana* (1980; see also Blakeslee and Blasing 1988; Campbell and Field 1968).

The influence of intensive survey projects on the study of trails, paths, and roads is particularly evident in the American Southwest. The famous Chaco roads, for example, were known only via brief comments before the launching of major survey research in the 1970s (Gabriel 1991; Hurst, Severance, and Davidson 1993; Kantner 1997; Kincaid 1983; Lekson 1999; Marshall 1997; Mathien 1991; Pattison 1985; Roney 1992; Schreiber 1997; Severance 1999; Snygg and Windes 1998; Stein 1983; Stein and McKenna 1988; Van Dyke 2008; Vivian 1997a, 1997b; Windes 1991). Despite a few earlier suggestions (e.g., Hartmann and Hartmann 1979; Steen 1977), systematic fieldwork on other Southwest paths, roads, and trails largely postdates the Chaco work (Adams et al. 1989; Becker and Altschul 2008; Darling, Chapter 4, this volume; Darling and Eiselt 2003; Motsinger 1998; Ferguson, Berlin, and Kuwanwisiwma, Chapter 2, this volume; Pattison and Potter 1977; Pitezel 2007; Snead 2002, Chapter 3, this volume; Snead and Preucel 1999; Swanson 2003). Trail studies drawing from ethnographic knowledge are increasingly influential, with detailed studies such as Stephen Jett's research on Navajo trails at Canyon de Chelly (2001), various projects associated with the Zuni Salt Lake (Berlin, Ferguson and Hart 1985; Ferguson, Berlin, and Hart 1995; Hart and Othole 1993), and research at Hopi (Ferguson, Berlin, and Kuwanwisiwma, Chapter 2, this volume; Zedeño 1997) demonstrating new opportunities.

Only a few research initiatives on trails, paths, and roads can be cited from elsewhere in North America. Formal features associated with the Hopewell culture of the Ohio River valley have recently attracted considerable comment and await more comprehensive fieldwork (Lepper 1995, 1996). A few studies of other precolumbian paths and trails in this region exist (Kapches 1992; Myers 1997). New North American initiatives emphasize the historic period, where interest in more recent roads and road networks has increased (Fisher 1999; Purser 1988; Raitz 1996; Schlereth 1997).

Oceania is a final area that has stimulated research on landscapes of movement. Fieldwork on roads and paths in Hawaii have benefited from ethnohistory (Apple 1965; Kaschko 1973; Mills 2002), and references to these features are intrinsic to discussions of the intricate archaeological record of the islands (e.g., Kirch 1992). Two recent studies, one focusing on Rapa Nui (Lipo and Hunt 2005) and the other on Raratonga (Campbell 2006), demonstrate the diversity of evidence for constructed roads in Polynesia. In the case of Micronesia, unpublished reports of trail features on Kosrae (Beardsley 2006) suggest that further fieldwork would pay considerable dividends. Evaluation of Aboriginal trails and paths in Australia draws heavily from the extensive literature on dreamtime or "The Dreaming" (e.g., Goodale 2003; Myers 1986, 1991; Price-Williams and Gaines 1994; Spencer and Gillen 1968; Tonkinson 2003). Archaeologists and ethnographers relate "dreaming tracks" to cognitive geography and routes of ceremonial and economic exchange (Glowczewski 2000 as reviewed in Lohmann 2004; Smith and Burke 2007:42–46).

This brief foray into the archaeological literature on landscapes of movement is not intended to be exhaustive, and is biased towards English-language sources. Nonetheless, the volume of research on trails, paths, and roads is clearly sufficient for this topic to be treated holistically. Scholars following these paths have adopted many different methodological and theoretical strategies, to which we next turn our attention.

METHODOLOGY

The complex palimpsest and often ephemeral evidence for landscapes of movement require distinct methods from those of traditional site-based archaeology. Some approaches inevitably derive from local topography, environment, and culture history; but some broad trends are evident. We will briefly review these here, with allusion to projects that make particularly lucid case studies.

Reconnaissance Survey

The traditional method for exploring trails, paths, and roads in the archaeological record is to follow them. Many scholars have noted that the logic of travel in particular settings is only evident on foot (e.g., Lynch 1993; Bell, Wilson, and Wickham 2002:185; Hyslop 1984). Simply walking a trail, of course, implies that it is there to be seen, not a trivial issue in most situations. Modern environment, terrain, and boundary issues present considerable obstacles, and walking a Maya *sakbeh* or an Amazonian causeway today requires considerable expertise with a machete. In some instances, linear arrangements of contemporaneous sites alone have been argued to reflect the presence of roads or paths (MacDonald 1988:212). An additional challenge is to link the road underfoot to a particular time period of construction and use. Much of the literature on road networks of the Eastern Desert of Egypt, for instance, focuses on identifying the builders and users of these systems, since there is often little physical modification of the routes themselves to interpret (compare Gates 2005a, 2005b; Sidebotham, Zitterkopf, and Riley 1991; Wright 2003).

Intensive Survey

Intensive pedestrian survey establishes the material context for human activities at increasingly greater scale, allowing associations to be made between multiple categories of evidence (Crumley and Marquardt 1987; Darvill 1999; Plog 1990). This approach has proven essential for the study of landscapes of movement because it emphasizes physical and temporal context at multiple scales and time periods. Thus, archaeologists can identify not only potential beginnings and endpoints of routes and their specific character, but also what they pass along the way. In the case of the trails of the Pajarito Plateau of the American Southwest, the results of a major site survey project (Powers and Orcutt 1999b) not only identified trails but also the thousands of features associated with them in the landscape, providing a deeper context within which movement along them in different eras could be evaluated (Snead 2002; Van Zandt 1999).

Of course, even the largest survey areas have arbitrary boundaries, and inevitably trails, paths, and roads will cross these and disappear into the distance. Surveys are scale-dependent, and relatively few operate at the macro level required to understand regional and interregional routes. In traditional archaeology, contextualizing landscapes of movement will remain a relatively localized option for the foreseeable future.

Remote Sensing

Our appreciation of landscapes of movement has been revolutionized by remote sensing. The aerial reconnaissance of the mid-20th century opened up new frontiers for road studies in various places, such as Rome's eastern frontier (Van Liere and Lauffray 1954–55; Kennedy 1982), the Peruvian coast (Kosok 1965), and Central America (Sheets and Sever 1991). Remote sensing allows for the identification of routes of movement in terrain that is difficult to survey, either due to topography, vegetation, or access (Lepper 1996; Madry 1987; Vermuelen and Antrop 2001).

Satellite imagery has added a potent tool to the remote sensing of trails, paths, and roads, a potential demonstrated by recent work in the Iraqi-Syrian Jezira by Jason Ur and Tony Wilkinson (Wilkinson 1993, 2003; Ur 2003, 2004, Chapter 9, this volume). Using CORONA satellite imagery, they have documented a particular form of "trackway" associated with settlements of the 3rd millennium BC, numbering in the thousands and clearly a major structural element of the Bronze Age countryside. This approach not only demonstrates the technical utility of a particular remote sensing platform but also breaks important new ground by using GIS to integrate such data and to use it to query interpretive models of Bronze Age society in the Near East.

Geographic Information Systems (GIS)

Study of landscapes of movement is one of the many aspects of archaeological research that has been transformed by the use of Geographical Information Systems (GIS). At one level, GIS analysis provides the opportunity to predict the course of trails, paths, and roads on the basis of topography when physical evidence for these features is lacking. Calculating such "cost pathways" is an increasingly common way to model movement through the countryside (Bell and Lock 2000; Bell, Wilson, and Wickham 2002; Frachetti 2006, 2008; Gaffney and Stancic 1996; Madry and Crumley 1990; Madry and Rakos 1996; Wiedemann, Antrop, and Vermuelen 2001).

For example, John Kantner's GIS study of Chaco roads (1997) tested the orientation of these features against a "rational" pattern of travel across the landscape. His demonstration that the Chaco roads of Lobo Mesa, New Mexico, were a poor "fit" for the model supports inferences that they were more than purely functional routes. In addition, Kantner was able to infer the presence of what may have been more functional pathways linking different Chaco sites, a contention supported by the presence of particular types of archaeological features along those routes. A second generation of GIS research on landscapes of movement is now emerging, which is more theoretical in orientation (Brett 2007; Harris 2000; Llobera 1996, 2000). As these approaches develop, some of the strictures of the "least cost" approach will be shed and more truly social models constructed.

Excavation

Despite the fact that trails, paths, and roads are notoriously difficult to excavate, a number of recent studies demonstrate that subsurface testing provides useful information. These include the Costa Rican pathways studied by Payson Sheets and his team, where excavation has revealed both the structure of the routes themselves and, through association with various layers of volcanic tephra, provided dates for their period of use (Sheets, Chapter 8, this volume). In the case of constructed features, testing can not only supply stylistic and chronological information but also contribute toward studies of construction and energetics, and an understanding of features associated with trails, paths, and roads (e.g., Cardale de Schrimpf 1996:161; Erickson 2000c, Chapter 10, this volume; Loendorf and Brownell 1980; Vermeulen and Antrop 2001).

A spectacular example of excavation in the context of landscapes of movement is provided by work in the Somerset Levels of southwestern England conducted over many field seasons by John Coles, Briony Coles, and their team (Coles and Coles 1986). Wooden trackways of a variety of construction types and ages have been unearthed in these drained wetlands, including the 1800-m-long "Sweet Track" dated to the late 4th millennium BC. Their detailed evidence has led them to numerous hypotheses about local and regional movement during this era, including construction and reconstruction strategy, labor allocation, and patterns of mobility in the landscape (Raftery 1990; Casparie 1987). Little of this information would have been available without excavation.

Additional Approaches

Other methods have been employed by archaeologists studying landscapes of movement. Many of these are adopted in the relative absence of specifically archaeological data, intended to model possibilities as much as to document realities. Thus the network analyses of routes in Central Mexico presented by William Santley (1991) is developed in the apparent absence of material evidence for actual routes of travel (see also Gorenflo and Bell 1991; Jenkins 2001). Graph analysis has been applied to the study of Roman roads using textual evidence for their routes (Graham 2006). Other potential methods for the study of trails, paths, and roads, such as space syntax, which uses a formal spatial grammar to define accessibility (Hillier and Hanson 1984), are rarely put into practice.

THEORETICAL AND INTERPRETIVE PERSPECTIVES

Studies of trails, paths, and roads increasingly draw on anthropological and archaeological theory, using landscapes of movement as components of broader discussions on the nature of the human past. These approaches are diverse, reflecting various research problems and intellectual trajectories. Here we profile several schools of thought that have either been influential on current research or show promise for the future.

Political Economy

Landscapes of movement "move" things, including people, livestock, and material goods. Such movement can reflect tribute, trade, and other elements that make political systems work. Interpreting trails, paths, and roads through the lens of political economy thus has a long history. In many related studies, this focus is implicit rather than explicit, but several scholars have drawn attention to the ways that our understanding of sociopolitical systems can be enhanced by considering the structure of movement (e.g., Ur, Chapter 9, this volume).

The work of Ross Hassig has been particularly influential in the incorporation of data from trails, paths, and roads into a discussion of political economy (1985, 1991). By developing a materialist model of transport costs in Central Mexico, Hassig identifies changing patterns of political integration and the mobilization across the late precolumbian/Colonial boundary. Some influential studies of Maya *sakbeob* examine how these features establish hegemony and control, whether on a local scale, as at the site of Cara-col (Chase and Chase 2001), or on a more regional level, as David Friedel and colleagues have interpreted the 100-km causeway connecting the Maya centers of Cobá and Yaxuna (Ambrosino et al. 2003; cf. Shaw 2001, 2008).

The integrative effects of trails, paths, and roads have also been used to question models of economic and political self-sufficiency. Peter Mills, for instance, suggests that the evidence for roads and paths connecting differ-ent *ahupua'a* on the island of Hawaii implies that interaction between these social/economic units may have been more common than traditionally thought (2002; Lee 2002). The relationship between political transforma-tion and the reorganization of landscapes of movement has been detailed for the Roman case by Jason Dowdle, using data from the influential Bur-gundian Landscapes project (1987), a case that is made by Erickson and Walker, Sheets, and Ur (Chapters 11, 8, and 9, respectively, this volume).

Phenomenology and Spatial Theory

Since the 1990s, phenomenological approaches to landscapes have had considerable influence. Drawing from a diverse range of 20th century theo-rists, these strategies are built on the principle that the human body is the principal, shared element in our *experience* of our surroundings (e.g., Casey 1996; Thomas 1993, 1996; Tilley 1994, 2004). Focus must thus be placed on how landscape shapes relationships through sight, sound, and feeling. As Julian Thomas observes, "The quality of place emerges out of the way in which spaces are inhabited by human bodies, gaining in familiarity through interpretation and sensuous experience" (1998:87). Culturalized spaces have a concrete reality and are formed by the interaction of human experience in Nature and ideology (Lefebvre 1991; Soja 1989).

The relevance of phenomenology for landscapes of movement has been most carefully articulated in Christopher Tilley's *A Phenomenology of Landscape* (1994; 2004), in which paths play a central role. "Paths," he writes, "form an essential medium for the routing of social relations, connecting up spatial impressions with temporally-inscribed memories" (1994:31). In the context of the British Neolithic, which is his particular concern, paths would have linked settlements and monuments and thus played a critical role in how these places were approached, effectively creating a "narrative" of experience.

Critiques of archaeological applications of phenomenology have appeared which express skepticism that we can actually share experience with our predecessors (Brück 1998; Fleming 1999). The passing of time and transformation of the landscape makes it certain that what they saw and what we see along the way are not the same thing. The idea that experience is in itself a social construct has recently been emphasized (cf. Myers 2000), generating additional difficulty in understanding experiences of people in other societies through the archaeological record.

With such caveats in mind, phenomenology has obvious utility for the study of trails, paths, and roads (e.g., Chadwick 2004). For instance, a phenomenology of Roman roads has recently been applied in Italy (Laurence 1999) and Britain (Matthews 2002; Witcher 1998), and to the Chaco roads (Van Dyke 2008). Ultimately, phenomenology and related spatial approaches inform us about alternate cultural systems of managing geographic information. These include song geographies (Darling, Chapter 4, this volume), the representation of social relations through metaphors of space, place, and paths (Myers 1986; Parmentier 1987:114–16), and the role of cognitive maps in wayfinding, particularly in unfamiliar environments (Golledge 2003; Bender 2001).

Practice Theory and Structuration

Poststructural approaches of social theory have influenced contemporary archaeology, providing powerful tools for understanding the dynamics, production, and reproduction of culture (e.g., Hodder and Preucel 1996). Practice theory (Bourdieu 1977) and structuration theory (Giddens 1984) provide explanatory frameworks for teasing out the complex recursive relationship between human agency and structure. Trails, paths, and roads are the creation of human agency and result from the physical alterations of landscape through the practice of everyday life. Once established, these same features structure the everyday life of agents by channeling their movement through physical structures that either enhance or inhibit circulation (Erickson, Chapter 10, this volume).

Although not explicitly applying practice theory, Tim Ingold's (1993, 2000) concept of taskscape and sensitive landscape perspective captures the interrelationship between movement, work, the seasonal cycle, and environmental transformation producing a highly patterned rural countryside, which in turn provides the mental and physical template for proper existence. Cynthia Robin (2002) applies practice theory to understand circulation and gendered movement of farmers in small-scale landscapes of precolumbian Maya households and their rural surroundings in Belize.

Ethnogeography

The utility of ethnographic discussions of trails, paths, and roads for the interpretation of archaeological evidence is increasingly clear. Not only do these sources provide literal sources for comparison about patterns of movement in different cultural settings, but they also contain considerable information about the significance and perception of such movement from an inside perspective (Abercrombie 1998; Brody 1981; Myers 1986; Nabokov 1981; Parmentier 1987). Ethnographic perspectives on landscapes of movement derive from various perspectives but in particular require working with indigenous concepts of space and place, and thus *ethnogeography* (Fowler, Chapter 5, this volume; Zedeño, Hollenback, and Grinnell, Chapter 6, this volume).

A recent example of the ethnogeographic approach is Stephen Jett's study of Navajo trails at Canyon de Chelly in northeastern Arizona (2001). This research places these features in context, with detailed descriptions of trail fabric and structure seasoned by discussion of the conceptual role of these features in Navajo culture. Such approaches need not be restricted to "non-Western" settings, since in a sense all pasts can be treated ethnographically. For instance, linguistic approaches to Maya roads (Keller, Chapter 7, this volume) are paralleled by work on movement terminology in classical languages. Yannis Lolos has summarized ancient Greek words for roads, paths, and related features, developing a frame of reference that can inform topographic research undertaken on landscapes of movement from that era (2003; Gates 2005a). Echoes of ethnogeography in other works about travel in the pre-modern Old World (e.g., Adams and Laurence 2001; Strassberg 1994) and cross-cultural studies from anthropologists such as Mary Helms (1988) are particularly useful for comparative study.

Other Theoretical Approaches

The utility of studying trails, paths, and roads in archaeological contexts can be seen in the numerous additional theoretical perspectives that have been employed in their interpretation. Such studies have been used as elements of broader cultural-evolutionary arguments, most influentially by Timothy Earle, whose cross-cultural analysis of organization and labor investment in landscapes of movement is widely cited (1991; Chapter 12, this volume). Carl Lipo and Terry Hunt (2003) analyze the "quarry roads" of Rapa Nui society from a selectionist perspective.

Diverse, "post-processual" viewpoints on trails, paths, and roads are increasingly common. Matthew Campbell argues that the particular significance of the Ara Metua road that once encircled Raratonga was in providing structure to ritual and memory (2006:107). The symbolic role of trails, paths, and roads has been given significance in several recent archaeological interpretations (cf. Snead, Chapter 3, this volume). The Chaco roads, which have been argued to primarily serve as a "cosmological" organization of landscape, are a good example (Marshall 1997; Sofaer, Marshall, and Sinclair 1989; Vivian 1997b).

CULTURAL HERITAGE

In the late 20th century, the presence of trails, paths, and roads in cultural landscapes came to the attention of land managers, who then grappled with associated issues of preservation, interpretation, and cultural heritage. Understanding how people moved through the country bears a direct relationship to the role that landscape played in a given social context, which in the modern era is potent information for establishing rights and obligations. Such information can also be culturally sensitive, even proprietary, since in many cases trails, paths, and roads remain in use for ritual practices, as mnemonic devices, and symbols of identity, all evidence that movement continues to be a political act (Ferguson, Berlin, and Kuwanwisiwma, Chapter 2, this volume).

Landscapes of movement have also become an important element of heritage tourism. Some well-known and maintained pathways in the British Isles are based on indigenous tracks, and such historical associations are part of the walker's experience (Johnson 2007). The popularity of initiatives directed at historic routes in North America such as the "National Road" (Raitz 1996) and the Camino Real between Mexico City and Santa Fe, New Mexico (Marshall 1991; Palmer 1993), indicates the public's perception of their importance. Various documentary, commemorative, and interpretive strategies have resulted. Roads were the theme of Kansas archaeology month in 2006, for instance, with associated teaching materials and outreach programs (Irvin and Cooper 2006). Both the Eurasian Silk Road and the primary Inka roads are the subject of international heritage initiatives (UNESCO 2004; Espinosa 2002).

The challenge with any landscape-oriented interpretive scheme aimed at the public is to establish the web of associations inherent in such a context. The "Santa Fe National Historic Trail" is essentially a network of separate installations dispersed across the Central Plains of the United States, unified (at least in theory) by their historic connectivity (Simmons 2001) but separated by the vast tracts of modern America. Every year thousands of tourists follow the Inka Trail to Machu Picchu and, increasingly, the Imperial Inka road network; but they probably do not envision the trip as it once was, a route lined with estates, administrative centers, waystations, and villages and traveled by messengers and laden llama caravans (Espinoza 2002). Instead, the trip engages the romance of hidden ruins in the jungle and high Andes, certainly an evocative journey but one that evokes European romanticism rather than Inka landscape organization. Ironically, although trails, paths, and roads may be an ideal focus for heritage tourism, the journey still belongs to the one making it rather than to those who passed before.

CONCLUSIONS

One of the principal conclusions of the Penn International Research Symposium on Landscapes of Movement is that archaeological research on trails, paths, and roads is relevant and timely. New tools and methods make such research much more feasible than ever before; innovative theoretical approaches have opened windows for us to comprehend these features in ways that make them meaningful on their own within their original context and to be incorporated into our perceptions of human society at a broader comparative level. Landscape is a liberating strategy, and the chapters in this volume make that case in creative ways.

The authors in this volume argue that the landscape paradigm breaks down artificial barriers between categories of archaeological information, linking research on trails, paths, and roads across regions and continents. Such connections are particularly critical at a time when the features we study face threats from multiple sources, including urban development, energy exploration, and even recreational overuse. Just as archaeologists need to think about what landscapes of movement mean to the people who used them, so we must also ponder how they can be made meaningful to their modern visitors.

Ultimately field research on landscapes of movement has its own particular appeal, what O. G. S. Crawford once described as the "unalloyed archaeological thrill . . . in finding and tracing a new piece of Roman road" (1960:18). Whether or not we can share the experience of the ancestors, walking in their footsteps can be a profound and engaging process. The chapters that follow pay homage to these different ancestors and to our own archaeological predecessors by drawing attention to the real value of trails, paths, and roads to the study of the human past.

2

Kukhepya:
Searching for Hopi Trails

T. J. FERGUSON, G. LENNIS BERLIN,
AND LEIGH J. KUWANWISIWMA

Kukhepya is a Hopi word that means to go along looking for footprints. In applying this concept to archaeology, footprints should be understood both literally as the tracks created by people traveling across the land and metaphorically as *itaakuku,* "our footprints," the ruins, potsherds, petroglyphs, shrines, and other archaeological sites that Hopi ancestors intentionally left behind during their long migration to the Hopi Mesas (Kuwanwisiwma and Ferguson 2004). For the Hopi people, *itaakuku* provide enduring proof that their ancestors occupied an area in accordance with religious instructions they had received from Màasaw, the deity who instructed them on how to find Tuuwanasavi, the center of the universe in their homeland on the Hopi Mesas. Such footprints, along with natural landforms associated with deities and historical events, provide the landmarks used to recognize and venerate Hopitutskwa (Hopi land). Hopitutskwa is symbolized by an area encompassing about 65,000 km² in northern Arizona, with its boundaries delineated by a series of shrines extending from the Mogollon Rim to the Colorado River, and from the Grand Canyon to the eastern slope of Black Mesa. Many important Hopi shrines lie outside of this heartland, however, and in a spiritual and historical sense, Hopitutskwa encompasses a much larger area, including all of the land where Hopi ancestors dwelled during their migration to the

Hopi Mesas. This migration took many centuries, and covered considerable parts of Mexico and the Southwest United States (Fewkes 1900; Kuwanwisiwma and Ferguson 2004).

Trails are an integral part of Hopitutskwa because they connect villages on the Hopi Mesas with resources and sacred areas in the surrounding region. Hopi trails have morphological, functional, and symbolic attributes that are similar to other trail systems documented in the Southwest, including those described by Darling, Fowler, and Snead in this volume. For the Hopi people, however, the trails associated with their ancestors have particular cultural values that stem from the physical inscription of tribal history on the land. Hopi trails run for hundreds of kilometers, matching the scale of the trail system of the neighboring Zuni Tribe (Bartlett 1940; Colton 1964; Ferguson and Hart 1985:55). In fact, the Hopi and Zuni trail systems grade into one another and they are both part of an even larger macro-regional trail system encompassing the entire Southwest United States.

Today the Hopi find themselves in the difficult position of needing to engage in *kukhepya* to locate and document ancestral trails. While many trails are referred to in oral traditions, knowledge of their precise location on the ground has waned. This is because Hopi aboriginal land was taken by the United States and either transferred to Federal agencies and other Indian tribes, or removed from the public domain and converted to private property (Ellis 1961). As regional patterns of land ownership changed, fences were erected across trails and the Hopi people lost access to many traditional areas. Today, distant shrines are still visited but Hopis travel to them along modern roads and highways in cars and trucks.

Centuries of use of Hopi trails left physical traces on the land but these are so subtle that archaeologists often fail to recognize them. As the pace of development in the American Southwest intensifies, these trails are increasingly threatened with destruction by the construction of modern roads, mines, reservoirs, and other land-modifying projects. This situation concerns the Hopi Tribe because ancestral trails embody sacred and spiritual qualities, and provide an important source of scientific information about the past.

Over the last decade, the Hopi Tribe has worked with an interdisciplinary team of archaeologists, historians, geographers, and tribal members to develop methods to identify and document trails. In this chapter, we review the cultural importance and historical development of Hopi trails and then describe the methodology the Hopi Tribe has used to discern the morphological and archaeological attributes of trails. We conclude by discussing the results this methodology has produced in the study of Hopi pilgrimage trails to the Grand Canyon and Zuni Salt Lake. Our study shows that trails have a discernable signature in the archaeological record. This signature can be faint, however, and easily overlooked if archaeologists focus solely on the concentrations of artifacts or architectural features conventionally designated as "archaeological sites." Identification of trails requires paying close attention to subtle modifications of the terrain surrounding and encompassing archaeological sites.

HOPI CONCEPTS OF TRAILS

Hopi trails were established in various ways. The most ancient trails are said to have been established by spiritual beings to connect Hopi villages with religious shrines and places of cultural importance. For example, the Hopi Salt Trail to the Grand Canyon is said to have been established by the Pöqangwnatupkom (Twin Brothers) when Salt Woman moved from the Hopi Mesas to Öngtupqa (Salt Canyon). After this trail was established, generations of Hopi men used the route during pilgrimages to collect salt and conduct rituals in the Grand Canyon (Bartlett 1940). Other routes were established to facilitate travel from one place to another for secular purposes, such as trade between the Hopi Mesas and the Havasupai in Cataract Canyon (Casanova 1967; Colton 1964). In some instances trails were used for both religious and secular journeys. For example, the Hopi trails to Zuni Salt Lake were used in ceremonial pilgrimages associated with the Wuwtsim ceremony and on trading expeditions to the Pueblo of Zuni.

For the Hopi people, trails embody spiritual values that complement their physical imprint on the ground. The cultural importance of trails is related to the ritual activities and shrines associated with them. For Hopis knowledgeable about tribal culture and history, the very act of walking along a sacred trail engages the meaning of the destination, recalling both spiritual purpose and the ancestors who preceded them on the path. Hopi values for trails thus resonate with Darling's research on Akimel O'odham songscapes and trails in southern Arizona (Chapter 4, this volume), and with Fowler's description of Paiute trails (Chapter 5, this volume).

Hopi depictions of trails provide cognitive maps that visualize the landmarks encountered during travel and the ritual activities undertaken during the journey. This is illustrated in a mural showing the Hopi trail to Zuni Salt Lake painted by Fred Kabotie in 1948 in a room at the Painted Desert Inn in Petrified Forest National Park (Figure 2.1). In this mural Hopi men are seen traveling from their corn fields on the Hopi Mesas to Zuni Salt Lake, passing springs and prominent landforms along the way, camping, and engaging in ritual activities. After collecting salt, the men are shown returning home via Zuni Pueblo, and finally arriving at their village where they are met by their aunts who have prepared a ritual feast. All of these activities are described in first-person accounts of the pilgrimage, including Don Talayesva's classic autobiography, *Sun Chief* (Simmons 1942:252–55; see also Kabotie in Livingston 1992:58–61, and Winslowe 1969).

Trails are important to the Hopi people because they have religious associations. Regional trails are like umbilical cords that spiritually link Hopi villages with outlying shrines and sacred features in a vast cultural landscape. The trails are revered because they physically connect the Hopi people with shrines and the deities they are associated with, such as the Pöqangwnatupkom (Twin Brothers) and Öng.wùuti (Salt Woman). Closer

2.1 Fred Kabotie mural of Hopi salt pilgrimage.

to home, within the Hopi villages, trails and pathways connect plazas and kivas to other places where ritual activities are conducted. The sacredness of religious pilgrimages and ceremonial routes is constant, even though the ritual use of these trails may be periodic. Some trails located near the villages are used daily for prosaic activities, yet these pathways always retain their religious significance, even though this significance may only be visible to the public when they are in ritual use. Hopi religious leaders want to protect ritual trails from the encroachment of modern development that impedes their ceremonial use.

Trails, like other ancestral sites, are considered to be monuments on the land that warrant preservation so these "footprints" can be used to teach young Hopi people about their cultural heritage. Hopi elders think that the management of trails through historic preservation compliance activities is increasingly important because the routes are no longer nurtured through regular, physical use. Given that trails play an important role in the retention and transmission of Hopi culture, the Hopi Cultural Preservation Office considers them to be significant traditional cultural properties.

Trails are associated with a number of important cultural features, including sacred springs, shrines, and trail markers. Springs are important in Hopi culture because they are linked to life and fertility (Fewkes 1906:370; Hough 1906:165–66), and they also provide the essential water needed during travel in an arid environment. *Tuutuskya* (offering places) and *tutukwmola* (trail markers) occur along trails and help define their routes. The ritual offerings deposited in *tuutuskya* and *tutukwmola* enhance the sacredness of trails. *Tutukwmola* in the form of cairns or rock monuments also serve a secular function in that they constitute prominent landmarks used to locate and sight the course of trails.

Many trails lead to ancestral villages that connect past and present Hopi use of the landscape. Low–density artifact scatters are often found along trail networks, as are temporary shelters, camps, and resting areas. *Tutuveni*, literally "writing," are images pecked into or painted on rocks, and these are frequently found in association with trails. Many petroglyphs and pictographs have semiotic functions marking the past use of an area by Hopi clans. The famous Hopi petroglyph site of Tutuventiwngwu along the Hopi Salt Trail exemplifies this (Bernadini 2007; Colton and Colton 1931; Michaelis 1981). At this site, more than 2000 petroglyphs were pecked into boulders by Hopi men participating in the salt pilgrimage to the Grand Canyon (Figure 2.2). Repetitive petroglyphs at this site mark multiple pilgrimages made by the same person or a member of the same clan.

2.2 Hopi petroglyphs associated with the pilgrimage trail to the Grand Canyon.

DEVELOPMENTAL HISTORY OF HOPI TRAILS AND ROADS

Many Hopi trails exhibit a historical progression in their use, which has implications for how these routes and their associated features can be recognized on the landscape (Ferguson, Berlin, and Hart 1995:26–31). Pedestrian routes, or foot trails, were established in ancient times before the introduction of burros and horses in the Southwest. These pedestrian trails are generally narrow in width, with tracks formed by people walking in single file. Where pedestrian trails run up steep escarpments or cliffs, as near mesa-top villages, steps or embankments were occasionally constructed to facilitate travel or decrease erosion. Pedestrian trails are generally characterized by straight routes that pass directly through rugged terrain.

After burros and horses were introduced, segments of many pedestrian routes were converted into pack trails, and eventually into formal roads that could be used by wheeled vehicles. Routes for pack animals and wheeled vehicles need increasingly wider tracks with more gradual gradients and curves to avoid breaks in topographical features. These engineering factors result in longer, less direct routes for pack trails and vehicular roads. The increase in route length is offset by increases in the hauling capacity of pack animals and wheeled vehicles, making longer journeys more economically efficient and increasing the density of social space by making it easier to move between distant settlements.

The theoretical dichotomy between informal trails and formal roads is not clear-cut (Hyslop 1984, 1991; Trombold 1991a:1). Some routes vary from simple paths to formal roads along their course. The developmental history of roads further complicates their classification. Segments of some pedestrian trails were later developed into roads, and roads constructed during one period may revert into pedestrian paths due to a lack of maintenance or to a change of purpose. In the Southwest, as in other parts of the world (Hassig 1991:18–19), multiple routes with various means of transportation were used concurrently. Older modes of transportation co-existed with newer, more efficient modes in a complementary fashion. Various types of routes were, and still are, used for different terrain or social purposes. On the Hopi Reservation, some foot trails continue to be used for religious processions and other pedestrian routes persist even though there are more modern and less arduous alternatives available.

Trail evolution on the Hopi Reservation is exemplified by Arizona State Route 264, a modern highway that bisects the entire Reservation, linking all of the villages. This route was initially developed as a pedestrian trail that gradually evolved into a pack trail and eventually into a wagon road. Portions of the original trail are still found near villages where the highway was relocated to avoid topographic features such as cliffs and large boulder fields. Segments of the earlier trail are still used by contemporary Hopi for travel by foot and horseback.

METHODOLOGY FOR IDENTIFYING HOPI TRAILS

Our research to identify Hopi trails has concentrated on developing a methodology to reliably identify individual trail segments. Although we are ultimately interested in the structural configuration of the linkages that constitute the entire Hopi trail network, meaningful research at local or regional scales of analysis cannot be undertaken until the individual segments that compose the system are known. The first step in the study of trails, therefore, has to be the accurate identification and documentation of trail segments. The study of Hopi trails thus requires a long-term research program.

The repeated use of Hopi trails has produced linear depressions which run across the land. These linear features are often associated with archaeological sites, including ancient villages, artifact scatters, and petroglyph panels. It is this archaeological signature that is sought during the process of *kukhepya,* searching for trails. Work to date has been funded in a piecemeal fashion by projects collecting information needed to pursue land rights or documenting cultural resources for compliance with Federal historic preservation legislation. Given the vagaries of historic preservation funding, most of the research has concentrated on regional rather than local trails. This includes the Hopi salt pilgrimage trails to the Grand Canyon and Zuni Salt Lake (Berlin, Ferguson, and Hart 1993; Ferguson 1998; Ferguson and Polingyouma 1993), and trails in the area between Hopi and Zuni (Ferguson, Berlin, and Hart 1995). The methodology we have developed includes a sequenced application of airphoto interpretation, ground verification, and ethnohistoric research.

Interpretation of Aerial Photographs

Airphoto interpretation to identify linear features associated with human use has proven to be an effective tool for locating Hopi trails. This research entails the acquisition of public domain aerial photographs (airphotos). For most projects, several series of photographs are available from the period between 1934 and the present. These multidate airphotos incorporate differences in scale, season, and film type (panchromatic or color infrared). Analyzing photographs taken at different points in time, with different lighting and vegetative conditions, reveals patterns than cannot be discerned in using a single series.

Four guiding principles facilitate the correct interpretation of identifying features on the aerial photographs that may represent trails. First, formal pedestrian trails tend to be straight over considerable distances and not deviate in direction for minor topographic obstacles. The advantage of this "straight as an arrow" route is a reduced travel time between two points. Second, a trail is likely to be preserved as a series of discontinuous segments (i.e., fragmented preservation), rather than as a continuously preserved feature over a considerable distance. Segments located in low-lying areas are often subject to erosional or depositional processes that can destroy or bury the trail. Thus, as with other types of archaeological remains, the older the trail, the less likely it is to be preserved as a continuous feature. Third, trails often have depressed surfaces as a result of heavy, long-term use, with perhaps additional deepening by surface runoff. This cultural wear pattern has been termed "troughing" by Sheets and Sever (1991:69). Fourth, portions of many trails are comprised of two or more parallel segments. The existence of parallel routes is a common attribute of many aboriginal trails in the New World (Robertson 1983; Obenauf 1991). Parallel routes may be due in part to the use of trails as transportation corridors, where people travel along a general course rather than walking or riding within a single, specific track.

Based on the guiding principles described above, the major interpretative task is to identify foot travel routes by identifying linear features or traces on the aerial photographs whose segments are aligned in a rectilinear or slightly curvilinear pattern and which ignore minor topographic irregularities (Figure 2.3). Use of these defining parameters helps to eliminate most misidentifications involving well-established stock trails, wagon roads, abandoned or contemporary two-track roads, and natural erosional features having a linear expression.

In addition, the following recognition elements, or indicator phenomena, can enhance the appearance of suspect trail traces on the aerial photographs: (1) linear depressions, or swales, perhaps with shadow enhancement; (2) anomalous drainage features, perhaps with shadow enhancement; (3) soil discolorations; (4) moisture marks; and (5) anomalous vegetation patterns, such as linear alignments relating to differences in type, density, or height compared to background.

Photointerpretation occurs in two phases. The first phase centers on a three-dimensional stereoscopic analysis of overlapping images. This is accomplished with a mirror stereoscope equipped with 1.5X magnification lenses. Stereoscopic analysis is especially useful for both detecting suspect trail traces and seeing their positions in a three-dimensional landscape. During the second phase, the aerial photographs are examined individually under 4X and 8X magnification and with a Ronchi diffraction grating (no magnification) to determine if any of the suspect trail traces can be extended or if additional traces can be identified. A Ronchi grating is a device

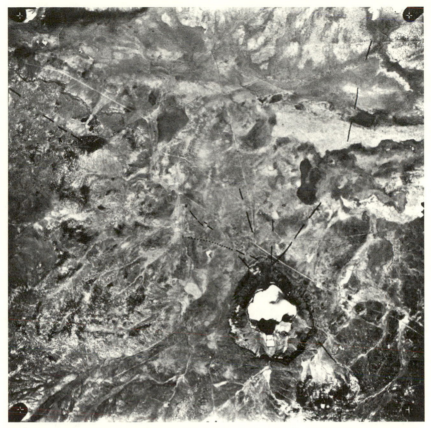

2.3 Black-and-white version of infrared aerial photograph marked with suspected trail segments leading to Zuni Salt Lake. (National Aerial Photography Program, EROS Data Center, U.S. Geological Survey)

consisting of a series of parallel black lines (typically 78 lines/cm) printed on either glass or clear plastic; both the line width and the distance between the lines are the same. When the grating is placed inside the near-field focus of the eyes and slowly rotated in front of an aerial photograph, linear elements parallel to the grating lines appear diffused (suppressed), while linear elements perpendicular to the grating lines are enhanced. A thorough discussion of the diffraction principles of a Ronchi grating for enhancing linear features is given by Pohn (1970) and Offield (1975).

Different lighting conditions are used to illuminate the transparencies and prints during the photointerpretation sessions. The color infrared positive transparencies and panchromatic negative transparencies are viewed with transmitted white light in a darkened room. Prints made from these transparencies are viewed with reflective light from an adjustable-arm fluorescent lamp.

Because of disparities in aerial photograph scales, the interpretive data are compiled on prints enlarged to a common scale of 1:24,000. This enables the suspect trail traces to be georeferenced to the appropriate USGS 7.5-minute topographic quadrangles. The interpretative data plotted on the enlarged aerial photographs and quadrangles are used to guide the fieldwork. Although numerous traces are identified for field inspection, only those that are field verified are described in technical reports.

Ground Verification

The interpretation of aerial photographs identifies possible trail routes that are then targeted for ground verification through archaeological fieldwork and independent historical documentation. We have developed thirteen criteria for identifying trail segments on the ground:

1. Pedestrian trails are wider than stock trails, but narrower than pack trails, wagon roads, and two-track roads.
2. When changing directions, pedestrian trails do so with an abrupt "dogleg" turn, rather than a broad, sweeping turn that is characteristic of pack trails, wagon roads, and two-track roads.
3. Pedestrian trails follow a straight course without deviation for most topographic obstacles. This is in contrast to stock trails and two-track roads, which can have winding to intricately meandering ("zigzag") courses.
4. Pedestrian trails often have parallel segments.
5. Pedestrian trails are often preserved in a series of discontinuous segments.
6. In the absence of erosion or reuse, preserved trail segments do not have "fresh" appearing surfaces, and their bed floors may be reverting to climax vegetation.
7. Trail segments may be expressed as linear depressions, with or without adjacent berms.
8. Trails have summit notches where they traverse hilly relief, including sand dunes.
9. Heavily used trails have "troughing" or depressed surfaces. In cross-section, these trail segments typically have concave profiles. This is in

contrast to wagon roads, which have flat-floored, rectilinear profiles with wheel ruts.

10. Trail segments may be expressed by linear drainage, soil, or vegetation patterns, which appear to be out of place in the natural environment.
11. The evidence for the existence of a trail is enhanced if: (a) artifact scatters are observed on or immediately adjacent to a trace; and (b) shrines and/or trail markers, such as cairns, are observed along a route.
12. Independent historic documentation provides corroborating evidence for the route of a trail.
13. Independent ethnographic information provides corroborating evidence for the route of a trail.

During fieldwork, the locations at which observations and measurements are made and recorded to verify trails are termed "documentation sites." This term is *not* synonymous with "archaeological site," because at some documentation sites there are no archaeological manifestations other than the trail itself. The term documentation site is employed solely as a means to provenience the locations at which ground evidence was collected. The measurement of morphological attributes (such as trail width, depth, and azimuth) is an important part of fieldwork because these data are useful in distinguishing foot trails, pack trails, and wagon roads.

Several of the project areas we have investigated are restricted to small tracts of land or long, narrow rights-of-way. Because trails often have discontinuous physical expressions, fieldwork must be conducted outside of these spatially restrictive areas in order to locate trail segments that are aligned on the same azimuth. In some project areas, the route of trails not visible on the ground surface can be projected by reference to verified trail segments in adjacent areas.

Historical and Ethnographic Research

Documentary history and ethnography provide independent sources of information that are used to corroborate specific trails. In the Southwest, historical maps from the Spanish Period (AD 1540–1821) and Mexican Period (AD 1821–1846), General Land Office Surveys and military maps from the 19th century, and early editions of USGS maps from the 20th century have all proven to be useful sources of information about trails. These are supplemented with written historical descriptions of trails when these exist.

Ethnographic research entails extensive interviews with tribal members coupled with collaborative fieldwork during or after the ground verification phase of research (Figure 2.4). Shrines and trail markers often have enigmatic physical expressions, and tribal cultural advisors have proven adept in helping to locate and interpret these archaeological features.

2.4 G. Lennis Berlin working with tribal advisor during ground verification of trails between Zuni and Hopi. (Photograph by E. Richard Hart, June 22, 1994)

Management of Sensitive Information

The Hopi Cultural Preservation Office manages information about trails and associated shrines so that it is not released to the public in a manner that would endanger the physical integrity of sacred places. There are many "New Age" adherents in the Southwest who throng to Native American sacred sites when these are publicized, and the fragile nature of trails and associated features needs protection from this type of inappropriate visitation. The UTM (Universal Transverse Mercator) positions and precise locational information collected during photointerpretation and ground verification is curated by the Hopi Tribe, and released to land managing agencies only when it is needed for decisions about land use and management of cultural resources. In addition, some of the ethnographic data collected during trails research is privileged information that is not appropriate for sharing with the general public. Much of this information is never translated into English, and field notes and tape recordings documenting ethnographic research are maintained by the tribe and shared with scholars on a need-to-know basis. The following summary of the results of our trails research represents general information appropriate for use in scholarly work that documents Hopi history and land use.

CASE STUDIES

We discuss two case studies to illustrate how the methodology for identifying Hopi trails is put into action in field research. Both of these case studies involve long trails to salt sources, one running 130 km to the Grand Canyon, and the other 200 km to Zuni Salt Lake in west-central New Mexico. These trails are both associated with religious pilgrimages and they were in use long before Europeans arrived in the Southwest in the 16th century.

Hopi Salt Pilgrimage Trail to the Grand Canyon

For centuries, the Hopi have used a salt mine located at the base of a cliff in the bottom of the Grand Canyon, 130 km to the west of the Hopi villages. Research on the Hopi salt pilgrimage trail to the Grand Canyon was sponsored by the Hopi Tribe to collect information needed to secure rights to continue use of the trail and its associated shrines.

Hopi salt pilgrimages to the Grand Canyon are associated with the culmination of Third Mesa Wuwtsim ceremonies when boys are initiated into manhood (Titiev 1937; Simmons 1942:232–46). The pilgrimage traditionally entailed an arduous and spiritually dangerous week-long journey, during which 37 shrines were visited. Young men demonstrated their prowess during this pilgrimage by climbing down a cliff in the Grand Canyon to collect salt from the Salt Mine along the Colorado River. Bearing a heavy load of salt, they then climbed back up the cliff to begin their journey home. The salt was brought back to the Hopi villages and distributed to relatives for ritual and domestic use. In addition to the Third Mesa pilgrimage, Hopis from First and Second Mesa also traveled along the trail on pilgrimages to the Grand Canyon for other ritual purposes. The Hopi people preserve a rich oral history about salt pilgrimages (Ferguson 1998:152–91).

The shrines associated with the salt pilgrimage trail provide known points along its route because these are still remembered and used by the Hopi people. In addition, segments of the trail along the Little Colorado River Gorge and Colorado River in the Grand Canyon were described in previous research (Eiseman 1959, 1961). While the general route of the pilgrimage was thus known, the precise location of the trail between known points could only be projected. The Hopi Tribe thus sponsored remote sensing and ground verification research with tribal members to document the physical traces of the trail from the western edge of the Hopi Reservation to the top of Salt Trail Canyon (Figure 2.5).

We found the Grand Canyon salt trail incorporates segments of pedestrian trails, pack animal routes, wagon roads, and modern unpaved roads used for vehicular traffic. The pilgrimage trail thus is best represented as a corridor rather than a single-file pedestrian track. Virtually the entire trail could be located on the ground except for a short portion that runs through a highly developed area adjoining Tuba City. In this area, the route of the trail was projected using historical information. The physical changes that have occurred in the salt pilgrimage trail to the Grand Canyon embody the history of changing modes of transportation in the region, and show how Hopi traditions have been maintained as the technology of travel changed. As pack animals and wagons became available, they were used during pilgrimages to travel over segments of the route, and over time the overall route between settlements was developed to facilitate secular use with modern methods of travel.

The salt pilgrimage trail to the Grand Canyon does not exist in isolation. It is part of a regional trail network whose exact configuration is only known schematically (Figure 2.6). The Hopi trail network in the Grand Canyon region incorporates several alternate routes to Öngtupqa (Grand Canyon), the Colorado River, and the Havasupai village that were historically used for trading, resource procurement, and ceremonial purposes. The research needed to delineate the physical location and archaeological attributes of these trails still needs to be accomplished.

Hopi Salt Pilgrimage Trails to Zuni Salt Lake

The Hopi also conduct a pilgrimage to collect salt at the Zuni Salt Lake in west-central New Mexico, located 200 km to the southeast of the Hopi villages (Figure 2.5). The Zuni Salt Lake is situated within a volcanic maar, where a briny crust forms on the surface, providing a pristine source of

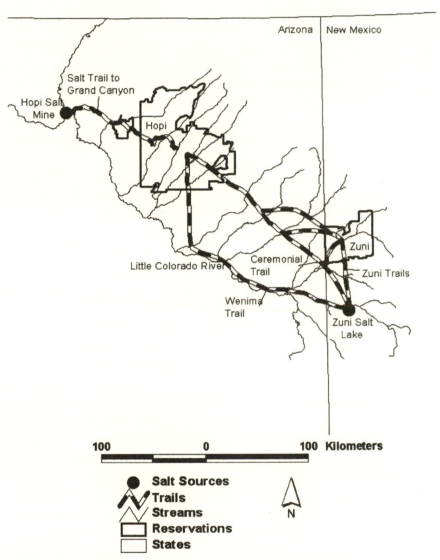

2.5 Schematic depiction of Hopi salt pilgrimage trails to the Grand Canyon and Zuni Salt Lake.

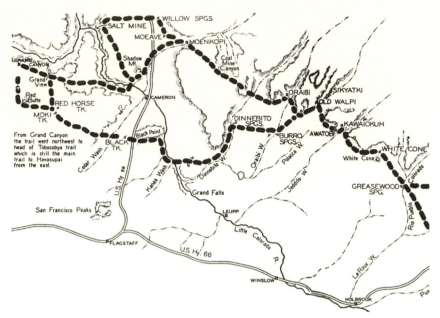

2.6 Schematic depiction of major routes in the Grand Canyon in the Hopi trail network; from Bartlett (1940:43). (Courtesy of Museum of Northern Arizona)

pure salt (Taylor 1954). The Hopi trail network encompassing Zuni Salt Lake entails multiple routes that were used by particular groups for various religious or secular purposes.

Research on Hopi salt pilgrimage trails to Zuni Salt Lake in New Mexico was sponsored by the Salt River Project (SRP) as a part of historic preservation compliance activities associated with the proposed development of a strip mine and associated railroad corridor. Hopi research on this project was one component in a larger project that also involved the Zuni, Acoma, and Navajo tribes. Research focused on the SRP project area north of Zuni Salt Lake along Largo Creek (Berlin, Ferguson, and Hart 1993). In this area, we documented the northern half of a transportation network with trails radiating outward from Zuni Salt Lake like spokes on a wheel (Figure 2.7). These trails lead to Hopi, Zuni, Ramah Navajo, Acoma, and Laguna settlements (Dittert and Minge 1993; Ferguson and Polingyouma 1993; Hart and Othole 1993; Mercer 1993). Additional trails radiating out of Zuni Salt Lake to the west and south were used by Apache tribes but documentation of this part of the network was beyond the scope of work funded by SRP.

While Hopi use of Zuni Salt Lake is well documented (Stephen 1936:994; Beaglehole 1937; Simmons 1942:252–55; Richardson 1991:9; Titiev 1972:39), research on the trails to Zuni Salt Lake was complicated by the occurrence of multiple routes used in different social contexts, and a relatively sparse oral history describing the explicit geography and shrines associated with the trails. The last Hopis who walked the old trails have all passed away, and Hopis who have made pilgrimages to Zuni Salt Lake since 1950 have all traveled in vehicles via modern highways and county roads. Another limiting factor in the research was that airphoto interpretation and ground verification of trails between the SRP area and the Hopi villages was beyond the scope of funding provided by the project sponsor, and the documentation of these trail segments was therefore solely based on historical and ethnographic research. However, short segments of these trails have been documented in subsequent projects (Ferguson, Berlin, and Hart 1995; Ferguson, Anyon, and Berlin 1999), and this has helped verify tentative conclusions based on the other sources.

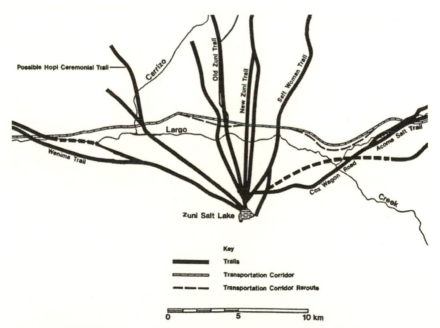

2.7 Trails leading to Zuni Salt Lake and their intersection with a proposed transportation corridor; adapted from Hart and Othole (1993: fig. 16).

The Hopi historically used two pedestrian routes to Zuni Salt Lake, each more than 200 km in length (Figure 2.5). These trails were used during ceremonial activities associated with First and Second Mesa villages. One of these trails, known as the Wenima Trail, headed directly south from Second Mesa and then followed the Little Colorado River upstream to the sacred site of Wenima (known to the Zuni as Kołuwala:wa). From there, the trail followed Carrizo and Largo creeks to Zuni Salt Lake. The second trail, known as the Ceremonial Trail, followed a southwesterly course from the Hopi Mesas, running in a more or less direct route to Zuni Salt Lake. Several springs and shrines along this trail help locate its general route. This second trail is said to have been used during the culmination of the Wuwtsim ceremonies at the Second Mesa village of Musangnuvi, at which time initiates were taken on a salt pilgrimage with many ritual activities comparable to those associated with the Third Mesa journey to the Hopi Salt Mine in the Grand Canyon. The use of these ceremonial trails avoided Zuni Pueblo, and thus provided privacy for Hopis while they were engaged in religious activities.

In addition to pilgrimages associated with ceremonial initiations, Hopis from all of the Hopi villages also made other journeys to Zuni Salt Lake to make ritual offerings if there was a drought and to collect salt for domestic purposes. On these trips to Zuni Salt Lake, Hopis often traveled via Zuni Pueblo, where they would stop to visit with friends and trade Hopi pottery, baskets, and textiles. Three trails were established that led from the Ceremonial Trail to Zuni Pueblo (Figure 2.5). A segment of one of these trails northwest of Hawikku is observed as a large linear depression with a deep summit notch, indicative of substantial use in the past (Figure 2.8). This trail appears to be an ancient route, and we believe it was also used by the Coronado Expedition and subsequent Spanish officials traveling between Zuni and Hopi villages.

Hopis traveling from Zuni Pueblo to Zuni Salt Lake followed two Zuni trails (Figure 2.8). One of these is named the Old Zuni Trail, because its narrow width and straight route indicate it was used as a pedestrian and pack trail. The other trail is called the New Zuni Trail, because its greater width and avoidance of steep topography indicate it was used as a historic wagon road. The New Zuni trail has a parallel segment along part of its route.

During investigation of trails in the vicinity of Zuni Salt Lake, we were interested in a feature that appears on many maps of the Chaco road system

2.8 Notch in crest of sand dune along the trail from Zuni to Hopi.

labeled as the "Salt Mother Trail" (e.g., Gabriel 1991:4; Lekson et al. 1988).
Our fieldwork at this trail segment, part of the Old Zuni Trail, indicates this
is actually a historic wagon road and not an ancient route associated with
the Chacoan period.

However, we did document a pedestrian trail that the Ramah Navajo
know as the "Salt Woman Trail," which runs several kilometers to the east
of the wagon road misidentified as a Chacoan Road (Figure 2.7). After this
trail ascends to the Zuni Plateau from Zuni Salt Lake, it branches into two
segments, with one running to Zuni Pueblo and the other to the El Morro
Valley. Our fieldwork along the prominent swale of what the Ramah Navajo
refer to as the "Salt Woman Trail" suggests it may have been constructed or
engineered, and its widths (measured at different points as 4 m and 8.5 m)
are within the size range of primary and secondary Chacoan roads. If this
is indeed a Chacoan road, it has been reused by the Ramah Navajo in more
recent times. Although the engineered attributes of the road may have been
degraded by erosion and deposition of sediments, the linear swale still provided a viable route that could be traversed on foot or horseback.

As with the Hopi salt pilgrimage trail to the Grand Canyon, the trail network in the vicinity of Zuni Salt Lake incorporates a complex superposition

of pedestrian trails, pack animal routes, wagon roads, and modern unpaved roads used for vehicular traffic. The trail system at Zuni Salt Lake thus reflects the complexity of the history of use by many tribes and the changing modes of transportation through time.

CONCLUSIONS

We find that the Hopi transportation network comprises a palimpsest, with trails and roads overlaid upon one another over time. This overlay is not entirely isomorphic, however, and short segments of earlier trail and road systems are often preserved where they deviate from the straighter and more highly engineered routes of modern roads. The task of documenting Hopi travel routes is made difficult by the fact that most trails have intermittent visibility. Geomorphological processes of alluviation and erosion have obscured some trail segments, and other segments have been obliterated by their subsequent incorporation into formal roads. It takes a diligent combination of remote sensing, ground verification, and ethnohistorical research to reliably identify trails and roads.

The need for reliable identification of trail segments prior to undertaking the structural configuration of the linkages that constitute an entire network is highlighted by what we think is the misidentification of a wagon road near Zuni Salt Lake as a segment of the Chaco road system. The strength of archaeological theories ultimately rests on the veracity of the facts used in their construction, and we need to make sure the methodology to identify trails and roads keeps pace with our developing ideas about the past.

In closing, we briefly mention two implications that documentation of the Hopi trail network has for archaeological research. First, we think the use of the Grand Canyon and Zuni Salt Lake salt pilgrimage trails by different Hopi villages is related to the complex history of clan migration. Although Fewkes (1900) was interested in correlating Hopi clan history with the archaeological record in the late 19th century, this research issue fell out of favor and has only recently been revived by young scholars (Bernardini 2005; Lyons 2003). As we amass more information about the trails that physically connect ancient sites and contemporary villages, we think these data will be increasingly useful in writing the history of the ancient past. Second, we think the scale of the Hopi trail network, extending over hundreds of kilometers, needs to be considered by archaeologists in bounding realistic study areas for past groups. Most archaeological study areas comprise relatively small locales compared to historical patterns of land use. We think Hopi ancestors traveled widely over the land, and paying attention to trail networks is one way to chart the area in which we should expect to find their archaeological remains and to understand interactions with other groups.

Anthropological and archaeological investigation of trails has had instrumental benefits for the Hopi Tribe. This research has helped provide the documentation needed to secure land rights for continued use of the pilgrimage trail to the Grand Canyon. It has also provided the Hopi Tribe with the information it needs for consultation with Federal agencies pursuant to the implementation of the National Historic Preservation Act.

We hope that research of Hopi trails continues so that these important features can be identified, documented, and preserved as Hopi footprints so that future generations of Hopis will know the tracks their ancestors left upon the land.

3

Trails of Tradition: Movement, Meaning, and Place

JAMES E. SNEAD

Every path I knew there too, and every little track running off from the paths,
the width of a single footstep, by which children ran to gardens of their own,
that they had found or made among weeds; but some of these paths had
altered in the long time since I was there. It was a long time.

— Lord Dunsany, "The Return"

The view from windows overlooking collegiate quadrangles almost anywhere incorporates a common perspective, including that of a representative landscape of movement. Open space between the buildings, filled
by grass, trees, or plantings, is bounded by sidewalks, some of which cross
open ground in crisp diagonals. Between classes students march along these
preordained routes toward their next destination. And yet some of these
strollers make their own way across the grass, a shared act of subversion
that over time blazes clear trails through the greenery. These strips of dirt
are as much part of the fabric of the quadrangle as are the brick-lined sidewalks, and tell us a great deal about movement, intention, and meaning.

Among the many incongruities that underlie the concept of a landscape
of movement—in effect, using a static, material signature to represent the
active passage of humans across the countryside—I am particularly concerned with how perceptions of formality and "permanence" shape our

Epigraph. 1954:173.

ideas about how we travel through the world. Archaeological research has focused on formal roads for the pragmatic reason that they are relatively straightforward to identify (see Chapter 1, this volume). It is often forgotten, however, that constructed features represent a specific mode of passage, one infused with the intent of authority rather than necessarily of those who use that route. In no case with which I am familiar are they representative or exclusive. Deliberate formalization of the process of travel may take place for numerous interesting reasons that have little to do with movement itself, and may reflect an effort to control or even subvert other ways of travel rather than evolving from convenience or efficiency.

The tension between formal and informal within landscapes of movement is expressed in university quadrangles and other spaces where control and response can be manifest. Students walking across the grass are effectively frustrating the designer's intent to convey a sense of order and decorum. The informal routes created in this way may be a result of preference and expediency, but it is also imaginable that they reflect some low-key resistance to a more grand design. The relationship between planners and the landscape is a reflexive one, however, and can involve barricades of signage and fencing. I have also seen quadrangles where the "unofficial" paths are ultimately paved over, representing acquiescence, cooption, or both.

Landscapes of movement thus embody multiple ways of moving, each with distinct structure, significance, and associations. Looking for these different contemporaneous features moves us towards understanding the way that landscapes as a whole are structured by practice and intent, representing multiple—and perhaps, conflicting—narratives, as has been done with various other types of archaeological landscapes (see, for example, Upton 1990). Studying movement in context can ultimately inform us about that context, often in unexpected ways.

MOVEMENT, MEANING, AND PLACE

Differences between apparently formalized and informal movement in specific cultural settings subvert the idea that formal "roads" are more inherently meaningful than informal "trails." Of course people have to get from point to point, and human beings do approach this in common ways. Yet considering informal movement as exclusively driven by "rational" concerns such as the minimization of cost is often to reduce it to insignificance, converting those who walk these ways into culture-free abstractions. A common element in many of the Boasian ethnogeographies is that paths and trails were more than simply means to an end. Instead, they were so infused with the significance of activity that took place along them—with movement, travel, connection, separation—that they became synonymous with such themes (see Harrington 1916; Loud 1918; Waterman 1920).

Ethnogeographical information thus indicates that trails are themselves *places,* with all that such a definition implies (i.e., Agnew 1989; Barrett 1999; Carson 2002; Low and Lawrence-Zuñiga 2003; Malpas 1998) (Figure 3.1). Wendy Ashmore has recently called for archaeologists to construct "life histories of place" (2002:1178), which requires examining complex relationships between function, meaning, and time. This presents a particular challenge for a trail/place that is not "lived" in the classic sense of the term.

We can address the relationship between trails and place by beginning with the idea that moving through a landscape is a process of engagement. As landmarks of topography and the built environment come into view, the traveler reaffirms relationships with those landmarks, and whatever associations come with them. Thus Keith Basso describes Western Apache cowboys reciting place names under their breath as they ride through the countryside, a process that makes reference to the entire complex of meaning associated with them (1996b). I cannot drive on highways traveled since my childhood without hearing the voices of grandparents instructing me about landmarks along the way. Since the trail itself makes that engagement possible, it would take on some related significance. I do not favor a strict phenomenology of trails (see Tilley 1994), since I follow Fred Myers (2000) in believing that landscapes are overwhelmingly social constructions, and that meaning emplaced in the landscape can create barriers just as impenetrable as those that are experienced physically. Thus interpreting trails must partake equally in the structures of culture and the structures of movement, an approach that I have called contextual experience (Snead 2008). From this theoretical perspective, context includes not only topography, architecture, and other factors of the physical environment, but also the cultural knowledge required to interpret such a setting. Gaining understanding of a place cannot come exclusively from "being there," but also requires constructing a perspective analogous to those for whom the place had significance. Contextual experience is a landscape archaeology of cultural traditions, an ethnogeography of the past.

3.1 Trails as places: a staircase leading to a mesa top in Garcia Canyon on the northern Pajarito Plateau, New Mexico.

Secondly, as Mary Helms (1998) has observed, there are strong cross-cultural patterns in the way that travel and distance are perceived. In cultural terms trails—at least those of medium distance—are liminal zones, with familiar associations interwoven with the possibility of something entirely new and unpredictable. The anthropological literature is filled with accounts of meetings along pathways, with associated risks and opportunities. Referring to seasonal travel, Barbara Bender writes that "a person part-knows the way, part-knows that each time of return there will be change and unfamiliarity; part-fears, part-revels in the chance encounter, the possible adventure. Arriving is important but so are the stories woven around the traveling" (2001:84).

Trails would also, of course, be distinguished by unique cultural referents. The "corpse roads" of sparsely inhabited parishes in northern England, along which the bodies of the dead were carried to isolated churches, are pathways of such distinctive meaning (Hindle 1998:10) that they linger in historical memory despite changes in function over time. Named trails in Canyon de Chelly are associated with the origins of particular Navajo ceremonials (Jett 2001). All indicate the rich cultural context for paths and trails as well as their nature as places in their own right.

Frames of Reference

Evaluating trails as places in archaeological contexts is enhanced by consideration of the two linked concepts of *inscription* and *materialization*. Inscription, used by various landscape theorists (e.g., Aston and Rowley 1974; Wilson and David 2002), describes the "marking" of landscapes both as an inadvertent result of people going about their daily lives and as a product of conscious action. Over time the landscape becomes a complex overlay of different marks from different eras that have been "overlain, modified or erased by the work of another" (Aston and Rowley 1974:14). This dynamic setting in turn exerts its own influence, less a passive "stage" for human activity and more an actor in the process.

Materialization, as formulated by Elizabeth Demarrais and colleagues (1996), is directly concerned with the relationship between ideology and material culture, of which landscape is a critical element. Through the construction of monuments and related features, perceptions of space can be shaped to highlight particular social and political relationships, thus linking the conceptual and physical worlds. In their argument, materialization is a tool used in particular by elites to naturalize their positions, serving to "strengthen the association of a group and a place" (1996:19). From my perspective the process is more fundamental and representative of a broader range of social relationships. Although such investments may transcend time, then, they are particularly linked to specific circumstances and ambitions.

Both inscription and materialization have direct relevance to the understanding of paths and trails. As movement through the land becomes more deeply inscribed, views and perspectives along the way become fixed, in effect framing the experience of the traveler. Over time this experience becomes more complex and more laden with meaning. As the relationship between movement and meaning becomes particularly associated with such an inscribed landscape, it creates an opportunity for materialization, since in effect the "signature" that has evolved can also be constructed. Investing labor into landscapes of movement can have the effect of replicating a landscape that would not otherwise have the deep associations of others that had been inscribed over time. The fact that the symbolism associated with such places, real or created, was experienced through constant movement strikes me as particularly important.

Examples of landscapes of movement that have been structured in ways that echo older, more inscribed places can be found scattered through the literature on paths, trails, and roads. The case of Roman roads has been articulated by Ray Laurence, who describes an elaborate, built environment associated with the road network, particularly on the approach to a town, where an array of constructions defined the experience of the traveler. "For those towns on the major roads from Rome, the opportunity to present an image of their city to a greater number of individuals passing through would seem to have had an importance that appears in their spatial arrangement. Equally, for the traveler to Rome, the towns and in particular the colonial settlements could represent an image of Rome's *imperium* as expressed through the medium of public buildings, statues and colonnaded streets" (1999:150–51).

Such materialized landscapes of movement are most typically visualized in association with "imperial" systems, where the mobilization of labor was an essential part of state control (such as the Inka example originally used by De Marrais, Castillo, and Earle 1996:29). This is accurate in terms of sheer scale, but otherwise there is no reason why such relationships be-

tween people and landscape could not have existed in less "complex" circumstances. Thus the "hundreds of rock cairns" erected along the Bad Pass
trail in Montana were created, non-functional features that structured the
experience of the generations of Native Americans who passed among
them (Loendorf and Brownell 1980:11; cf. Blakeslee and Blasing 1988).
Since a rock cairn is as tangible as a tomb along a Roman roadside, ideology is as imbedded within paths and trails as in imperial highways. In fact, I
think it is only by looking at trails and paths through frameworks that allow
them to be considered as influencing an experience as inscribed landscapes
and as potential materialized ideology that we can more fully appreciate
their nature.

TRAILS IN THE PAJARITO LANDSCAPE

To further examine meaning in landscapes of movement, I turn to the Pajarito Trails Project, begun in 1991 as an exploratory survey of Ancestral
Pueblo trail networks on the Pajarito Plateau of north-central New Mexico.
The Plateau itself is a consolidated pyroclastic flow of Pleistocene date associated with the Jemez volcano (Ross, Smith and Bailey 1961). Erosion
of this friable bedrock has created topography dominated by flat-topped,
steep-sided, linear mesas or *potreros* divided by sheer-walled canyons. These
conditions have also proved beneficial for the preservation of trails, which
in many instances have been worn into the rock by the passage of feet (see
Snead 2002, 2008).

Although humans have used the Pajarito for thousands of years, the trail
system is generally thought to have originated during the AD 1100s, with
the movement of large numbers of Pueblo people into the region. Over
the subsequent centuries a considerable population developed, farming the
canyon bottoms and mesa tops. An initial pattern of many small communities, each organized into clusters of small residences adjacent to agricultural
fields, evolved into a smaller number of spatially extensive communities,
each centered upon a single large "community house" surrounded by hinterlands with seasonally occupied field houses. By the AD 1600s most of the
permanent population had shifted a few kilometers eastward to the Rio
Grande lowlands, but hunting and gathering continued on the Pajarito until
modern times (for an overview, see Powers and Orcutt 1999a).

The spectacular preservation of the archaeological landscape of the Pajarito has attracted considerable interest over time, and the trails have had their share of attention (summarized in Snead 2002, 2008). Our fieldwork between 1991 and 2001 recorded 173 trail segments representing dozens of different trails, totaling more than 11 km in length. This represents only a fraction of the total system, which must extend for hundreds of linear kilo-meters (Snead 2002, 2005, 2008).

In this chapter I will focus on trails in the Tsirege group, a settlement cluster of the central Pajarito (Figure 3.2). Approximately 10 km from north to south, the Tsirege Group is dominated by the Classic-period community houses of Otowi, Tsankawi, Navawi, and Tsirege, each a multi-storied ma-sonry structure containing hundreds of rooms. These and the associated field houses, petroglyphs, gardens, and other associated features date to the post–AD 1300 era, but many smaller residential groupings from the preced-ing centuries can be found nearby. The well-preserved trails of the Tsirege group form one of the most impressive aspects of this landscape. Here I will make some general remarks about the trail network in this area before discussing some specific aspects of trails directly associated with the com-munity houses.

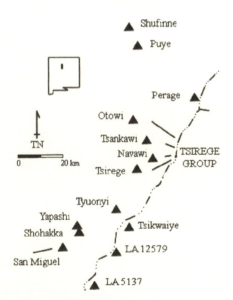

3.2 Major archaeological sites of the Pajarito Plateau, New Mexico, illustrating the location of the Tsirege Group.

Movement, Tradition, and the Pajarito Trails

The Pajarito landscape is inscribed by trails at local, community, and regional scales. In the most spatially restricted context, trails form an intricate and redundant network, taking people through a range of daily activities that are almost entirely within hailing distance of their homes. As recorded in the Tsankawi Community, where preservation conditions are ideal, local trails are dense and bewildering, with some segments only a few meters in length. The trail network at the more-extensive community scale, linking the community house and associated features with nearby fields and activity areas, shows a comparatively consistent structure. Steep terrain permits only a few routes up and down the mesa on which the community house is located, and the evidence indicates that these trail and stair segments were used over relatively long periods of time. The regional trails, connecting the Tsankawi Community with others in the Tsirege Group and beyond, illustrate travel over greater distances and have even greater time depth. Some regional trails are marked by deep ruts reflecting patterned movement across many centuries (Figure 3.3; Snead 2008).

The significance of trails as places would have been different at each scale. The local trails established a context for life in the community houses, representing complex relationships among the people who used them, coming in and out of use as these relationships changed over the years. Individual segments may have had limited significance, only in the aggregate representing the social web of the community. Regional trails, worn by generations, were more discrete, permanent elements of the landscape, routes as familiar to the travelers of the 13th century AD as to their descendants 500 years later.

I assume that the Ancestral Pueblo inhabitants of the region had a world view similar to that of the modern Tewa (Ortiz 1969, 1979), one in which the world is organized as a series of spatial zones configured by topographic landmarks and constructed shrines with villages at their centers (for a discussion, see Snead 2008; Snead and Preucel 1999). Moving through a world defined by mountains, springs, and other meaningful topography would have structured the experience of such landmarks. Walking the trails would have emphasized continuity with the natural order, and with the human history that it encompassed. Thus people crossing the Pajarito would have been surrounded by both natural landmarks and more explicit evidence of their own history, walking through pueblos teeming

3.3 Segment 3 of LA 66885, the Sandia Mesa Trail network, illustrating deep surface wearing of trails used for travel at a regional scale.

with life and past grass-filled plazas of older settlements that were no longer lived in on a regular basis but still part of the community fabric.

From my perspective it was the regional trails that made the lived places
of the Tewa world into a cohesive whole. Richard Parmentier has noted
that seemingly disparate elements of the Palauan landscape in Micronesia—
"sacred stones, trees, valuables, place names, and titles"—are made into
comprehensible systems by the paths that connect them (1987:109). In this
regard the inscribed trails of the Pajarito—the deeply worn ruts, tangible
footsteps of the ancestors (see Chapter 2, this volume)—would have been
particularly powerful symbols, in effect "trails of tradition." Trails effectively shaped the experience of movement for all who used them and thus
represented the order itself. Such tradition would have been generated not
through individual intent but by the cumulative impact of the inscribed
landscape.

Place, Materialization, and the Pajarito Staircases

The local and regional trail networks acquired meaning in large part
through use, but it is at the intermediate, community scale that the role
of human intention in shaping trails and their significance is most evident.
Many of these routes were designed to connect outlying nodes of the communities, such as shrines, with residential areas, and as such illustrate "created" relationships between constructed features of the landscape. The
investment of labor into such trails thus provides insight into the intent of
their builders.

One common strategy evident in the Pajarito trails at the community
scale was the construction of staircases on the flanks of the mesas and
potreros (see Figure 3.1). We have recorded more than a dozen of these,
each comprised of numerous steps and handholds deeply incised into the
bedrock, some with petroglyph trail markers on an adjacent cliff face (Figure 3.4). Much of this labor strikes modern observers as counter-intuitive.
In some cases parallel sets of steps climb steep faces adjacent to each other,
or formal steps have been constructed on relatively gentle slopes where they
are not strictly necessary. There are several staircases associated with each
community, but typically one of these is significantly more elaborate than
the others and directly associated with the community house. These appear
to have served as formal entryways into the heart of these settlements, and
I have described them as "gateway trails" (Snead 2002, 2005).

3.4 Petroglyph "trail marker" along the Kwage Mesa trail network (LA 21602).

The most elaborate gateway trail/staircase yet recorded on the Pajarito is the Bayo Staircase (LA 21585; Figure 3.5), associated with the Otowi Community House (LA 169). Otowi, composed of a few hundred rooms in several linked roomblocks, is located on a low ridge in the middle of a relatively open valley flanked by higher, steep-walled potreros, with several associated trail networks (Snead 2001). Traveling north of the community house required climbing a nearly sheer cliff out of Bayo Canyon, a route to the summit that can be intermittently traced via eight distinct segments for 176 m that we have called the "Bayo Staircase" (Figure 3.5).

3.5 Lower segment of the Bayo Staircase (LA 21585). (Photograph by H. Newman)

The Bayo Staircase is highly formal, with dozens of steps and handholds cut into the tuff (Figure 3.6). These would have assisted the climb, given the steep slope, but there are also at least two parallel routes, often running only 20 m apart. The formality of the Bayo Staircase is particularly evident when compared with the segment of the trail as it continues northward, as the staircase descending into the next canyon is much less elaborate. This implies to me that some of the labor invested in the construction of the stair exceeded the strictly functional requirements of getting up and down the cliff.

3.6 Middle segment of the Bayo Staircase (LA 21585), illustrating formal construction.

In addition to the stairs themselves, several formal features are associated with the Bayo Staircase. These include a large petroglyph trail marker high on the cliff face above the lowest segment, apparently a circular "sun" figure that when originally cut into the cliff face would have been visible from far down the slope. A cairn is also associated with the summit of the stair, a point where the view to the north captures the probable onward route of the trail in that direction across a pass between potreros.

A second gateway trail is associated with the Tsirege community house itself (LA 170; Figure 3.7). Located on a relatively low, flat mesa overlooking substantial agricultural land and with an estimated 600 masonry rooms, Tsirege is the largest and latest precolumbian residential complex on the Pajarito. Archaeologists have long noted the presence of trails at Tsirege (see Hewett 1904), and our brief reconnaissance in 2004 identified nine different staircases along the rim of the mesa.

The most prominent of these is the Tsirege Staircase, which descends the 6-m cliff face down to the valley floor on formal, tread-like steps cut into the rock, passing through a natural gap between the cliff face and a free-standing outcrop incised with petroglyph trail markers. People climbing through the gateway in the 15th century AD would have faced the high

3.7 Tsirege, the largest community house on the Pajarito Plateau.

western wall of the community house, which does not appear to have had entrances. The other staircases associated with Tsirege are less formal, and several probably linked the community house with multi-storied structures built into the cliff face.

Gateway trails represent the conspicuous investment of labor into an otherwise utilitarian feature. Functional explanations for this work have been suggested, such as the possibility that they assisted people climbing with burdens. As far as we know fields and hunting grounds used by the inhabitants of the community houses were scattered throughout the vicinity, so if staircases made it easier to bring corn home from the harvest or deer back from the hunt I would expect most of those within a community to be of a similar formality. We do not have a clear sense for how commodities—including pottery or raw materials—were moved about the countryside at a larger scale, but I do not perceive such exchange to have occurred at a scale that would have encouraged local communities to make such travel easier. The parallel routes and repeated reconstruction of the gateway trails is also difficult to explain in functional terms. It does not seem likely that there was sufficient traffic to require multiple routes, nor does it appear that the original staircases deteriorated rapidly over time. I am also struck by the overt symbolism implied by the trail markers, which are not exclusively associated with the gateway trails but are quite conspicuous in these places. The *awanyu* (horned serpent) figure associated with the Tsirege Staircase is one of the most striking petroglyphs on the Pajarito.

I am thus persuaded that the gateway trails were "overbuilt" to enhance their symbolic value, and that such acts represent materialization. The suite of characteristics associated with gateway trails means that they were experienced differently than other routes, and such modification would have been obvious to the traveler. These staircases were statements, possibly associated with territoriality and/or community identity, and their construction was the result of decisions by members of local communities to establish such symbols.

It is also likely that the *practice* of making the staircases was as important as the result. Repetition is central to Tewa ritual, both in terms of specific actions and in the constant re-establishment of ceremonial features such as the paintings on kiva walls, which Elsie Parsons has described as enforcing a "sense of order or of achievement through order" (1996 [1939]: 490). There are several other archaeological examples of this process, and the progressive repainting and reconstruction of kivas has been documented on the Pajarito and elsewhere (see Smith 1952). Crown and Wills have recently described refiring of vessels and reconstruction of kivas at Chaco Canyon as reflecting a process of "ritual renewal" (2003:523), and an analogous process seems to be represented by patterns of activity on the Pajarito. In the case of trails, building formal staircases was as important for the act itself—the laborious pecking of steps into the bedrock—as for the message it sent to the residents and travelers alike who climbed them.

Finally, investing labor into staircases as I have described it here returns us again to the concept of trails as meaningful places. The gateway trails at Otowi and Tsirege confirm the impression—derived from elsewhere on the Pajarito—that these features are more than simply functional aspects of the local trail networks. Their careful construction would have channeled traffic along specific routes, and associated symbols would have conveyed particular meaning to those passing through.

DISCUSSION

The precolumbian Pajarito Plateau was part of an orderly world structured by deep concepts of place. Movement played a role in the construction and maintenance of that order, reinforcing tradition through consistent travel along ancient routes. Worn deep through use, these trails became places in and of themselves, as fundamental to world view as mountains and springs.

This order was more than simply received wisdom, however, and could be modified through action and intent. Naturalizing human motivation by linking it to universal processes—embodied by historicized topography—is a broadly cross-cultural strategy (e.g., Ashmore 2004:104; Bradley 2000; Sahlins 1992). A widely cited example is provided by "roads" associated with the Chaco system, built features that—in some cases—link places occupied in different times, a process that archaeologists have dubbed "roads through time" (Roney 1992), "roads to ruins" (Van Dyke 2003:192), and "time bridges" (Fowler and Stein 2001:117; see also Kantner 1997). Although there is disagreement on their significance, these Chaco roads are widely seen as attempts to structure the landscape in such as way as to provide historical grounding for local ambitions.

Such materialization associated with landscapes of movement is present in the Pajarito trails as well. The trail markers seen widely across the plateau are an example of the overt construction of symbols that were thereafter indelibly associated with the trail passing by. The gateway trails at Tsirege and elsewhere represent a more labor-intensive version of the same symbol-making process. Constructing such elaborate features—monuments, in a different vocabulary—materialized the ambitions of the builders, linking those motivations to the tradition represented by the pathways. Archaeological examples of using trails and roads to "invent" traditions (cf. Hobsbawm 1983) outside the Southwest are scarce. The symbolic relationship between worn pathways and the construction of entrenched entry features described by Sheets (Chapter 8, this volume), however, is quite similar, and suggests that further comparative research would be productive.

In the Pajarito case the building of gateway trails would have been a literal association with tradition, since the constructed stairways physically resemble the worn trail segments produced by generations of movement. The investment of effort into stairs that symbolized relationships between the social and natural orders is particularly interesting because they are associated with an overall transformation of the settlement system. Tsankawi, Tsirege, and the other new community houses that arose in the 14th century and thereafter are often described as part of a widespread process of "aggregation" that resulted in larger populations concentrated in fewer communities (cf. Cordell, Doyel, and Kintigh 1994). For present purposes, however, it is interesting that multiple lines of archaeological evidence are indicating that this period was characterized by increasing levels of competitiveness between communities (i.e., Powers and Orcutt 1999a; Snead, Creamer, and Van Zandt 2004; Snead 2008; Vint 1999; Walsh 1998). Other aspects of the trail network, including the construction of guard pueblos at strategic junctions (Snead 2002, 2005), can also be seen as responses to competitive pressure.

Whatever the interpretation of this social transformation, placing the gateway trails in a competitive context clarifies the symbolism of their construction. It was an uneasy time, and we can imagine the friction involved with the removal of large parts of the population into new centers. Justification for such a shift to those enduring it—and the defiant symbolism of the benefits of the transformation to those outside—can be seen in the new entrances. Walking up the trail to Tsirege it would have been forcibly apparent that the former easy gradation from countryside to community had been discarded in favor of an overtly stylized transition, one that was couched in the symbolism of the trail.

Considering trails as places using the theoretical frameworks of inscription and materialization provides one avenue for addressing the question of meaning in landscapes of movement. Working in a context associated with a living tradition—such as the Pueblo Southwest—and in a setting that has been well documented by archaeologists offers the opportunity to take such an approach. The Pajarito trails, and the thousand other pathways slowly vanishing in the wind and rain, offer us the opportunity to glimpse what Kathleen Stewart has described as "the past and present as sensed, tactile places that remember and haunt" (1996:148).

Acknowledgments

My research on the Pajarito trails is conducted with the guidance and permission of staff at Bandelier National Monument and ESH-20 at the Los Alamos National Laboratories. In particular I would like to thank Michael Elliott, Rory Gauthier, Steve Hoagland, John Isaacson, Bruce Masse, Elizabeth Oster, and Brad Vierra. Significant funding has been provided by the Friends of Bandelier through their Bob and Pam Massey Fund, and I am indebted to Dorothy Hoard for this and other support of my Pajarito work. Thanks also to my trails recording crews and to Bob Powers, who introduced me to the Pajarito trails.

4

O'odham Trails
and the Archaeology of Space

J. ANDREW DARLING

A path is a prior interpretation of the best way to traverse a landscape,
and to follow a route is to accept an interpretation, or to stalk your predecessor
on it as scholars and trackers and pilgrims do. To walk the same way is to reiterate
something deep; to move through the same space the same way is a means of
becoming the same person, thinking the same thoughts. It's a form of spatial theater,
but also spiritual theater, since one is emulating saints and gods in the hope
of coming closer to them oneself, not just impersonating them for others.

— Rebecca Solnit, *Wanderlust. A History of Walking*

Edward Soja defines historicism "as an overdeveloped historical con-textualization of social life and social theory that actively submerges and peripheralizes the geographical or spatial imagination" (1989:15). This chapter is a contribution to Soja's cause, an engagement in archaeological "spatial theater" (Solnit 2000). I consider two concepts, landscape and *space*, in a discussion of trails archaeology and the identification of social spaces in the past. *Infrastructure* also plays a part as a subset of the built environment, which involves the interplay of ideas and facilities, in this instance trail systems, that allow a society to function.

Definitions of landscape and space are derived from the work of Tilley (1994) and Lefebvre (1991). However, perhaps more like Lefebvre and less like Tilley, I wish to examine the way in which the social intersection of

---
Epigraph. 2000:68.

trails (as facilities for travel and mobility) and traditional song cycles (as expressions of geographic knowledge and cognitive geography) serve to produce and reproduce social spaces.

I will consider the role of Akimel O'odham (Pima) song series (or cycles) in the generation of social space in the arid southwest of central and southern Arizona and northern Sonora. One series, known as the Oriole Songs, serves as a primary example of the way in which social space is created through geographic itineraries expressed during song performances and corresponding travel on trails (Figure 4.1).

Travel is a geographical and a social phenomenon which is strongly tied to cognitive perceptions of landscape, the relationship of social spaces to physical places, and socio-cultural requirements for mobility (Darling, Ravesloot, and Waters 2004:283; Kelly 1992:44–49; Urry 2000:3). Tilley (1994, 2004) provides a synthetic approach that stresses phenomenological aspects of landscape including active or experiential dimensions. This includes dynamic sociological processes such as *agency* and *praxis,* which link actor, event, and place with ideological and cognitive systems. Tilley defines

4.1 Historic trail segment in the Maricopa Mountains, Arizona.

landscape as ". . . a series of named locales, a set of relational places linked by paths, movements and narratives. It is a 'natural' topography perspectivally linked to the existential Being of the body in societal space" (1994:34). Social space—its history, production, and manipulation—is a major theme in postmodern sociology and critical geography, and contributes significantly to Tilley's work.

If landscapes are composed of relational places (conceived by Tilley as arrays of socially constituted spaces), then it is reasonable to assume that social spaces can be reconstructed archaeologically through a study of trail systems, particularly when trails, as regionally extensive places, transcend social spaces or territorial boundaries (Snead, Chapter 3, this volume). This chapter, in part, seeks to examine the relationship of social space to archaeological trails.

For Henri Lefebvre, space is a social product that, like place, has a concrete reality exhibiting both abstract and physical properties (1991:26–27). "Socially-produced space is a created structure comparable to other social constructions resulting from the transformation of given conditions inherent to being alive" (Soja 1989:80; see also Foucault 1986; Sheridan 2006). Social space emerges from a "multitude of [material, social, and ideological] intersections," composed of *spatial practice, representations of space,* and *representational spaces* (Lefebvre 1991).

Lefebvre's conceptual triad contrasts sharply with formulations of perception and experience common to landscape studies, which are often viewed as perfect dualistic oppositions such as front-back, up-down, inside-outside, and right-left (Tilley 1994:16). For some critical geographers and sociologists the dualistic view subverts or limits the real connections between physical spaces in nature and ideational space. Lefebvre's multi-dimensional view, his conceptual triad (identified above), acknowledges that societal space exists in three corresponding, sensual realms, the *perceived,* the *conceived,* and the *lived* (1991:39–40). This multi-dimensional approach "shatters" traditional dualism, and leads critical geographers to conclude that the "material space of physical nature and the ideational space of human nature have to be seen as being socially produced and reproduced[,] . . . as ontologically and epistemologically part of the spatiality of social life" (Soja 1989:120).

The *built environment* is an example of social space, which includes not just the physical properties of architecture, or the spaces they contain, but also the ideology that serves to define social spaces within artificial (built) constructions (Soja 1989). Trails and trail systems are elements of the built environment that interact directly with physical and social space. They are different, because, unlike buildings which act as containers, trail systems define social spaces that are external to them. Journeys begin when spaces are identified (through which travel will occur), routes are selected, and trails are experienced (according to preconceived notions of travel and trail use).

Infrastructure links measurable facilities such as trail networks to pre-existing sets of cognitive social spaces (associated with certain activities and purposes) and geography. For example, travel to perform a religious function may require movement along sacred paths that interconnect shrines or other elements of the built environment dedicated to religion. Travel for trade, on the other hand, may imply movement along the same or different combinations of segmented pathways (now perceived as trade trails), which could include visits to trading partners or locations where items for trade are acquired or produced.

Viewing trails as Native infrastructure is a theme that appeals to concepts of how communities function as collections of interconnecting ideological and material systems. Knowledge of trails—not just of where people were but how they got there—provides an important dimension for understanding the location and distribution of sacred sites and settlements, and their relationship to trails. It also provides insights into the regular flow of resources (energy and information) among traditional communities through or between social and physical spaces (Gorenflo and Bell 1991; see also several chapters in this volume).

INFRASTRUCTURE AS TRADITION

The arid Southwest provides us with a unique natural landscape where trail segments, some as old as 10,000 years, are still visible in the desert (Figure 4.2). For the O'odham of central and southern Arizona, traveling is more than going from one place to another. It is a part of tradition and it is a metaphor for life. In fact, the way of life of the O'odham is illustrated by the Pima Maze or Sehe'e Ki (Elder Brother's home), the symbol used most often to identify O'odham heritage (Figure 4.3).

The Maze represents a significant spatial moment. As a life symbol, it is

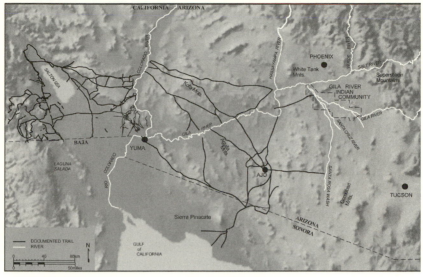

4.2 Major trail networks in the arid Southwest and northern Mexico.

composed of four roads or four stages of life. Everyone's life on this land is a cycle, generations of cycles, meeting over and over again on the way to other life journeys (Canouts, Allison-Ray, and Ravesloot 2002). Trails and travel are an intrinsic part of those journeys. The Maze also is a depiction of Elder Brother's mountain home, which exists simultaneously in four locations, each associated with one of the four directions. These include South Mountain, north of the Gila River Indian Community, Baboquivari Peak, the Sierra Pinacate, and one other. As a world symbol, the Maze identifies the four cardinal directions or the universe of creation in which life is enacted in concert with divine spirituality.

In a similar sense, *himdag* is the O'odham word meaning "tradition"; but it also can mean "heritage" or for the purposes of this discussion, "infrastructure." *Himdag* also can be translated as "to walk a (good) path." *O'odham himdag,* while acting as a covering term for Pima tradition and cosmology, appeals to qualities of travel or journeying also conceived as life's process. In a cosmo-geographical sense, the journey of the sun and moon, from the east (*Si'alig weco*), to the sunset or west (*Huduñig*), through the staying earth (*Ka:cim jewed*), describes a horizontal plane sandwiched by the sky above (*Da:m ka:cim*), and the fire below (*Mehi weco*)—a universal space defined as intersecting horizontal and vertical planes. Mountains, caves,

4.3 The O'odham Maze or *Sehe'e Ki.*

and shrines are places within the staying earth where humans and spirits (who reside to the west) may communicate. In the east (the direction of the sunrise) the spirits of the deceased may return to the staying earth to visit and to teach their living descendants about curing and shamanic practices (Kozak and Lopez 1999:65–66).

Song and power acquisition through dream journeys to spiritual places recapitulate travel and cosmo-geography. They are fundamental to the relationships between the ideology of travel and the actual trails that certain songs or song series may represent (or the journeys they entail). Songs may be sung separately when singers find themselves at a particular place or when referring to it (Darling and Lewis 2007). However, complete song series or cycles are performed during all-night "sings" at social dance grounds. Many song series, when "properly" performed, reenact the journey of the sun and moon and are temporally consistent with the all-night dances of which they are a part. In this way, "sings" provide a basic form by which journeys are preconceived metaphorically as cognitive or spiritual maps. In the case study that follows, these maps relate critical geographical knowledge, which may be vital to desert travel and survival.

MOVEMENT AND O'ODHAM SOCIAL SINGING

Donald Bahr has presented a wide range of studies related to O'odham curing practices and the ethnopoetics of O'odham song (Bahr 1986; Bahr, Giff, and Havier 1979; Bahr and Haefer 1978; Bahr et al. 1974; and Bahr, Paul, and Joseph 1997). Two abstract categories of O'odham song are identified, subsistence songs and social songs. Subsistence songs are those "aimed at improving the future material condition of the tribe" (Bahr, Giff, and Havier 1979:176), and can include curing songs or songs of divination. Social songs, such as the Oriole, Swallow, and Ant songs, accompanied traditional Pima "stomp" dancing held at all-night social events. Whether for sacred or secular functions, songs are never authored by Pima singers and instead are composed by the animals, spirits, or ghosts who teach the songs verbatim through dreams or visions. As a result, the songs are identified by the divine or spiritual author but can be passed on from singer to singer through performance and imitation (1979:172).

Traditional all-night dances require lengthy sings. These consist of a long series of brief songs strung together to create a mood and a particular story. Bahr typically translates individual songs in five to eight lines as demonstrated by these two examples from the Oriole series (Songs 16 and 17) (Bahr, Paul, and Joseph 1997:123):

(16) Iron Mountain.
Iron Mountain.
Uninvitingly sounds.
Wind runs there,
Then Stands,
Then hoots.

(17) Many people gather there
While I here
Sorrily die.
This my feather tip,
Already dead.

In general, songs from different song series (or divine authors) are not mixed, and as a result there is a consistency of source and theme during performances. Sings have a narrative structure with a beginning, middle, and end resembling prose myths. Each song in the series conveys some quality of action or geographic place. Unlike myths, however, which do not vary in plot, the order or sequence of songs may change at each performance. Such improvisation is essential to creating a mood or narrative sense that is conveyed across the entirety of the performance, even though the fixed sequence of events and places described may change (1997:70–72).

Bahr has focused his analysis on the ethnopoetics of sings and the sequencing of songs. The uniqueness of each performance lends the sing a character and expressiveness that is tied to an intimate knowledge of geography. "It is well to think of social dance song sequences as postcards sent from someone on an impassioned journey. On receiving the card one speculates about the mood of the sender, about all that was happening at the moment of the message . . . , and what the next step in the journey might be" (Bahr, Paul, and Joseph 1997:77).

As Bahr suggests, the geographic itineraries of a sing are created through song sequencing and establish the metaphorical domain of an imaginative journey to which physical travel (or its remembrance) is related.

Oriole Songs

The Oriole Song series was shared by Vincent Joseph, a member of the Gila River Indian Community in central Arizona, and consists of 47 individual songs recorded on three occasions from 1983 to 1985 (Bahr, Paul, and Joseph 1997:107–13). Bahr structures his analysis on the second sing, which he then subdivides into eight parts or thematic segments according to the song order. These include: Mythological Prelude (Songs 1–8); The Westward Journey (Songs 9–22); Birds (Songs 23–29); Calamities (Songs 30–32); Sunset (Song 33); Medicine Men (Songs 34–39); Whores (Songs 40–45); The Last Two Songs (Songs 46–47).

The itinerary or journey of Vincent Joseph's performance was geographically consistent, and as Bahr comments, this was an important organizing principle used by Joseph to memorize and later recite the songs. Two directional principles apply. First, the overall structure of the Oriole series follows the path of the sun and moon across the sky above (east to west) and fire below (west to east), without which no song series would be complete.

Second, the journey itself is subdivided into two separate axes of travel or orientation. The first axis is the Mythological Prelude, which follows a circuitous route encompassing areas north to south and back again, describing a ceremonial counter-clockwise cycle along an ethereal path clearly referencing the O'odham story of creation (Bahr et al. 1994; Lloyd 1911).

In this first thematic segment, the path of the Mythological Prelude proceeds as follows (Figure 4.4):

Song 1   Song (The singer sits surrounded by Oriole people)
Song 2   Where the Sun Is Newly Made (Casa Grande Ruin)
Song 3   East Shining Great House (As seen from Casa Grande Ruin)
Song 4   Witch's Making Place or Witch's Bed

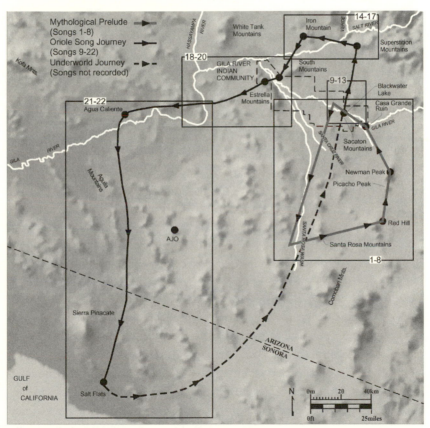

4.4 Oriole Song itinerary including the Mythological Prelude (Songs 1–8) and the Oriole Song-Journey to the West (Songs 9–22). The dotted route represents the journey through the underworld for which no songs were obtained.

Song 5   Children's Burial (Santa Rosa)

Song 6   Red Rock Hill

Song 7   Chief's Great House

Song 8   Chief's Great House (Feeler Mountain, also known as Newman Peak)

The second axis of travel begins with Song 9 and shifts the movement to
east-west outlining the first half of a counter-clockwise course connecting
various iconic mountains and springs (see Figure 4.4):

Song 9   Black Water Lake (in the Gila River Indian Community)

Song 10   White Pinched Mountain (Gray Hill as seen from there)

Song 11   Zig-zag Mountain

Song 12   Crooked Red Mountain (identified by Bahr as Red Bent
Mountain)

Song 13   Long Gray Mountain (Santan Mountains)

Songs 14–15 Remainder Bent Mountain (Superstition Mountains)

Song 16   Iron Mountain (Vainom Doag, also known as Piestewa Peak)

Song 17   Thin Mountain

Song 18   Greasy Mountain (South Mountain)

Songs 19–20 Broad Mountain (Estrella Mountains)

Song 21   Agua Caliente Hot Springs

Song 22   Spongy Water (Gulf of California, Salt Flats)

Bahr was unsure as to the location of the mountains identified in the
songs, although one consultant, Blaine Pablo, was able to point out many
of them from his house located in Sacaton Flats in the Gila River Indian
Community (Bahr, Paul, and Joseph 1997:120–21). The locations identified
to the north and west, which Bahr could not place specifically, such as Agua
Caliente Hot Springs and the Salt Flats, I have identified on the basis of discussions with Akimel O'odham singers.

The relationship between the two thematic axes defines two connected
journeys in cognitive and physical space. The Mythical Prelude establishes
the spatial and temporal context of the song-journey, which is reminiscent
of "The Dreaming" or Australian aboriginal concepts of dreamtime (Smith
and Burke 2007:42–46; Chapter 1, this volume). The Mythical Prelude
also situates the traveler (and the singers) in the world of named places,

which were the homes of significant medicine men or spiritual leaders. The prelude orients the listeners to the objective of the journey and the song performance, which is the acquisition of spiritual knowledge through the sacred journey to gather salt.

The second thematic segment charts a journey in geographic space, beginning at Blackwater Lake, a spiritual place of emergence located in the east end of the Gila River Indian Community not far from the home of the singer, Vincent Joseph. As a place of emergence, Blackwater Lake is both the starting and ending point of the journey. According to O'odham tradition, the salty waters of Blackwater Lake are said to originate or connect with the waters of the Gulf of California. The salt flat described in Song 22 is the halfway point, where the return passage or spiritual trail through the underworld from west to east begins. As discussed below, Vincent Joseph did not or was unable to share this portion of the underworld journey with Bahr and his colleagues.

Vincent Joseph's performance of the Oriole Songs appears to lack as many as 30 or more segments of the Oriole Song series, which were either left out or unknown (Bahr, Giff, and Havier 1979). My own discussions in 2005 with one O'odham elder suggest that these missing songs may have included elements of the journey that chart the path of the sun from west to east through the underworld (fire below). In Vincent Joseph's mind, it may have been inappropriate or irrelevant to recite the underworld segment in the context of social singing (a different cognitive space).

O'odham song performance, including the Oriole Songs, may vary among singers based on the context of the sing, where they live, and how they learned the songs. This presents a potential obstacle among groups composed of singers from different reservations or backgrounds with different cognitive geographies (Amadeo Rea, personal communication, 2005). In this case, the logical conclusion of the Oriole Song-Journey is the completion of the ceremonial counterclockwise movement of the sun at Blackwater Lake, where the journey began. As noted above, Blackwater Lake is thought to be physically connected with the Gulf of California. Participants in the sing would have been well aware that after visiting the salt flats, the travelers would return from the west both spiritually charged and potentially dangerous.

Once the journey is complete, the remaining segments of the series published by Bahr and his colleagues provide other thematic elements not directly related to the journey (and are therefore not part of the current discussion). Nearing the end of the series, Song 33 describes the death of the Sun at sunset, and establishes a moment of finality in this particular Oriole Song-Journey, but sets the stage for the unrecorded journey through the underworld. The penultimate song of the Oriole series initiates the conclusion with Song 46 (Bahr, Paul, and Joseph 1997:143):

And now we stop singing and scatter.
Here on our seats our poor scraping sticks lie,
With song-marks marked where they lie.

Bahr and colleagues interpret "song-marks" (*o'ohon* or *o'ohadag*) as drawings, inscriptions, writings, or even petroglyphs. Their remarks are compelling since "scraping sticks" or musical rasps (*hiifkut*) can be decorated with flowers or other decorations, which are emblematic of the spiritual qualities of the songs performed. "Song-marks" may be translated alternately as "song flowers." These pictures or representations embody the spiritual essences of the songs performed and for the Oriole series memorialize the spiritual journey that has just taken place. So, too, petroglyphs occurring along trails may also commemorate a place mentioned in the songs (Darling and Lewis 2007).

TRAILS AND SONG GEOGRAPHY

The song performance of Vincent Joseph offers one version of the Oriole Songs and therefore a single consistent song itinerary. Archaeological reconstruction of the journey in the field, however, is challenging since there are numerous possible trails or routes available which could link the landmarks identified in the series. Trail segments recorded during recent archaeological survey are related to elements of the Oriole Songs enumerated above (Darling and Eiselt 2003).

During the survey, the following general principles were maintained concerning trails in the arid deserts of the American Southwest. First, trails are the product of humans repeatedly traveling across preexisting game trails, natural corridors between resource areas (such as water sources), or along purposefully constructed or established routes of travel (Becker and Altschul 2008; Fowler, Chapter 5, this volume; Snead, Chapter 3, this volume). In some instances trails exhibit characteristics of casual clearing of stones and debris by travelers and intentional engineering. Geographic and environmental considerations also determine the location, appearance, and duration of trails.

Second, physical or geographic space has both etic and emic properties, in the same way that Lefebvre (1991) describes social space as having a reality, which is both abstract and sensory. Travel for Native American societies in the Southwest, prior to the latter stages of contact, was travel without Western forms of maps, or at least not the written or printed kind. Mapping was situated within the same mental process that determined the appropriate ordering of a song series or the retelling of myths replete with geographic references. Experience of travel and the qualities of place were reinforced in the repeated performance of songs and the telling of stories. As a result, one who knows the songs may be viewed as someone who knows where they are going and, more importantly, of the dangers along the way (Darling and Lewis 2007).

Finally, preliminary analysis of trails in the Southwest reveals that many routes of travel crosscut major drainage systems rather than paralleling river courses or streams (Darling and Eiselt 2003) (Figure 4.5). Movement along trails between zones of settlement and relative security (Zone A) to dangerous mountains/spiritual domains (Zone B), where loss of life and possessions is coupled with spiritual empowerment, is typical of cross-country travel in the desert Southwest. In Zone B, greater frequency of artifacts on the trail, especially broken pottery jars, as well as shrines, rock art, and other features attest to the dangers of travel where treacherous, steep terrain offers numerous threats to life and property.

ORIOLE SONG ARCHAEOLOGY

Oriole Song archaeology begins with the axes of travel represented in the two major segments of the Oriole Song series. In the Mythological Prelude, the geographic location expressed in each song revolves around events in ancient time, which appear in the O'odham creation story, but is not connected by archaeologically identifiable trails or trail segments. Each location, however, can be tied to an archaeological site, intaglio, or shrine mentioned in O'odham stories of creation (Bahr et al. 1994). These sites are not described in detail here. Instead, I focus on the trails associated with the

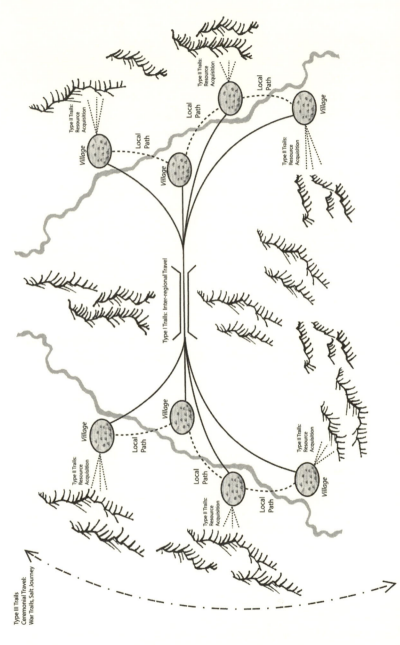

4.5 Trail networks often crosscut drainage systems, dividing the landscape into settled zones (Zone A) and hinterlands (Zone B). Type I trails serve in intra-regional travel between major drainages, whereas Type II trails are for local resource acquisition. Type III trails are ceremonial, inter-regional trade trails, or war trails that may bypass settlements.

westward journey, which can be traced from the Gila River Indian Community to the Gulf of California, an approximate distance of 460 km.

Westward Journey: Trails in the Santan Mountains

The westward journey begins at Blackwater Lake (Song 9) and in subsequent songs (Songs 10–13) proceeds northward in the direction of the Superstition Mountains. The series describes several mountains in the Santan Range located on the northern border of the reservation including White Pinched (To-hai-we-ñi-w-li-ke), Zigzag Connected (Ju-ñula-ñi-ñi-ka), Red Bent (Crooked Red) (We-gyu-na-ko-na-ke), and Long Gray (Ce-wesi-ko-mani). These are each mentioned in terms of their spiritual qualities or as places where songs may be learned (Bahr, Paul, and Joseph 1997:121–22, 150–51) (Figure 4.6).

As shown in Figure 4.6, Santan Trail #1 evolved into a wagon road and ultimately was used by motorized traffic. Santan Trail #2 traverses a much narrower canyon where foot traffic and the passage of horses and livestock were possible. Each of these trails exhibit artifactual evidence of continuity

4.6 Trails in the Santan Mountains (Songs 9–13; see Figure 4.4). Trails #1 and #2 pass frequent rock art panels and are flanked by numerous lookouts shown as circles.

with earlier prehistoric, Hohokam use (AD 950–1450). Intact trails are normally 30–50 cm wide and vary in expression depending on their location. Where they cross desert pavement, a clear track or multiple parallel tracks are often visible. As the trail rises into the Santan Mountains or that portion known as the Malpais Hills, the trail becomes incised into unconsolidated rocky talus that displays evidence of piling and removal to clear the path. Artifacts, mostly ceramic jar fragments, often in the form of potdrops, offer further confirmation of the validity of the trail and also the increased risk of loss as the traveler climbs higher into the mountains.

Additional landscape features associated with the Santan trails include numerous lookouts of dry-laid circular or defensive walls on flanking ridgetops overlooking the main passes. These served as defenses during the period of Apache raiding in the 19th century. The lookouts also served as signaling stations to keep the settled villages on the Gila River informed of the coming and going of O'odham retaliatory war parties, who used the same trails to track the Apache back to their home territories (Figure 4.7; Mallery 1881:339, 538).

While the Santan Range remains to be surveyed systematically, several trails have been identified (Adams et al. 1989; Adams, Howard, and Macnider 1989). According to the Oriole Songs, these trails follow a course leading to the next destination described in Song 14, or Remainder Bent (Wi ka me na ko na ke), also known as the Superstition Mountains. The Superstition Mountains can be easily seen from the trails in the Santan Range and offer a clear point of orientation while traveling (see Figure 4.2). For the next three songs, Songs 14–17, identification of the trails is hampered significantly by the presence of greater metropolitan Phoenix, although further investigation may still identify segments in the landscape.

The Komatke Trail

From the Santan Range, the Oriole Song itinerary proceeds through a series of mountainous destinations and continues to the Superstition Mountains, then west to Iron Mountain (Vainom Doag), Thin Mountain, and finally to South Mountain (Greasy Mountain or Moahdug). Archaeological evidence of the westward trail(s) picks up again at Song 18 (Bahr et al. 1997:123–24) (Figure 4.2). Here, several trails intersect at the western terminal ridges of South Mountain. Some trails lead into the South Mountain to access upland resources, while others lead to shrines, includ-

4.7 Lookouts in the Santan Mountains north of the Gila River Valley as depicted by Mallery (1881: fig. 339).

ing those dedicated to Elder Brother (Se'ehe) who keeps his home there. As the Oriole Song dictates, from South Mountain the trail proceeds across the Gila River Valley to a location in the foothills of the Estrella Mountains (Broad Mountain), where rock art and geoglyphs are present (Songs 19–20).

From the eastern side of the Estrella Mountains, across a high pass, and for a distance of 36 km, archaeological evidence of a trail to the west appears in segments as it traverses the Rainbow Valley to a pass in the North Maricopa Mountains, effectively crosscutting the large S-curve in the Gila River, which ends at Gila Bend (Figure 4.8). This portion of the trail identified as the Komatke Trail was described by Fr. Eusebio Francisco Kino, who traveled it from west to east in the winter of 1699 (Kino 1948).[1] Archaeo-

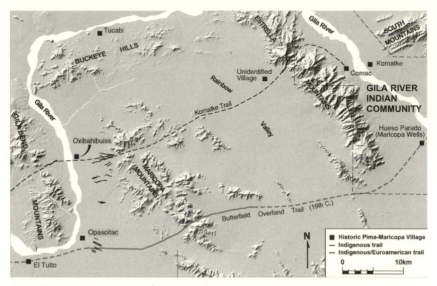

4.8 The Komatke Trail (Songs 18–20; see Figure 4.4) showing trail segments identified in passes in the Estrella Mountains, the Maricopa Mountains, and the Gila Bend Mountains.

logical evidence indicates that it was a more significant route of travel for prehistoric and historic Native Americans.

Field identification of portions of the trail through passes in the Estrella Mountains, Maricopa Mountains, and Gila Bend Mountains provides evidence that this route extended from the central Hohokam region, dominated by archaeological sites such as Snaketown, to its western periphery. During the Historic Period, the trail communicated between Yuman (Patayan) areas along the river inhabited by the Cocamaricopa, the Opa (including Pima and Opa living in mixed villages in the Gila Bend), the Maricopa, and the Pima (Ezell 1963; Darling and Eiselt 2003; McGuire and Schiffer 1982; Waters 1982).

Unusually good preservation of the trails west of the Maricopa Mountains reveals extensive branching as the main Komatke Trail split into numerous smaller trails accessing villages scattered along the length of the valley north of Gila Bend. Rock art and several shrines include one distinctive travel shrine in the Estrella Mountains, where the Komatke Trail begins, consisting of a tall, natural rock column with numerous ceramic offerings at its base (Figure 4.9). Visible trails are approximately 30–50 cm wide where they cross desert pavement, accompanied by linear artifact scatters consisting mostly of isolated sherds and ceramic potdrops (Figure 4.9). Artifacts recorded near the point where the Komatke trail enters into the Gila River Valley beyond the North Maricopa Mountains include one unmodified *Glycimeris sp.* shell, suggesting prehistoric movement of trade goods from the Gulf of California to the middle Gila drainage. This also anticipates the final portion of the journey to the west as depicted in the Oriole Songs.

4.9 Features along the Komatke Trail: bifurcating trails lead out of a pass in the Maricopa Mountains, an intact marine shell dropped along a trail in the same area, and a large trail shrine in the Estrella Mountains.

From Gila Bend to the Gulf of California

There is no correlation between the number of songs and distance traveled. The 153-km journey from Blackwater, on the Gila River Indian Reservation, to the Estrella Mountains required 20 songs, but only 2 songs (Songs 21–22) spanned the greater distance to the Agua Caliente Hot Springs and onward to the salt-gathering locations on the coast of the Gulf of California. Unlike the earlier portions of the journey westward, this latter segment of the trip resembles the spiritual travel of the Mythical Prelude.

Several scholars have described in detail the O'odham ritual journey to gather salt (Lumholtz 1912; Rea 1997; Underhill 1946). Along the northern beaches of the Gulf of California, the high tides deposit salt in a largely uninhabited and waterless landscape. The Tohono O'odham, and formerly the Akimel O'odham, make pilgrimages to the salt flats usually in summer following trails across the desert that connect the few hidden natural tanks holding rain water. Salt pilgrimages were significant religious events made by young men and experienced male leaders. Salt Journeys also presented some of the same hardships and dangers as going to war, with many opportunities for dreaming and acquiring spiritual power.

Reconstructing the trail network associated with these journeys is complex, in part because different O'odham communities utilized different salt flats. A logical continuation of the Komatke trail passes through the Gila Bend Mountains to Agua Caliente; however, other possible routes may have followed the Gila River Valley (Hayden 1967) (Figure 4.10). From the Tohono O'odham Nation (Papago), one trail took a total of four days, leading west through Ajo and then southwest to the Sierra Pinacate (Black Mountain), one of the homes of Elder Brother, and on to the coast (Underhill 1946). The shorter route only took two and a half days and ran to the south from Quijotoa to El Nariz, Quitovac, the Chujubabi Mountains, and finally the salt flats (Lumholtz 1912; Underhill 1946).

Tohono O'odham still make the Salt Journey today. However, the journey described by the Oriole Song cycle identifies a route that is uniquely tied to the Gila River Indian Community or the Akimel O'odham. This suggests that the northernmost O'odham living along the Gila River may have undertaken their own version of the Salt Journey, which included travel to the hot springs at Agua Caliente prior to traveling south to the Gulf of California.

DISCUSSION

In this chapter, I have related the O'odham Oriole Song series recorded by Bahr, Paul, and Joseph (1997) to segments of trails identified in the field through archaeological survey (Darling and Eiselt 2003). The ideological domain of O'odham song is mapped onto the domain of experience (and vice versa) via the facilities or trails that make journeys possible. Infrastructure results from the overlap or cross-domain mapping of ideology with places and trails in the landscape. Spiritual journeys are expressed through the combined metaphorical rendering of song, and the occurrence of fa-

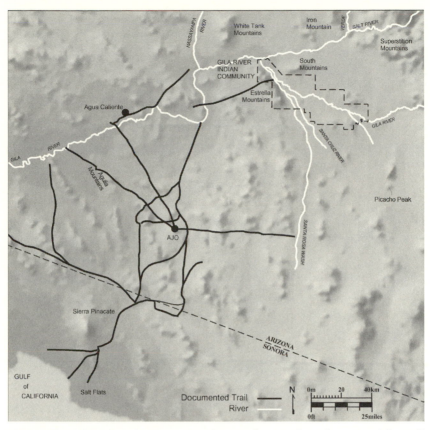

4.10 Trails to the salt-gathering areas (after Hayden 1967) on the coast of the Gulf of California (Songs 21–22; see Figure 4.4). Trails originating near Aguacaliente west of the Gila Bend are feasible routes.

cilities or trails on which journeys may be enacted. These are some of the relationships and spatial practices that lie at the core of O'odham infrastructure, which define the role of trails and dream travel in the acquisition of spiritual power.

As Borgo observes in reference to musical performance, "Cross-domain mappings do not simply 'represent' one domain in terms of another. They are grounded in our bodily experiences and perceptions and create precise, inference-preserving mappings between the structures of both domains . . ." (2004:180; see also Lakoff and Johnson 1980, 1999). O'odham cognitive geography is generated, in part, by cross-domain mappings of experience and representation through traditional and repeated song practice. In the case of the Oriole Songs, cognitive geography relates abstract domains (spiritual places) conveyed through song performance to familiar or concrete domains (geographical spaces) experienced through acts of travel. Song performances invoke social spaces in the form of journey imagery, which can be enacted in whole or in part by following well-used trails.

As archaeologists begin to recognize the thousands of kilometers of trails that once existed in the prehistoric and historic arid Southwest, it becomes apparent that numerous possible routes of travel once existed that would link as many or more places. Based on this analysis of the Oriole Songs, I propose that cognitive maps encoded in song journeys identify generic routes of travel between places or mountains, which can be used as mental reference images for planning other journeys. Knowledge of songs implies that certain song leaders had knowledge of geography and ceremonial travel. In the case of the Oriole Song series, spiritual enrichment requires that the journey proceed through several ideologically significant locations culminating in the journey for salt. However, when traced out in the field it is clear that other kinds of travel also took place on the same trails. These include acts of warfare and counter-raiding, trading expeditions, and travel between valleys and settled areas (see Devereux 1961:427–28 for a discussion of Mohave motivations for travel).

Native infrastructure is based on the corpus of traditional knowledge that relates ideas and facilities including cognitive mappings of social and physical space. The regular performance or retelling of songs and myths serves more than simply to educate a larger populace about the geographical configuration of places and things. Such performances also generate a shared sense of infrastructure and social space, a topic which remains to be examined in greater detail.

Networks of trails are part and product of a functioning infrastructure which relates social space to landscape. Trails, in turn, can be related to places including rock art and shrine sites along them. The chronology of the songs and trails is also interesting, since the social space defined by the Oriole Songs, recorded ethnographically, also correlates with the older Hohokam landscape (Darling and Lewis 2007). Trails, rock art, shrines, and linear artifact scatters offer tangible evidence that physical journeys between locations enumerated in song were routine for at least a thousand years prior to Vincent Joseph's recordings (Darling and Eiselt 2003).

CONCLUSION

I have attempted to relate theoretical concepts of space, landscape, and in-frastructure as a means for analyzing geographical referents and itinerary contained in the O'odham Oriole Song series. In particular, I suggest that repeated song performances generate shared cognitive mappings or a sense of spatial geography among the performers and listeners. It is helpful for O'odham singers to have a well-developed sense of space and geography. Listeners also benefit through the repeated association of certain songs with places arranged along trails. As a result, the organization and relevance of certain archaeological trail networks is made possible through the re-construction of landscapes of relational places (socially constituted spaces) identified in song and infrastructure (trail systems) (see Basso 1996b and other chapters in this volume).

Further consideration of song traditions like those of the O'odham and other southwestern desert cultures (Fowler, Chapter 5, this volume) may reveal a variety of ways in which geographic information is managed and perpetuated with ample opportunities for cross-cultural comparisons, par-ticularly with groups exhibiting complex dream cultures (see, for example, in the western Pacific and Australia, Lohmann 2004). Such studies may prove useful in the future reconstruction of cognitive geographies and their relationship to places and trails observed in the archaeological record.

NOTES

1. Ironically, the actual location of the route followed by Kino and his companions on March 1–2, 1699, was later misidentified by historians and archaeologists—first by Bol-ton in Kino (1948 [1919]), and subsequently by Karns (1954), Schroeder (1961), and Bur-rus (1971).

5

Reconstructing Southern Paiute–Chemehuevi Trails in the Mojave Desert of Southern Nevada and California: Ethnographic Perspectives from the 1930s

CATHERINE S. FOWLER

People are perhaps by nature wanderers and explorers. How else to find natural resources, establish good places to live and work, meet, greet, and trade with neighbors, and ultimately claim and hold places? Viewing a new landscape from an elevated vantage point allows one to observe potential routes of travel for these purposes: natural land contours, mountain passes, stream courses and other drainages, game trails, and ecotones. Although rarely defined by straight lines, these potential pathways into an area at a minimum provide a linear orientation to a landscape and perhaps further reduce it to a scale more manageable for human memory. All groups also develop mechanisms for orienting themselves in physical spaces, including some universal principles (Brown 1983) as well as ones taken directly from their geographies. Once a region is explored, human orientation systems help straighten kinks and meanders in pathways and further define routes based on various locators and known objectives. Over time, and with increased experience, people also develop elaborate systems of nomenclature for remembering or "mapping on" to those parts of their landscapes that they find significant. These, too, are conditioned by specific geographies, languages, and cultures of orientation (Boas 1934; Sapir in Mandelbaum 1958). By these several mechanisms, peoples and societies become comfortable with places, give them life through story, and turn them into "homelands" or places with unique cultural content and spiritual significance (Basso 1996b; Golledge 2003).

But the history of a people's explorations and particularly their actual routes of travel in a given area (paths, trails, even roads) are often obscured by time both physically and mentally. Sometimes they are set down in oral tradition or in written form, but perhaps more often older routes are forgotten as travel modes and goals change. Occasionally trails (physical manifestations of routes) or other travel features are rediscovered as physical remnants through archaeological investigation or through memory ethnography (Snead 2002; Darling and Eiselt 2003; Darling, Chapter 4, this volume; Ferguson, Berlin, and Kuwanwisiwma, Chapter 2, this volume). Systems of nomenclature, including toponyms or place names for landscapes, sometimes survive better (Basso 1996b), so that with even some knowledge of names and the principles they encode, it is possible to reconstruct something about the mental and physical world of travel for an area that people may have largely forgotten.

This chapter attempts such a reconstruction using some of the rich data on place names and travel routes collected by ethnographer Isabel Kelly from 1932 and 1934 among the Southern Paiute people of the Great Basin of western North America (Figure 5.1). More specifically, my analysis focuses on Kelly's data for the Las Vegas Southern Paiute and Chemehuevi (a Southern Paiute sub-group) in the southern and central Mojave Desert, one of the harshest landscapes in North America, but one known to have been heavily traveled (Davis 1961; Heizer 1978). Kelly recorded more than 500 place names as well as other travel data from a few elderly individuals in these groups, people who had long been displaced from their lands but who remembered the old days and older means of travel. She attempted to map them as best she could given the reference materials available to her at the time. She also recorded their memories of travel and trails between these locations, and she recorded pieces of songs and other data relating to sacred journeys, some of them following routes perhaps more mental than physical.

Some of Kelly's data for the Chemehuevi correlate nicely with those collected by Carobeth Laird (1976) from the 1920s into the 1940s from her husband, George Laird, a Chemehuevi who knew the area in his youth. In turn these accounts link with others involving places and routes used by

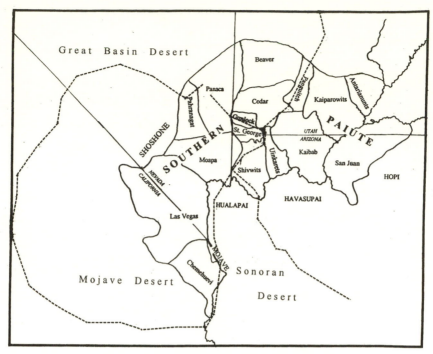

5.1 Southern Paiute territory (after Kelly 1934).

other Mojave Desert people and by early Euro-Americans traversing the region (Casebier 1972; Farmer 1935; Harner 1957; Johnston and Johnston 1957; Kroeber 1951; Rogers 1941). Taken together these data add additional depth to our knowledge of travel networks in the Mojave Desert and beyond that were so important for many types of cultural exchanges over millennia (Colton 1941; Davis 1961; Haury 1976; Heizer 1941, 1978; Sample 1950). They also illustrate the value of combining ethnographic memory data with other materials to provide a broader perspective and a richness of detail on travel and trails in a region than archaeology alone has been able to achieve.

TRADE ROUTES AND SACRED TRAILS

The Mojave Desert, with its vast areas of sparse vegetation and exposed soil surfaces, shows clear evidence of many traverses likely over thousands of years (Figure 5.2). Archaeologists and ethnographers have tied some of the trails and related features (such as rock cairns) to specific human activities, and are continuing to document more (Farmer 1935; Johnston and Johnston 1957; Kroeber 1925, 1951; Pigniolino, Underwood, and Cleland 1997; Rogers 1941; Spier 1933; Von Werlof 1988). Trail features are often found near other puzzling but important features of the human occupation of the region, such as linear rock alignments and the great mazes of the Mojave and Colorado deserts (Von Werlof 1987, 2004).

Several major routes and trails were developed at various points in the past for the shell trade and other trafficking between the Pacific Coast, the interior of southern California, and the Southwest (Heizer 1941, 1978). Artifacts along trails indicate that some may have been in use 5,000 or more years ago, while others date around AD 1000 (Harner 1957). Several of the major routes were still in use by the Mohave, River Yumans, and Chemehuevi during the Contact Period (1770s) to furnish trade goods such as shells, but also food stuffs, rabbit-skin blankets, salt, pottery, and basketry to each other as well as to the Cahuilla, Pai groups, other Southern Paiute, and

5.2 Trail across the Mojave Desert. Note petroglyph on the left. (Photograph courtesy of Ann Ettinger)

Navajo (Davis 1961; Sample 1950). Stories about small groups of Mohave men running along these desert trails, often traveling at night to avoid the heat and guided by reflective white stones as markers, are among the most impressive of southern desert travel narratives (Kroeber 1925, 1951; Weldon Johnson, personal communication, 1985; Sample 1950). They often ran 100 miles a day, reaching coastal destinations in three to four days (Stewart 1983). Several modern transportation routes cover or parallel these trails even today (Davis 1961: map 1).

The sacred trail system is no less impressive. Although physical manifestations have been documented for parts of it, the sacred system is at least in part a mental phenomenon. The literature tying ancient songs, stories, and dreams to geography is well known for the Mohave people (e.g., Kroeber 1925:754ff), with whom the Chemehuevi and Las Vegas Southern Paiute have long been in contact (see also Darling and Eiselt 2003; Darling and Lewis 2007; Darling, Chapter 4, this volume; Ferguson, Berlin, and Kuwanwisiwma, Chapter 2, this volume). The Chemehuevi and Las Vegas Paiute people likewise have several of the same song cycles related to ancient stories of great journeys by spiritual beings and ancestors, at least some of which were used to establish hunting and other territorial rights for their hereditary owners. Both Kelly (1932–34) and Laird (1976) recorded versions of the better-known cycles, including the Mountain Sheep Song, Deer Song, Salt Song, and Talk Song. Kelly also recorded fragments from individuals of the Chemehuevi and Las Vegas Paiute tribes covering more localized areas. The songs and stories contain numerous place names for mountains, water sources, valleys, and other geographic points of interest, many of which are also physical points on known trails. In a few ancient stories, the places and the place names are actually first established in the distant time, by various beings. For example, Southern Fox shoots four arrows as he begins his journey, each of which creates a well-known spring when it strikes the earth and is pulled out (Laird 1976:159f). One of the versions of the Salt Song recorded by Kelly (1933:18:106f) tells of the grand journey of two birds up the eastern side of the Colorado River from roughly the Blythe area to the salt caves beyond the great bend of the river to the north and then back south through the Las Vegas valley and Ash Meadows, ultimately returning to their point of origin. They then follow the Bill Williams River, ultimately ending their journey by entering a large cave. The narrator reported to Kelly that "they sang en route and as traveling along—named everything they saw, mountains, water, everything." Although neither Kelly nor Laird was able to record any of these cycles in full, it is clear that the sacred telling and singing allowed the storytellers and listeners to journey to many specific named places in their minds, memorizing routes, springs, foods, stopping places, and camping locations along the way. The songs were owned by specific individuals and passed down to their heirs. But they could be sung by others who had memorized them, and likely were repeated often enough to become potent learning devices. Mental maps of this kind keep geography fresh in a person's memory, perhaps making it easier to follow a particular route when needed, even if a person may not have physically visited an area before. Most trails and trail complexes in this region today no longer have such associations, although at least some clearly once did. A few, such as the Salt Song Trail, are at least partially known (Salt Song Project 2005). But sorting sacred from secular routes may never have been significant to these indigenous travelers, as such a dichotomy rarely divided other aspects of thought in life (Kelly 1932–34; Laird 1976; Miller 1983). The specific mechanisms involved in singing and storytelling likely made memorizing the routes and details easier as well. This tradition was clearly fading by the time Kelly and Laird were in the field, but enough of it remained to illustrate its obvious importance.

CONSULTANTS

Isabel Kelly recorded most of her data on Chemehuevi trails and attendant place names from Charlie Pete (AKA Mataviam) during fieldwork at Fort Mohave and Parker, Arizona, in 1933. Mr. Pete lived most of his life at Fort Mohave, which apparently had been principally within Mohave territory prior to the mid 1800s (Roth 1976). His father was from Ivanpah Valley and his mother from the Old Woman Mountains, both to the west in the Mojave Desert. Mr. Pete had also lived at Pahrump and at Ash Meadows within the territory of the Las Vegas Southern Paiute and thus he knew that region well and was able to map part of it. Although we do not know how Kelly worked with Mr. Pete on his map of place names and trails, apparently the map was drawn by him more or less from memory, with some reference to a map of springs in the Mojave Desert compiled by Walter Mendenhall (1909). Kelly also may have used some of the few existing USGS maps. She checked some of the data provided by Mr. Pete with other

Chemehuevi men, including Tom Painter and Ben Paddock, and especially with Las Vegas Paiute Daisy Smith (Kelly 1932–34). Mrs. Smith provided her own map of the Las Vegas valley and some of its trails, but the detail is not as rich as on Mr. Pete's map for Chemehuevi country. Mrs. Smith was born in the Las Vegas valley and lived in and around the area most of her life.

Carobeth Laird began recording information on Chemehuevi places and trails from her husband George Laird beginning in 1919 at Parker, and then continuing after they moved away from the area a few years later (Laird 1976). Unfortunately, Laird's maps were lost, but her remarkable volume on Chemehuevi culture and history contains a reconstruction of some of the trail and place name information (Caylor 1976). Although the Kelly and Laird materials are primarily from only three people, and admittedly only fragmentary, they help to document what must have been an extensive network of trails linked to an elaborate system of landscape nomenclature, song, and story. They also coincide with other fragments from historical, archaeological, and other sources to give a broader understanding of the region's cultural geography (e.g., Ahlstrom 2003; Duke 2006; Zedeño et al. 2006).

GENERAL ASPECTS OF TRAVEL

Charlie Pete described general principles of travel to Kelly in the following way:

> Travelers packed everything on their backs, and wore any kind of footgear. Children always wore shoes; if the children were too small to walk, their parents took turns carrying them. They also took turns packing the water jar, which was carried in a burden basket (*aɨs*) or a net. Blankets, etc., were taken. Women took cooking utensils, including manos, but not metates. Men took weapons and walked ahead. Dogs accompanied the party. Children were given something to carry—perhaps a small skin sack, but not a burden basket or net. Travel along certain routes had to be timed so that people could be sure that there would be water available in drier sections. Timing was particularly important if some of these sources were tanks and sandstone potholes. (Kelly 1934:23:7)

According to Tom Painter (Kelly 1934:24:26), Chemehuevi travelers always stopped at certain piles of rocks (cairns) along the way: "there were many of these, all in the mountains." They broke off twigs of creosote bush and placed them on top of the pile with a stone to cover. Then they stood on the stone for 10 to 15 minutes talking to the stone pile and asking to be refreshed, saying: "'I do this that my limbs may not be tired.' Only older people did this—they never passed up one." Mr. Painter did not think that the cairns were necessarily part of a sacred trail system. Rather, he felt that the stone piles were part of the regular travel network, but that they got their power from particular "doctors," persons with special supernatural powers. Nor did Mr. Painter associate cairns in particular with the distinctive mazes (geoglyphs, linear and non-linear arrangements of rocks and/or cleared areas, sometimes in the form of humans or animals) in the region, telling Kelly that the mazes were present in the area before the Chemehuevi arrived (see Von Werlhof 2004 for Mohave and River Yuman accounts of their origins). According to Mr. Painter, good Chemehuevi runners could run all day, covering the distance from Fort Mohave to Yuma (more than 100 miles) in 24 hours, thus certainly rivaling the feats reported for Mohave runners.

George Laird related similar material to Carobeth Laird (1976:135f), noting that although conditions of travel had been altered by the late 19th century, choice of trails differed depending on whether men were traveling alone or with families. Men often took more direct routes (and more short-cuts) through drier country as they could travel more rapidly and cover more distance between water sources. Trails chosen by family groups or weaker persons had more water stops and potential camping places, as did more modern horse trails. But for the most part, according to George Laird, all persons followed established trails. The only exceptions were hunters in direct pursuit of game (Laird 1976:136). Mr. Laird apparently did not comment on rock cairns or any other trail markers.

EXAMPLES OF ROUTES AND TRAILS

As noted earlier, the routes mapped by Kelly and Laird provide but a fragmentary record of what was likely a very complex network for travel along the Colorado River, and across the Mojave Desert, one of the hottest and driest regions in North America. Routes and specifically trails in the desert usually linked named water sources, many of them permanent springs, but also more ephemeral ones such as smaller sandstone tanks and pot-holes (locally called *tinajas* after the Spanish term). Most were in the desert ranges, and thus travel routes link these "islands" in the desert. Although many water sources were known in the collective wisdom of Chemehuevi and other Southern Paiute people, a few examples with their linkages will serve as illustrations. A comparison of Charlie Pete's with George Laird's accounts show several correlations, if not in exact routes, at least in place names and descriptions of the country traversed along the way. The actual trails used have not been verified by archaeological survey.

Example 1: Chemehuevi Valley to the New York Mountains

According to Mr. Pete (Kelly 1933:23:7b), there were two alternative trails from Chemehuevi Valley (Sɨwavats, "Gravel Water") on the Colorado River to the New York Mountains (Kaiva, "Mountains"), a place visited for hunting, for collecting "greasy" pine nuts (*Pinus edulis*), and occasionally for mining turquoise (Figure 5.3). The first route (see dark line, Figure 5.3) took four days and ran along the base of Paiute Mountain (Anpanikaiv, "Call-Out Mountain"), past Clipper Mountain (Tukumpavits,"Wild Cat Chop-up"), and up the west face of the Providence Range to the New York Mountains. The first night's camp was on top of the Turtle Mountains (Nantapɨaxantɨ, "Having Large Mescal"; Figure 5.3 #1) and was apparently a dry camp, al-though Mr. Pete named four springs on the mountain. The second night people stayed at a spring on the north end of the Old Woman Mountain (Mamapukaibɨ, "Old Woman Mountain"; Figure 5.3 #2) where he named six springs. The third night's camp was made at a spring on the north end of Clipper Mountain (Tukumpavits), likely at a spring called Pagampɨgantɨ ("Has Cane [*Phragmites*] Spring"; Figure 5.3 #3). The fourth night was spent at the South Providence Mountains (Tɨpisaxawats, "Blue-green Stone Place," Figure 5.3 #4), where there are five major springs, and on the fifth night the party would reach New York Mountain (Kaiva, Figure 5.3 #5). The second route was a day shorter with the second night spent at the north end of Old Woman Mountains (Figure 5.3 #2), the third at a spring at the north end of Paiute Mountain (Figure 5.3 #3a), and then reaching New York Mountain (Figure 5.3 #5) on the fourth day.

George Laird's (1976:137) route from Chemehuevi Valley, called Siwáavatsi ("Place of Mortars"), to the New York Mountains is less clearly

5.3 Charlie Pete's trails from Chemehuevi Valley to the New York Mountains. (Map by Karen Byers)

defined overall (see solid and dashed lines, Figure 5.3) and camping places
are not mentioned. But it went first to West Wells (Hawayawi—no etymology; Figure 5.3 A), then to Mohawk Spring (Siwayumitsi, "Coarse Sand
Caves In"; Figure 5.3 B) in the Turtle Mountains, then to Paiute Mountain
(Ampanigyaivya, "Talking Mountain"; Figure 5.3 C), then to Old Woman
Mountain (no name provided; Figure 5.3 #2—same as Mr. Pete's), then to
the South Providence Mountains (Tɨmpisagwagatsitci, "Green Stone"), perhaps by way of Arrowweed Spring (Figure 5.3 D; it could be accessed from
either side of Clipper Mountain; see also Table 5.1), and finally north to the
New York Mountains (Kaivayáamanti; Figure 5.3 E). With the exception of
a possible reverse order in stops at Paiute and Old Woman mountains, and
no mention of Clipper Mountain, the routes are largely the same (see Table
5.1 for comparison).

Table 5.1. Place Names Along the Chemehuevi Valley to New York Mountains Route: Charlie Pete and George Laird Versions

CHARLIE PETE	GEORGE LAIRD
Chemehuevi Valley: Sɨwavats, "Gravel Water"	Chemehuevi Valley: Siwáavatsi, "Place of Mortars" West Well: Hawayawi (no etymology)
Turtle Mountains: Nantapɨaxantɨ, "Having Large Mescal"	Turtle Mountains: (not named) A spring: Siwayumitsi, "Coarse Sand Caves In"
Old Woman Mountains: Mamapukaibɨ, "Old Woman Mountain" (2nd stop)	Old Woman Mountains: (not named) (3rd stop)
Paiute Mountains: Anpanikaiv, "Call Out Mountain"	Paiute Mountains: Ampanigyaivya, "Talking Mountain"
Clipper Mountain: Tukumpavits, "Wild Cat Chop-up" At spring: Pagampɨgantɨ, "Has Cane Spring"	Clipper Mountain: (not mentioned) (but spring Pagangkwitcunni, "Bunched Up Cane," in South Providence Mountains)
South Providence Mountains: Tɨpisaxawats, "Blue-green Stone Place"	South Providence Mountains: Tɨmpisagwagatsitci, "Green Stone"
New York Mountains: Kaiva, "Mountains"	New York Mountains: Kaivayàamanti, "Mountain __"

Sources: Kelly 1932–34; Laird 1976

Example 2: Chemehuevi Valley to Parker

A second example from the materials recorded by Kelly from Mr. Pete involves travel from Chemehuevi Valley to Pa'siva'u (no etymology), a farming community on the Colorado River below present-day Parker, Arizona, a distance of roughly 40 miles. Four alternative routes between these two points were possible (Figure 5.4). Three trails went over the Whipple Mountains (Wiato), and the fourth, the easiest, followed the river. The first trail (Figure 5.4 #1) over the mountain passed by Spring 1 (circled on Figure 5.4), called Kwiar‡mpaxant‡ ("Screwbean Water"), and was a very hard trail with steep cliffs used only by men when hunting or in a hurry to get to the village. Kelly remarked that the trail was apparently still visible, and included a series of steps near the top. A second spring, called Avatakan ("Many Caves," circled on Figure 5.4), was also on this trail, east of Monument Peak. The second trail also accessed the same two springs but was further west (Figure 5.4 #2). The third trail (Figure 5.4 #3) apparently went around the west side of the mountain passing two additional springs which were not permanent: Sagab‡axat‡ ("Has Willows") was midway along the top of the mountain but apparently was sometimes dry; and Sawapits ("Arrow Grass Water") that may have been near Whipple Well in Whipple Wash, but was also unreliable (neither is marked on Figure 5:4).

George Laird, when charting a longer route from Cottonwood Island north of Chemehuevi Valley to Fort Yuma (opposite the mouth of the Gila River in Arizona), recounted the following about part of this route:

> Leaving ?Opinyawit‡m?ma, the next water is ?Owasopiyamant‡ [Salty Tasting], after that a spring the name of which was not recalled, then Hawayawi [West Wells]. Here the trail divides again, one route going over Wiyaatuwa [Whipple Mts.] and the other passing around it to the west. The old high trail from Hawayawi over Wiyaatuwa is one which time has not obliterated. Where the ascent begins, there is the watering place called Pagoosovɨtsi [Guatamote Spring]. Further on the pitch approaches the perpendicular, and near the summit stones have been piled to form crude steps. There are springs at intervals along the top of the range, but the next named and located water is Sohorah [Notched Post, Chambers Well].

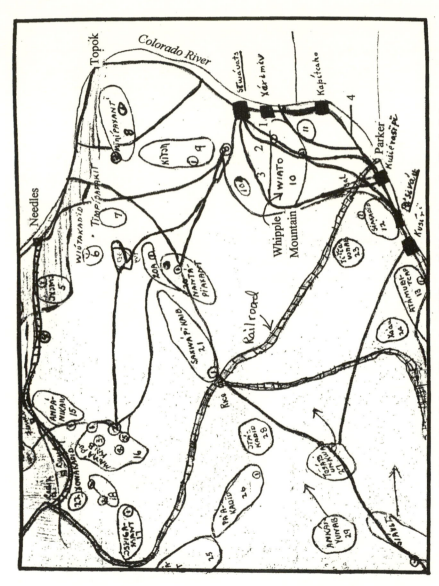

5.4 Map of trails from Chemehuevi Valley to Pa'siva'u drawn by Charlie Pete.

The two trails Mr. Laird describes over and around Whipple Mountain seem close to those reported by Mr. Pete (his #1 and #3), including the difficult assent for the first one. The differences in spring names suggest that they either stopped at different water sources or that the springs had alternative names. Given that the accounts of both of these men were recorded many years after they had traveled these trials, they still show a remarkable correspondence.

Jay Von Werlof (personal communication, 2004) describes walking what may be the same trail with two Mohave companions in 1980, but in reverse, and finding a trail shrine near the summit. A friend had told him of a trail from below Parker (perhaps Mr. Pete's Pasi'va'u) up into the Whipple Mountains. The friend noted that near the crest travelers would place a stone alongside the trail as they neared the summit. Von Werlof and companions followed the trail (being careful not to walk directly on it) "from near Earp [California] across from Parker [Arizona] on up-sloping terrain some 12 miles (?) to the crest, heading to the Whipples." Near the summit they found the rock cairn which he described: "The cairn by then must have contained thousands of river-worn cobbles (probably brought purposefully from the river), standing some 10–12' high and a diameter of perhaps 20'." Von Werlof adds: "The trail is a Chemehuevi trail, and one of the major ones out of the Mojave Desert to their friendly hosts at Parker." Although he does not mention steps, these would have been on the other side of the summit, which he did not descend.

Example 3: The Mojave or "Old Government" Road

A third trail, described in part by Charlie Pete and George Laird and mentioned in historical accounts going back to at least 1860 (Casebier 1972), is the more heavily traveled route from Fort Mohave, on the Colorado River, west across the desert to the San Bernardino Mountains. This trail follows one of the old trading trails from the Colorado River to the Pacific Coast that was heavily used in pre-contact times (Farmer 1935; Johnston and Johnston 1957). The U.S. Army and supply trains used it in the 1860s. This route was probably modified from the Native foot trail to accommodate horses and wagons, but it is clear that at least parts of it followed the older Mohave/Chemehuevi trails and stopped at known Chemehuevi water sources. I add this account not only to show the points of agreement between Charlie Pete, George Laird, and historic accounts, but through the added detail provided in a military reconnaissance, to illustrate that the Native trail system was probably even more complex than the route information documented in the memories discussed thus far (Figure 5.5).

The route as described by Mr. Pete went from Fort Mohave (Figure 5.5 #1) to Paiute Springs (Paasa, Figure 5.5 #2), then on to Rock Springs (Tooagah, "Center of Boulders," Figure 5.5 #3), then to Marl Springs (Figure 5.5 #4), then to Soda Springs (Figure 5.5 #5) on the west side of Soda Lake, down the course of the Mojave River and beyond to the San Bernardino Mountains. George Laird described this same route as leaving the river at "Owl Ear Tank" (Muhunankavkyavo?o), passing on to Paiute Springs (Paasa, Figure 5.2), then to Rock Springs (Tooyagah, Figure 5.3), and north to Kessler Spring (?aipavah, "Boy Water," Figure 5.5 #6, dashed line), past Soda Lakes (Figure 5.5), on to the Mojave River and ultimately to San Bernardino Mountain (Kukwnɨyagantɨ). The two accounts agree on most important places on this route, except the addition of Kessler Spring which is to the north of the more direct track that became the Mojave Road or the "Old Government Road" (Casebier 1972).

A Military Reconnaissance in the District

From April 30 to May 10, 1860, Lieutenant M.T. Carr, an army officer under command of Major J. H. Carleton and assigned to chase and kill supposed hostile Chemehuevi/Paiutes in this part of the Mojave Desert, made a reconnaissance through sections from where the trail left the Mojave River near Camp Cady (Figure 5.5 'A') to and around Soda Lake, Rock Springs, Marl Springs, and the Providence Mountains. The report, which is a day-by-day account, frequently mentions "Indian tracks" and "Indian trails," including many more than any "main route" might suggest, as well as camps and water holes. Carr's account from Camp Cady is summarized as follows (Casebier 1972:18–25) (Figure 5.5 'B' through 'F' indicate areas of march; frequent returns to Soda Springs were for water and forage for horses):

Day 1. Cienega of the Mojave to Soda Springs: crossed two Indian trails going in the direction of the Providence Mountains.

Day 2. Across Soda Lake: saw two Indian tracks following the main road, and another going north at the sand hills.

Day 3. Followed one of the trails, found a camp and gave battle, killing and capturing four people and taking several basketry water jugs filled

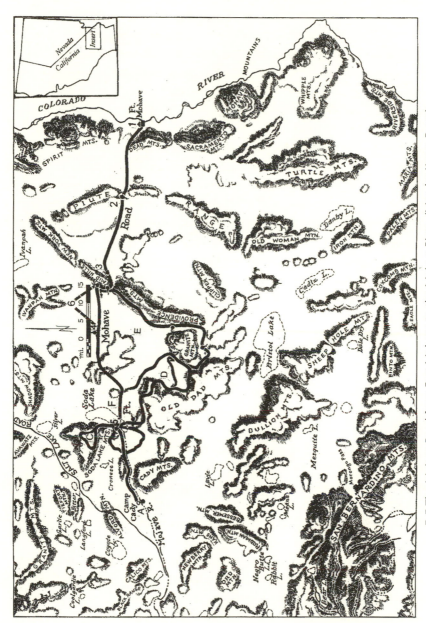

5.5 The Mojave Road from Fort Mohave to the Mojave River. (Map by Karen Byers)

with "clear, cool, mountain spring water"—although they could not find the source.

Day 4. Back to Soda Springs: found another trail but was unable to follow it up.

Day 5. Left Soda Springs for Marl Springs, following an Indian trail but losing it in the dunes; saw additional fresh tracks at Marl Springs, and Indian and horse tracks at foot of Cornese Mountains.

Day 6. Followed an old trail south to an abandoned rancheria that may have had 60 Indians and 10–12 horses; crossed three more trails going south.

Day 7 and 8. Back to Soda Springs and out again to Rock Spring, crossing more trails and finding rock holes full of water, fresh tracks.

Day 9: Out of Marl Springs, saw several old trails, including ones leading toward the Colorado River and north to Bitter Springs.

Day 10. Followed another trail from Soda Springs to Bitter Springs, and then returned to Camp Cady via the Cienega of the Mojave River.

Although Carr's troop sometimes saw Native people in the distance, the one battle was the total return for their ten days of effort. Carr provides this interesting note on the day of the battle, after not being able to find the water source at the camp with the water jugs: "There must, of course, be water near the rancheria, but no person but an Indian, who knows exactly where it is, would ever be likely to find it, as these springs are covered over with large stones and these covered up with drift sand. Indians who know the country well, know every spot to go to and scrape the sand off to get at the water" (Casebier 1972:20).

Carr's account not only validates much of the main route described by Pete and Laird, but hints at the numerous additional trails and alternative routes present in even a small district such as this. Major Carleton found similar patterns later in 1860 during his reconnaissance of the region north of Soda Lake to Las Vegas, Nevada, while hunting for supposed renegades (Casebier 1972). A complex of trails and tracks connected all of the permanent and ephemeral water sources in the region, not just the main routes. Big horn sheep trails and human trails would likely coincide for many routes in higher country, but lowland trails may have been exclusively human. Although the trails and place names recorded by Kelly and Laird are significant to putting a human face on this landscape, the ethnographic memory they recovered is likely but a pale reflection of true travel and trail systems in the region in pre-contact times.

Example 4: The Las Vegas Valley

A similar situation is evident in the data provided to Kelly by Daisy Smith and others of Las Vegas regarding trails in that part of Southern Paiute country. Kelly and Mrs. Smith produced a sketch map with several place names, especially for important water sources (springs, ephemeral streams, seeps, and tanks), and some indication of the routes and trail links between them (Figure 5.6). Her detail is best for the Las Vegas Valley and immediate vicinity, including the east slope of the Charleston Range, and

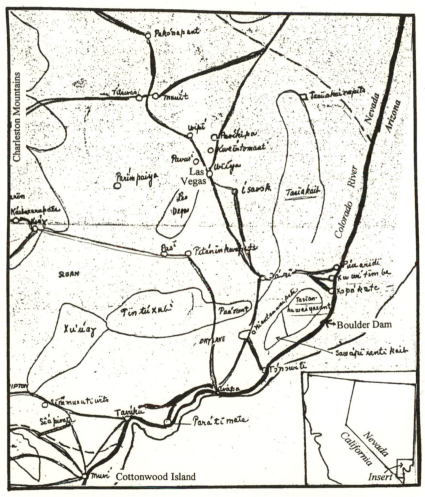

5.6 Map of Southern Paiute territory drawn by Daisy Smith.

the west slopes of the Sheep Range and Sunrise Mountain, the heartland of Las Vegas Southern Paiute territory. Her knowledge extended both east and west of this central area, and included place names for the Pahrump Valley, Ash Meadows, the Indian Springs area, the Desert Range, and the Colorado River. Mrs. Smith drew lines connecting several of these points, suggesting that there were trails between and among them, but the map details are not as rich as those provided by Charlie Pete. Although Kelly does not comment on the issue of gender and knowledge of trails and travel, women may have known little about trails associated with hunting territories. They would rarely be the singers or inheritors of songs and stories tied to such places, although women would certainly hear them performed (Laird 1976).

Some archaeological evidence of trails in this Southern Paiute region has been identified in recent years. In 2003, Heritage Research Associates of Las Vegas discovered what appeared to be a short segment of an old trail at the base of the Sheep Range, near Corn Creek, the site of one of the important 19th century Southern Paiute settlements. This feature correlates with one of the trail lines drawn by Mrs. Smith that runs along the Sheep Range as far as Indian Springs. The trail was difficult to follow beyond that short segment (Roberts, Warren, and Eskenazi 2007:57). An additional set of trails, some of which appeared to be footpaths linking water sources, was located in a survey of the Sloan Canyon area southeast of Las Vegas Valley (Duke 2006). Zedeño et al. (2006) also recorded archaeological evidence of trails in the Charleston Mountain and Belted Range region together with comments by contemporary Southern Paiute and Western Shoshone elders about their use. Some of these also link with places and trails named by Mrs. Smith (see Figure 5.6).

Kelly also recorded fragmentary versions of the sacred trail system for the Las Vegas area, particularly as expressed in variants of the Deer Song, Mountain Sheep Song, and Salt Song (Kelly 1932–34). A portion of her account of the Deer Song serves to further illustrate the power of these materials for providing knowledge of geography. Kelly says:

In the deer song, the deer travels around Charleston range looking for food. The snow is deep and it goes from place to place. It starts up on top of Charleston Peak; then it comes through the snow, finally out of the snow and down the valley. Comes through *tsoriuway*

(Joshua Tree Valley), between Charleston Range and Tule Springs. They sing all this in a song; name every place he stops, everything he eats. (1933:18:122)

Kelly then gives two samples of parts of the song, both of which name three places that the deer stops, two of them springs. She notes that one singer, who sings until midnight, takes the deer around Charleston Peak and down about half way to the valley. A second singer, who starts after midnight, covers all the places the deer stops when it comes down the rest of the way and emerges from the snow into the valley. Kelly (1933:18:122) reports that an abbreviated version of this song was sung for dances and funerals, but that hunters who owned it sang the full version upon request by other hunters who were about to go out for game. This indicates that the proper singing must have been an exceedingly rich and informative experience, both in terms of the places named and visited as well as the foods for the deer: a virtual environmental inventory. Although such journeys when sung were more mental than physical, at least some paths and trails may have been associated with connecting the points of reference in the songs, perhaps to actual deer or other big game trails. Today we can only correlate the songs with broad corridors of movement, but archaeologists are on the alert for the places and other features mentioned that may be connected by other, more mundane trail networks. For both physical trails and mental journeys, certainly one key is the location of water resources: of the 230 place names Kelly collected from Mrs. Smith and others for the Las Vegas territory, 92 are the names for springs and other water sources, 70 are for mountains or mountain-related features (perhaps for overall orientation), and the remainder are other geographic features.

CONCLUSION

The ethnographic data collected by Isabel Kelly from the Chemehuevi and the Las Vegas Southern Paiute, in tandem with those collected by Carobeth Laird and given in historic sources, illustrate a complex set of linkages for travel in the Mojave Desert. On the practical level, these included various types of local trails, attendant place names, and probably at least some trail markers. Locating and remembering water sources within one's own territory was clearly emphasized. Discovering and establishing reasonable travel routes between these sources, both for families on the move as well as for hunters who might better be able to take more direct routes or go longer distances between water sources, was also important. In addition to more localized routes, several very well known trade routes extended across the Mojave Desert crossing tribal boundaries, and these likely were used over very long periods as communication linkages and major avenues for moving goods over the whole of the Desert West and Southwest. At least portions of these have been documented on the ground by archaeological surveys and continue to show promise of further definition (Duke 2006; Johnston and Johnston 1957; Rodgers 1941).

Equally important in this region, and again part of the memory ethnography of Kelly and Laird, are the sacred trails, which invested symbolic importance in corridors of movement and perhaps specific trails. Knowledge of the system was kept in song and stories, and gave the mental maps to be handed down through generations. These were likely excellent devices for learning one's own hunting territory as well as those of others, and became mechanisms for further attaching oneself to the land and its resources. Although we are aware of only fragments of these lengthy and detailed traditions today, as many slipped into disuse long ago, we can still marvel at the hints of their richness recovered by ethnographers in the 1930s (see also Darling, Chapter 4, this volume; Ferguson, Berlin, and Kuwanwisiwma, Chapter 2, this volume; Zedeño, Hollenback, and Grinnell, Chapter 6, this volume). Specifically, the correlation between these symbolic systems of geographic knowledge and more practical routes of travel to and through the Mojave Desert may not have been isomorphic, as the mental journeys could cross areas that might be impractical to access (e.g., Laird's [1976:157f] abbreviated journey of the Southern Fox). However, the two systems reinforced each other and provided people with the means to learn about their country, to travel through and live within it. Although many of the data presented here require more work, including more archaeological and ethnographic verification, they remind us of the importance of views of the world of travel and landscape through mental images as well as physical. The study of the oral tradition of place, including trails, place names, and the songs, stories, and metaphors that go with them, is receiving new attention of late (Basso 1996b; Feld and Basso 1996; Hunn 1994; this volume), so perhaps from this combined approach something of the soul of these materials might be better recovered and understood, to the benefit of the indigenous communities as well as other place seekers.

Acknowledgments

Work on this project has been funded in part by the Wenner-Gren Foundation for Anthropological Research, and is by permission of Robert Van Kemper, Southern Methodist University, Kelly's literary executor.

6

From Path to Myth:
Journeys and the Naturalization of
Territorial Identity along the Missouri River

MARÍA NIEVES ZEDEÑO, KACY HOLLENBACK,
AND CALVIN GRINNELL

I was scout of the war parties. I was a good runner, hardy and enduring, and
that is how I came to know the names of those hills and other landmarks in the
country. I know that I am right because I have seen these places. A person who
tells the stories without seeing the places, should anyone see the account will
be laughed at. Some have been farther than I and know more. I can also tell the
names of the chiefs of the parties and the ponies stampeded.

— Crow's Heart, "Geography of a War Party"

Narratives of travel, ranging from origin and migration traditions to
personal accounts such as that told by Mandan warrior Crow's Heart
to anthropologist Martha Beckwith in the 1930s, provide a unique opportunity to explore the many dimensions of landscape movement from an indigenous perspective. In this chapter we combine the information contained
in native maps and sketches with narratives of origin, migration, war, and
ritual to examine the role of journeys in the formation of territorial identities among the historic Siouan-speaking Hidatsa and Mandan of North Dakota (Figure 6.1). The central tenet of the chapter is that movement across
the landscape both generates and constantly reinforces identities through

---

Epigraph. From Beckwith 1938:303.

the fulfillment of social and ceremonial obligations, as well as ownership rights connected to specific physiographic features and natural resources. To pursue this line of thought, we begin by outlining the dimensions of movement across the landscape by individuals and groups. Second, we discuss different types of journeys to illustrate the varying scales of landscape movement among the Hidatsa and Mandan and the relative contribution of these journeys to identity formation. And third, we reflect on the extent to which travel, narrative, and ritual led to the rise of territorial identity in this modern tribe.

DIMENSIONS OF LANDSCAPE MOVEMENT

Understanding the relationship between journey and identity formation requires the isolation of two distinct but complementary aspects of landscape movement: behavior and memory. The first aspect refers to the act of traveling and to all the interactions a traveler may engage in with people, nature,

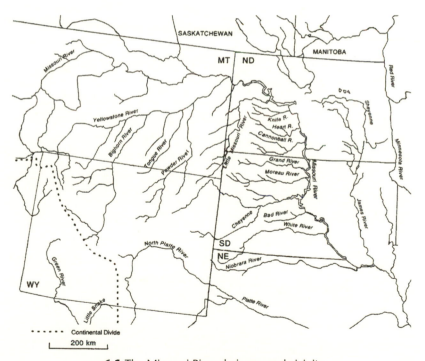

6.1 The Missouri River drainage and vicinity.

and the supernatural (Kelly and Todd 1988; Malouf 1980; Rockman 2003; Zedeño and Stoffle 2003). The second aspect denotes the internalization of landscape knowledge acquired during traveling (O'Hanlon and Frankland 2003; Golledge 2003; Levinson 1996) and the inscription of old and new knowledge through symbols and stories (Lowenthal 1975; Rappaport 1985). Behavior and memory ultimately contribute to the formation of identities by generating "place-worlds" that humans come to identify as their own or as their nature. As Basso explains, "if place-making is a way of constructing the past, a venerable means of *doing* human history, it is also a way of constructing social traditions and, in the process, personal and social identities. We are, in a sense, the place-worlds we imagine" (1996b: 6–7). We further add that trails, as places in their own right (Darling, Chapter 4, this volume; Fowler, Chapter 6, this volume; Snead, Chapter 3, this volume), play a unique role in the construction of territorial identities embodied in Basso's "place-worlds" because they foster connectivity, reinforce the right to move freely about the homeland, and provide a means to organize, delimit, and monitor movement (Ur, Chapter 9, this volume). More importantly, trails help to situate people, events, and stories in particular geographic contexts and temporal frames that all together contribute to the naturalization of nation.

To characterize the interplay of journeys and identity formation among the Hidatsa and Mandan, we apply a multi-dimensional approach to landscape movement that addresses connections among place, travel, memory, and identity. Behavioral interactions that occur during travel may be explained by three dimensions: formal, relational, and historical (Zedeño 2000; Schiffer 1999). Recollections of landscape features and events, as well as the consolidation of newly acquired knowledge and past experience, may be explained by cognitive and inscriptive dimensions (Tilley 1994; Whittlesey 1988, 2008; Van Dyke 2003).

BEHAVIORAL DIMENSIONS OF LANDSCAPE MOVEMENT

Given that behavioral interactions cannot occur without reference to place, time, and participants, the formal, relational, and historical dimensions help identify and describe contexts of landscape movement (Zedeño 2000:107). Briefly, the formal dimension corresponds to the physical characteristics of these contexts; the relational dimension addresses the interactive links (economic, social, political, and ritual) that develop while traveling; and the historical dimension describes the progression of landscape learning that results from successive journeys.

The contexts of landscape movement encompass at least two key formal elements: route and path. Route refers to the direction, mode, and distance of movement, whereas the path refers to the physical and cultural properties of the route. Paths, traces, roads, or trails are also used as synonyms to describe the material imprint left by frequent travel along a given route. But the concept further applies to dream journeys: during a vision quest, for example, an individual may travel through unknown lands by leaping from landmark to landmark or following an actual trail (Brody 1981; Darling, Chapter 4, this volume). As connections between travel behavior and recollections of travel experiences unfold, the distinction between route and path may be either blurred or sharpened as needed to draw attention to a certain area of knowledge or to derive a fable from the experience.

Routes and paths have performance characteristics or interaction-specific capabilities (*sensu* Schiffer 1999) that allow travelers to accomplish the original purpose of their journeys as well as to opportunistically benefit from these capabilities. Visibility, for example, allows travelers both to see far and to be seen; seclusion, on the other hand, prevents travelers from having to confront physical danger; accessibility and proximity help travelers to obtain needed resources or to arrive at their destinations with relative ease. Along the Missouri River and its tributaries, notably the Knife River, it is still possible to discern the tracks left by horse travois used for transporting heavy loads. Other, more subtle paths have been obliterated by natural and cultural formation processes, but associated material remains made by their users, such as petroglyphs or cairns, may still be visible along them.

Classic examples of purposeful and opportunistic interactions among travelers and between travelers and other resources abound in the northern Plains ethnographic literature; the most common is that of chance encounters between groups of antagonistic hunters that escalate into warfare. The North Dakota journals of Lewis and Clark (1804–1805) contain almost daily observations of Mandan, Hidatsa, or Arikara hunters being attacked or attacking Sioux war parties and hunting groups (Jenkinson 2003). Hunting and warfare were in fact complementary activities that took place in the same season. A journal entry by William Clark (Jenkinson 2003:108) describes a humorous instance of a Sioux attack on a hunting party that took place in the depth of winter. Ready to counterattack, Clark was nonplused when the Mandan chief told him that it was too cold to go on the warpath and so they could wait until the spring to avenge their hunters.

When planning a journey, travelers may consider the relative merits of different routes and paths according to their performance characteristics. The need for safety, for example, may be more important than proximity to a destination; or, the need to find water may override safety. Golledge (2003:27) observes that, when selecting routes, travelers are less concerned with optimization than with satisfactory compromise; generally, a route that takes people where they want to go is good enough. Paths that are frequently traveled owe their popularity to especially attractive properties and performance characteristics; there, travelers may engage in repeated in-teractions with other travelers, with natural resources, or with spirits. Pop-ular paths often are naturally well marked by conspicuous physiographic features and do not lend themselves to being easily ambushed. Movement effectiveness increases when the terrain becomes familiar enough that trav-elers can devise short-cuts or alternative routes (LaMotta 2004), or when they can use the specific properties and performance characteristics of a given path for accomplishing multiple tasks.

Intentional or otherwise, interactions or experiences lived on the path offer unique place-making opportunities; whether exploring, settling, or guarding the homeland or simply going about cyclic activities, journeys are at the core of territorial identities. For example, the discovery of new re-sources and fallback lands optimizes the potential for survival and economic growth; friendly encounters with other people help expand social networks through trade and marriage; or violent encounters can potentially increase one's reach into another's homeland and resources through war, raid, and slavery (Zedeño and Stoffle 2003). Not in the least, spiritual journeys enhance personal power and wisdom (Myers 1986). A particularly blessed dream or song obtained during a vision quest or any other journey could cause the dreamer to enter an existing religious group or to develop new rites and cer-emonies and may, on occasion, bring about transformative knowledge, as is the case of prophesies (e.g., Carroll, Zedeño, and Stoffle 2004).

Even when following a familiar route, therefore, a traveler may bring home new and valuable information and experiences that become linked to specific places and resources along the path. The progression of "landscape learning" and "wayfinding" (Rockman 2003) leads to the evolution of particular places or suites of places into landmarks. Landmarks may be likened to "pages" in the history of landscape because they often mark singular events, serve as cartographic devices for wayfinding, and help recall particularities of stories and myths (Zedeño 2000:107). Devil's Lake, the Turtle Mountains, or the mouth of the Yellowstone River in North Dakota are types of conspicuous landmarks recognized by different ethnic groups in the northern Plains as key points in north-south and east-west travel routes. Such landmarks contain archaeological, cartographic, and narrative evidence of their use history. Along well-known routes one may find landmarks that are placed sequentially or that form clusters at specific trail points. Narratives of travel illustrate how the accumulation of different interactions linked to individual landmarks, landmark sequences, or landmark clusters forms the fabric of cognition and representation of the "place-worlds" travelers create to justify their search for land-based social identity.

REMEMBERING JOURNEYS: COGNITION AND REPRESENTATION

What makes people remember journeys? Across cultures, narratives of a distant past—for example, migration traditions—commonly recount how, at the time when people's survival depended on their ability to read the landscape for its resource potential as well as for its unseen dangers, travelers keenly studied the horizon, committing to memory shape, direction, and orientation of different features. They took note of animal traces, nests, and dens; vegetation and all potential indicators of the presence of water; minerals and rocks; and all signs of the presence of other human and nonhuman beings. Upon their return, they described to others (orally or in writing) what was observed and learned. Salient landforms and other features would have been described by their appearance, their proximity to other features, or by the specific experience lived or event observed at or near them.

Whether referring to physiographic characteristics or to intangible qualities, descriptions of route and path may be readily noted as the first and most significant form of internalizing or "cognizing" the context of landscape movement. Most Native American place names and linguistic expressions, in fact, are quasi-pictorial descriptions of form, content, or event. To illustrate, the Ojibway name for the present site of De Tour Village, Mackinac County, Michigan, is Giwideonaning or "point where we go around in a canoe." Vogel (1986:136) notes that this descriptive name is not only a navigational indicator different from portaging or crossing a specific waterway, but also a descriptor of a shoreline feature such as a point or a bend. Naming is inseparable from remembering, as descriptive names help people identify landmarks and resources they have not seen before. Naming and describing are also crucial in educating children about navigation; for example, contemporary Blackfeet hunters who take children with them usually teach them how to recognize a landmark by describing its appearance from different directions so that the budding hunters will not get lost if separated from the adults (Zedeño et al. 2007).

While descriptive naming is a common practice among Native Americans and other societies, the actual inscription of names and places is usually encoded in culturally specific frameworks. According to Golledge (2003:30), "Cognitive mapping is generally understood as the deliberate and motivated encoding of environmental information so that it can be used to determine where one is at any particular moment, where other specific perceived or encoded objects are in surrounding space, how to get from one place to another, or how to communicate spatial knowledge to others." To his definition we may add the deliberate and motivated encoding of individual and group interactions with supernatural beings. The mode by which people encode new landscape information into existing categories of knowledge, create new categories, and later reckon these from memory is bounded by language as well as by cultural training and experiences (Keller, Chapter 7, this volume; Levinson 1996:353). This is evident in Crow's Heart's "Geography of a War Party" narrative:

> Where the Mouse river makes an elbow and flows north is a high hill they call Mouse-river-corner butte. Following up the Mouse river you come to a high yellow sandstone bank which they call High-hill-with-picture-writing. In early days war parties going north when they came to this side of the cliff would draw pictures of events that had happened. If they killed an enemy they drew a picture of a man lying down, if they took horses they would draw horses' hoofs. (Beckwith 1938:306)

Whereas narratives by Mandan and Hidatsa warriors focus mainly on the act of taking the warpath and its social and political consequences

(Bowser 1963:225–67), Crow's Heart's stories not only provide an insight into the mode of traveling and route navigation by scouting parties, but also identify connections among warfare, journeys, landmarks, knowledge acquisition, and identity. His scouting activities apparently took him from the Mouse River and Devil's Lake area northeast of his village to the Black Hills in South Dakota; the narrative is filled with details of the country. As Crow's Heart describes the landmarks and the significance of their names, he also recalls the associated activities, including fasting, self-torture, offerings made for good luck, war paint gathering and ritual body painting, interactions with spirits, and event-recording (Bowers 1950:171–73). Overall, the cultural dynamics expressed in scout stories, particularly the opportunistic relationship between landmark proximity and ritual practice, are representative of a wide range of socially sanctioned activities incorporated into travel at various scales and levels of participation.

Individual narratives of journeys, therefore, are generally inscribed or represented to others by appealing to elements that are shared by the society. Surviving a lightning storm at a particular place during a journey, for example, could be recounted by a Hidatsa individual in reference to the power of thunder, the home of the mythic thunderbirds, the Water Buster bundle, or Thunder Nest Butte (Zedeño et al. 2006). According to Brody (1981), dreaming about old and new paths and traveling experiences is another device that allows people to integrate old and new information in reference to movement across landscapes not yet experienced by others and to justify decisions and actions regarding future travel or other activities.

Both historical and contemporary narratives of landscape and travel among the Hidatsa and Mandan (Zedeño et al. 2006) indicate that cognition and inscription of the contexts of landscape movement are not only culture-specific but they also operate at different levels of participation—individual, community of practice, institution, faction, and polity—and at varying spatial and historical scales. By appealing to shared elements of inscription, the reckoning of individual journeys and the experiences, knowledge, and moral lessons they provide may be reclaimed by any or all participant constituencies, eventually becoming integral to their right-of-being and right-of-possession of a territory.

SCALES OF MOVEMENT AND LEVELS OF PARTICIPATION

Connections between journeys and identity formation among the Hidatsa and Mandan (and numerous societies worldwide) involved various scales of movement, from local commutes to continental excursions (Zedeño and Stoffle 2003). Macro-geographical movement involved migration, pilgrimage, resource gathering, trade, and warfare, and potentially encompassed vast areas of land well outside what would become the Hidatsa and Mandan traditional homeland of historic times. Each of these events and activities contributed uniquely to identity formation. Memories of migration, for example, are at the core of establishing right-of-being as a people who once shared experiences and were blessed by the company and gifts of the creator and other primordial beings who interacted with humans while they were searching for their final destination. Memories of warfare, on the other hand, show the close connections that exist between individuals or communities of practice attempting to gain status and the faction or the polity asserting rights over contested lands and defending its territory. Like warfare, long-distance trade and adoption of individuals of a different ethnicity further affirmed a group's identity by allowing the group to portray itself in a certain manner and to be seen by others accordingly (Spicer and Spicer 1992).

Traditionally, micro-geographical movements involved travel within the homeland, including seasonal village moves, summer and winter hunts and resource gathering, and ceremonial activities such as vision quests, eagle trapping, fasts, offering placement, and replenishing of ceremonial bundles (Bowers 1950, 1963; Wilson 1928). We suggest that these types of movement contributed to identity formation at different levels of participation, from individual to polity, by constantly reinforcing the unique and critical role each level had in the well-being of the society and the culture as a whole. Many of the activities associated with micro-geographical movements are practiced today. While this chapter does not review the entire range of interactions and activities that stimulated or required movement within the homeland, it includes examples of activities most frequently portrayed in Native American cartography and narratives of travel.

LANDSCAPE MOVEMENT ON THE MISSOURI RIVER

For thousands of years, the Missouri River formed the main artery of travel for many groups inhabiting or making use of its banks and tributaries. In addition to offering travelers a clear path across the prairie, from the western fringe of the woodlands to the Rocky Mountains, and from Hudson Bay to the Mississippi River, its timbered coulees and breaks furnished protection from natural elements and enemy groups, as well as an abundance of plant and animal resources. Likewise, the river and its tributaries cut through geological features exposing fossils, clays, pigments, gypsum crystals, and many other useful mineral resources. The seasonal regime, with its characteristic long winters, high winds, violent storms, and clear summer days, set a dramatic stage for life and travel.

Native Americans were heavily dependent on the Missouri drainage system to navigate the northern Plains even after the adoption of the horse in the mid-1700s. Migration traditions of the southern Mandan, for example, describe movements and events in direct relationship to rivers, leading to their final destination near the confluence of the Heart and Missouri rivers (Beckwith 1938; Bowers 1950). While the nomadic as well as the semi-sedentary upper Missouri tribes were accustomed to traveling long distances with dog travois or dog packs, the need to maintain a balance between proximity to water sources and accessibility to buffalo herds likely determined their choice of travel routes. Whereas the horse did not have the same impact on Hidatsa and Mandan society and culture as it did on the nomadic Plains tribes (Ewers 1980), it certainly contributed to the development of a macro-geographical dimension of movement across the landscape. Less burdened by travel time and distance, equestrian hunters, traders, and warriors were able to take their journeys across the vast prairies and as far west and south as the Cimarron River and the Arkansas River (Roe 1955:91). Except for the 19th-century military expansion of the Lakota Sioux, this macro-geographical reach was seriously curtailed with the advance of Euroamerican colonization and settlement, and formally terminated with the institution of the reservation system (Hamalainen 2003:26).

Migratory Movements

Macro-geographical movement among the peoples of the northern Plains, including ancestors of the Hidatsa and Mandan, was of continental proportions. Historical linguistics addressing the evolution of Siouan dialects suggests that the mutually unintelligible Hidatsa and Mandan split from the ancestral Siouan-speaking population and from each other several millennia ago. In fact, at the time of European contact speakers of Siouan dialects could be found across the mid-continent from the Yellowstone River to the Appalachian Mountains (Grimm 1985), thus supporting the idea of early population separation and geographical drift. Narratives of long-distance unidirectional movement toward the Missouri River also hint at macro-geographical knowledge of unknown antiquity.

The northern Plains is one of the few culture areas in the Unites States where continuity in ethnic identity from prehistory to history was established early by scholars who sought to integrate archaeology, history, and ethnography in reconstructions of the past (e.g., Libby 1908; Bowers 1948; Lehmer 1971; Wood 1993; Ahler and Thiessen 1991). However, many issues regarding the origin and development of the earth-lodge tribes on the Missouri River remain unresolved archaeologically (Toom 1992, 1996; Ahler 1988, 2003). Several versions of Mandan and Hidatsa migration stories were recorded by explorers and fur traders (e.g., David Thompson, in Tyrrell 1916), travelers (Catlin 1965; Maximilian de Wied in Thwaites 1906), government agents (Matthews 1877), and ethnographers (e.g., Beckwith 1938; Bowers 1950, 1963). In many of these accounts key informants acknowledged that different versions of the story reflected separate origins of Mandan and Hidatsa ancestors and, in the case of the Hidatsa, separate origins for the historic sub-groups—a fact that has proven difficult to determine archaeologically.

Despite the wealth of archaeological information on the Missouri River trench, all that is known with some certainty is that groups of Mandan ancestors arrived at the Heart River sometime before AD 1250 from the south (perhaps not too far south) and may have encountered nomadic or semi-nomadic groups already using the area on a seasonal basis. Groups of Hidatsa and River Crow ancestors likely arrived to the Knife River from the northeast after AD 1450 to join a related group already in the area since early times, with the Crow splitting and moving west before European contact. The question of whether Mandan and Hidatsa joined or replaced existing nomadic groups who inhabited that segment of the Missouri River drainage, or developed locally, continues to be explored (Ahler 2003).

The modern Hidatsa and Mandan acknowledge descent from a number of self-identified and named groups, many with their own version of the origin or migration story. Broadest in its geographical reach is the Mandan migration tradition told by Wolf Chief to Alfred Bowers:

> A long time ago the Missouri River flowed into the Mississippi River and thence into the ocean. On the right bank there was a high point on the ocean shore that the Mandan came from. They were said to have come from under the ground at that place and brought corn up. Their chief was named Good Furred Robe . . .
>
> In this early time when they came out to the ground, Good Furred Robe was Corn Medicine, and he had the right to teach people how to raise corn. The people of Awigaxa asked him to teach them his songs so as to keep the corn and be successful in growing their corn. Good Furred Robe also had a robe which, if sprinkled with water, would cause rain to come.
>
> When they came out of the ground, there were many people but they had no clothing on. They said, "We have found Ma'tahara." That was what they called the river as it was like a stranger. It is also the word for "stranger." (Bowers 1950:156–63)

Wolf Chief's story describes in detail the subsequent movement of the ancestral Mandan—including groups named Nu'itadi ("from us"), Awi'gaxa, and Nu'ptadi—along the Mississippi River, their contact with people who made and used shell bowls and spoons, their trading of red-painted rabbit hides and meadowlark breasts, and the acquisition of useful knowledge and items, such as the bull boat, the bow and arrow, snares, buffalo corrals, and ceremonies and ritual objects from First Creator, Lone Man, and the animal people. Explicit references to travel and navigation abound in his narrative, for example: "Good Furred Robe also owned a boat that was holy. It could carry twelve men. Each time they wanted to trade in the other village, they would take the red rabbit hides and the yellow meadowlark breasts and float over. There was a rough place in the middle, and they would drop some of these objects into the water, and then the water would calm" (Bowers 1950:156).

The narrative contains rich description of landscape features as well as of floral and topographic variation, with details on the appearance of the Missouri River. Of particular significance in Wolf Chief's version is the mention of three stopping places where there are archaeological sites sometimes attributed to ancestral Mandan populations: Pipestone in Minnesota, the White River or White Clay River, and the Cheyenne River, both in South Dakota. Other places mentioned in the migration story, including the "place where turtle went back" on the Cannonball River near Standing Rock, the White High Butte near the Turtle Mountains on the Canadian border, and Eagle Nose Butte, are associated with the acquisition of the rituals of the Okipa, the most sacred ceremony of the earth-lodge tribes (Catlin 1965; Matthews 1877; Thwaites 1906).

From the Mandan migration tradition as recalled by Wolf Chief, one learns that their movement toward their final homeland near the confluence of the Heart and the Missouri rivers followed the course of the Mississippi River upstream to the mouth of the Missouri River, and then continued along the Mississippi River, cutting across the prairie toward the White River of South Dakota. Each or all of the Mandan bands named in the story built villages and grew corn at different times and locations along the route, occupying them for a few years at a time. Separation from the main body of the tribe and regrouping are acknowledged, and references to the passage of time and its effects on language variation are noteworthy (Bowers 1950:157). The knowledge that band-specific villages existed and that the identities of these bands persisted into historic times is evident from independent historical sources, including the journals kept by David Thompson (Tyrrell 1916), Prince Maximilian de Wied (Thwaites 1906), and by George Catlin (1965), among others.

The Hidatsa origin and migration traditions, first recorded by Thompson in the 1780s (Tyrrell 1916:225) and later by Lewis and Clark in 1804, are thought to derive in part from those of the Mandan (Bowers 1963); however, they have an altogether different geographical context. The story begins in time immemorial somewhere in the underworld below the lacustrine woodland-prairie ecotone of the Red River to the northeast, with special emphasis on the connection to Devil's Lake, the Hidatsa primordial homeland. Like the Mandan, the Hidatsa origin and migration stories have numerous places and events explicitly associated with one or more linguistically similar (but dialectically different) subgroups, namely, the Mirokac or Hidatsa-River Crow and the Awaxawi. Their migration took them as far north as the Turtle Mountains during the flood and west to the Yellowstone and Powder Rivers. In contrast, the story of another subgroup known as Awatixa lacks specific references to macro-geographical movement and thus may represent a more localized population with attachments to the Missouri River that predated the arrival of the Mandan and the other Hidatsa subgroups (Bowers 1963:300), but who still spoke a Hidatsa dialect.

The Hidatsa story, which is rich in detail about group identity, social distance, and rights to land and resources, acknowledges the prior presence of the Mandan on the Heart River as well as the Awatixa on the Missouri River, but affirms that corn, buffalo, and tobacco were given to Awaxawi and the Hidatsa-Crow while they were still living at Devil's Lake. Therefore they owned these resources independently from the Mandan. Overall, the migration story and other origin traditions of the Hidatsa-Crow and Awaxawi portray an ancient lifeway that came to characterize the natives of the northern Plains, with far-reaching movements and frequent contact with other groups including the Chippewa, Cree, Assiniboine, and Blackfoot.

A complex of stories associated with the Awatixa—also known as the Myths of the Sacred Arrow—while not including references to physical travel, reveal the powers of mystical travel and the significance of ritual in identity formation. The traditions speak of a village in the sky and the expression "sacred arrow," which refers to the mode of travel used by the sky village people and their leader, Charred Body, and his ability to change into an arrow (Beckwith 1938). The themes center on Charred Body's selection of 13 sky village couples to settle the earth, their movement from the sky to the earth and its consequences; war and competition for the right to live on the Missouri River; crime and punishment; and the acquisition of a liturgical order as the marker of the end of strife and the beginning of a new society. These stories of change and becoming are full of symbolism that provided a rationale for their ritual calendar and many other actions.

An eloquent explanation of the historical trajectory imbedded in these myths was given to Bowers by Hidatsa informant Bears Arm. Drawing a sketch in the shape of the letter Y, Bears Arm indicated that each of the upper forks represents, respectively, (1) the making of the earth and the exodus from the underworld and (2) the settlement of the lands by people from the sky. The stem symbolizes the acquisition of social and ceremonial obligations once the villages were established, the Crow had left, and people had learned how to cooperate. At different points throughout this journey, Bears Arm explained, the ancestors acquired ceremonies that follow one another like "knots on a string" (Bowers 1963:304). These ceremonial obligations, in turn, connected people to landmarks and resources in the new homeland, and at the same time linked the new homeland to their ancestral origin places.

Many of the ancestral landmarks mentioned in the origin and migration myths are noted on Sitting Rabbit's map of the Missouri River, including villages or "towns," many of which do have archaeological referents (Thiessen, Wood, and Jones 1979:154–56). Sitting Rabbit, a native of the Fort Berthold Indian Reservation, completed in 1907 a map of the Missouri River, from the modern North Dakota-South Dakota border to its confluence with the Yellowstone River. The map was commissioned by then secretary of the State Historical Society of North Dakota Orin G. Libby, who offered to pay five dollars for the labor involved in this project. Prepared in consultation with several Mandan and Hidatsa elders, the map depicts the location of village sites and other natural and cultural features, including 38 place names and notations in the native language. Many of these places correspond to narratives of migration, colonization, and settlement (Thiessen, Wood, and Jones 1979:45). This map is invaluable not only because it renders in canvas an emic view of the Missouri River at the turn of the 20th century, but because most of the features in it are under the waters of the modern Lake Sakakawea.

Among Sitting Rabbit's landmarks located below the known Mandan towns on the Heart River are ten villages (Figure 6.2), at least six of which

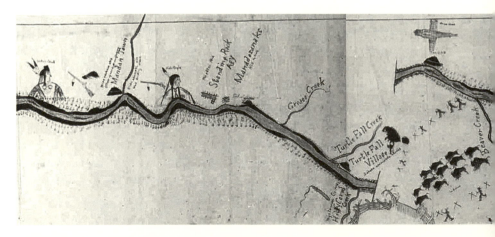

6.2 Detail of Sitting Rabbit's map showing features mentioned in the Mandan migration story.

correspond to known prehistoric sites. Most villages are named individually. Also depicted is a "mysterious corral" near Holy Corral Creek, which apparently represents the buffalo corral built by Lone Man during the migration to save the Mandan from the flood (Bowers 1950:162). Other landmarks that likely allude to events told in the migration story include the Turtle Fall Creek and Village, the Eagle Nose Village, and the mythical Awatixa village of the Arrow People, known archaeologically as the Flaming Arrow Site (Will and Hecker 1944). Numerous historically known landmarks associated with the other Hidatsa subgroups and with Euroamericans are also depicted on the map.

Although Sitting Rabbit used river charts provided to him by Owen Libby, to the Western eye his sequential arrangement of the charts and the placement of landmark depictions on either bank of the river seem backwards and upside-down. Yet, such cartography shows the way in which the Mandan map maker and his consultants culturally understood the river: historically, beginning in the south and ending in the north, and geographically, as it appeared to them from their turn-of-the-century homes. The sequences and clusters of landmarks that Sitting Rabbit chose to depict in the map and their corresponding icons follow the historical trajectory of the Mandan from their migration to the establishment of the reservation. The map further encodes culturally ordained information about the relationship among Indians and non-Indians, the landscape,

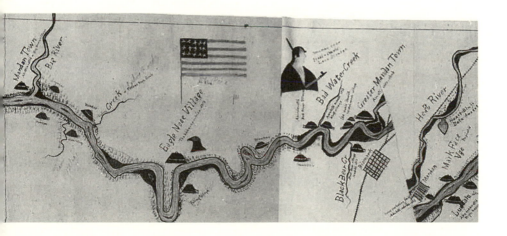

and the spirit world, thus showing a clear sense of differentiation between "us" and "the other."

LANDSCAPES OF WAR AND TRADE

Until the devastating smallpox epidemic of 1837, the Hidatsa along with Mandan and Arikara warriors were in the habit of taking long-distance journeys to fulfill visions and attain prestige (Meyer 1977:69). In fact, during his 1832 visit to the villages Prince Maximilian de Wied noted that "The Mandans and Minataries [Hidatsa] make excursions as far as the Rocky Mountains, against their enemies, the Blackfeet, and against the Chippeways, to the country of Pembina. Their other enemies are the Sioux, the Arikara, the Assiniboins, and the Chayennes. They are at peace with the Crows" (Thwaites 1906:353).

The main westward route was drawn on a sketch of the upper Missouri country made by the Mandan chief Sheheke or White Coyote for William Clark in 1805 (Jenkinson 2003:179). Clark later recorded this path in the general expedition map drafted by Nicolas King. It is shown with the characteristic dotted line of a footpath paralleling the south bank of the Missouri River, crossing the Yellowstone River just above its mouth, crossing the Missouri River below the Three Forks, and penetrating the Rocky Mountains (Tucker 1942: Plate 31A) (Figure 6.3). Another "road to war" was drawn by the Assiniboine in the mid-1800s (Figure 6.4). The Assiniboine route traverses the same region as the Hidatsa route, and also penetrates the Rockies, but it parallels the Missouri River on its north bank. The path begins at Fort Union on the mouth of the Yellowstone River and follows the river course closely; it then turns northwest along the Milk River where it forks, one path going to the Fort Benton Trading Post on the Marias River and the other, labeled "warpath," deviating toward the north side of the Sweetgrass Hills and then turning south to the heart of Blackfeet territory in East Glacier, Montana (Warhus 1997: pl. 64). Both routes reflect similar landscape movement behaviors but different territorial identities and perhaps different tribal allegiances: whereas Hidatsa warriors traversed Crow territory relatively safely, the Assiniboine warriors could do the same across Gros Ventre lands.

Macro-regional pathways of movement are clearly laid out in a map of the world made by Ac ki mok ki, a Blackfoot chief, in 1801 at the request

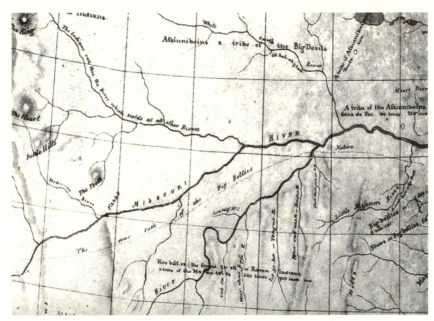

6.3 Detail of William Clark's 1810 map showing the Hidatsa "Big Bellies" war path (from Tucker 1942: pl. XXX1A).

of Hudson's Bay Company trader Peter Fidler (Warhus 1997: fig. 56). This map, which encompasses a 1,200 mi² area virtually unknown to White explorers, depicts a portion of the "Old North Trail" that ran parallel to the Rocky Mountain Front from the Upper Saskatchewan River in Alberta to, arguably, the city of Santa Fe in New Mexico (Ewers 1980). This map also sketches the Missouri River watershed, from the Continental Divide to the mouth of the Yellowstone River, noting the existence of the river villages just to the east of this landmark (Figure 6.5). Ac ki mok ki's map became the key to the Western territories as it depicted the route Lewis and Clark would soon follow.

The continental routes known to Ac ki mok ki likely had facilitated long-distance trade since prehistoric times. Manson (1998:386) notes that the development of trade networks that crisscrossed the plains and linked groups ranging from the Pacific Ocean to the Mississippi headwaters may be traced to the 11th century, with evidence of long-distance-movement obsidian and shell dating to Hopewell or the Middle Woodland Period (AD 1–400). Upper Missouri River networks predate the arrival of Mandan ancestors to the

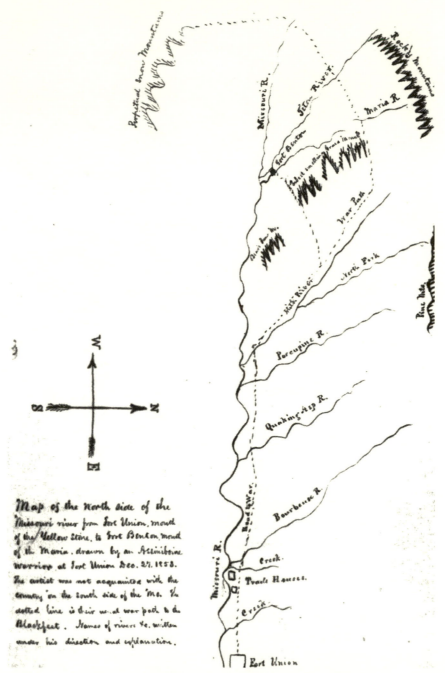

6.4 Assiniboine map of a war path (from Warhus 1997).

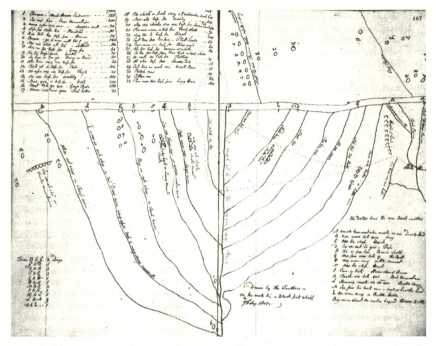

6.5 Blackfoot map of the world depicting the Missouri River drainage and trails (from Warhus 1997).

Heart River, which after AD 1250 became the main center of trade activity in the northern Plains. At its height, or before the smallpox epidemic of 1781, the network articulated with several strategically located rendezvous trading centers that connected distant and often enemy tribes to the Mandan depot (Ewers 1968; Manson 1998:389; Wood and Thiessen 1985). The trade evolved historically from subsistence/ceremonial gifting to firearms, horses, and other European imports, and to the fur trade (Thiessen 1993), but its role in mediating interethnic political relationships and social and geographic boundaries among traditional enemies remained central.

Control of the trade network helped to shape the identity of the Mandan as rich, fabled people with fortified towns of almost surreal quality—not unlike the seven cities of Cibola in the Southwest. During his Missouri River voyage of 1719, French explorer Bernard La Harpe heard of these "famous towns" from the Osage, Pawnee, and Wichita (Wedel 1971). A similar fame among the subartic hunters attracted Pierre Gautier Varennes sieur de La Verendrye and his sons to travel from the Lake of the Woods to the Missouri

River, where they met the Mandan in 1738 (Wood 1980). Trade continued even after the smallpox reduced the Mandan to a few thousand and forced them to abandon some of their villages. Explorers such as Antoine Tabeau, a chronicler for Spanish envoy Jacques d'Englise, described in 1791 that "all the rivers, which empty into the Missouri above the Yellowstone, are frequented by a swarm of nations with whom, at the post of the Mandanes, a trade, as extensive as it is lucrative, can be carried on" (Abel 1939:161). Even after the Corps of Discovery had returned from their expedition in 1806 and the fur trade was taken over by American Fur Company's upper Missouri outfit, Euroamerican writers pondered the magnificent villages, describing and painting portraits of their picturesque vistors (Abel 1997; Catlin 1965; Twaites 1906). The trails to the Rocky Mountains continued to be used by the nomadic tribes for warfare and trade throughout the life of Fort Union Trading Post at the mouth of the Yellowstone River (1829–1866) until the Reservation Period. Tracks of a barely visible travois trail remain outside the modern Fort Union Trading Post National Historic Site.

PATHWAYS OF THE HOMELAND

With the advance of Euroamerican colonization and concomitant expansion of the Sioux into the northern Plains after the epidemic of 1837, long-distance movements of the Hidatsa and Mandan were reduced, both due to the danger of traveling outside their territory and of leaving the villages undefended. Yet, raids and revenge attacks continued throughout the 19th century. By the late 1880s short-distance trade trips to the main posts and episodic raiding against the Sioux and the Arikara occurred mainly near American trade and military posts. A pictorial sketch made by Lean Wolf in 1881 recounts a horse raid against a Sioux encampment near the site of Fort Buford at the mouth of the Yellowstone River (Figure 6.6). In contrast to earlier maps, Lean Wolf's sketch depicts a country bounded by the White man, from Fort Buford to Fort Berthold. Recall that Sitting Rabbit's map of 1907 (see Figure 6.2), while depicting the most ancient storied places, does so from the perspective of his reservation village, Like-a-Fishhook, on the north bank of the Missouri River. These instances, and the reservation-era narratives discussed throughout the chapter, demonstrate the enduring role of movement in an individual's search for a rightful place in society, and its material and symbolic contribution to building territorial identities.

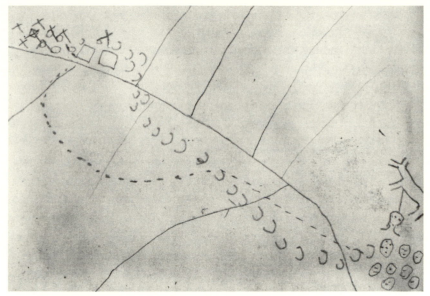

6.6 Detail of a horse raid by Lean Wolf (from Warhus 1997).

The homeland and its boundary markers were sketched by Hidatsa warrior Bears Arm in the early 20th century (Figure 6.7). Within its boundaries, the homeland contains pathways linking myriad places and resources that embody territorial identity at all levels of participation; many of these pathways were used throughout prehistory and history (Simon 1982). Although Bears Arm's sketch may not have exactly matched the boundaries of the homeland of all Hidatsa and Mandan subgroups, it provides a framework for understanding the connection between journeys and identity at a time of tremendous change and loss of freedom. Among the most significant landmarks noted by Bears Arm, which are associated with movement within the homeland, are the buttes where visions were sought by individuals who needed power in order to achieve good social standing. Connections made between vision quests, warfare, and political leadership are clear in the narrative by Crow's Heart that Bowers recorded in the 1930s:

If a man goes out on the hills to fast and suffer and some holy person or animal comes to him and tells him that he will be lucky and kill an enemy, but when he goes out as leader, the enemy kills one of his party instead, he will come home crying because the people will think that he didn't fast right or that his dream wasn't real. Brave men will start fasting again and seek an even stronger god by fasting longer and offering their flesh to the Sun . . . It is often hard to get men to follow an unlucky leader. If he goes out a second time and kills or strikes an enemy, the people will say, "You have a real protector now, one that is going to be a great help to you." (Bowers 1950:170)

The locales named in the map or mentioned in the narratives of war are but a few of those linked to important beings, stories, persons, factions, events, and activities that mark the history of the Hidatsa and Mandan people since Creation. For example, the Dog Den Buttes are associated with the origin of the Dog Societies (Bowers 1963:195); the women's Goose Society has connections with all features and ancestral sites belonging to the Awatixa and to the legendary Mandan leader Good Fur Robe, particularly the Missouri River (Bowers 1963:201). A cluster of landmarks—Rainy Butte, Buffalo Den Butte, and Children's Den Butte along the Little Mis-

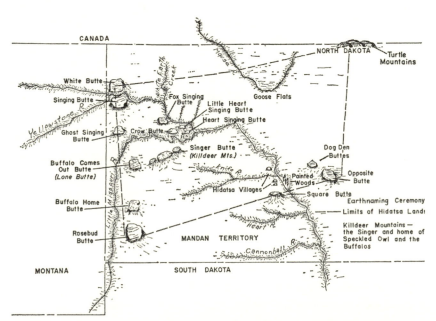

6.7 Bears Arm's map of the Mandan and Hidatsa homeland with landmarks mentioned in Crow's Heart's narrative (from Bowers 1963).

souri River—are considered the homes of human and nonhuman spirits. The Little Missouri, Knife, and mouth of the Yellowstone rivers contain eagle-trapping locales that are yet another critical set of territorial markers with far-reaching geographical, ceremonial, and mythical connections among people, land, and sky (Bowers 1950:215; 1963:468; Wilson 1928). Last, there are the places where important resources must be procured for subsistence, medicinal, and ceremonial purposes. In particular, named locales where clay and mineral pigments abound are closely associated with origin traditions of specific society bundles and ceremonies (e.g., Beckwith 1938:303; Bowers 1950:172). Tragically, many of the locales that were once along the Missouri River were destroyed by the construction of the Garrison Dam.

RECALLING JOURNEYS AND BEHAVING ACCORDINGLY

The notion that the memory of a distant journey, as recalled in oral tradition, is not simply alternative history but a dynamic tool for transferring the rudiments of behavior and preserving the social order (Vansina 1985) is explicitly or implicitly understood by the members of native societies such as the Hidatsa and Mandan (Grinnell 2004). This is most evident in the malleable configuration of origin and migration myths, war epics, and liturgy. As Beckwith notes (1938), versions of a story vary according to the narrator's whim for organizing all the critical pieces. Such freedom is acceptable as long as the moral of the story is driven home or the ritual associated with the story is effective.

Stories evolve through time because they are dependent upon experience and training of the narrator as well as collective change; yet, without permanent anchors stories would drift and lose their reason for being remembered. Place and landmark, especially when named descriptively, have the power of anchoring memories so that people can appeal to a familiar referent when making decisions as to how to approach the unknown (Basso 1996b). Likewise, trails and paths across the homeland and beyond connect people to their past and allow them to organize their present and future actions. For this very reason, journeys, memories of journeys, and the actual routes followed occupy a central place in the social order. Origin and migration myths, too, incorporate landmarks and experiences that reflect the distance between the ancestors and the generation recalling the myth, the knowledge accrued in the intervening time and space, the legitimacy of the story for claiming god-given rights, and its relevance for substantiating decision-making processes in the present. For example:

> According to the Mandan creation myth, as told to Arthur Mandan by his mother Calf Woman, when First Creator and Lone Man decide to make the world from mud brought by a bird to the surface of the water, Lone Man chooses to create the east whereas First Creator chooses [to] create the west, leaving a space between, in the water, which becomes the Missouri River . . . First Creator makes the west side: broad valleys, hills, coulees with timber, mountain streams, and springs with buffalo, elk, mule deer and white tails, mountain sheep and all other creatures useful to mankind for food and clothing . . . Lone Man makes the east side: mostly level country, lakes and small streams with rivers far apart and his animals were beaver, otter, muskrat, moose and other animals with cattle of many colors with long horns and long tails.
>
> First Creator and Lone Man meet and compare their creations: They first inspect what Lone Man has created . . . First Creator disapproves: "the land is too level and affords no protection to man. Look at the land I have created: it contains all kinds of game. It has buttes and mountains by which man can mark his direction. Your land is so level that a man will easily lose its way for there are no high hills as signs to direct him . . . The lakes you have made most of them have no outlet and hence become impure. Look at the cattle you have created with long horns and tail, of all colors, with hair so short and smooth that they cannot stand the cold! Lone Man realizes his dilemma: "The things I have created I thought were the very things most useful to man. I cannot very well change them now that they are once created. So let us make man use first the things that you have made until the supply is exhausted and then the generations to come shall utilize those things which I have created." (Grinnell 2004:24)

This conflation of time, place, and event in a single argument, a seamless story, is essential to the naturalization of territorial and group identity. In a fashion similar to narratives of origin and migration, where a story describes the ways in which the ancestors, whether alone or alongside primordial creatures, transformed the unknown into the familiar, the tales of war expeditions and victories also serve a crucial role in generating and perpetuating identities. By recalling the wisdom and status acquired from experiencing the landscape and appropriating it from others, people construct a coveted "place-world" and subsequently modify it; with the passage of time, the repeated affirmation of rights to place-worlds through action and story leads to their becoming a part of the natural world.

MOVEMENT, MEMORY, AND IDENTITY TODAY

The Missouri River has changed drastically since William Clark sketched it from Sheheke's memory in 1805 and since Sitting Rabbit completed his map in 1907. The modern river landscape is, by and large, a product of the construction of six dams in the 1930s and 1940s. The remains of its use history and the imprints of the foot and horse paths that closely followed its course are now under water. Many of the landmarks mentioned by Crow's Heart no longer bear their original names. Yet, the upper Missouri tribes and particularly the Hidatsa, Mandan, and Arikara Nation maintain their intimate connection to the river. As many other native groups do (e.g., Ferguson, this volume), they continue to travel along the highway paralleling the old route to find work, to attend social, political, and religious functions, and to pay homage to ancestral sites. Gossip, news, and gifts spread quickly and widely through the age-old social networks, and arguments ranging from the ethnic identity of Sakakawea to tribal water rights are as aggressive now as trade and warfare were in the past. Today, a recreation complex complete with a bridge, hotel, casino, museum, and marina in the busy "New Town" at the Fort Berthold Indian Reservation has replaced the bustling earth-lodge villages that sheltered the Corps of Discovery in the winter of 1805. Yet, change and modernity are inseparable from Hidatsa and Mandan identity, because they were anticipated by First Creator and Lone Man when the world was young and the Missouri River and surrounding plains had just begun their existence.

Calf Woman's prophetic story shows how, to the modern tribes, the Missouri River serves as a dividing line and as a measure of distance between two worlds—First Creator's representing precolonial identity and traditional lifeways, and Lone Man's the reservation life. Rather ironically, by taking a strong initiative in the celebration of the Lewis & Clark Bicentennial (2004–2006), the upper Missouri tribes are reclaiming the river and its history to assert their own identity. For the Mandan, Hidatsa, and Arikara Nation the Missouri River remains a "time-line" in the construction of individual and group identities, because it encompasses both a literal and a symbolic journey through land and time, and a place-world where this nation has found itself anew.

7

A Road by Any Other Name: Trails, Paths, and Roads in Maya Language and Thought

ANGELA H. KELLER

What is a man on a road?

Time.

— Maya riddle, in Munro Edmonson, *Heaven Born Merida and Its Destiny: The Book of Chilam Balam of Chumayel*

Across a vast tropical rainforest, the Maya built masonry roads of a quality unsurpassed in the preindustrial world. Many Maya causeways are monumental in scale, measuring 3 m to 50 m wide, and some 1 m to 3 m tall. These massive constructions, the longest of which runs 100 km between the Yucatecan sites of Coba and Yaxuna, required an enormous outlay of labor for their initial construction and an ongoing program of cleaning and refurbishing. Until recently, though, the prehispanic roads of the Maya were poorly recorded and rarely excavated. Using satellite imagery and targeted pedestrian surveys, archaeologists today are documenting scores of new roads and road networks across the Maya lowlands. Researchers have mapped large, complicated systems of roads around the sites of Calakmul (Folan et al. 2001), Caracol (Chase and Chase 1987, 1996, 2001), El Mirador (Hansen 1991; Sharer 1992), Chichen Itza (Cobos and Winemiller

---

Epigraph. Translated by Munro Edmonson (1986:50).

2001) and Coba (Benavides Castillo 1981; Folan, Kintz, and Fletcher 1983). At hundreds of other sites, from the small site of Mopan 3-Este in southeastern Guatemala (Gómez 1996) to the massive site of Tikal (Coe 1988), archaeologists have mapped hundreds of shorter roads as well. In fact, the elevated stone causeway, along with the temple pyramid and ballcourt, is emerging as one of the most conspicuous and enduring features of elite Maya architecture from the Preclassic period to the Conquest (Reid 1995; Shaw 2001, 2008).

Despite the increased archaeological interest in Maya roads, we are still hampered by a lack of associated artifacts and the effort involved in excavating these large constructions. Consequently, many scholars have focused on the formal spatial analysis of causeway alignments and site plans (e.g., Benavides 1981; Carrasco 1993; Folan, Kintz, and Fletcher 1983; Gómez 1996; Kurjack and Andrews 1976; Kurjack and Garza 1981; Maldonado 1995). In these spatial studies, the roads are simply lines on a map connecting various residential and public spaces. The interpretative emphasis, then, shifts from the roads themselves to the structures and places connected by the roads. The resulting analyses typically focus on the integrative potential of Maya causeways as conduits of social interaction, transportation, commerce, and political control (e.g., Carrasco 1993; Chase and Chase 1987, 1996, 2001; Cheetham 2004; Cobos and Winemiller 2001). Lost in these analyses is an appreciation of Maya causeways as problematic constructions worthy of investigation in their own right.

What did roads and road building mean to the Maya? Firsthand accounts from Spanish chroniclers writing early in the Colonial period uniformly, and emphatically, stress the spiritual and ceremonial significance of the Maya roads (Bolles and Folan 2001; Bustillos Carillo 1964; Folan 1991; Freidel and Sabloff 1984; Keller 2006; Saville 1930, 1935; Thompson 1930; Tozzer 1941; Villa Rojas 1934). Although most researchers agree that prehispanic Maya causeways had both prosaic and ceremonial functions, the interrelationship between these, the relative weighting of one to another, remains an open debate.

One little-explored avenue of research is the detailed investigation of the words used by the Maya themselves to talk about their roads (Bolles and Folan 2001). As archaeologists, we cannot speak with the people of the past, but we may arrive at a closer approximation of their beliefs if we do not rely solely on English words and categories. Linguist Anna Wierzbicka (1997:34) cautions, "what people regard as 'common sense' is bound up with a particular language," and often serves to "reify" the concepts of that language. A critical use of Mayan vocabulary may help us construct a more Mayan "common sense" approach to the past.

In this chapter, I examine the historical development of the Mayan terms for what we would call trails, paths, and roads in English. I augment the information gleaned from dictionary entries with a variety of use examples from contemporary and historical sources. By carefully tracking the uses and modifications of the Mayan terms, I hope to approach a Maya understanding of roads.

TALKING ABOUT ROADS IN MAYAN

Researchers studying paths and roads often make a qualitative distinction between the category of "trail" or "path" and that of "road," pointing to the greater formality, directness, and labor investment evident in the latter (Earle 1991:11; Hyslop 1984). This heuristic distinction, though sensible in English, is muted in the Mayan languages. Whereas in English we have a whole host of discrete terms for paths and roads—street, boulevard, promenade, avenue, lane, trail, drive, highway, turnpike, thoroughfare, and so on—in all of the Mayan languages there is only one common root term which is pronounced *beh* in Yucatec Mayan, *bih* in Cholan Mayan, and variously *bej, bey, be,* and *bir* in the other Mayan languages (Dienhart 1989:528–30). This root term may be modified with adjectives to specify the nature of the route in question, but the distinctions between these types are more a matter of degree than kind.

To understand the nature of the Mayan concept of *beh* as distinct from the English concepts of trail, path, or road, we must look at specific use examples. For this study, I have worked from the richer data of the modern and Colonial periods back into the more fragmentary records of the prehispanic past. The collected dictionary entries and textual examples are synthesized and grouped by meaning senses to approximate emic Mayan dimensions of *beh*. The discrepancies and concordances between Mayan and English revealed in this study highlight potential areas of cultural misinterpretation as well as agreement, if not conceptual universality.

Modern Meanings

In modern usage, *beh* means trail, path, or road, but it can also mean life course, destiny, matter, and affair. Through its incorporation in everyday words and expressions, *beh*'s metaphoric meanings appear equally as important as, if not more important than, its literal meaning of 'road' or 'path' (for simplicity's sake, I will gloss the primary meaning of *beh* as 'road', although it means something more like 'trail, path, or road'). Modern ethnographers have noted that *beh* "means more than 'the road you can see with your eyes,' for it is the road of life" (Tedlock 1992:118). As William Hanks (1990:312) eloquently observes, "one's road is where one has been and is heading."

Commonly today, Yucatec Mayan speakers ask, 'How is your road?' (*bix a bèel?*), meaning 'How are you?' or 'How's it going?'. Important tasks, obligations, or endeavors are also roads, and to accomplish a goal is to 'finish a road' (*ts'oksah beh*). Similarly, to get married is to 'finish one's road' (*ts'okan u bèel*) in the sense that one important goal has been accomplished and now a new road has begun. This new, married road is called the 'husband road' (*icham beel*) for women, and the 'wife road' (*atan beel*) for men. Extending the metaphor, community elders that act as matchmakers and general advisors are called 'road guides' in both Quiche Mayan (*k'amol be*) and Yucatec Mayan (*ah bebesah beh*).

Analogous to the use of *beh* to symbolize one's life course is the incorporation of *beh* in everyday terms referencing time and segments of time. To talk about today, the day after tomorrow, and the day after that, as well as right now, Yucatec Mayan speakers use *beh* as the root for 'day'. Thus, 'today' is *beh-hé'ela'e'* (commonly contracted *behlá'e'*), meaning literally 'the road right here'. Similarly, the day after tomorrow is 'two road' (*ká'a beh*), and the day after the day after tomorrow, three days away, is 'three road' (*oxbeh*) (Bevington 1995; Hanks 1990; Tedlock 1992). In an interesting twist, the terms for 'now', *beora*, and 'right now', *beorita*, are Spanish-Mayan hybrids, mimicking the Spanish constructions *ahora* and *ahorita* (Bevington 1995:89–90; Hanks 1990:312). These examples, although not exhaustive, develop the important personal and temporal dimensions of *beh* for modern Mayan speakers.

Colonial Dictionary Meanings

Mayan dictionaries compiled in the Colonial period contain all of the modern uses of *beh,* and many more terms and expressions which have either dropped out of use or occur less frequently in modern parlance (Barrera Vásquez 1995). William Folan and colleagues have profitably mined this wealth of terms to construct a typology of prehispanic Maya roads (Folan et al. 2001; Bolles and Folan 2001). My focus here is somewhat different. I hope to approach an emic Mayan understanding of roads by exploring the term *beh* as a literal and metaphoric concept. Therefore, I have been less selective in my analysis of the Colonial period dictionary entries and collected more than one hundred distinct terms (Table 7.1). I have distilled the collected terms into four core meaning senses:

1. *Road:* including the concepts of trail, path, transit, canal, or spirit path
2. *Day:* meaning either a calendar day or the length of a journey in days
3. *Work:* including one's occupation, good works, or government office
4. *Life:* incorporating the concepts of well-being, prosperity, life course, and destiny

Despite their analytic separation, all four meaning senses blend together in practice. When a Mayan speaker uses an expression which entails the day, work, or life meanings of *beh*, the road sense necessarily comes to mind and, of course, the reverse is also true. Still, the metaphoric senses of *beh* are more numerous, and are implicit even when an actual road is referenced.

The Maya recognized a variety of trails, paths, and roads, including 'straight roads' (*t'ubul beh*), 'crossing roads' (*xay beh*), 'narrow roads' (*ch'ux beh*), 'great roads' (*noh beh*), 'side roads' (*xax beh*), 'main roads' (*ch'ibal beh*), 'rocky roads' (*bok'olbok' beh*), 'overgrown roads' (*lob beh*), and 'white, constructed roads' (*sakbeh*). Further, several terms in the dictionaries refer to the act of creating a road or path through the forest (*hats' beh, hol beh, tah beh, top' beh*), as well as the maintenance of a road after its construction, indicating the importance of these activities. Local communities maintained and swept the paths and roads (*mis beh*, lit. 'sweep road') as part of community service. The clearing and maintaining of trails, paths, and roads between villages and outlying cultivated lands was surely important to the basic survival of dispersed farmers living amid a tropical forest. As cultural entities, these rural roads created networks of cultured space through the untamed forest, and imposed cultural order on the decidedly messy expanse of lowland jungle and scrub.

The Yucatec Mayan term *sakbeh* (also spelled *sacbe* and *sakbeob,* plural),

Table 7.1. Selected Terms and Expressions
Containing *Beh* from Colonial Period Yucatec Dictionaries

MEANING/SENSE

YUCATEC TERM	LITERAL TRANSLATION	ENGLISH GLOSS	COMMENTS
I. Road			
IA. TRAIL, PATH, ROAD			
bok'olbok' beh	beaten/mixed road	rocky, rough road with many hills and dips, not level	
but'bil beh	filled road	road constructed with fill, probably refers to raised, stone-filled roads	
ch'akat beh	crossing road	road that has many forks and crossings	described as a difficult road to follow, the *ch'akat beh* is contrasted with a direct route or straight road
(u) ch'ibal beh	(its/his/her) lineage road	large or principal road from which smaller roads emerge	metaphorically likened to the direct male line of descent, this road is considered a large, primary road from which smaller roads branch off
ch'ux beh	narrow road	narrow road	
ek' beh	black road	rough, narrow road or path	
hats' beh	whip road	to open a path through thick undergrowth, or the path itself	
hol beh	mouth/to open road	to open or make a new road through the mountains or forest	a related term is *hol che' beh* (lit. "open tree road"), "to make a road through trees and hills"

Table 7.1. Selected Terms and Expressions
Containing *Beh* from Colonial Period Yucatec Dictionaries

MEANING/SENSE

YUCATEC TERM	LITERAL TRANSLATION	ENGLISH GLOSS	COMMENTS
(u) hol beh[a]	(its) mouth/hole road	the entrance onto or beginning of the road	
hola'an beh	open road	open road	synonymous or derivative terms are *holoknak beh* and *homoknak beh*
kan beh	four road	crossroads	found repeatedly in the *Chilam Balam* texts
koch babe'en beh	wide road	a wide, open road	a synonymous term is *koch babaknak beh*
lob beh	overgrown road	rough or impassable road thick with weeds	
lut' beh	narrow road	path, lane, small road	synonymous with *nut' beh*; also recorded as *lulut' beh*; the related term *lut' ximbal* (lit. "narrow walk") means "to walk in a jumping fashion," or "to trot"
matan mis beh	charity/alms sweep road	a section of road to be swept by a particular town, barrio, or person	
nak beh	near road	close to or adjoining the road	also the name of a major Preclassic Maya center in the Peten
noh beh	great road	royal, principal, great, wide road	used in reference to the largest and longest roads of Yucatan, and the main roads into cities; a related term in Quiché is *nima be*, "high, main road"

**Table 7.1. Selected Terms and Expressions
Containing *Beh* from Colonial Period Yucatec Dictionaries**

MEANING/SENSE

YUCATEC TERM	LITERAL TRANSLATION	ENGLISH GLOSS	COMMENTS
sakbeh	white road	white road, constructed stone road, main road	see secondary meaning as "Milky Way" (below)
tul beh	full road	path	
t'ubul beh	sinking road	straight road	*t'ubul* is also used with *k'in* (lit. "day/sun") to mean the setting of the sun
t'ul beh	narrow road	narrow road	a synonymous term is *x-t'un t'ul beh* (lit. "drop" or "dot road") which has the added connotation of being a narrow pedestrian road through the mountains
xax beh	side road	road that goes around or to the side of something	use examples indicate that *xax beob* go around things like towns and crosses
xay beh[a]	divided/crossed road	divided or crossed roads	a synonymous term is *xayah beh*; two related terms are *xayankil beh*, "the crossing and dividing of the roads," and *xaybesah*, "making the crossings and divisions of the road"
xoy beh	roundabout/circling/ turning road	detour, shortcut	a synonymous term is *nach xoy beh* (lit. "far turning road")

Iʙ. Tᴜʙᴜʟᴀʀ ᴏʀ Cᴀɴᴀʟ-ʟɪᴋᴇ Rᴏᴀᴅ

(u) beel bah	(its) road mole	the tunnels of moles underground	
(u) beel buts'	(its) road smoke	chimney	

Table 7.1. Selected Terms and Expressions
Containing *Beh* from Colonial Period Yucatec Dictionaries

MEANING/SENSE

YUCATEC TERM	LITERAL TRANSLATION	ENGLISH GLOSS	COMMENTS
(u) beel ha'	(its) road water	canal	synonymous terms are *bekan, bebek*
(u) beel it	(its) road ass/anus	line between the gluteal muscles, or anus	
(u) beel k'ab	(its) road hand	line(s) on the hands	
(u) beel k'íik'	(its) road blood	vein, artery	synonymous terms are *(u) beel nohol* (lit. "its road south"), and *(u) beel nah* (lit. "its road house," or possibly "its road mother")
(u) beel luk'	(its) road mud/clay	sewer of the house	
*(u) beel pach*ª	(its) road back	depression between the shoulder blades running down the back	
(u) beel pol	(its) road head	part in the hair	generally used in reference to a child's hair or a woman's elaborate hairstyle
(u) beel wiix	(its) road urine	urethra	

Ic. Astral Course

(u) bèel ek'ob	(their) road the black ones	orbit of stars	
*(u) beel kaan*ª	(its) road sky/heaven	the road of the sky	this term may refer to the course of the sun across the sky or to the Milky Way
sakbeh	white road	Milky Way	a synonymous term is *kuxan sum* (lit. "living rope"), meaning "umbilical cord" and "Milky Way"

**Table 7.1. Selected Terms and Expressions
Containing *Beh* from Colonial Period Yucatec Dictionaries**

MEANING/SENSE

YUCATEC TERM	LITERAL TRANSLATION	ENGLISH GLOSS	COMMENTS
II. Day/Journey			
ká'a beh[a]	two road	the day after tomorrow, the day before yesterday	
tan beh	middle road	middle of the road, middle of the day, middle of the journey	a synonymous term is *tan k'in* (lit. "middle day/sun"); the connotation of both terms is midpoint of the sun's journey through the sky along its course or road
ox k'in beel	three sun/day road	third day	meaning "three days from today," similar to the modern term *oxbeh*
III. Work			
(Occupation, Office, Responsibility)			
(u) atan beel	(his) wife road	married life, for husband	
(ah) belbesah beh	(he of the) guide road	a person who opens the road where another will travel, road guide, trailblazer; a matchmaker	sometimes contracted to *belbesah*; a similar term is *(ah) payal beh* (lit. "[he of the] guide road"), meaning "road guide"; an analogous term in Quiche is *k'amol be* (lit. "road guide"), a daykeeper specializing in matchmaking
(ah) beel nal[a]	(he of the) road ear of corn	administrator, local government official	this term seems to refer to local, Mayan-speaking officials during the Colonial period

Table 7.1. Selected Terms and Expressions
Containing *Beh* from Colonial Period Yucatec Dictionaries

MEANING/SENSE

YUCATEC TERM	LITERAL TRANSLATION	ENGLISH GLOSS	COMMENTS
(u) beel tah beel[b]	(its) road ownership road	to administer, to be an official	a synonymous term is *beelancil*
ch'a beh[a]	to carry road	to accept a job or an office	
(u) icham beel	(her) husband road	married life, for wife	
(ah) kanbal beh	(he of the) teaching road	novice, generally in an art-related field	
(u) p'omal u beel	(his/her) selling road	merchant	
*(u) sabin beh*b	(its) weasel road	sentinel or spy	Tozzer (1941:205) notes that the "weasels [*sabin*] of the army were the scouts or spies"; two related terms are *(u) sabin k'atun* (lit. "[its] weasel *k'atun*/war"), meaning "war spy," and *(ah) ch'a' beh*, "sentinel, spy, or scout"
tah beelankil[b]	owner's roadship	to elect to an office	
(ah) tohol beh	(he of the) true road	good and virtuous person (who does good works)	a synonymous term is *(ah) tibil beh*
ts'oksah beh	finished road	to finish a job or a piece of work	
tus beh[a]	false road	to commit a sin, idle entertainment, preoccupation, diversion	today in the area around Coba, *tus bel* means "errand," without the negative connotations of the Colonial term (Bevington 1995:173)

**Table 7.1. Selected Terms and Expressions
Containing *Beh* from Colonial Period Yucatec Dictionaries**

MEANING/SENSE

YUCATEC TERM	LITERAL TRANSLATION	ENGLISH GLOSS	COMMENTS
IV. Life, Destiny			
(u) beelil k'aak' chakawil	(its) road fire/ burning	it's natural for the fire to burn	
bix a beel	how (is) your road	how are you	
hok'ol beh[a]	go out onto road	to go from one road to another, to become infamous; to be born[b]	also noted in Classic period hieroglyphic texts where it means "to be born" or "to appear" (Coggins 1988:71)
ma' tu ch'a'ik beh	not taking one's road	not prospering, not thriving	
ts'o'okan u beel	end one's road	to get married	
ts'ola'n beh	ordered road	order or mode of life, history, chronicle	
(u) ts'ola'n beel maak	(his) ordered road man	biography	
(u) ts'ola'n beel santosob	(their) ordered road saints	chronicle of the saints	the contracted form is (u) beel santosob
xik'bul u beel ch'iich'	fly its road bird	it's natural for the bird to fly	

Notes: For a complete list of collected terms, see Keller 2006. Unmarked entries collected from Barrera Vásquez (1995). Parentheses are used around optional but generally present particles; alphabetization disregards these particles.
a. Terms also found in *Chilam Balam* and other Yucatec texts reviewed for this project.
b. Collected from Andrews Heath (1980).

has a special place in the Maya archaeological literature where it persists as a synonym for causeway. The Colonial-period dictionary compilers glossed *sakbeh* with the Spanish term *calzada* ('main road, highway, causeway'), suggesting a major road that is well constructed and somewhat elevated. Amplifying this interpretation of a *sakbeh* as a well-built road is the synonymous term *betun* ('stone road'), which was also listed as a translation of *calzada*. Both *sakbeh* and *betun* refer to raised roads that are constructed of stone (*tun*) and usually covered with a white (*sak*) surface of lime plaster or crushed marl. Another analogous term is *but'bil beh* ('filled road'), which refers to raised rubble-filled roads like those constructed by the Maya.

Sakbeh is also one of the Mayan names for the Milky Way. This *sakbeh* of the heavens is conceived as a celestial highway that spans the length of the night sky and runs down to the earth as a sort of spiritual conduit through which the initiated may converse with supernatural and ancestral beings (Tozzer 1941:174). Thus, the term *sakbeh* references the color and construction of the ancient roads, as well as their reputed cosmological meaning and ceremonial function.

In addition to actual paths and roads, *beh* can also be applied to road-like things, particularly tubular or canal-like features. A blood vessel is 'the road of blood' (*u beel k'iik'*), a chimney is 'the road of smoke' (*u beel buts'*), a mole's tunnel is 'the road of moles' (*u beel bah*), and a canal is 'the road of water' (*u beel ha'*). This canal-like connotation of *beh* is reminiscent of the construction of some central lowland causeways with low parapet walls that contained the flow of human concourse much like a canal or a chimney contains flowing water or smoke.

When associated with individuals, the term *beh* is exclusively metaphorical. In the Colonial period, one's road was one's well-being, occupation, and destiny. The dictionaries contain terms for several occupations, such as sentinel or spy (*u sabin beh*), local official (*ah beel nal*), and merchant (*u p'olmal u beel*), as well as expressions related to the acceptance of political office (*ch'a beh, tah beelankil*). One's road might be either good or bad, but the collected use examples suggest that a good, true road exists from which people occasionally lose their way and therefore do not prosper (*ma' tu ch'a'ik be*, lit. 'not taking one's road'), or become preoccupied with falsehoods (*tus beh*, lit. 'false road'). This true road is a person's life and life-works, and the ideal is a long, orderly, straight journey marked by birth, marriage, work, and death.

Other uses of *beh* associated with life and destiny include expressions for 'birth' (*hok'ol beh*, lit. 'step onto road'), 'death' (*ok beh*, lit. 'to enter road'), and 'life history' (*u ts'ola'n beel maak*, lit. 'the ordered road of a man') (Coggins 1988:71; Freide, Schele, and Parker 1993:77). Further, the course of the sun was thought of as its road, just as the orbits of the stars are their roads (*u beel ek'ob*, lit. 'their road the black ones'). In these cases, *beh* refers to the linear transit of these astral bodies across the sky, as well as their metaphoric destinies.

In summary, from the Colonial period to the present, *beh* has a relatively stable meaning, integrating life-cycle, temporal, and vocational meanings with the image of a physical road. The most significant change appears to be a constriction of use contexts over time, as well as a marked de-emphasis of the work meaning in modern speech. In the Colonial period, one's life course, destiny, well-being, and occupation all coalesced in the term *beh,* but today work is more commonly discussed as *meyah,* or as *tràabaho* from the Spanish word for work, *trabajo.* This may have something to do with a shift to wage labor from the traditional work of farming, food processing, craft production, ritual specialization, and political office, all of which were understood as one's fate or destiny, rather than simply one's paycheck.

Colonial Contextual Meanings

Despite their richness, these dictionary entries provide few of the whole "sentences, in which words are meaningfully put together," necessary for a contextual semantic analysis (Wierzbicka 1997:27). To place the word *beh* in a broader semantic context, I have reviewed several texts written in the Colonial period by Maya scribes for a Mayan-speaking audience. The selected texts include Yucatec Mayan divinatory calendars and historical chronicles (Craine and Reidorp 1979; Edmonson 1982, 1986; Roys 1965), and Quiche Mayan epic tales (Edmonson 1997; Tedlock 1996, 2003). These texts are concerned with religion, myth, divination, curing rituals, calendrics, and a Maya-centered history in which the Spanish conquistadors are rarely mentioned (Restall 1998:35). Many were "deliberately kept secret from the Spanish," and they stand as some of the only existing books "produced exclusively by and for the Indians themselves" (Farriss 1987:580). They are also poetic works written in a traditional semantic couplet format with extensive use of metaphor (Edmonson 1982:xiv). The meaning of *beh* gathered from these texts, therefore, is skewed toward the poetic and metaphorical. In these ritual texts, the Maya scribes elegantly developed numerous metaphoric linkages between roads and time, incorporating the allied concepts of life, obligation, and destiny (Table 7.2).

As with the dictionary examples, I have grouped the textual use examples of *beh* into four core meaning senses:

1. *Road:* encompassing trails, paths, spiritual or metaphoric paths, and crossroads

2. *Day:* limited to the expression *kabeh,* 'the day after tomorrow'
3. *Work:* meaning one's political position, religious office, or vocation
4. *Destiny:* incorporating the concepts of fate, life-course, well-being

These meaning senses are similar to, but do not exactly duplicate, the dictionary meaning senses. All collected use examples converge on a ritual sense of *beh* as a spiritual thread of destiny and communication between realms. This meaning sense is heightened in these texts as compared to modern speech and the Colonial-period dictionary entries. Frequently, the destinies of polities or people are described as their *beob,* their 'roads'. Several passages refer to rulers and gods who take, step onto, or are seen on a metaphorical road of destiny, thereby accepting the burden of power (Edmonson 1986:121).

Not surprisingly, the *beh* of these Colonial period ritual texts is rarely a literal road, but more often a mythical or metaphorical construct. Time is born on a road, ancestors and gods communicate with the living via roads, calendrical cycles such as the *k'atun* (a period of 20 years, analogous to our decades) are celebrated on roads, and the cosmos is organized by the intersection of four roads which form a crossroads. The image of the crossroads, typically expressed as 'four road' (*kan beh*) in Yucatec Mayan and 'four crossed roads' (*kajib xalkat be*) in Quiche Mayan, was the most frequent and salient use of *beh* in the Colonial-period texts reviewed here.

The crossroads is both a physical place and a metaphoric device signaling order, centrality, and the concordance of spiritual and mundane topographies. In the Quiche epic, *Popol Vuh,* the crossroads is the location of transition and transformation where the mythical Hero Twins (Hunahpu and Xbalanque) take the 'black road' (*q'eqa be*) to the underworld (Tedlock 1996:95, 116). In the Yucatec *Chilam Balam* texts, the crossroads is also associated with the underworld and the ancestors, as well as with insignia of power and sacrificial offerings. When the mantle of rulership is conferred upon a city, the 'burden' (*kuch*) of power is 'lowered' (*emom*) over the crossroads. When political rivalries erupt, the traditional images and icons of power are 'removed' (*ok'om*) from the crossroads, thus vitiating the authority of the city. The crossroads is a mythical place of power where this world and the spirit world collide; a place where communion and transformation are possible, and where the gods and ancestors are present.

The Yucatec Mayan references to the crossroads are quite consistent, usually invoking first the 'crossroads' (*kan beh*) and then the enigmatic places

Table 7.2. Selected Phrases Including *Beh* from Colonial Period Yucatec Texts

MEANING/SENSE

YUCATEC PHRASE	ENGLISH GLOSS[a]	SOURCE[b]
I. Road		
Way	Here	Chumayel (p. 181)
Ti luum beh	On the road of the land	
Yum e he y ok haa e	Father, this is the water ditch	Chumayel (p. 201)
Ti yx y an te u iknal e	And it is here on me	
Heklay u bel yn pach e	It means the spine [road] of my back	
He ix ah ximbalte	And there are the travelers	Tizimin (p. 133)
Y etel ah numul beob e	And those who suffer the roads	
Y an bin kimik ob I	They will die	
Kimlahak	And must die	
Ia. Spirit Path		
Emom suum	Descended was the cord	Chumayel (p. 209)
Emom tab	Descended was the rope	
Tal ti kaan u thanil	From heaven was the word [of God]	
Ma tusbil beh	Of the undeviating path	
Naak-hom tibil beob kanal	Raising fear of the paths of heaven	Tizimin (p. 30)
Emom lobol beob	Descending the evil paths	
T u tz'u luum	To the marrow of the earth	
Ib. Crossroads		
Ok'om bul kum	Gone is the bean bowl	Chumayel (p. 213)
Y etel yax kach	And the green fly	
T u ho kan beh	From the gate of the four roads [crossroads]	
T u ho kan heleb	From the gate of the four changers	
T u kan helebil kaan	In the four changes of heaven	Tizimin (p. 67)
T u kan helebil beh	In the four changes of the road	
Ox k'ok'ol tzek'	Three stone rattles	Tizimin (p. 76)
Auatnom yax kach	The green fly screeched	
T u ho kam beh	At the entry of the four roads [crossroads]	
T u ho kan luub	At the entry of the four rests	
T u k'in	On the day	Tizimin (p. 88)
U ch'aik u matan	He took his request	
Hol kan beh	At the gate of the four roads [crossroads]	

Table 7.2. Selected Phrases Including *Beh* from Colonial Period Yucatec Texts

MEANING/SENSE

YUCATEC PHRASE	ENGLISH GLOSS[a]	SOURCE[b]
Hol kan lub	At the gate of the four rests	
Ti emom	Which lowered	
U kuch witz	The burden of the mountain	
y okol may ku l	Over the cycle seat	

II. Day

Samal kabehe	Day after tomorrow	Chumayel (p. 118)
Ti tali	It will come	
Bayen ob i ti samal kabeh e	So be it, on the day after tomorrow	Tizimin (p. 187)
Ch'a ex a ba ex	You will take yourselves	

III. Work

(Office, Burden, Assumption of Power)

Y an chek' beh k'atun	There was the pacing of the *k'atun* road	Tizimin (p. 37)
Xoipahom t u chak'anil	Making the circuit of the fields	
T u ch'aik u bal	They take office	Tizimin (p. 90)
Ah kan tziknal	The four honored ones	
Ka'a u kah	Taking their place	
T u bel	On the road	
Lik u talel	As he comes	Tizimin (p. 91)
T u p'at beh k'atun e	To the remainder of the road of the *k'atun*	
T u ch'aik u bel	Then to take office	
Talel u kah	One may come to settle	Tizimin (p. 108)
U ch'a beh k'atun	And take the road of the *k'atun*	
Ah pop	The man of the mat	
Ah tz'am	The man of the throne	

IV. Destiny, Life

Bin ix k'uchuk t u k'in	For when there arrives the time	Chumayel (p. 169)
U holol u bel	Of the beginning of his road	
Ka u satah ob beh	They destroyed the road	Tizimin (p. 7)
Kak'an Putun	of Champoton	
Y an ychil u kuch	That is its burden	Tizimin (p. 173)
Y etel u bel	And its road	

Table 7.2. Selected Phrases Including *Beh* from Colonial Period Yucatec Texts

MEANING/SENSE

YUCATEC PHRASE	ENGLISH GLOSS[a]	SOURCE[b]
Y an ychil u kuch hab i la e	That is the burden of the year	
Sakiapan, u hetz' k'atun	Valladolid is the seat of the *k'atun*	
Ma wil bal u bel	If you don't follow the road	Tizimin (p. 189)
A tz'aik a pol ex ti	You'll give your heads to the Archbishop	
arsobispo e		

Notes: For a complete list of collected phrases, see Keller 2006.
a. English gloss translations follow those presented in the source texts.
b. Source abbreviations refer to the following texts: Chumayel=*Heaven Born Merida and Its Destiny: The Book of Chilam Balam of Chumayel*, trans. Munro S. Edmonson (1986); Tizimin=*The Ancient Future of the Itza: The Book of Chilam Balam of Tizimin*, trans. Munro S. Edmonson (1982).

called 'four rest' (*kan luub*) or 'four change' (*kan hel*). Munro Edmonson (1982:76–77) believes that the four rest/change places refer to actual "rest stops, platforms on which one may temporarily deposit one's burden," and "ceremonial platforms of this sort at the entry to a central plaza." Examples of such roadside platforms exist around modern Maya towns and at numerous archaeological sites (Coe 1965; Keller 2006; Konrad 1991; Redfield and Villa Rojas 1934:114; Tozzer 1941).

The largely spiritual texts from the Colonial period reviewed here contain only a few of the various *beh* terms recorded in contemporary dictionaries, but they nonetheless provide a vivid glimpse of the metaphorical manner of Maya thought and speech. Turning now to an examination of the hieroglyphic texts, I suggest that the metaphoric meanings of *beh* have deep roots in the prehispanic past.

Prehispanic Meanings

Compared to the diverse documentary materials from the Colonial period, the corpus of deciphered prehispanic texts is more limited in size and subject matter. Concerned primarily with political affairs, the hieroglyphic texts nonetheless contain numerous instances of the term *beh,* or *bih* in Cholan Mayan, the *lingua franca* of the Classic period and the presumed language of most of the hieroglyphic texts.

The Classic-period glyph for the term *beh/bih* was the image of a quincunx: four corner dots and one in the center, like the five on gaming dice (Figure 7.1a). A synonymous glyph from the Postclassic period suggestively took the form of a human footprint (Tozzer 1941:170), but the quincunx glyph was apparently the primary glyph for *beh/bih* in the Classic period. This quincunx glyph is hardly road-like unless we imagine it as a crossroads, with each corner dot marking the four roads at their resting places, and the center dot marking their crossing point. Thus, the crossroads may have been the fundamental image of '*beh*-ness' for the Classic Maya.

The quincunx glyph, also known as Thompson's glyph T585, is found in the monumental inscriptions of over 20 sites and on many polychrome painted codex-style vases (Thompson 1962:209–13). Like most glyphs in the prehispanic Mayan writing system, the quincunx glyph occurs both as a lexeme (as the word *beh/bih*), and as a phonetic complement (supplying a /b/ or /bi/ sound to a phonetically rendered expression). The most famous use of the quincunx glyph occurs in the text adorning the sarcophagus of Pakal I, the illustrious ruler of the site of Palenque (Figure 7.1b). In a passage discussing Pakal's death, the quincunx glyph is paired with a glyph translated as *och* in Cholan, or *ok* in Yucatec, meaning 'to step' or 'to enter'. In this instance, epigraphers translate the expression into Cholan as *och bih,* 'to enter the road', and interpret it as a metaphor for death (Coggins 1988; Freidel, Schele, and Parker 1993:76–78; Stuart 1998:388, fig. 9a). Since the initial decipherment of Pakal's sarcophagus, epigraphers have identified several other examples of *och bih* death expressions at Palenque and surrounding polities (Harris and Stearns 1992:88; Martin 2001:181; Taube 2004:80). A related expression including the quincunx glyph is *hok'ol beh* (lit. 'to go out onto the

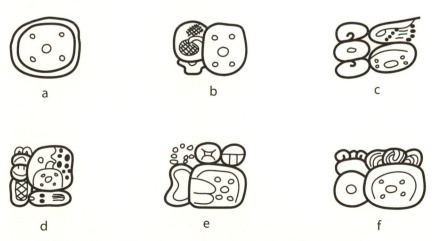

7.1 Examples of the quincunx glyph from various Classic period texts.

road'), which Clemency Coggins (1988:71) has interpreted as 'birth' or 'to be born'. In the Colonial period, the same expression meant 'to appear' or 'become infamous', as well as 'to be born' (Andrews Heath 1980:241), and was used to describe the metaphoric rebirth of rulers upon taking office.

In addition to its use as a lexeme, the quincunx glyph appears as a phonetic value in combination with other hieroglyphs. The glyph occurs repeatedly on fine polychrome painted vases as part of the so-called wing-quincunx and fire-quincunx collocations (combinations of several glyphic elements in one glyph block signifying a single term) (Figure 7.1c). Although scholars have offered a variety of translations for these two common collocations (e.g., Coggins 1988:76), they are now convincingly translated as *y-uch'ib* ('his drinking vessel') and *u-ts'ib* ('to write/paint', or 'his paint'), respectively (Houston, Stuart, and Taube 1989; Reents-Budet 1994:114–15). In each instance, the quincunx glyph supplies the final /b/ sound. In addition, Maya scribes regularly used the quincunx glyph as part of the term *waybil* (Figure 7.1d), meaning 'lineage shrine' (Freidel, Schele, and Parker 1993:190–92) or simply 'domicile' (Stuart 1998:fig. 1).

Finally, perhaps the most instructive use of the quincunx glyph has only recently been identified by David Stuart (2006; see also Houston, Stuart, and Taube 2006:262). On the six inscribed stone panels found along the 100-km-long causeway that connects the sites of Coba and Yaxuna, Stuart (2006:1) has identified a collocation combining the quincunx glyph with the glyph for 'white' (*sak*), which he reads as *sakbih,* or 'white road' in Cholan (Figure 7.1f). All of the inscribed panels bear dates, indicating to Stuart (2006:1) that they were "dedication markers for the causeway," and further that the term *sakbih* indeed refers to the causeway with which the monuments are associated. Stuart has also collected a handful of new references to roads in Classic-period texts, including hieroglyphic passages from the Copan site containing the term *kan bih,* 'the four roads' or 'crossroads'. These passages may refer to actual causeways at the site, but Stuart suggests that the crossroads of the Copan texts is metaphorical and cosmological like the crossroads of the later Colonial-period texts.

These are but a few examples of the quincunx glyph in the Classic period, and more epigraphic work remains to be done. Nevertheless, this cursory review illustrates the continuity of meaning from the Classic period to the present, particularly the longevity of the terms *sakbeh* and *kan beh,* and the longstanding interrelation of roads, life, and destiny.

ARCHAEOLOGICAL IMPLICATIONS

Working from the modern era back into the prehispanic past, I have traced both continuities and subtle shifts in the meaning of the term *beh*. How, though, does this exercise help us better understand the archaeologically documented Maya causeways? For archaeologists, the three most significant implications of this study may be (1) the pervasive temporal quality of roads, (2) the importance of the crossroads and associated change or rest places, and (3) the profound significance of movement along roads for Mayan speakers.

The temporality of roads in Maya language and thought is striking. Roads are associated with journeys, the passage of time, important life events, and the celebration of calendrical ceremonies, particularly the *k'atun* and other period-ending rituals. Archaeologically, we see the association of roads and time in the frequent placement of dated stone monuments along and at the ends of causeways (Keller 2006; Stuart 2006). Classic period rulers may have processed along their roads to mark time in the physical world, much like the rulers of the Colonial-period texts 'paced the *k'atun* road' (*chek' beh k'atun*) to mark temporal cycles while surveying the extent of their polities. In this regard, the Colonial materials suggest that cruciform arrangements of four roads, or crossroads, were particularly significant.

Crossroads and Change Places

The mythical crossroads of the Colonial-period texts may be physically reflected in the cruciform causeway patterns of sites such as Coba (Benavides 1981), Ek Balam (Bey, Hanson, and Ringle 1997), Yaxuna (Stanton and Freidel 2005), Seibal, Xunantunich (Keller 2006), and La Honradez, among others (Coggins 1980; Mathews and Garber 2004). Seemingly incomplete cruciform patterns with roads oriented to some, but not all, of the cardinal directions are even more common. Numerous sites have roads running to the east or north of the site core, and a smaller number have south- or west-oriented roads. Typically, these roads are aligned roughly to the cardinal directions following the often skewed orientations of the sites with which they are associated (Keller 2006). Just as modern Yucatec Mayan speakers conceive of their villages as having four roads associated with the cardinal directions which are rarely oriented exactly to the east, west, north, and south of the village (Redfield and Villa Rojas 1934:114), so too might the prehispanic Maya have been flexible in this regard. In the physical world of caves and mountains, of lakes and streams, the crossroads may have been stretched and warped to fit.

In the Colonial-period texts, the crossroads are consistently paired with the 'four rest' (*kan lub*) or 'four change' (*kan hel*) places. If we accept Edmonson's (1982:76–77) interpretation of the *kan lub* and *kan hel* as actual structures, they may have direct archaeological corollaries at numerous prehispanic sites: small, seemingly out-of-place structures along causeways. Examples of such roadside structures exist at numerous archaeological sites, including notable examples at Copan, Ixkun, Naranjo, Tzum, Yaxuna, and Xunantunich. These structures are commonly small, low platforms adjacent to or astride causeways at their entrance to major plazas. Some of the structures are suggestively associated with stone monuments that mark the completion of calendrical cycles.

In the 16th century, Bishop Diego de Landa described similar roadside structures, or "heaps of stone," erected at the four cardinal entrances of Maya towns. During the annual Year Ending (*Wayeb*) ceremony, the Maya placed upon these rock platforms "a statue of a god" representing the New Year (Tozzer 1941:139–41; Coe 1965; Sharer 1994:547–51). Michael Coe (1965) analyzed the Year Ending ceremony described by Landa and concluded that the rites involved the processions along roads and the rotation of four calendrical god images, known as year-bearers, each associated with a different cardinal direction. Each year, a new year-bearer presided over the year and the god's image was taken to its cardinal place along the roads. In this manner, the location of the year-bearer's image shifted counterclockwise each year, manifesting the metaphoric rotation of time as an actual physical rotation of images around the town (Coe 1965; Thompson 1934). Anthropologists working with lowland and highland Maya groups have documented analogous calendrical rituals involving cardinally oriented roads and associated platforms and shrines (Farriss 1987:577; Fox 1994:160; Konrad 1991; Redfield and Villa Rojas 1934; Tedlock 1992; Vogt 1970, 1976). The physical rotation of calendrical cycles along roads is apparently an enduring feature of Maya ritual life from the prehispanic era to the present day. The collected words and writings of the Maya, though, suggest that *all* movement along roads held a strong ceremonial and symbolic significance.

Movement

By moving through their landscape along prescribed routes, the Maya came to understand not only the contours of the world, but also the contours of their own bodily and perceptual presence in the world (cf. Zedeño, Hollenback, and Grinnell, Chapter 6, this volume). This process of self-recognition is today described through the metaphor of a person traveling along a road, as in the common Yucatec Mayan expression, 'How is your road?' (*bix a beel?*), meaning 'How are you?', wherein the concept of road is equated with a person's well-being, life-course, and destiny.

In contemporary Maya thought, movement has a spiritual character and a generative power. Many modern ritual practitioners diagnose and cure illness by tracing the movement of various forces in the world and within individual bodies (Hanks 1990:343; Tedlock 1992:138). The movements of spiritual forces create illness, and only through the counter-movements of the ritual specialist is a cure affected. William Ringle (1999:200) observes that we find this "widespread concept, the belief in the efficacy of motion," expressed in ritual activities ranging from curing rites and house dedications, to community-wide processions and long-distance pilgrimages. The act of walking—whether around a house lot or to a shrine—imparts substance and power upon a ritual undertaking. What should be apparent in this discussion is that Maya movement is not merely a receptive activity, but a generative act capable of effecting change in the world. The Maya are not alone in this regard. In many cultures movement, and especially processional movement, is a uniquely potent activity (e.g., Basso 1996b; Coleman and Eade 2004; Coleman and Elsner 1994; Morinis 1992; Orr 2001; Poole 1991; Stanley 1992; Turner 1974; see also Ferguson, Berlin, and Kuwanwisiwma, Chapter 2, this volume, and Sheets, Chapter 8, this volume).

Considering the efficacy of movement in Maya thought, we should not be surprised that Maya rulers made the control of movement a fundamental aspect of urban design from the Preclassic period forward. Maya architects had many means at their disposal to direct movement, such as walls, stairs, the opening or blocking of passageways, but constructed roads were a particularly overt tool. With their roads, Maya rulers controlled the movement of people and power within and between their centers (cf. Snead, Chapter 3, this volume). The largest and most impressive causeways also likely functioned as stages for royal display (Ringle 1999). By stepping onto a causeway, a ruler stepped into time, destiny, and his rightful place in the world. He stepped onto a *beh,* with all its many and layered meanings.

CONCLUSIONS

The importance of the term *beh,* from the Classic period to the present, suggests the deep and abiding importance of trails, paths, and roads in Maya life and thought. As Munro Edmonson (1982:76) explains: "The image of the road is central to Yucatecan cosmology. Life is a road. Fulfilling one's road is achieving one's destiny. One form of doing so is marriage: *k in tz'ookl in bel,* 'I finish my road', is 'I marry'. The sun and the gods also follow their roads, which intersect in the center of the community, which is the center of the universe."

Although the fundamental meaning senses of the term *beh* appear to have changed little from prehispanic to modern times, subtle shifts in significance have occurred. From the Colonial period to today, *beh* has lost some of its inclusive power to convey a person's life, occupation, social and spiritual obligations, and destiny in one coherent package. Over time, the 'work' meaning of the term has lost its relevance, such that today, Maya speakers rarely use *beh* in discussions of their daily work. From the Classic to the Colonial periods, I suspect that there was a comparable shift in meaning related to the profound social and political transformations wrought by the Conquest. Road terms and concepts pertaining to the ruling elite, such as *ch'ibal beh* ('main road' or 'lineage road'), may have lost some of their currency with the reduction of the traditional ruling class. My feeling is that many of the large, archaeologically documented stone roads, particularly those attached to major centers, were intimately associated with the power and the person of the ruler. The *noh beh, ch'ibal beh,* and *sakbeh* were the ruler's roads reflecting the flow and extent of divine power.

Revisiting the riddle posed at the beginning of this chapter, "What is a man on a road?," we can now sense the logic behind the answer: "Time." The association of roads and paths with time is a metaphoric device common to many cultures and languages (Potter 2004:324). By walking on a road, one senses the passage of time physically: what is behind me is in the past, what lies ahead is in the future. Few concepts could be more fundamental.

For the Maya, however, the conflation of roads and time entails not only a linear path from there to here, but also multiple, interwoven cycles of time that form the fabric of life. The road of life is likened to the roads of the sun, moon, and stars that run in great circles around our everyday world, forming transits in the sky and tunnels through the underworld. By walking along their roads, the Maya performed time. They displayed the passage of time, and the transition of temporal cycles as spatially rooted entities. The English words 'path', 'road', and 'causeway', although formally descriptive, fail to capture the meaning of the Mayan word *beh*. As Eva Hoffman (1989:204) elegantly describes, between languages "there are shapes of sensibility incommensurate with each other, topographies of experience one cannot guess." As archaeologists, we may use the shapes of sensibility revealed by the study of native languages and local histories to approach the past with a greater sensitivity to long-forgotten topographies of experience.

Acknowledgments

This chapter evolved out of a portion of my dissertation research on Maya roads, which was funded by a National Science Foundation Dissertation Improvement grant, a Fulbright/IIE award, a William Penn fellowship and grants from the University of Pennsylvania. I am happily indebted to Clark Erickson and James Snead for asking me to be a last-minute participant in the Penn Museum International Research Conference Seminar from which this volume developed. Thanks also to the other seminar participants, who helped me to think more critically about trails, roads, and journeys cross-culturally. I am grateful to James Snead, Clark Erickson, J. Andrew Darling, Jason Ur, Wendy Ashmore, and a particularly helpful anonymous reviewer for their critical reading of draft versions of this paper. Their wise suggestions have improved the clarity of the final version. Any remaining shortcomings are my own.

8

When the Construction of Meaning Preceded the Meaning of Construction: From Footpaths to Monumental Entrances in Ancient Costa Rica

PAYSON SHEETS

In human societies, the control of energy constitutes the most fundamental and universally recognized measure of political power. The most basic way in which power can be symbolically reinforced is through the conspicuous consumption of energy. Monumental architecture, as a highly visible and enduring form of such consumption, plays an important role in shaping the political and economic behaviour of human beings. This explains why, as systems based on inequality evolved, monumental architecture loomed so large in the archaeological record.

— Bruce Trigger, "Monumental Architecture:
A Thermodynamic Explanation of Symbolic Behavior"

The Arenal Research Project in northwestern Costa Rica has documented human occupation and human movement in the landscape over the past ten thousand years (Sheets and McKee 1994). Apparently, human movement across the landscape in times of low population density, such as the PaleoIndian, Archaic, and early sedentary periods, was oriented to specific tasks at particular times. That movement was therefore sufficiently randomized to have left no permanent record that we have detected.

However, a different form of movement began around 500 BC in the

Epigraph. 1990:128.

Arenal area, as people began burying their dead in cemeteries separated from their villages. Simultaneously they began following precise paths that connected villages with cemeteries, and cemeteries with the resources used in them for construction and for feasting. The "proper" cemetery-associated movement was single file along the same path used by parental and earlier generations, resulting in compaction and erosion of the path itself.

These paths were the product of this structured pattern of movement, and we have never found any evidence of construction along any path. When people trod the same path on slopes over $10°$, the channel formed by many footsteps began to erode. With time, concomitant erosion on either side of the path deepened it dramatically. Generation after generation of path use resulted in entrenchment of the paths 1, 2, 3, or more meters below the surrounding ground surface, and in one case over 7 m deep. Thus the sustained use of a straight path entering a cemetery had the unanticipated consequence of causing a sunken entryway.

I contend that this incidental entrenchment of paths created a culturally meaningful landscape of movement. The ritual standard presumably developed that the preferred way to enter a cemetery was along a sunken narrow straight path, and then when people entered the special place it opened up in front of them. It might have emulated the birthing process, or emergence into the otherworld.

The formation and use of these sunken entryways in the Arenal area date from 500 BC to AD 1300. After AD 500, and especially after AD 1000, a series of more complex societies developed further east. Along with inherited inequality came the "mentality of monumentality" and chiefs chose to impress their commoners and visitors with large constructed entryways into their special places. I suggest that the monumental entryways of the later chiefdoms had their origins in the earlier inadvertent sunken entryways to cemeteries of simpler societies.

What became a cultural standard with no construction effort in simpler times, as people constructed the meaning of special places and how to enter them, apparently was "writ large" into a constructed monumentality in later times. The unanticipated results of repeated activities eventually became impressive indeed. And what a wise choice by a chief seeking monumentality, to seize on a long-valued concept of sunken entry, to legitimize their centralized authority by exploiting a value embedded in antiquity. The regularly repeated movements embedded meaning in the landscape that was later co-opted by leaders in need of monumentality to control behaviors of construction, maintenance, and use.

THE ARENAL RESEARCH PROJECT

The Arenal Research Project has been operating in northwestern Costa Rica since the early 1980s (summarized in Sheets and McKee 1994). Funding from the National Science Foundation, National Geographic, and the University of Colorado has supported research. NASA has provided abundant remotely sensed imagery from aircraft and satellite platforms, in both analog and digital formats (McKee, Sever, and Sheets 1994) (Figure 8.1).

Certainly the most surprising, and most important, research result is the realization that we can detect ancient footpaths in the remote sensing imagery, and we can confirm them by excavations and careful attention to stratigraphy (Sheets and Sever 1991). Most linear anomalies can be identified as recent or modern features, such as roads, fencelines, property boundaries, or trails, by inspection of the imagery and by verification on the ground. However, many have proved on excavation to be ancient paths eroded and entrenched by centuries of use. Our ability to evaluate these features is enhanced by the presence of a thick tephra deposit produced by one of the greatest of the precolumbian eruptions at about AD 1450, providing a useful separator between ancient and historic features.

Early Occupations and Task-oriented Movement in the Landscape

We have not detected any preserved footpaths from our earliest time spans, from PaleoIndian through Archaic and the early sedentary (Tronadora phase) occupations. That covers the majority of time that we have documented people living in the area, from approximately 10,000 to 500 BC. My assumption is that task-oriented travel predominated, wherein people perceiving a need to obtain a food or other resource, visit kin, or conduct a ritual generally would travel least-cost routes on an individual task basis, sufficiently randomizing foot travel across their countryside so that entrenched paths did not develop. In fact, it is indeed fortunate that every footprint of people moving across the landscape does not preserve, or there would be very few of us able to live in a thoroughly trampled world.

Tronadora-phase (ca. 2000–500 BC) villages were small, probably less than 100 people, in round houses with (presumably) thatch roofs. The

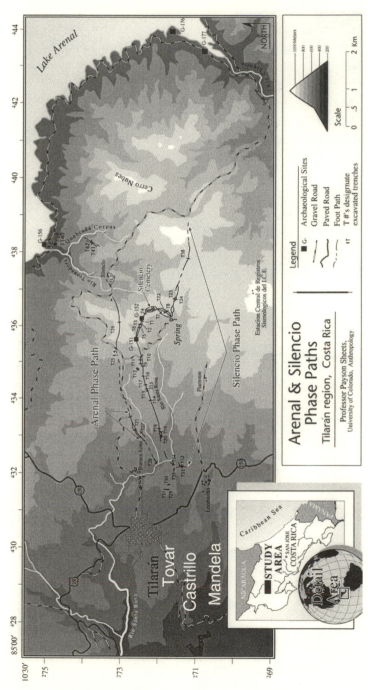

8.1 Map of the Arenal-Tilaran area, with the Arenal and Silencio phase paths and the sites they connect. The earlier Arenal path leads from the G-156 village on the lakeshore, uphill over the pass, and down westward to the complex of cemeteries in the Castrillo-Mandela area. The later Silencio paths lead south from the Silencio cemetery to the spring, and then east. Their terminus likely is a village or villages, and two likely candidates are in that direction along the lakeshore. The path leading westward from the cemetery passes two repositories of construction stone and continues to the Tovar source of that stone. The path likely continued to a village or villages.

ceramics were highly sophisticated, and were accompanied by basic and efficient chipped and ground stone tool assemblages. Manos and metates probably were used for grinding maize and other seeds, and both macro-fossils and pollen indicate that some gardening of domesticates was done. However, the bulk of the diet probably derived from wild species of trees, bushes, vines, and other plants, along with hunting and fishing.

Burials were secondary, in small rectangular pits just outside the driplines of house roofs and often accompanied by ceramic vessels. We have closely examined all analog and digital remote sensing imagery in and around these villages, and found no linear anomalies that could be ancient footpaths. In terms of social organization, all material indicators consistently point toward egalitarian societies throughout the thousands of years from PaleoIndian through Tronadora times.

The Arenal Phase and the Emergence of Ritually Directed Movement

The population density during all precolumbian phases of occupation of the Arenal area remained quite low by Mesoamerican, Andean, and even by overall Costa Rican standards. It probably never exceeded a few people per square kilometer. However, the Arenal phase (500 BC to AD 600) had the largest settlements and the highest regional population density of any phase in our research area. Villages were composed of houses similar in size and construction to the earlier phase, but many more of them, with more ceramics and heavy tools such as manos and metates.

In terms of social organization, societies during all phases of occupation prior to the Arenal phase were egalitarian, based on the uniformity of housing, artifacts, and grave goods in the Tronadora phase as well as evident uniformity in the two earlier phases. Housing and household artifacts do not show any differentiation during the Arenal phase, supporting the interpretation that egalitarian societies continued. However, some Arenal phase burials show differentiation that could reflect status differences, but it also could derive from gender or age differences and the society thus have remained egalitarian.

In a dramatic variance from earlier periods, Arenal Phase burials were placed in cemeteries separated from the villages, in some cases by only a few hundred meters, but usually many kilometers distant. A good example of an Arenal phase cemetery is the Bolivar site, located on a hill 150 m southeast of the associated village (Hoopes and Chenault 1994). Although we detected no remains of a path at Bolivar, the cemetery itself is instructive as to burial procedures and post-interment rituals (Hoopes and Chenault 1994). Burials close to the ridge top received considerable post-interment attention. The primary burials were placed in pits dug about a meter below the ground surface, and occasionally accompanied with grave goods (stone axes). The pits were filled in with dirt and then outlined with elongated stones on the surface, and then rounded river stones were harshly smashed onto the entire surface, creating a low mound of rock. That was followed by extensive feasting and smashing of hundreds of complete pottery vessels and dozens of decorated metates and other artifacts in post-funerary rituals throughout the cemetery.

Only 10 m down the gentle slope was a different kind of cemetery, covered with much more fragmentary and eroded sherds and a few broken ground stone artifacts. We concluded that these artifacts were scavenged from a midden and redeposited over the burials, a "poor person's" imitation of the more elaborate cemetery nearby. If these differences are not reflective of variation in gender, age-grade, or other similar factors, they could be indicative of the beginnings of social inequality. The lack of skeletal preservation in all Arenal phase cemeteries is due to high soil acidity and mean precipitation of about 3000 mm per year. Unfortunately, that means no gender or age studies of the deceased can be performed.

Paths dating to the Arenal phase have been recorded elsewhere in our Arenal research area. The shortest known path (Figure 8.2) is only 250 m long, and its positioning helped us understand how important entrenched paths were to ancient people in this area. It is between a cemetery (G-184) and a village (G-180) that are 1.1 km apart (McKee, Sever, and Sheets 1994:144–46). The easiest transit between the village and cemetery is on the flat floodplain of the Rio Piedra, along an almost straight line. However, the path runs up and over the hill, increasing the distance of travel slightly and the effort significantly. In addition to movement, this entrenched path also structures associated views in interesting ways. Traveling from the cemetery, one would be in the entrenched path up and down the hill, but as one reached the bottom of the hill and the entrenched path disappears, the village would open up to view.

Wherever we suspect we have detected an ancient path in the imagery or on the ground, we excavate it to determine its age and nature. On the north side of the hill the path had eroded down to about 1.5 m below the

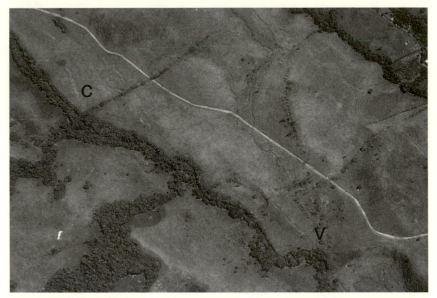

8.2 Aerial photograph of the Rio Piedra area, just west of Lake Arenal. The Rio Piedra flows from the upper left corner down to the lower right, under the gallery forest. The "V" denotes the Rio Piedra village, and the incised path is visible on the hill immediately to the northwest. That path points directly toward the cemetery "C". The easier route between village and cemetery would be to pass on either side of the hill. Horizontal distance of aerial photograph is 1.6 km.

surrounding ground surface, while other parts of the trench on both sides of the hill had eroded to an estimated 2 m below the surrounding ground surfaces. Such an entrenched path would only have formed under particular conditions, one being movement restricted to that specific route.

Cultural/ritual prescription of travel along precisely the same path, year after year, from village to cemetery and back, would have generated the signature we see for this and other Arenal phase paths. The first effect of sustained walking was linear compression, and inclinations greater than 5°, and especially over 10°, provided sufficient slope for moving water to erode the path itself. The actual "walked surface" is consistently only about 0.5 m wide, and that can only be formed by single-file use. Because the tephra layers and the juvenile soils on them are so unconsolidated in the Arenal area, their angle of repose under these conditions is a slope on either side of the path of approximately 30° from horizontal. Thus, as the path surface erodes downward, it takes a broad V shape of surrounding surface down with it. Thus the prescription on path use in sloping areas resulted in the inadvertent entrenchment, which I believe became a cultural standard of the proper way to traverse between special places.

Although none of the paths of the Arenal phase were themselves constructed, associated constructed features do exist. On the hilltop above Rio Piedra two low stone platforms flanking the path were built of subrounded river cobbles, presumably carried from the river nearby. It is possible that people with special ceremonial roles stood on the platforms as processions passed single file between them. These features may be pregnant with importance, as they may be the forerunners to elements of monumentality in later chiefdoms (see below). The smashed ceramic vessels found on top of, and between, the stones are reminiscent of ritual pottery-breaking in Arenal phase cemeteries on both sides of the divide.

The longest Arenal phase path discovered to date is over 10 km long, leading south from village site G-156 on the south shore of Lake Arenal, and dated by ceramics, stratigraphic associations of the soil on the volcanic ash unit when path use began, and the ash unit that fell after the path was abandoned (Hoopes 1994) (see Figure 8.1). The path runs across the grain of the land with little regard for terrain, ultimately bending westward, crossing the mountain range that divides the Caribbean from the Pacific drainage. The path has been traced and confirmed to where it crossed the Rio Santa Rosa 1 km east of Tilaran, at the left side of Figure 8.3, and 6.4 km from the village (straight line distance). That segment of the path was confirmed by excavating Trenches 21 and 28. What appears to be a section of the same path, but farther west, was recently discovered at the juncture of the *fincas* (ranches) of Callan Vargas and Hilma Jenkins, 8.8 km from the village in a straight line.

Finding that segment led our survey into what must have been a special area of some two dozen Arenal phase cemeteries 1 to 2 km farther west (see Figure 8.4). This supports our contention that entrenched paths connect villages and cemeteries. That entrenched footpaths began during the Arenal Phase, and not before or after, brings up two key questions, for which I can offer only possible answers.

Cemeteries Separated from Villages

Why separate village from cemetery? A potential answer is provided by ethnographic accounts from lower Central America. First we consider

8.3 Black-and-white version of infrared aerial photograph showing rainforest (dark) and pastures (light), with earlier Arenal phase path confirmed by Trenches 21 and 28. The path is the single darker line at Trench 28 that runs uphill (northwest), and divides into two parallel paths at Trench 21. Horizontal distance is 1.5 km.

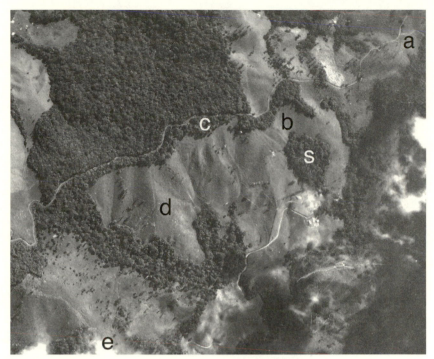

8.4 Silencio phase paths radiating from the Silencio cemetery ("c") atop the mountain, dividing the Pacific from the Caribbean drainages. Three paths ("b") lead down to the spring ("s"), and then continue northeastward to "a" and presumably a village or villages. Another path heads south to "d" and bends around a stone repository, and then southwest to cross the small stream and climb the steep slope to "e". This path leads to the source of construction stone at Tovar, just west of Tilaran, and probably on to a village or villages. Horizontal distance of aerial photograph is 2.3 km.

the present-day Cuna in Panama (Dillon 1984), the most traditional Native Americans in lower Central America. The Cuna bury their most prominent village members (civic leaders, heads of prominent households, shamans, curers) in cemeteries at or near ridge tops visible from the village but many kilometers away. When asked why the cemetery is so far away, the Cuna respond that the spirits of the dead are less bothered by the noise, smoke, and children of the busy village, and the living are happier with the spirits of the formerly powerful people buried at a distance. The body of a powerful person may have stopped functioning, but their spirit has not and it must be dealt with appropriately. As the Cuna travel from village to cemetery and visit the graves of deceased ancestors for extended times, they consume food and drink, burn incense, and make offerings to the deceased.

The most traditional Native Americans in Costa Rica are the Bribri, described by Skinner (1920) and Bozzoli de Wille (1975). The Bribri believe that people leave a part of themselves in everything they touch, or in every place where they lived or to which they have traveled (Bozzoli de Wille 1975). Both ethnographers mention the Bribri concern for evil spirits at the time of death. After death, the soul-spirit of the deceased will revisit all those places, and to find those places the assistance of the living is essential (Bozzoli de Wille 1975). She describes (1975:95) an example of a cemetery on a hilltop 2 km from the village and the processions carrying the bones (presumably from the platform) to the cemetery. The spirit, following the bones and the procession, needs guidance. The women tie string along the path to help guide the spirit, which of course causes a path segment to follow a straight line. If similar practices existed in ancient times in the Arenal area, perhaps by tying vines, this could explain why so many of our path segments are so straight. Elaborate funerary rituals occurred from the time of death to the interment.

Why travel such a precisely prescribed route? James Snead (2002) provided important insights that could help answer this question in his study of ancestral Pueblo trails of northern New Mexico. He found that meaning as well as practical and economic factors were intrinsic to ancient paths in the Bandelier area. In a paradigm-changing insight into how differently Westerners and Native Americans can view a trail, Snead provides a quote from Waterman about the Yurok of California: "Trails are sentient, and must be traveled with urbanity. If you step out of a trail and in again, and fail to preserve decorum, the trail becomes resentful" (2002:756). Although the geographic and cultural distances between Arenal people and the Yurok are great, I believe the former might have considered their paths as sentient, or at least so special that people did not step out of the path.

Pertinent here is the concept of materialization (De Marrais, Castillo, and Earle 1996), also discussed by James Snead (Chapter 3, this volume). Materialization focuses on the relationship between material culture and ideology, within the framework of landscape. It relates the physical to the conceptual world. As generations of Arenal villagers processed single file along the same ritual pathways to their cemeteries, their perception of the gradually entrenching paths changed, as did their perception of the landscape. The separation of village and cemetery appears suddenly in the archaeological record. Simultaneously, people determinedly maintained their precise paths linking village to cemetery, thus enforcing connections between the living and the deceased. As those paths entrenched during later centuries, a new value emerged, that of the ideal way to transit the landscape and enter a special place. Generations of processions of Arenal people along their paths constructed meaning.

It remains unclear why the shift to prescribed paths occurred during the Arenal phase, but the separation of cemetery and village space is clearly important. It is possible that the belief in the supernatural power of the spirits of the deceased had somehow blossomed around 500 BC, and therefore separation of village and cemetery was necessary, as well as prescribed passage between them. Single-file processions were involved, and a sense of place, as well as the tradition of going to the cemetery precisely as one's parents and grandparents did.

The Silencio Phase and Continuity in Ritually Directed Movement

The tradition of separating village from cemetery, as well as the cultural prescription of following the same path between them, continued during the subsequent Silencio phase (AD 600–1300). The continued forming and using of entrenched paths is one of several indicators of continuity between two phases. Overall population declined, however, and villages were smaller (Sheets and McKee 1994). The principal change in funerary practice from Arenal to Silencio phases involves the shift from rounded river rocks to flat slabs of rock (called *laja*) used to make stone box tombs.

A good example is provided by the Silencio cemetery (G-150) perched atop the divide between Atlantic and Pacific drainages (Figure 8.4). Evidence in the cemetery of feasting and other ritual activities associated with the deceased and their spirits included great numbers of thermally fractured stones using in cooking, many cooking vessels, dispersed maize pollen possibly indicating corn grown in the cemetery, carbonized foodstuffs, and pine pollen (Sheets 1994). The cemetery was connected to a village (or villages) and to exploited resources by paths that headed downslope into both drainages, to the east and west.

The path headed westward from the Silencio cemetery has been traced for 3.7 km (straight-line distance) to near Tilaran where it disappears in relatively flat-lying terrain that has had major agricultural disturbance (particularly sugar cane) and a lot of recent construction. However, the path heads straight toward the Cerro Tovar laja source, the principal source of stone slabs and headstones for the Silencio cemetery. The straight-line distance from the Tovar source to the cemetery is 7.3 km. Other confirmation that the path was intended to access the laja source is provided by the two laja repositories that lie along the path (G-151 and -152) on the west side of the cemetery.

Because the amount of trail use is proportional to the amount of erosion (holding slope constant), one can estimate relative amounts of foot traffic on portions of these Silencio phase paths. The volume of erosion of the path headed westward from the cemetery is about as great as the erosion of the path headed eastward. One function of the westward path was transporting stone for construction of tombs from the Tovar source southwest of Tilaran. However, the amount of erosion (i.e., foot traffic) on this path is considerably greater than that expected if it were used only for occasional access to the laja quarry. Therefore, I believe it is probable that a village connected to the Silencio cemetery lies to the west of the Tovar source.

Traffic on the eastward path can be divided into two segments: the section connecting the cemetery to the spring, and the continuation of it farther east (Figure 8.4). Well over twice the erosion, hence foot traffic, traversed the paths between cemetery and spring, than traversed the continuation eastward. People involved in funerary rituals frequently descended to the spring and returned, more often than they walked the distance from village to cemetery. It is virtually certain that a village, or villages, participating in cemetery rituals lies at the terminus of this eastward path. We have yet to confirm the path all the way to that terminus, despite years of trying.

The Tilaran Phase

The Tilaran phase is the final precolumbian phase in the Arenal area, dating from AD 1300 to 1500. The population decline of the earlier phase continued and even accelerated, leaving scattered hamlets across the countryside and no evidence of cemeteries separated from villages. The settlement pattern is like that of the Tronadora phase, the earliest sedentary phase, but probably with even lower regional population.

We could find no evidence of Tilaran phase footpaths, despite the fact that their higher stratigraphic position would have meant fewer sources of disturbance than the older footpaths. It is thus probable that ritually prescribed travel had been eliminated from the culture. There is other evidence for significant cultural discontinuity from the preceding tradition, as the local cultural traditions were replaced by a Central Highlands-Atlantic Watershed culture (Sheets 1994). An actual immigration and population replacement may have taken place.

AND THEN, THE MENTALITY OF MONUMENTALITY

By AD 1000 a series of larger sites emerged to the east of the Arenal area, in the Atlantic drainage of Costa Rica. I would characterize them as ranked societies or chiefdoms, with their central places distinguished by large, bilaterally symmetrical architecture that exhibits monumentality. The sites often have long roadways paved with cobbles called *calzadas* that lead into formal plazas ringed with barrier structures, large mounds, and occasionally aqueducts, pools, and bridges (Snarskis 1981:63). As Snarskis states, Guayabo de Turrialba is the largest and best known of these chiefly centers, which also include Las Mercedes, Anita Grande (a.k.a. Parasal), Fortuna, Cutris, Costa Rica Farm, and La Cabaña.

In all cases the entryway into the special place is constructed to be impressive. One approaches the Guayabo de Turrialba site via a 20-m-wide and straight calzada that passes between two imposing stone structures or "guard towers" (Figure 8.5) (Fonseca 1981:106). However, on either side of the "guard towers" I could find no natural or constructed feature that might hinder someone circumventing this entrance. The view down the calzada between the guard towers toward the center of the site is precisely oriented on the distant Turrialba volcano. I suspect the intended effect was to create the impression of monumentality and to display chiefly power to those walking the calzada, making a statement of authority and connectivity or rulership.

According to Mauricio Murillo (2002), a long stone-paved calzada has been traced and confirmed heading north-northeast out of Guayabo for over 4 km, linking it with other sites on the way and a site complex at its northern end (Figure 8.6). This feature cuts across tremendous topographic variability in order to maintain an almost straight line.

Fortuna and Cutris are the centers of chiefdoms located in a topographic

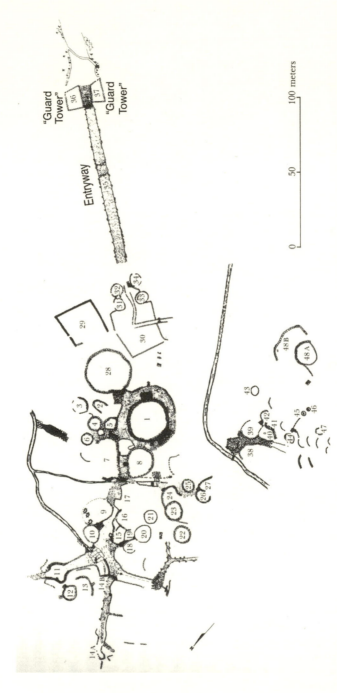

8.5 Map of the chiefdom site Guayabo de Turrialba (after Fonseca 1981:105). The entryway on the right leads up a large stone-paved stairway, between two "guard towers" of stone, and along a long stone-paved walkway to the center of the site. The entryway aligns directly to Turrialba volcano to the west, past the principal Mound 1.

setting quite different from Guayabo, as they are beyond the steep rocky terrain of the volcanic slopes. Unlike Guayabo, they lacked easy access to large construction stone, as they are in a gently sloping alluvial environment of finer sediments. Instead, their impressive entryways are earthen constructions. Large labor gangs created these entryways by digging a few meters down into the fine river alluvium and piling the sediment up on both sides, creating a long sunken road with long straight berms on both sides. Recent research on Cutris shows that the site is earlier than expected (Vazquez, Guerrero, and Sanchez 2003). Other chiefdoms in Costa Rica have been dated to Period VI, between AD 1000 and 1500. Cutris reached its apex during Period V, between AD 500 and 1000. The 50-hectare site center is like the later chiefdoms, with some 86 identified features, largely platforms and

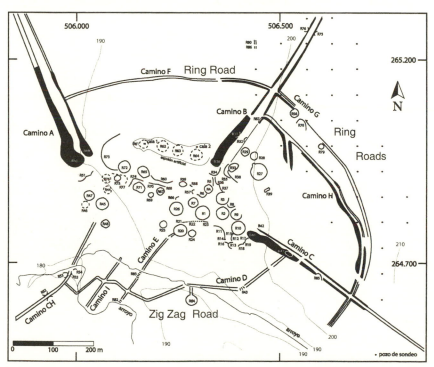

8.6 Map of the Cutris chiefdom site (after Murrillo 2002), with the beginnings of the four roads radiating outward (denoted as Camino A, B, C, and CH). Roads A, B, and C are interconnected with ring roads. The mounds in the site center were used for public performances, residences, and burials. The zigzag road at the bottom connects roads C and CH.

mounds of which some have river stone in facings and stairs. Illicit excavators have found both gold ornaments and carved jade.

The monumental sunken roadways radiating from Cutris are impressive. Vazquez, Guerrero, and Sanchez (2003) have found that each terminates in a smaller village, from 6.7 to 9.4 km from Cutris. The roadways are of earthen construction, and are visible in aerial photography (Figure 8.7). The roadways average 6 m in width, and they broaden dramatically in the final kilometer approaching the site center. They broaden to 35 to 40 m in width, and are deeper than before, perhaps some 5 m below the surrounding ground surface.

The emotional impact of walking along such a sunken roadway is notable, and even today some are sufficiently deep to hide the surrounding countryside. One's attention is thus focused on the distant objective ahead. Anticipation builds as one walks in the progressively deeper and wider entryway, and then as one enters, the full site center is suddenly in view. If the modern visitor can have such an emotional reaction and be so removed from the ancient inhabitants by centuries, culture, language, and belief, one can only imagine the effect on the traveler who is fully informed and experiences the entrance process from within the relevant cultural context.

According to Juan Vicente Guerrero (personal communication 2003) small stone platforms were built along either side of the entryway close to the site center, atop the berms, every few hundred meters. Is it possible that the stone platforms beside the naturally eroded path atop the hill near Rio Piedra might have been an egalitarian forerunner to these stone platforms flanking the broad, deep entryway?

Two sets of ring roads connect three of the radial entryways at Cutris (Figures 8.6 and 8.7), and are 2–3 m wide (Vazquez, Guerrero, and Sanchez 2003) and about that deep. These secondary roads could have provided access to other major roads without entering the site center. Perhaps not all processional participants were allowed entry to the site center. Why the southern secondary road follows a zigzag route is totally unknown.

Broad entrenched entryways radiating some 4 km from a site make no sense as defensive features. I think the most likely functional explanation is in the ritual domain, as monumental processionways and materialized power (De Marrais, Castillo, and Earle 1996). These roadways can readily be interpreted as chiefly displays, demonstrating their control of energy through human labor to construct and maintain these huge systems that

8.7 Aerial photograph of the Cutris chiefdom center at "C", and roads radiating outward at "A" and "B". Horizontal distance of aerial photograph is 2.5 km.

shape perception of space to advance political and social agendas. Chiefs could display their control of human activity through processions using the entryways, demonstrating their hierarchical power before their subjects and before visitors from other centers.

The relationship between these chiefly centers and the Arenal area is unclear. A population movement from Arenal eastward to these sites is possible, but there is no evidence of it. It is also possible that rulers in the more complex societies adopted the idea from the Arenal area. Perhaps more likely is a widespread religious conversion of people in all these areas, resulting in establishing distant cemeteries and paths that entrenched through time. No earlier simple eroded paths have yet been found east of the Arenal area that would support this interpretation. A ruler initiating control of labor to construct, maintain, and use monumental entryways would be wise to exploit a valued cultural norm that had existed for centuries before, rather than inventing something entirely new.

COMPARISON WITH OTHER PATHS OR ROAD NETWORKS

The pattern seen in Costa Rica of central places connected by calzadas with "ring roads" is also known in other areas of the tropical lowlands in South America. They also have some similarities with constructed roadways in ancient North America. These patterns reflect common expressions of monumentality and processions/pilgrimages.

Heckenberger et al. (2003) report on complex regional settlement patterns of native Amazonians in the Xingu area of Brazil from ca. AD 1200 to 1600. They found 19 major ancient settlements an average of 4 km apart, and they were linked with broad straight roads detectable in Landsat TM imagery. Some of the excavated ditches in and around the settlements were up to 2.5 km long and 5 m deep. The major roads were 10 to 50 m wide, with berms on each side, and often ran into plazas.

The pattern of a central place with radiating principal entrenched roads, with smaller concentric rings of ditches, is strikingly similar to Cutris. The rings could have functioned as roads linking the radiating primary roads, or some of them could have been part of ditch-and-palisade fortifications. The radiating roads must have served practical functions for communication and trade, but their width as they approach the site centers indicates more of a ritual/processional function. To some degree this widening could have practical aspects, as Ur (Chapter 9, this volume) found. However, I believe the degree of widening at Xingu and the Costa Rican chiefdoms is much greater than the rather small populations would warrant for purely practical purposes. Heckenberger and colleagues (2003) estimate residential populations in the larger centers as between 2500 and 5000 people, or regionally at 6 to 12.5 people per square kilometer.

Similar patterns can be seen in lowland Venezuelan sites associated with chiefdoms, which developed earlier than most of those in Costa Rica and the Amazon (Spencer 1994:38). Calzadas came into use between AD 500 and 1000, linking several of these centers. The settlement pattern, density, radiating calzadas and ring roads, and central places are quite similar to Atlantic lowland Costa Rica. Large and small mounds and an oval "ring road" similar to Cutris, for instance, characterize the Gavan site. Three calzadas radiate toward other sites as well (Spencer 1994).

In Ohio the "Great Hopewell road" (Lepper 1995) has been traced for some 90 km as a straight entrenched roadway from the Newark earthworks south-southwest to the High Banks works in Chillicothe. The width of the roadway is impressive at about 60 m, a bit wider than the Cutris entryways. The earthworks at both ends are huge enclosures that are somewhat reminiscent of the plazas in the large Costa Rican sites. Although they are in a dramatically different arid landscape, the Chaco roadways in the Southwest United States (Lekson 1999; Sever and Wagner 1991) also share characteristics with the roadways at Cutris and other chiefdoms.

All of these constructed cases share roadways that become more formal and wider as they get closer to "downtown." Similar characteristics include berms and a general tendency toward straightness despite topographic obstacles. They also share roadway entrances that are much wider than can be explained by economic needs. Although never historically connected, the commonalities of these types of roads imply similar patterns of materialization (De Marrais, Castillo, and Earle 1996) as sustained use embedded ideology into the landscape. The quote that begins this chapter on labor control and monumentality is pertinent here. Snead (2002; Chapter 3, this volume) develops the concept of a "gateway trail" among the ancestral Puebloans, which shares important features with many of these built entryways, but without the monumentality.

SUMMARY AND CONCLUSIONS

As our research has documented, precolumbian populations of the Arenal area of Costa Rica are notable for social stability and continuity across more than 10,000 years. Residents avoided the population explosions of Mesoamerica and the Andes, and they avoided state level societies with their concomitant chronic warfare, environmental degradation, reliance on intensive cultivation of a carbohydrate staple crop, nutritional deficiencies, and other hallmarks of civilization.

Human movement across the landscape throughout 80% of the precolumbian occupation of the Arenal area was sufficiently randomized to leave no trace that we can detect by remote sensing, pedestrian survey, or excavation. That movement is here interpreted as task-specific and thus was not routinized in place for long periods of time. However, this pattern changed at about 500 BC, and for almost two millennia people separated their cemeteries from their villages. They traveled in single file between them on straight routes. Regular processional use of the path must have invested it with increasing meaning and sanctity.

Use of the same precise path resulted in linear compaction. Where the path traversed a slope, an unintended consequence was erosion. Although the actual path surface was never wider than a half meter, the downward-eroding path eroded its sides as well. Use sustained over a few centuries resulted in paths entrenched a few meters below the surrounding terrain. A person traveling an entrenched path loses sight of surrounding terrain, and vision is inevitably focused on the objective at the end of the path.

I suspect the deep meaning of the path became associated with travel through such a deep entrenchment, which opens up when one enters the special place at the terminus. That inadvertent consequence permanently engraved procession routes into the landscape, and into social memory. Such entrenched passageways became the "right" way to enter sites of sacred character.

I propose that in later centuries, when chiefdoms developed to the east of the Arenal area, and chiefs needed to exercise their authority by mobilizing labor to make large nonutilitarian features, they adopted the symbolism of entrenched entryways for their monumental architecture. Thus they built features such as the ca. 8-km-long entrenched earthen roads at Cutris, and later the long paved calzadas with monumental entryways into sites such as at Guayabo de Turrialba. Thus, the egalitarian societies developed the principles that were "writ large" when the mentality of monumentality developed among more complex societies. When leaders of nearby chiefdoms needed a "hook" to get commoners to engage in large work gangs to construct monumental features, they wisely chose sunken pathways that had a high cultural value recognized by all.

Acknowledgments

Without the assistance of Tom Sever (NASA) the Arenal project would have been traditional, short-lived, and focused on chronology, settlement patterns, and the effects of explosive volcanic eruptions. Tom opened the door of remote sensing, which had the unanticipated consequence of the footpath discoveries fundamentally enriching our research. All hyperboles are warranted.

I thank Juan Vicente Guerrero for taking the Arenal project members to the big chiefdom sites of Fortuna, Cutris, and Parasal during the 2003 field season. It was during that trip that the little "light bulb" finally ignited and I perceived a possible relationship between the inadvertent erosional paths in the Arenal area and the monumental entryways in the big sites. I greatly appreciate the invitation by James Snead, Clark Erickson, and Andrew Darling to join their inaugural Penn Museum International Research Conference Seminar, and the resultant volume, on this under-researched topic. I am deeply indebted to the comments on an earlier version of this chapter by my esteemed colleagues at the seminar, as they have helped my thinking on the topic, and improved this final written version. Jason Ur was particularly helpful.

I greatly appreciate the support for this field research provided by the National Science Foundation, National Geographic, and the University of Colorado. The dedication of many field crews has been impressive, second only to their determination to get to the beach on weekends. I am deeply appreciative of my CU archaeological colleagues' comments on an earlier draft of this chapter, especially Art Joyce and Cathy Cameron. James Snead gave an earlier draft a careful reading, and his suggestions have greatly improved many a convoluted expression. An anonymous reviewer was exceptionally helpful in pointing out redundancies and unclear sections. All errors of omission or commission are mine.

9

Emergent Landscapes of Movement in Early Bronze Age Northern Mesopotamia

JASON UR

O ne of the positive effects of the landscape approach to the human past has been the dismantling of the notion, often implicitly held, that settlements were islands in the midst of a sea of uninhabited or unused space. This notion has been subconsciously reinforced by settlement pattern maps wherein sites are depicted as black dots on a vacant white surface. The advent of sedentism did not bring to an end movement through the broader landscape beyond the settlement, but rather concentrated it in ways that have made it easier for archaeologists to detect. At the most mundane level, agriculturalists and pastoralists had to move between settlements, fields, and pasture. In addition to these subsistence-related activities, complex societies required movement for exchange in non-local materials used for marking and maintaining status differences.

Centralized polities cannot remain integrated without continuous interactions between political centers and their hinterlands. A holistic landscape approach not only recognizes the importance of these movements but also develops methods to document their traces and integrate them into economic and sociopolitical models.

As the material manifestations of movement through the landscape, the surviving traces of roads and paths have much to tell us about past societies. These features manifest both repetitive social, political, and especially economic activities but also can serve as models of social order (Earle 1991:10).

With regard to this distinction, any study of movement must engage the critical issues of intentionality and constraint.

All human movement is of course intentional; at no time was directionless wandering a systematic part of past social action. Movement may have been at all times purposive, but the associated landscape features may not have been deliberately created. Here we must make the important distinction between constructed and non-constructed features. The former are planned or even "overengineered" built features. The construction of a road does not automatically mean it was heavily traveled; they occasionally tell us more about where movement was intended to go rather than where it went. Furthermore, these intentions may be linked to a small subset of society (i.e., the planners and labor mobilizers) who may have also limited access to roads.

On the other hand, non-constructed paths owe their existence to continued use. Rather than being imposed by decision-makers, they emerge from the cumulative actions of many individuals. These movements are certainly purposive, but the formation of the path is never the explicit intention. Unlike constructed features, which may or may not have borne much traffic, the very existence of non-constructed paths is a testament to their use. Their width and depth are indicators of their span of use and the intensity of movement along them. This binary opposition between imposed constructed and emergent non-constructed features is not so simple, however; a broad range of variation exists in both, and non-constructed paths can be formalized into built roads (Hyslop 1991; Trombold 1991a). From an evolutionary perspective, non-constructed features may be closely associated with less complex societies. Large-scale formal features are a product of political action under chiefdoms and states, although most mundane economic movement still takes place on paths (Earle 1991).[1]

The second issue is of constraint: what keeps the traveler on the route? Constraint can be external or internal. Constructed roads can have parapets or curbs that act to restrict traffic to the surface between them, or they may move through areas of walled fields (see examples in Hyslop 1984). Elsewhere it may be the presence of dense forest or marshlands. These constraints are external to the traveler, who is prevented from straying or strongly encouraged to stay on the path by the inefficiencies of traveling off of it. It is uncommon, however, to be so physically constrained. Far more common are internal cultural constraints in the form of property rights, legal restrictions against trespassing, or socio-religious values about the proper way to travel. The degrees to which these elements of social practice are part of an individual's cognitive structures determine whether he or she adheres to the path. For example, the depressed footpaths of the Arenal region in Costa Rica formed presumably because of the widely held belief that travel to and from cemeteries should be on elevated paths along ridges (Sheets, Chapter 8, this volume). Other, less identifiable cognitive constraints are operative in the southwestern United States today as well as in the past (Snead 2002; Ferguson, Berlin, and Kuwanwisiwma, Chapter 2, this volume).

This case study will focus on movement as manifested in the earliest phase of widespread urbanism in the Upper Khabur basin of northern Mesopotamia during the Early Bronze Age (EBA) (Figure 9.1). These settlements emerged simultaneously with an elaborate network of almost 2000 km of roadways. I will describe this archaeological landscape and then move to what it can tell us about political economy. First, however, I present an overview of EBA society and review the sociopolitical frameworks that have been employed. EBA society was the dynamic product of both bottom-up and top-down structures. My own understanding of the composition of society places a much greater emphasis on the bottom-up, or emergent, structures than do the most widely cited models. In the case of the agricultural and pastoral landscape, these structures included the widespread motivation to intensify production held by most or all households, and the imposed system of land tenure within which they were constrained in their activities. The deeply inscribed network of roadways was the unintended result of the recursive interaction of these forces.

THE SOCIOPOLITICAL CONTEXT OF
EARLY BRONZE AGE LANDSCAPES OF MOVEMENT

Urban settlement in northern Mesopotamia appeared abruptly in the mid-3rd millennium BC.[2] At the top of the settlement hierarchy were a series of mudbrick settlements of 65–120 ha. Most were composed of a high mound of 10–15 ha where non-urban settlement had existed previously, in some cases for millennia. These high mounds were surrounded by extensive lower settlements, which resulted from the abrupt demographic growth around 2600–2500 BC. By the end of the 20th century AD, excavation had

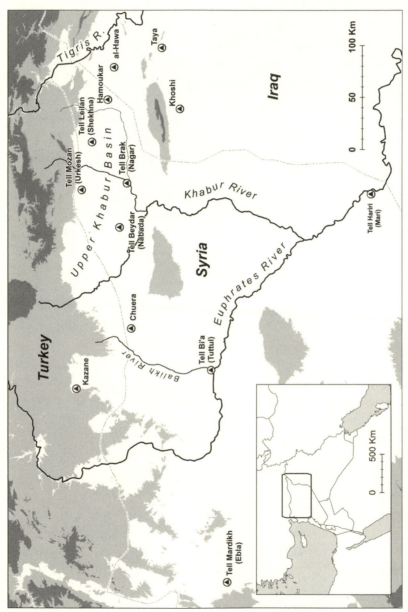

9.1 Urban settlements of the Early Bronze Age (mid- to late 3rd millennium BC) in northern Mesopotamia.

taken place at most of these sites, allowing us to make some generalizations about society at the time (e.g., Akkermans and Schwartz 2003; Stein 2004). Research has concentrated on the elite high mounds, revealing monumental temple and palace constructions. Specialized craft products included metalwork in bronze, gold, and silver, and mass-produced ceramics. Artistic styles and administrative technologies (clay sealing and cuneiform writing) were regionally distinct but clearly emulated those of the elites in the cities of southern Mesopotamia. In the infrequent times when archaeologists have investigated the non-elite lower settlements for this period, they have revealed dense but variable residential housing, packed tightly along narrow debris-strewn alleys (Pfälzner 2001). Although non-urban settlements have rarely been excavated, surveys have shown them to be generally in the range of 1–5 ha, with a few intermediate towns in the 10–25 ha range. The nature of settlement on these smaller sites is poorly understood, but is assumed to have been primarily agricultural with some pastoral component.

Publications on EBA northern Mesopotamia have often focused on issues of chronology and local developmental sequences, but a few regional syntheses have appeared, most prominently emanating from research at Tell Leilan and its region (Weiss 1997, 2000; Weiss and Courty 1993; Weiss et al. 1993). The approach adopted is ecosystemic, based around a highly centralized and hierarchical state that had incredible power over all aspects of society. According to this model, elites maintained their status by controlling the staple economy, in particular through the centralized storage and redistribution of cereals in standardized ration vessels. Cereal and animal production was intensified to sustain this political economy. Aspects of craft production, including elements as mundane as ceramic production, were also under the direct control of the state. The state could and did occasionally redistribute the rural population for purposes of economic efficiency and political control. In classic ecosystemic fashion, this model contends that EBA society remained in a stable equilibrium until forced to change by external factors (in this case, collapse at the hands of abrupt climate change). Other studies often implicitly adopt aspects of this centralized model.

Ecosystemic approaches have been criticized for underemphasizing conflict and competition within society (e.g., Brumfiel 1992; Brumfiel and Fox 1994; Stein 1998; Yoffee 2005). Michael Dietler has stated succinctly how archaeologists often assume that:

once symbols of political power and status have been 'materialized' and authority has become institutionalized, that somehow stability and permanence have been achieved and the work of relational micro-politics is made redundant and unnecessary. This is, of course, the dream and the ideological projection of every state apparatus: a kind of institutional fetishism that displaces contingent relations between people into stable relationships between people and permanently reified 'objects.' But nothing could be farther from the truth. The nasty little secret of history is that states and empires are very fragile, volatile, and transitory—far more so than their buildings and monuments. They are a fluid *process* rather than a durable thing, and they depend on constant hard work in the micro-political struggles of negotiation and legitimation to survive and operate. (2003:271–72; emphasis in original)

Far from being locked into a durable equilibrium state, complex society is to a large extent emergent from these processes of social and political renegotiation (van der Leeuw and McGlade 1997).

The sociopolitical model employed here attempts to address these critiques of hierarchical ecosystemic models. Instead of assuming a rational bureaucratic elite, it incorporates an emic social model that frames social and political relationships within the metaphor of the household at multiple levels of society. "House societies" have been well studied in recent decades (Carsten and Hugh-Jones 1995; Joyce and Gillespie 2000), but with some exceptions (e.g., Gillespie 2000) these have mostly been small-scale societies. Analyses of Sumerian, Akkadian, and Egyptian kinship terminology used in political contexts now demonstrate that the household has been a pervasive organizing metaphor for large territorial states in the Near East and Egypt since at least the 3rd millennium BC (Gelb 1979; Schloen 2001; Lehner 2000a, 2000b). The Patrimonial Household Model (PHM) of Near Eastern society (Schloen 2001) describes a society of nested households of various scales, ranging from the individual domestic unit to the extended lineage to temple households and up to the entire kingdom.

The PHM recognizes the limitations of political power and economic control in these early complex societies and reintroduces agency, history, and contingency. At first glance this arrangement of nested households might seem rigidly hierarchical. In fact, being based on continuously renegotiated personal relationships rather than an inflexible bureaucratic structure, the vertical and horizontal connections between various households were highly dynamic, and are better characterized as heterarchical (Crumley 1987, 1995). To the extent that these relationships in the Near Eastern Bronze Age had a material basis, they revolved around commensalism (Dietler and Hayden 2001; Pollock 2003) rather than staple redistribution. Thus, if a staple-based political economy (e.g., D'Altroy and Earle 1985) could be said to have existed, it involved small-scale exchanges of prepared food and drink for immediate communal consumption, rather than centralized storage and redistribution of bulk unprocessed cereals. To a considerable extent, however, these interpersonal relationships were probably based on exchange in high value items or non-material factors such as personal charisma and learned political skills (Schloen 2001). They are therefore based to a far greater extent on consensus-building between rulers and local elites and lineage heads than has been appreciated.

The necessity of continually reproducing the social hierarchy shifts emphasis from reified social units to the individual actors involved, a focus on agency that is increasingly common in archaeology (Brumfiel 1992; Dobres and Robb 2000; Dornan 2002). While the activities of specific individuals may be difficult or impossible to recover from the archaeological record, the dynamic structure of the PHM offers a set of goals and motivations that would have been widely shared across society, in particular the expansion of one's household (in both the literal and metaphorical senses) and the acquisition or intensified production of any material resources which would aid such an expansion. In this sense, the PHM employs the "generic" individual (Bell 1992), perhaps at the expense of the possibility of resistance and individual creativity (Dornan 2002:315). We can envision these widely held motivations as the local rules which ultimately produce the global order of early urban society. In this sense, the PHM echoes new directions in research on complexity, which developed in the physical and natural sciences and is now increasingly being applied in the social sciences (Adams 2001; Lansing 2003; Kohler and Gumerman 2000; Wilkinson et al. 2007a). The totality of these social actions is the society itself. Since the heads of households of various scales are continuously renegotiating its structure, society is constantly in a state of unpredictable endogenous change. This "bottom-up" view of society is proving to be a powerful approach in archaeology (Erickson 1993, 2006b).

I frame my study of settlement and movement in northern Mesopotamia during the Early Bronze Age within the PHM and a landscape approach. Contrary to the expectations of the long-dominant centralized and
hierarchical ecosystemic approach, I see the elaborate landscapes of movement as emergent from the activities of individuals within longstanding
structures of land tenure.

THE ARCHAEOLOGICAL LANDSCAPE

The cultural landscape of the Early Bronze Age in northern Mesopotamia is
spectacularly preserved. This situation is surprising for two reasons: its great
age means that cultural and natural taphonomic processes have had more
opportunities to remove archaeological traces, and its agricultural potential
inevitably attracts destructive resettlement (Wilkinson 2003; Williamson
1998). The primary reason for this preservation is that land use in northern Mesopotamia has cycled between sedentary agriculture and pastoral
nomadism. For example, northern Syria has been occupied by low-density
sheep and goat nomads for the last millennium (Lewis 1987). The archaeological consequence of this cycling is a preserved landscape of almost 2,000
km of roadways, most dated to the Early Bronze Age (Figure 9.2).

In this chapter, I focus on the Upper Khabur basin of northeastern Syria
and adjacent areas of northern Iraq. The basin consists of deep soils of alluvial origin, although today all drainages are downcut into the plain, which is
no longer aggrading (Courty 1994). The mainstay of the agriculture today
and in the past is rainfed winter cereal cultivation; however, pockets of irri-
gated summer crops, mostly cotton for the international market, have been
steadily growing since the 1950s.

The Physical Traces of Past Movement: Roadways

The surviving roadways, variously called hollow ways, tracks (Ur 2003),
or linear hollows (Wilkinson 1993), are broad and shallow linear depressions across the landscape (Figure 9.3). The features are similar to the paths
of the Arenal region in Costa Rica (Sheets and Sever 1991; McKee, Sever,
and Sheets 1994), but denser and of a larger scale. The northern Mesopotamian features were formed by alternating processes of compaction in the
wet season and aeolian erosion in the dry season (Tsoar and Yekutieli 1992).
The majority are between 60–100 m wide, up to 2 m deep, and range in pre-

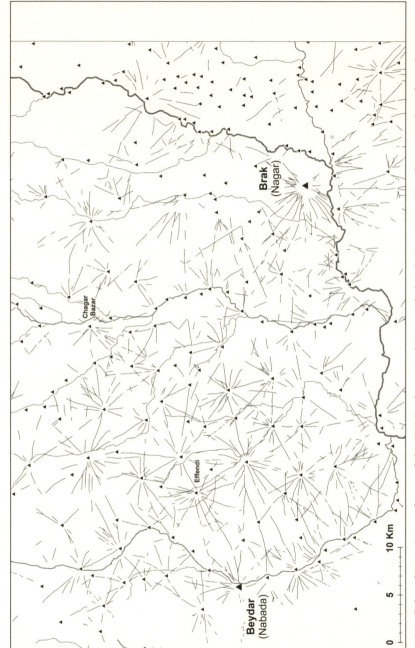

9.2 Radial and intersite roadways of the EBA in the central Upper Khabur basin. Large triangles are major urban sites; smaller triangles are other mounds.

served length from several hundred meters to more than 5 km (Figure 9.4). However, precise measurements are difficult, since what survives on the surface are not the roadways themselves but rather the surface signatures of features heavily transformed by natural and cultural processes. In some cases the depressed track has been filled with locally eroded sediments, and in other cases, has been deepened by channeled surface runoff. In the former situation, the lack of topographic expression is offset by a signature of denser vegetation growth (i.e., crop marks; Wilson 1982). In the latter, the depressed topography collects moisture, which translates into darker soil in the fall and, again, more abundant crops in the spring.

Ground recognition of roadways is often difficult, so historically these features have been studied from above. Pre-modern roads were photographed opportunistically by the pioneer of aerial archaeology Antoine Poidebard (1934), although he was primarily interested in Roman military installations.

9.3 Roadways viewed from the ground. Top: oblique view of a 1.2-m-deep roadway near Hamoukar (October 2000). Bottom: oblique view of a roadway near Chagar Bazar in the early Spring (April 1999; note the denser vegetation in the depression).

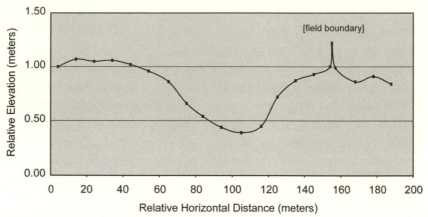

9.4 Vertically exaggerated profile across a roadway (Figure 9.3, top) near Hamoukar. Spike at right represents a low earthen field boundary.

In the 1950s, the government of Syria conducted an aerial survey in the process of developing the northern plains for agriculture. A Dutch soil scientist involved in this survey, Willem Van Liere, teamed up with the archaeologist Jean Lauffray to systematically map the roadways which were so apparent on the imagery (Van Liere and Lauffray 1954–55; Van Liere 1963). Recently, I have used declassified intelligence satellite photographs from the U.S. CORONA program to map roadways across northeastern Syria (Figure 9.5) (see Fowler 2004; Ur 2002a, 2003; Ur and Colantoni in press).

Roads and tracks are notoriously difficult to date; indeed, the great landscape historian and expert on Roman roads Christopher Taylor was one of the most pessimistic about the chances of success in this endeavor (1979:xii). Van Liere's somewhat speculative dating of the linear features was confirmed through intensive systematic surface survey by Tony Wilkinson in adjacent areas of northern Iraq (1993; Wilkinson and Tucker 1995). Most typical broad linear features have particularly strong associations with sites of the Early Bronze Age (ca. 2600–2000 BC). This association was initially recognized by Van Liere and Lauffray and later confirmed by intensive survey in northern Iraq (Wilkinson 1993; Wilkinson and Tucker 1995) and in the Upper Khabur basin (Wilkinson 2000; Ur 2002a, 2003). A small subset of features can be dated by association with the late Antique to early Islamic period (ca. AD 500–900); these features are distinguished by their narrower width (around 50 m) and will not be discussed further here.

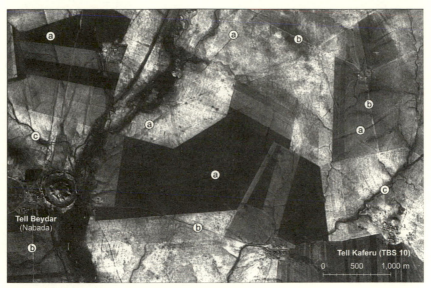

9.5 CORONA satellite photograph of modern and pre-modern roads and tracks east of Tell Beydar, CORONA 1102-1025DF006 (Dec. 11, 1967). (a) Depressed linear roadway features (premodern); (b) modern dirt or gravel tracks; (c) natural meandering drainage features (wadis).

The survival of EBA roadways is a patterned product of closely related cultural and natural factors. Within the Upper Khabur basin, they are disproportionately preserved in the central and western areas. This uneven distribution is the result of the basin's climate and settlement history. Rainfall is high in the northern and eastern parts, where the foothills of the Taurus Mountains to the north trap moisture. The reliable rainfall results in local movement of sediments that obscure tracks. Another consequence of higher rainfall is reliable agriculture, so settlement has been nearly continuous, leading to greater attrition of landscape features. In the southern basin, lower rainfall encourages pastoralism, rather than agriculture, as the dominant economic mode. Elsewhere, taphonomic processes have had localized effects. For example, few roadways survive in the narrow floodplains of the major north-south seasonal drainages (wadis) because of long-term sediment aggradation. Subsequent pre-modern land use has taken a toll as well, especially around the Roman-Byzantine city of Nisibin (modern Qamishli), where an elaborate irrigation system probably erased evidence of roadways.

Spatial Patterning in EBA Roadways

Because sites in the Upper Khabur basin were constructed of mudbrick, their eroded remains offer few surface clues about the interface between settlements and roadways. Around smaller sites, roadways appear to have originated around 100–200 m from the base of the site and radiate in a linear fashion. Around larger settlements, points of origin are clearer. At Tell Beydar, roadways articulate with gaps in its eroded outer wall and gullies in the central mound; these locations are probably the gates into the settlement (Lebeau 1997; Wilkinson 2000). More complex patterns of access can be discerned around the largest urban centers such as Hamoukar (Ur 2002b:25–26) and Tell Brak where roadways bifurcated as they approached the site; each bifurcation leads to a discrete point of access into the settlement.

Beyond the settlement, the roadways display different patterns at different scales of observation. At the regional scale, intersite roadways connect sites of the EBA throughout the basin. They tend to be straight but not rigidly so, and often they go around topographic impediments. At the local scale, roadways are composed of interconnected radial networks centering on individual sites. Unlike the intersite routes, whose destinations were other settlements, these local roadways disappear 3–5 km from their origin before reaching any identifiable destination. It would be misleading, however, to label these local features as "roads to nowhere." Wilkinson (1993) argues that the radial roadways led farmers and draft animals to and from the fields, and shepherds and their flocks to the pasture beyond.

ROADWAYS AND THE ECONOMIC LANDSCAPE

To date, archaeologists have used these scalar roadway patterns exclusively to reconstruct the economic landscape, particularly with regard to the production of staples (cereals and animals) in the context of EBA urbanism. By the 1950s, Van Liere and Lauffray (1954–55:136) interpreted the radial patterning as an indicator of a society of autonomous and self-sufficient agricultural towns and villages. In fact, the radial patterning is similar to what would be predicted by geographic studies of traditional agriculture in Europe (e.g., Chisholm 1962) and modern agricultural towns in the Near East (Wilkinson 2003: fig. 6.13).

Such roadways represent efficient movement of labor and livestock to agricultural fields and pasture, and of agricultural and pastoral products back into the settlement. Traffic would have included not only human foot traffic, but also the sheep, goats, and donkeys documented by zooarchaeology and recorded in administrative tablets. More difficult to assess is the significance of wheeled traffic. Although no physical remains of carts or chariots survive, they are a common motif carved into cylinder seals in the basin (Figure 9.6) (Jans and Bretschneider 1998; Matthews 1997), and clay models of wheels and carts frequently occur in the EBA (Moorey 2001; Oates 2001). The scenes on cylinder seals are military or ritual in nature, but the frequency of cartwrights (*nagar* ^{giš}*gigir*) in the administrative tablets from the site of Tell Beydar (Sallaberger 1996:95) implies that wheeled vehicles were used regularly for more mundane purposes.

9.6 Wheeled vehicles depicted on EBA cylinder seal impressions from Tell Brak, based on drawings by Helen McDonald (Steele et al. 2003: fig 6.72 nos. HP 27, 29).

These patterned economic movements were probably typical of all phases of agricultural settlement in northern Mesopotamia, yet radial roadways are disproportionately associated with sites of the EBA, and to a much lesser extent with sites of the late 1st millennium AD (Ur 2003). The reason why the roadways of the EBA proved to be more deeply incised into the landscape, and therefore more durable, is the key to understanding the uniquely intensified nature of the EBA staple economy.

EBA Roadways and Agricultural Intensification

In placing the roadways of the EBA in their economic context, it is important to recognize that these features were not created to increase the efficiency of transportation. They formed as human, animal, and wheeled traffic alternately compressed the fine-textured soils in the wet season and then disturbed them in the dry season, which allowed for aeolian erosion (Hindle 1993:11; Sheets and Sever 1991:58–63; Tsoar and Yekutieli 1992; Wilkinson 1993:556–59). At certain times of the year, roadways did provide a more compact surface for pedestrian, animal, and wheeled movement, but during the rainy season, their depressed linear morphology collected runoff. In the winter in the Upper Khabur basin today, roadways hold standing water and are avoided; instead, movement shifts to parallel routes across fallow fields.

If the roadways were muddy and inefficient for movement in the winter, why were they continuously used? In the case of northern Mesopotamia, movement was constrained onto roadways by the presence of cultivated fields bounding the tracks, or more accurately, by patterns of land tenure and social norms regarding trespass (Figure 9.7). Such constraints explain the patterning of the radial roadways. Within the cultivated zone, farmers, shepherds, and their flocks adhered to the roadways to avoid trampling crops. In the basin today, harvested fields are still valuable for the stubble they contain, the grazing rights to which are sold to pastoralists. If post-harvest fields were similarly valuable in the past, flocks would have been restricted year round, rather than only during the growing season, and roadway-forming disturbance would have been even more focused on the linear spaces between them.

At a certain distance, generally 3–5 km from the settlement, roadways reached the limits of the zone of cultivation and the start of the zone of pastoral land use. At this point, movement was no longer restricted by the presence of fields and thus could disperse. Dispersed movement meant dispersed compaction and disturbance, and therefore the depressed roadways did not form (Wilkinson 1994:492–93.)

The amount of pasture land beyond the cultivation fluctuates throughout the basin. In areas of low-density settlement, substantial pastoral land existed, whereas in other areas, such as the central basin between Beydar and Brak, the cultivated zones nearly abutted each other. In the latter case, more pasture probably existed but decreased as cultivation was expanded. This sequence would have had significant ramifications on the pastoral economy.

We can use radial roadway patterning to make inferences about the staple economy. Setting aside taphonomic issues, we can assume that the terminal ends of the roadway networks represent the boundary between the zone of cultivation within and the zone of pasture or non-agricultural land

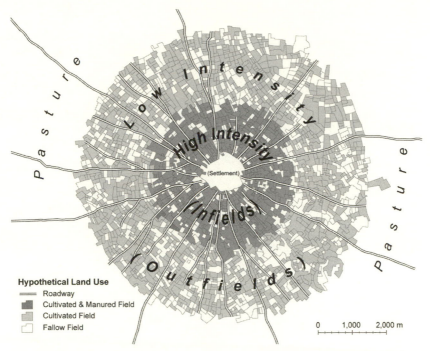

Hypothetical Land Use
- ═══ Roadway
- ▓ Cultivated & Manured Field
- ▒ Cultivated Field
- ☐ Fallow Field

0   1,000   2,000 m

9.7 Schematic plan of settlement, roadways, and land-use zones in EBA northern Mesopotamia. Field patterning based on CORONA interpretation of field systems around Qaraqosh, northern Iraq, Dec. 1969.

beyond it. Therefore, we can estimate the size of agricultural catchments and compare them to population estimates based on settlement size (Figure 9.8). Settlements whose agricultural catchments are larger than necessary to sustain their own populations were surplus producers, whereas those with catchments smaller than necessary would have been surplus consumers. Tell Beydar, a small center of 17 ha, would have had to import food, while the towns in the surrounding region could have produced surpluses (Wilkinson et al. 2007a). Using the same method, major urban centers like Tell Hamoukar (98 ha) would have needed to import up to half of their cereal needs (Ur 2002b; 2004:222–31).

These calculations assume biennial fallow, a practice that serves to ameliorate the loss of soil moisture and nutrients as a result of cultivation. The landscape evidence presented here, however, can be interpreted to demon-

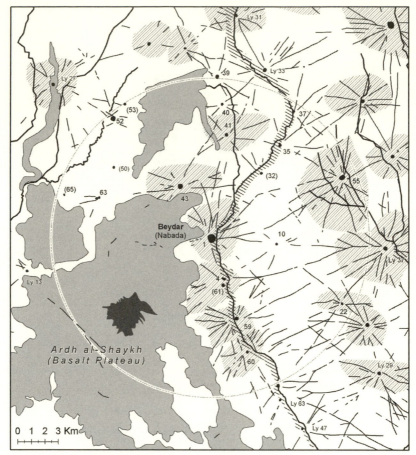

9.8 Cultivated areas around EBA sites in the Tell Beydar Survey area, derived from terminal ends of roadways. Sites with labels in parentheses feature minor or seasonal occupation.

strate that cultivation was intensified by violating fallow at the height of the EBA urban phase. If fewer or no fields were left fallow, movement would be constrained to the linear spaces between fields to an even greater degree; the intensified disturbance would result in deeper roadways than those created during a fallowing regime. Thus the formation of deeply depressed roadways may be a tangible landscape manifestation of the reduction or elimination of the fallow. According to Esther Boserup (1965), fallow reduction is the classic form of intensification, but it has been difficult to document archaeologically (Morrison 1994).

The continuous distribution of abraded pottery that covers the areas between sites, with greatest density around EBA settlements, is further evidence of intensification. These "field scatters" have been documented from England to Oman (Bintliff and Snodgrass 1988; Wilkinson 1982) and now are recognized in the New World (Killion 1992). Although such off-site scatters can result from a number of processes, continuous distribution is best interpreted as the remains of past manuring practices (Wilkinson 1982; Miller 1984; Charles 1998). Settlement-derived wastes were collected and deposited onto the fields as fertilizers. The organic component has long since decayed, but the incidental inorganic component (mostly potsherds, but also lithics) remains in the topsoil. Dense scatters surround EBA sites in northern Iraq and northeastern Syria (Wilkinson and Tucker 1995; Ur 2002a). The combined evidence of urban settlement patterns, deeply incised radiating roadways, and dense field scatters suggests that the agropastoral economy was intensive.

Bottom-Up and Top-Down Structures in the EBA Staple Economy

Proponents of hierarchical ecosystemic models might be tempted to interpret this intensification as the result of increased coercion and extraction from a growing elite based on a staple political economy. A review of the landscape evidence and excavation data, however, does not support this interpretation (Ur and Colantoni, in press). Excavations of monumental palace and temple households in northern Mesopotamia have not identified large-scale cereal storage beyond what was required to sustain their own household members.

The analysis presented here suggests that EBA roadways were not constructed by a coercive central authority but rather emerged from the actions of individuals as they maintained their fields and took their animals to pasture. Similarly, field scatters marking manured zones are an aggregation of actions by generations of farmers fertilizing their fields. No evidence for state-controlled collection and redistribution of manure for intensification of agriculture has been documented. On the other hand, waste disposal within urban residential areas was highly localized. Household debris was thrown into the streets immediately outside of the house (a pan-Mesopotamian practice; Stone and Zimansky 2004:55), and animal wastes were possibly collected in sumps within courtyards (Ur and Colantoni, in press). Manure was readily available to all farmers without the help of central authorities.

If the large elite institutions were not micromanaging the staple economy, what accounts for the clear evidence for agricultural intensification? Within the Patrimonial Household Model, the urban social fabric was composed of a dynamic arrangement of competing households of various scales; thus, intensification can be understood as one component of the continual renegotiation of the social hierarchy. Although status in EBA cities was not based primarily on the redistribution of staples, exchange in agricultural products played an important role at a more intimate scale. Communal consumption events involving alcohol and meat were important for the continual construction and maintenance of sociopolitical relationships. Archaeological studies of commensalism have focused on large-scale feasting events (Dietler and Hayden 2001), but if eating and drinking events were the arena in which these micropolitical processes played out, then every household had the motivation to produce more. Although the discussion has emphasized cultivation, animal production was also important. Indeed, the dramatic expansion of barley cultivation in the EBA may have been for fodder and meat production, as well as for human consumption (Charles and Bogaard 2001:325–26).

The focus thus far has been on the non-centralized aspects of the EBA economy and the possible motivations of politically ambitious actors within it rather than top-down control by elite households. To some extent, this is an attempt to redress the historical imbalance prioritizing top-down explanations such as the dominant ecosystemic model. The formation of the elaborate EBA systems of roadways, and more generally, the operation of the agropastoral economy, should be seen as a dynamic product of both emergent and imposed structures. The elite households certainly did extract surplus agricultural and animal products from dependents, but to a much lesser extent than supposed by traditional interpretations (Ur and Colantoni, in press). On the other hand, the top-down approach best explains ownership of agricultural land.

Although no textual sources on land tenure from the Upper Khabur basin have been recovered, data exist for contemporary southern Mesopotamia (Renger 1995) and Ebla in western Syria (Grégoire and Renger 1988); the latter is especially likely to be comparable, given its cultural and environmental similarities. Although individuals could own movable property and house lots, all agricultural land was considered to be "owned" by the large elite households. Land was rarely "sold" but rather usufruct rights were granted, generally in exchange for a small portion of the yield. These usufruct rights could be regranted down the hierarchy of households. Ideally ownership was retained by the largest household, but in practice lower-ranking households maintained practical control of land and it could even be "inherited." Only in the rare times of high centralization (e.g., the Ur III state) was the ideal form of exclusive elite ownership active (Renger 1995). Normally, de facto ownership lay elsewhere in the lower levels of the hierarchy of households (Schloen 2001).

In addition to land tenure, top-down economic control was probably limited to small-scale transfers of cereal and animal surpluses from small households to the larger ones which controlled agricultural land. These surpluses were probably consumed by the members of these larger households and expended in prepared form at communal events, rather than redistributed in bulk. The elite households were content to extract the apparently modest amount necessary for their own operation, rather than micromanaging a staple economy that ran quite smoothly on a household basis. Within this framework, the roadways of northern Mesopotamia formed primarily as the result of the movements of individual farmers and herders, acting primarily in the interests of their own households.

POLITICS AND MOVEMENT WITHIN THE KINGDOM OF NAGAR

Although not entirely separate from the economic sphere, we can place the roadways within the context of political action, which, much like the staple economy, was probably less centralized than assumed by ecosystemic reconstructions. As noted by Bell (1992), it is far easier (although still not unproblematic) to impute economic motives to individuals in the past than other motivations such as politics in the absence of explicit textual records. Fortunately, by the EBA, elite households in the urban centers of northern Mesopotamia had adopted cuneiform writing long in use in southern Mesopotamia. Although tablets are rare, we now have enough records from the sites of Tell Mardikh (ancient Ebla), Tell Beydar (ancient Nabada), and Tell Brak (ancient Nagar) to outline the political structure (Eidem, Finkel, and Bonechi 2001; Ismail et al. 1996; Sallaberger and Ur 2004).

Within the Upper Khabur basin, Nagar was the most important city and considered to be the political equal of the kingdoms of Ebla and Mari (Figure 9.1). The son of the ruler of Nagar married the daughter of the king of Ebla (Biga 1998), and the two royal households exchanged high-value luxuries such as silver, textiles, and specially bred equids (Archi 1998). The ruler of Nagar's control over the central and western parts of the basin is likely. He is mentioned in the tablets found at Nabada, and Nabada is listed as a dependent town of Nagar in the administrative tablets of Ebla. However, neither Tell Mozan (ancient Urkesh) or Tell Leilan (ancient Shekhna) appear as dependents of Nagar; therefore the eastern basin might have comprised one or more kingdoms independent of Nagar at the end of the 3rd millennium BC (Sallaberger and Ur 2004).

Our best interpretation of the internal operation of the Nagar polity comes from the more than 200 economic tablets from the site of Tell Beydar/Nabada, which primarily record lists of men, allocations of draft animals, and quantities of sheep and cereals (see Sallaberger 1996; Van Lerberghe 1996). Envisioned as a hierarchical, staple-financed state, one might expect these tablets to record the movement of cereals and animals from the "province" of Nabada to the central authority at Nagar. In fact, no material transfers of any kind between Nabada and Nagar are mentioned. Quantities of people, sheep, and draft animals are small and probably only describe the holdings of the major ruling household of Nabada itself, which appears to have operated independently of the nominal ruler of Nagar, at least in economic terms (Sallaberger and Ur 2004). The political relationship between Nagar and Nabada did not include exchange of staple products.

In ways closely connected to the landscape of movement in the basin during the EBA, the relative ranking of the ruler of Nagar and the elites in the major household of Nabada is documented in these tablets. The tablets record the allocation of cereals as feed for the donkeys of the ruler of Nagar for the number of days of his stay at Nabada, and they often mention his visits to other towns and shrines in the immediate area (Sallaberger 1996:95). The tablets list some 17 visits, averaging 3–4 days each; his donkey teams included up to 50 animals. The large quantities of cereals involved suggest that these must have been provisions for the ruler and his retinue in addition to donkey fodder (Widell 2004).

We can now imagine the ruler of Nagar moving along the roadways of his kingdom with a large entourage. Reading between the lines of these terse administrative tablets, we perceive the relatively decentralized nature of the kingdom, and the ruler's somewhat tenuous hold on power.

Most tellingly, the ruler of Nagar was obliged to visit the provincial elites within his kingdom, rather than vice versa (although our textual sources are potentially unrepresentative). As with the dynamic web of social relationships comprising the fabric of urban settlements described above, the ruler had to make the rounds of the polity, cementing his political ties with face-to-face interactions. During the brief era documented by the Beydar tablets, the ruler was a frequent visitor to the provinces. Rather than being institutionalized, the relationships upon which the kingdom of Nagar was built required continuous renegotiation.

In his movement across the plains of northern Mesopotamia, the ruler and his retinue must have passed by the farmers and herders as they took the same routes to and from their fields and pastures. The ruler's regional travel between the capital at Nagar and the provincial center at Nabada may have followed the system of roadways mentioned above (Figure 9.2). The indirectness of his movements is evidence of the limitations on centralized power. In other cases, powerful elites were able to impose straight roads onto the landscape as in the case of the Maya rulers (Keller, Chapter 7, this volume), or possibly the causeways and canals of the Bolivian Amazon (Erickson, Chapter 10, this volume), and the administrators of the Roman empire (Greene 1986:34–39). Such power appears to have been beyond the ruler of Nagar. Within his kingdom, he moved from settlement to settlement, respecting the local roadway networks as well as the local sociopolitical hierarchies and patterns of land control from which they emerged (Sallaberger and Ur 2004:69–70).

CONCLUSIONS

The extensive EBA network of roadways in northern Mesopotamia survives as a durable but unintended consequence of a unique phase of social complexity and demographic growth. Around the major centers and smaller towns alike, intensification of crop and livestock production left a distinct and deeply inscribed mark, literally and figuratively, on the landscape.

The subsistence demands of an expanding population did not single-handedly drive this intensified staple economy and its associated network of roadways, however. Within the towns and cities, household heads jostled for political advantage and worked to maintain their existing relationships. This required personal interaction in the context of commensal events, some large and elaborated but probably mostly small-scale and routine, as when a patriarch played host to his extended family, or when the head of a neighborhood lineage entertained the heads of other locally important families. Animals and cereals were a critical element of this household-level staple-based political economy. Cumulatively, these events placed a demand on the agro-pastoral system for the staples that greased the social gears: cereals for bread and beer, and livestock for meat consumption. These social and corresponding agricultural demands ultimately resulted in the linear features that remain etched into the landscape of northern Mesopotamia. This landscape was thus the product of a unique historical phase of emergent intensification within the constraints of the structure of the system of land tenure.

In northern Mesopotamia, the culturally familiar patterning of interconnected radial networks prevented Western researchers from venturing beyond economic interpretations. In some places, roadways can be interpreted as delimiting paths of movement through liminal or transitional zones, inspiring relief at homecoming in some and trepidation in others (Snead 2002). Although the roadways of the Early Bronze Age certainly held meaning to those who traversed them, it is inadvisable at present to speculate upon what it might have been. None of the laconic cuneiform texts available touch upon the kind of non-economic matters which would allow such insights.

Perhaps we might draw some conclusions on these aspects from the ultimate fate of this society. At the end of the 3rd millennium, all of the urban settlements were either abandoned or dramatically reduced in size. Although individual cities did reappear, urbanism on the scale of the Early Bronze Age experiment was never to return to the plains. When agricultural intensification returned, the emergent form, as manifested by roadways and field scatters, had been replaced by imposed varieties, road and irrigation systems stamped onto the landscape by the planners of the Neo-Assyrian, Seleucid, and Roman-Byzantine empires. Perhaps the competitive political economy, and its social environment, were ultimately found not to be worth the cost, and only with these later territorial empires were new landscapes of intensification again created. The EBA landscapes of movement, however, were never to be replicated.

NOTES

1. A terminological distinction is often made between non-constructed informal *paths* and intentionally constructed *roads* (Trombold 1991a:3; Hyslop 1991:29; Crawford 1953:60–62). The features discussed in this chapter are non-constructed, but I refer to them as "roadways" for several reasons. Unlike most informal paths, individual features are linear and non-redundant. Furthermore, the term "path" has connotations about size (small-scale) and means of transport (for humans, mostly foot traffic) that do not necessarily apply in this case study.

2. The long history of research in this area has produced competing and confusing variations in geographical and chronological terminology that will be mostly passed over in this chapter. Geographically, this region falls into northeastern Syria, northern Iraq, and southeastern Turkey, and is often referred to as Northern (or Upper) Mesopotamia or the Jazira (Arabic for "Island"). In absolute dates, the urban settlement phase began around 2600 BC and lasted until around 2000 BC (although these dates, particularly the end, are fiercely debated). In the most general Near Eastern chronology, this time spans the later Early Bronze Age (EBA). In the southern Mesopotamian historical chronology it would be considered the Early Dynastic III through Akkadian periods; and in the new "Early Jazira" chronology, it would be designated EJ III–IV (and possibly into EJ V).

10

Agency, Causeways, Canals, and the Landscapes of Everyday Life in the Bolivian Amazon

CLARK L. ERICKSON

Built environment provides an excellent medium for addressing issues of space, place, landscape, agency, flow, circulation, and interaction of human agents within physical structures laden with cultural, social, political, economic, and symbolic meaning (e.g., Atkin and Rykwert 2005; Lawrence and Low 1990; Low and Lawrence 2003; Moore 2005). The concept of built environment addresses issues of aesthetics, design, planning, function, and meaning of architecture. Traditionally, built environment meant formal buildings, monuments, and cities, although in more recent years, vernacular architecture and landscape are included. Because built environment is often highly patterned and physical, a form of material culture or human artifact, archaeologists can document, analyze, and interpret its origins, function, evolution, and meaning in much the same way as traditional objects of archaeological study are employed to understand the past.

In this chapter, human agency and structure that are embedded in the cultural or anthropogenic landscape, a particular form of built environment, are examined through practice theory. My research focuses on mundane landscapes, the landscapes of everyday life including farming, daily economic activities, routines of work and sociality. These environments have been transformed to such an extent through applications of technology and mobilization of human labor and energy that I refer to them as anthropogenic or engineered landscapes. Although often ignored in favor of large urban centers and monumental sites, these cultural landscapes are as constructed and planned as formal architecture anywhere on Earth. I document the patterned practices of everyday life that are physically embedded in a precolumbian and historical cultural landscape of the Baures Hydraulic Complex in the Bolivian Amazon. In this case study, ubiquitous landscape features such as causeways and canals provide a means of understanding complex landscapes of movement and social interaction through the perspective of practice theory and landscape.

AGENCY AND STRUCTURE IN CULTURAL LANDSCAPES

Pierre Bourdieu's (1977) practice theory stresses the dynamic relationship between the agency of individuals and groups and structure, the interface of which he labeled *habitus*. Bourdieu's concept of habitus is particularly relevant to archaeology because of his focus on the built environment, space, and the practices of everyday life (e.g., Barrett 2001; Bintliff 2004; Dobres and Robb 2000, 2005; Dornan 2002; Joyce and Lopiparo 2005; Llobera 1996, 2000; Smith 2001; Robin 2002). Bourdieu's original case study was the Berber house, a highly structured physical entity that is both a model of and a model for society. Human individuality and creativity produces cultural innovations that can become habitus (or structure) if adopted in human routines of life. Over time, habitus become an active force for shaping human activity. In turn, individual agents through daily practice can alter those structures of everyday life.

The complex recursive relationship between practice and structure creates the patterns that we recognize in the archaeological record and identify as aspects of long-term traditions; local, regional, and cross-cultural variation; and continuity and change over short and long temporal scales. Landscape is a valuable medium to read the nuances of practice, agency, structure, and habitus. Landscape archaeologists read the physical, patterned "residues" of accumulated human routines and practical knowledge or habitus. We do landscape archaeology through recognition of context, association, pattern, continuity and discontinuity, anomaly, palimpsest, landscape capital, inhabitation, and historical ecology (Anschuetz, Wilshusen, and Scheick 2001; Ashmore and Knapp 1999; Balée and Erickson 2006; Wilkinson

2003). With fine-grained analysis, even ephemeral patterning is detectable. Anomalies and disjunctures reveal discrete agency and spatial and temporal groupings and boundaries, which often relate to socio-political organization on the ground or changes over time (e.g., Erickson 1993; Walker 2004).

Trails, paths, and roads may be the best built environment media for highlighting the contributions of the archaeology of landscapes due to their materiality, longevity, permanence, patterning, and multiple functions and meanings. Trails, paths, and roads connect people to people, people to re-sources, or in the case of ritual roads and pilgrimage, people to their gods and sacred places. As complex networks of human relationships, routes map communication, transportation, interaction, and social, political, eco-nomic organization (e.g., Ingold 1993; Tilley 1994, 2004; Wilkinson 2003). On the other hand, where trails, paths, and roads do not go can demarcate territories and boundaries between groups occupying the same landscape. The multiscalar thinking about time and space in a landscape approach is relevant for understanding the archaeology of movement, which can in-clude anything from local short-term events to regional phenomena with deep histories and beyond. The size and complexity of movement network may reflect the scale and intensity of interaction (Earle, Chapter 12, this vol-ume; Appendices 1 and 2). Short, ephemeral trails and paths and circulation within households may relate to individual or small group activity (e.g., Robin 2002; Stahl and Zeidler 1990). In contrast, nested, bounded networks of road communication may reflect either hierarchical or heterarchical or-ganization of society (e.g., Crumley 1995; Crumley and Marquardt 1987). In other cases, vast networks of informal trails and paths of small, relatively non-complex societies may cover entire regions, subverting assumptions about scale and socio-political stages (Snead 2002, Chapter 3, this volume; Darling, Chapter 4, this volume). In addition to mundane practical everyday use, trails, paths, and roads may serve important functions of performance during processions, rituals, and pilgrimage (e.g., Abercrombie 1998; Bauer 1998; Inomata and Coben 2006; Moore 2005; Morrison 1978; Ferguson, Berlin, and Kuwanwisiwma, Chapter 2, this volume; Keller, Chapter 7, this volume). Approaches to the archaeology of movement range from descrip-tions and functional analyses of trails, paths, and roads, often through the lens of process, political economy, evolution, and cultural ecology (e.g., Espinoza 2002; Hyslop 1984; Kantner 1997; Oyuela 2000; Wilkinson 2003; Ur, Chapter 9, this volume) to studies of the interpretation and meaning of these features framed in phenomenology, practice, memory, interpretation, and semiotics (e.g., Aveni 2000; Chadwick 2004; Keller, this volume; Llobera 1997, 2000; Snead and Preucel 1999; Sofaer, Marshall, and Sinclair 1989; Tilley 1994, 2004). As the result of intentional activities of everyday life, repetitive movement creates physical structure over time. Once established, this highly patterned structure often determines later activities through features that facilitate and impede movement. Because of this recursive relationship, trails, paths, and roads can be models of and for society or Bourdieu's habitus.

The practices of everyday life and social interaction, in particular human movement through space, simultaneously create and are structured by the built environment and cultural landscape. Repetitive bodily movement through space and the physical structures that result from and channelize this movement create a tight recursive relationship. Places determine networks of movement and these networks structure new places. Informal movement creates paths and trails which over time grow and become more complex through accretion and formalization. Although "entrenched" over time, these movement networks can be transformed through changing needs, new technology, and the shifting of places of origin and destination. Although movement through already established routes is often unconscious, circulation through most space involves decision making (consideration of slope, natural obstacles, least resistance, and other physical contingencies of movement), negotiation (where you can and you cannot go because of neighbors, land tenure, and other social contingencies of movement), and meaning (the aesthetics, symbolism, ideology, metaphor, and other interpretations of movement). In extreme cases, movement can be highly structured through designed roads, bridges, and stairs that facilitate and direct traffic, and walls, barriers, gates, and other cultural obstructions that impede or control circulation.

THE ENGINEERED LANDSCAPES OF
THE BAURES REGION OF BOLIVIA

The Baures Region is a remote corner of the Llanos de Mojos (Moxos), a vast landscape of seasonally inundated grassland savannas, permanent wetlands, lakes, gallery forests, forest islands, and closed canopy forest in the Amazon Basin of northeast Bolivia (Figure 10.1). Much of the country is submerged beneath a thin sheet of water during the wet season. Rivers and lakes are filled with fish and other aquatic species throughout the year and migrate across the savannas during floods. The flooding of the wet season is in sharp contrast to the dry season when water can be scarce. Scattered "forest islands" rise a meter or two above the surrounding savanna, ranging in size from several hectares to many square kilometers and sustaining settlements, ranches, gardens, and fields within the populated areas to the north and west. Unlike the anthropogenic (human created) forest islands in central Bolivian Amazon, those in the savannas of Baures Region are natural formations produced by upwelling of the Brazilian Shield.

The Baure probably were the last indigenous group to be subjugated by

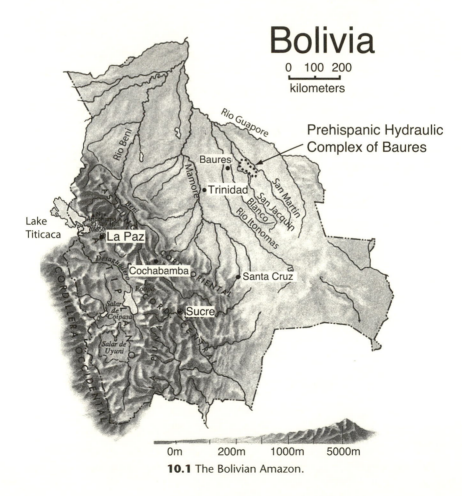

10.1 The Bolivian Amazon.

the Spanish in Bolivia. After a brief bloody retribution by the Spanish army for killing their first missionary, the Jesuits established control in the early 1700s. The Jesuits were impressed by what they recognized as a remarkable civilization: elaborate dress, large settlements, political organization, intensive agriculture, and monumental earthworks associated with the Baure people (Anonymous 1743; Eder 1888, 1985; Métraux 1942; Denevan 1966, 1991; Block 1994). Baure settlements were distributed in the Itonama, Blanco, Negro, San Joaquin, San Martin, San Simon, and Itenez (Guaporé) river drainages. In addition to groups speaking dialects of Baures (Baure, Muchojeone, and Paikoneka), smaller dispersed groups such as the Sirionó, Itonama, and Guarasug'we also occupied the Baures region. Population was estimated to be 40,000 dispersed in 75 to 124 large settlements (Altamirano 1891:117; Block 1994; Denevan 1966; Eguiluz 1884:22). Over time, native populations sharply declined due to Old World diseases, wars with the Portuguese, slavery, and other abuses following the expulsion of the Jesuits and later during the Rubber Boom and Chaco War. While some successful Jesuit mission towns such as Concepción de Baures continue to the present, many failed and were abandoned during the Mission Period.

I use the term "Baure" for the contemporary, Colonial, and precolumbian native peoples of the region, "Baures" for the mission and contemporary administrative center town, "Baures region" for the areas of archaeological features and contemporary occupied landscape (Figure 10.1), and "Baures Hydraulic Complex" (BHC) for the engineered landscape in the savannas between the San Joaquin and San Martin rivers (recognized as the Kenneth Lee Archaeological Reserve by the National Government of Bolivia) (Figure 10.2).

The inhabitants of the Bolivian Amazon imposed their agency and structure on the environment through permanent and significant engineering. Various scholars have highlighted the importance of causeways and canals (CEAM 2003; Denevan 1966, 1991; Erickson 1980; Métraux 1942; Michel 1993; Pinto Parada 1987; Plafker 1963; and specifically for the Baures region: Orbigny 2002; Lee 1979, 1995; Nordenskiöld 1916, 1918, 2001; 2003). Various sites in Baures, Magdalena, Bella Vista, and along the Itenez/Guapore River were briefly investigated by archaeologists (Becker-Donner 1956; Calandra and Salceda 2004; Denevan 1966; Dougherty and Calandra 1981, 1983, 1984; Kelm 1953; Prümers 2006; Prümers, Betancourt, and Plaza 2006; Reister 1981). As part of the Agro-Archaeological Project of the Beni (University of

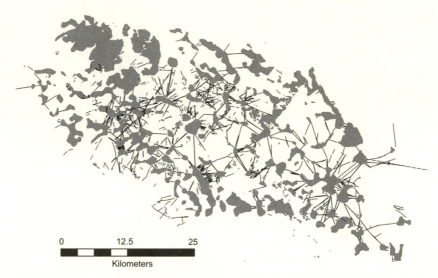

10.2 Major Causeways-Canals, Minor Causeways-Canals, and forest islands in the savannas of the Baures Hydraulic Complex, Bolivia.

Pennsylvania and National Institute of Archaeology), we investigated sites and earthworks including raised fields, fish weirs, water management structures, settlements, artificial river meander cut-offs and inter-river channels, causeways, and canals between 1995 and the present (Erickson 1995, 2000a, 2000b, 2000c, 2001, 2002, 2006a; Erickson et al. 1995; Erickson, Winkler, and Candler 1997; Vranich 1996).

MAPPING AGENCY AND STRUCTURE
IN A LANDSCAPE OF MOVEMENT

The study region is unpopulated today; thus, the earthworks are remarkably well preserved in contrast to areas subject to heavy cattle grazing. All surveyed forest islands larger than 1 km² have ring-ditch sites of diverse size and shape: octagons, hexagons, squares, rectangles, "D" shapes, circles, ovals, and irregular shapes (Erickson 2002, 2006a, 2008; Erickson, Winkler, and Candler 1997; Vranich 1996) (Figure 10.3). Large forest islands have multiple, evenly spaced, ring-ditch sites. Ditches are often several meters deep and steep sided and some extend 1–2 linear km and include multiple concentric rings. The Jesuits described these features as forts with deep

10.3 D-shaped ring-ditch site at the Buen Retiro Ranch, Bolivia.

moats and palisades (Anonymous 1743; Eder 1985) (Figure 10.4). Although few have been investigated archaeologically, ring-ditch sites may have been cemeteries, sacred spaces, elite residences, settlements, and/or defensive structures. These features also are documented for Riberalta, Bolivia (Arnold and Prettol 1989), and the Acre and Upper Xingu River regions of Brazil (Heckenberger 2005; Pärssinen and Korpisaari 2003).

10.4 Reconstruction of a ring-ditch site. (Artwork by Daniel Brinkmeier)

Although similar in shape and scale to the large circular villages with central plazas of the Central and Eastern Amazon basin (Wust and Baretto 1999; Heckenberger 2005, 2008), the ring-ditch sites of the Baures region, Riberalta, and the Acre region tend to lack evidence of domestic activity, which suggests non-residential use. The Jesuits were impressed by the larger settlements, but also describe dispersed, dense occupation throughout the forest islands. As an early strategy of control and indoctrination, the Jesuits resettled peoples in their new mission towns, a settlement system that continues today. Archaeologically, settlements are difficult to document due to thick vegetation and soil cover and the ephemeral nature of Amazonian residential structures. Today, individual households often maintain several houses in different locations for farming and resource collection.

A vast network of raised earthen causeways and canals provided a landscape of movement to connect these important places. A causeway is defined as a formal, intentionally raised road, usually of locally obtained earth. A canal is an intentionally excavated linear feature intended to hold water seasonally or permanently or simply the result of building causeways. Causeways and canals are usually associated as combined landscape features in the BHC. Causeways and canals vary in length from tens of meters to many kilometers. Most causeways and canals are straight. Many form radial patterns from a common source, usually located on a forest island. Most causeways and canals are associated with low-lying, seasonally or permanently inundated savannas or wetlands, although some penetrate the higher ground of forest islands. Causeways and canals can be divided into Major and Minor types based on scale, energetics, design, and context.

Major Causeways are highly visible as tree-lined features flanked on one or both sides by canals filled with dark aquatic vegetation, which stands out against the grass-covered savanna (Figure 10.5). The adjacent water-filled canals block annual savanna burns, allowing trees to flourish on causeways after abandonment. Major Causeways range in width from 1 to 10 m and elevations vary from 0.5 to 3 m tall; Major Canals are comparable in dimensions. Most Major Causeways-Canals are straight and extend up to 7.5 km, although most are several kilometers long. Pedestrians used the elevated causeways and canoe traffic circulated in the adjacent canal(s) (Erickson 2000a, 2000c, 2001, 2006a; Erickson and Walker, Chapter 11, this volume). Major Causeways-Canals represent the longest inter-forest island connec-

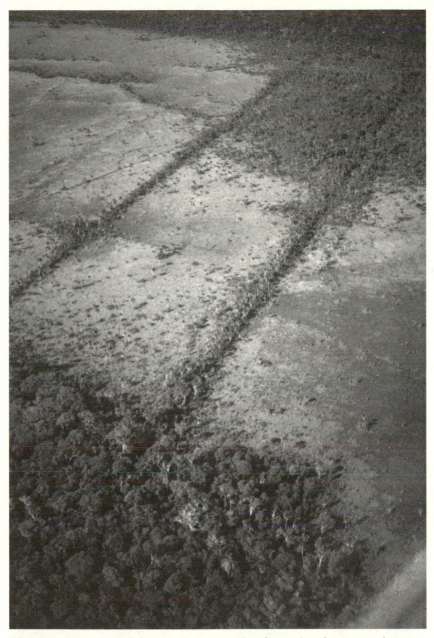

10.5 Tree-covered parallel Major Causeways-Canals crossing the savanna between forest islands.

tions. These works often are monumental in design, labor, and scale; most appear on satellite imagery from space and are formal roads. Some are particularly labor intensive in scale of earth moved and we recorded many double and triple parallel causeways-canals (Figure 10.5). Construction was done using simple wooden digging sticks and earth moved in baskets and/ or carrying cloths.

The more common Minor Causeways-Canals were also laid out in straight alignments but are shorter in length and required less construction than the Major Causeways-Canals. These features consist of a single shallow canal (1 m wide and less than 0.5 m deep) with low causeways or berms alongside ((Figure 10.6). My informant-guides and I interpret these shallow canals as precolumbian canoe paths: channels for paddling or poling large canoes across the shallow inundated savanna during the wet season. During the dry season, the channels could be used as routes for pedestrian traffic through savanna grasses. Repeated paddling, poling, or dragging a large canoe through the shallow water can create canal-like depressions over time with minimal planning or labor (Figure 10.7). The irregular scar of annual

10.6 Minor Causeway-Canal or canoe path (dark line) crossing the savanna in tall grass between Largo and Paralelo forest islands.

10.7 Poling and paddling a large dugout canoe across the flooded savanna of the Baures Hydraulic Complex.

canoe transit of my native guides is a good example of what a few hunters can do through even irregular routines over many years. Their paths have been permanently etched on the landscape as a modern layer of palimpsest. I can trace their recent canoe path across the savanna to their forest island camp on satellite imagery, a distance of 7 km. The sinuous irregular courses of these recent canoe paths stand in contrast to the straight trajectory of Minor Causeways-Canals, which implies concern with trajectory during the initial shallow channel excavation. Although simple constructions, Minor Causeways-Canals share the straightness and precision of layout of the larger Major Causeways-Canals.

The project Geographic Information System (GIS) of the Baures Region includes Digital Elevation Models, Landsat ETM scenes, CORONA images, aerial photographs, topographic maps, and vector maps of cultural features, classified vegetation, and landuse. Numerous flights in low-flying aircraft provided opportunities for oblique photography. Two short seasons of pedestrian survey, mapping, and excavation in the Baures region were conducted in 1995 and 1996. The GIS documents over 1000 individual artificial linear features representing 994 linear km in total length (averaging 1 km) in the 500–700 km² of the BHC (Figure 10.2). Most are Minor Causeway-Canals. A remarkable concentration of Minor Causeways-Canals is found in a 3–4 km² area of savanna between and around two large forest islands: the San Martin Forest Island Complex (Figure 10.8). In this small subset of the GIS, I detected 168 linear features, of which the majority are Minor Causeways-Canals of 1 km or less in length. Eleven Major Causeways-Canals extend to the south and north.

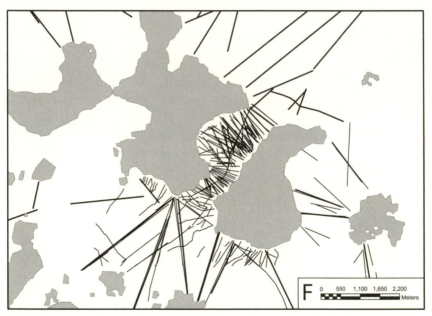

10.8 Major Causeways-Canals and Minor Causeways-Canals of the San Martin Forest Island Complex.

PREHISTORY, ETHNOHISTORY, AND ETHNOGRAPHY OF MOVEMENT IN THE AMAZON

As agency and structures of everyday life, the causeways and canals of the Baures region can be understood through archaeological context informed by the spatial patterning in the GIS and fieldwork and, to a limited extent, through historical and ethnographic analogy, and comparison to similar phenomena in the Llanos de Mojos and Amazonia. Although archaeological studies of causeways and canals are scarce, trails, paths, and roads are reported for the Amazon region. Large urban settlements with circular plazas bounded by concentric arcs of ditch and embankment that are connected by wide radial roads of several kilometers in length are documented in the Upper Xingú River basin (Heckenberger 2005, 2008). Located in uplands, these roads are defined by earthen curbs rather than raised roadways and excavated canals. While sharing straightness, radial patterning, and associations with ring-ditch sites, these roads are less numerous, of lower density, and easier to construct than those of the BHC. Archaeologists also have documented a precolumbian network of causeways in the Venezuelan savannas associated with chiefdoms (Garson 1980; Spencer, Redmond, and Rinaldi 1994) and networks of wide curbed roads in the Upper Xingu region (Heckenberger et al. 2008). Although individual causeways and roads are similar in size and length to those of the Baures region, the network is smaller in geographic scale and of lower density.

Although dispersed settlements, trekking, long-distance trade, reciprocity, and competitive feasting are emphasized in native Amazonian ethnography and history (e.g., Descola 1994; Posey 1983; Rival 2002), scholars have largely ignored the ubiquitous trails, paths, and roads that made this interaction possible. During early exploration along the Amazon River (Solimões River) by the Orellana Expedition of 1541–1542, Carvajal (1988) reported large riverine villages with wide avenues or streets radiating from plazas far into the hinterlands. An early account of the Paresi, a group linguistically related to the Baure, describes long, wide avenues between their many villages (Pires de Campo 1862). Nimuendajú (1939, 1946) discussed everyday and special ritual roads used by the Apinayé and the Eastern Timbira for processions, log races, and other rituals associated with initiations and community. Fabian (1992) discusses roads and plazas of the Bororo of Central Brazil as key elements for structuring of cosmological and spatial order.

The Spanish soldiers, missionaries, and colonial authorities observed the use of precolumbian and contemporary causeways and canals in the Bolivian Amazon (Altamirano 1891; Anonymous 1743; Castillo 1906; CEAM 2003; Denevan 1966, 1991; Block 1994; D'Orbigny 2002; Lizarrazú 1906; Marbán 1889; Métraux 1942). Many early Spanish expeditions penetrated the region using the vast network of trails, paths, and roads, most of which were still in use during the Mission Period. Jesuit Father Francisco Eder pro-

vides a rich eyewitness account of causeways and canals during the Mission
Period in the mid-18th century.

> [M]ost of the year the savannas are covered with high water. Boats
> are the only way to get from one forest island to another. Since most
> of the natives have no boats (either due to laziness or because they
> don't know how to make them), but they still find it necessary or
> enjoyable to go visiting their neighboring friends, usually for the
> purpose of drinking, they built a certain kind of bridge or dam-like
> structure of earth by digging a ditch on two sides and piling earth in
> the middle. These causeways generally remain dry in the floods and
> are wide enough for Spanish two-horse carriages. The water filled
> ditches created by their construction are also used for canoes. Dur-
> ing the hot dry period and burning of the savannas, these ditches
> retain enough water so that maize and other goods can be trans-
> ported. These causeways were mostly used by the Baure tribe; al-
> though they are found elsewhere. Nowadays, however, few are in
> use, partly because the lack of canoes at the disposal of the Indians
> and partly because after all these years of disuse, the causeways have
> become ruins. (Eder [1772]1985:104–5; Eder [1772] 1888:36; Boglar
> and Bognar 1973–81)[1]

The Baure efficiently combined causeways for terrestrial traffic and
canals for aquatic circulation into an integrated landscape of movement.
While we tend to focus on causeways as platforms for pedestrian movement, Eder clearly points out that canoe traffic in the associated canals may
have been more important. Native peoples in this region and throughout
Amazonia relied heavily on water transport. The canoe was a key characteristic of Tropical Forest Culture (Lathrap 1970; Lowie 1948). A complex network of natural and artificial waterways connects most of Amazonia with
neighboring drainage basins (Nordenskiöld 1916). Canoe travel by Amazonian peoples played a key role in alliances, warfare, slaving expeditions, and
trade during the Colonial Period (DeBoer 1986) and contemporary daily
life (Smith 1999). The artificial enhancement of water routes through canal
digging and river meander cut-offs is well documented (Abizaid 2005; Raffles and Winkler-Prins 2003). In describing the Mojo, Block (1994:23) states
that they "lived in their canoes" and an early vocabulary of Mojo Arawak

"is filled with watery words, including seven separate expressions for river, describing various sizes, colors, and textures." Canoe transportation is still highly valued in the Baures region. My informants and guides repeatedly tell me, "We would rather paddle or pole a canoe than walk any day."

The desire to travel by canoe has shaped the Baures landscape in other major ways. The obsession with straightness was also applied to the vast meandering rivers of the region. Nordenskiöld (1916) and D'Orbigny (2002) documented a number of river meander short cuts or cut-offs and canals, which connect the main channels of adjacent rivers or their headwaters, many of which were still functioning. More recently, additional canals designed to reduce travel time and canoe portage have been documented (Denevan 1966, 1991; Erickson, Winkler, and Candler 1997). My informants state that the historical and modern river cuts are the product of and "owned" by local communities. Erland Nordenskiöld (1916) cited informants who stated that these artificial canals could change mighty river courses over time. In the Baures Region, members of the Tujeré Community excavated a 0.25 km canal to cut a river meander in 1995 (Erickson, Winkler, and Candler 1997).

Contemporary farmers, hunters, ranchers, and cattle use informal paths to cross the savannas and wetlands, easily recognized by their irregular, sinuous trajectories despite the flat topography and open savanna. Although sometimes producing worn trench-like ruts in the landscape over time, these informal sinuous foot and canoe paths contrast sharply with the straight precolumbian causeways-canals. In travels within the BHC, my guides consider the overgrown Major Causeways-Canals as obstacles where their canoes must be portaged or a canal must be cut through the feature with shovels. In contrast, precolumbian Minor and Major Causeways-Canals rarely cross or intersect, suggesting a memory of and respect for preexisting features when new routes were created or added.

THE CREATION OF A LANDSCAPE OF MOVEMENT

Obsession with straightness and radial patterns is common in the cultures of the Americas. In the ethnography of the Central Amazon, straight roads are sacred axes of circular plaza villages dedicated to ritual uses such as the log racing of the Bororo and Gê (Nimuendajú 1939, 1946; Fabian 1992), in addition to trails and paths of mundane, everyday travel. The basic functions of causeways and canals were for transportation and communication: moving people, goods, and information between settlements in the savanna and rivers of the BHC. Canals were particularly useful for moving heavy and bulky agricultural produce from field to settlement and connecting people with resources such as game, fish, construction materials, firewood, and orchards. To move pedestrians or long, heavy canoes between two points in the flat landscapes of the BHC, direct paths are the most effective. On the other hand, constructing ruler-straight formal Major and Minor Causeways-Canals are beyond what is necessary for efficient movement. Other elements emphasize overengineering and expense such as the existence of multiple parallel causeways-canals when a single causeway-canal would suffice. These formal patterns suggest the agency of individuals, families, hamlets, and communities who agreed to create a local and regional infrastructure of direct communication based on a shared aesthetic of intense social interaction, straightness, and order.

The chronology for causeway and canal use begins around 600 years ago in the Central Bolivian Amazon (Erickson 2000c). We have a single corrected radiocarbon date ranging from AD 1490–1630 for a Major Causeway-Canal in the BHC (Erickson 2000c; Erickson, Winkler, and Candler 1997).[2] Based on these dates and palimpsest and context of earthworks, most Major and Minor Canals-Causeways probably were built and used in the late precolumbian or protohistoric periods before Spanish conquest and missionization of Baures in the early 1700s. With the introduction of Old World diseases, slavery, and wars between Spain and Portugal over this region, native populations collapsed, the region was depopulated, and the earthworks were largely abandoned.

How did the landscape of the BHC come to be and how does the historical process inform us about agency and structure? Despite our lack of direct dates of earthworks and settlements, the GIS shows a complex historical process of landscape formation that can be "read" through palimpsest and patterning. Superposition, intersection, and disjuncture of landscape features across space give us clues to help to sort out the complex construction of this built landscape. In particular, the rare intersections where earlier earthworks are "cut through" by the construction of later features provide clues about chronology and use. When this evidence is present, we can assume that either gradual replacement is occurring or some earthworks have fallen into disuse.

The straightness and uniformity of individual Major and Minor Causeways-Canals also argues for a single construction episode. The lack of evidence of segmental or incremental construction of individual Major and Minor Causeways-Canals is additional evidence of overall design and structure on the landscape. Straight Major and Minor Causeways-Canals were planned from the beginning. Few, if any, irregular paths, trails, or canoe paths can be dated through palimpsest as precolumbian. The cutting of these straight features by recent irregular trails and canoe paths suggests a disjuncture in patterns of movement. Thus, Minor and Major Causeways-Canals predate the modern features. Most are recently created by seasonal hunters and wild animals such as peccaries, agouti, deer, and tapirs moving between forest islands parallel to the overgrown earthworks, thus are not the evolutionary predecessors of the more formal features.

We find no evidence of mistakes, corrections, and/or experimenting in the design and patterning. The Major and Minor Causeways-Canals appear fully developed on first appearance and throughout their construction and use. The formal design emphasizing precision and straightness applies to all levels of the landscape of movement from Minor Causeways-Canals representing the efforts of individual households living in dispersed hamlets to the Major Causeways-Canals of large communities and supra-communities living in villages and towns and possibly a polity at the regional scale. A shared belief in structure clearly dominated formation of this landscape from the beginning and was passed down through generations as memory, inhabitation, and landesque capital (discussed below).

The majority of the Major and Minor Causeways-Canals do not cross or intersect their neighbors (Figure 10.2). The predominant radial pattern of the Major Causeways-Canals insures autonomy. When Major Causeways-Canals intersect, one usually terminates at the juncture, indicating contemporary use and respect for preexisting structures. Because of their number and density such as the San Martin Forest Island Complex, Minor Causeways-Canals are more likely to intersect, especially where crowded on the landscape (Figure 10.8). Their more ephemeral nature and simple construction suggests that these features regularly went in and out of use according to the needs of individual households, in contrast to the Major Causeways-Canals, which are more permanent and used by larger groups of people. The palimpsest relationship between Major and Minor Causeways-Canals provides details about the creation process of the landscape. The

cases of Major Causeways-Canals intersecting ("cutting through" and physically perforating) Minor Causeways-Canals outnumber cases of the reverse.
Thus, the Major Causeways-Canals were built after the establishment of
many Minor Causeways-Canals, but the evidence also suggests overlap in
use period.

Earthwork construction profoundly transforms soils, water, and vegetation in highly patterned ways. The design and construction process
is "additive" in that, once established, earthworks are permanent. Major
Causeways are literally additive in that earth is piled up to create them.
Minor Causeways-Canals are superimposed on earlier features as palimpsest, much like a messy, unerased blackboard. Although the features are
eroded remains today, we have no evidence of removal of earthworks
through destruction, leveling, or erasure. Thus, established earthworks do
not disappear through disuse and abandonment, but rather become landscape features of "inhabitation" (e.g., Barrett 1999a) whereby the occupants
of the landscape at any point in time are surrounded by and immersed in
the works of their ancestors. This inhabitation has important implications
for long-term memory, local history, a sense of pride, place, and community, agency, and structure. As an additive or accumulating landscape, the
BHC was continually under construction and undergoing a "filling" process
that has implications for agency and structure. Certain rules of design were
respected during the complex process of landscape creation. Whether the
avoidance of building new Major Causeways-Canals across preexisting features reflects respect for past tradition and structure, or simply a decision
to save time and energy by not dismantling old features is difficult to determine. Both choices show the increasing dominance of multigenerational
group structure over individual agency as the landscape becomes filled.
Through accumulation of generations of labor into permanent landesque
capital (Erickson and Walker, Chapter 11, this volume), the built environment appears overengineered. The occupants built more Major Causeways-
Canals than necessary, often double, triple, or parallel and many are wider
and taller than needed for a society without wheeled vehicles and draft
animals. Their sense of order and magnitude in the landscape approaches
a monumentality commonly associated with more ostentatious complex
societies (Trigger 1990).

Despite sharing straightness, individual Major Causeways-Canals vary
greatly in terms of length, width, and height. Although common in the

BHC, complexes of radial causeways-canals show little similarity in number of rays, orientation, and scale. This supports the idea that individual Major and Minor Causeways-Canals were planned according to a shared structure in mind, builders had considerable leeway in the execution and imposed their agency accordingly. These variations also support a more bottom-up construction and organization of the earthworks.

The numerous and repetitive Minor Causeways-Canals may be the result of long-term landscape-accumulation as households migrated across space through deaths, house replacement, fissioning of communities, and population growth; thus, Minor Causeways-Canals would have been abandoned and replaced as needed. Amazonian houses are impermanent structures that need maintenance and replacement; the lifespan of a typical Amazonian house is short due to post and thatch decay. The dispersed households and multifamily hamlets documented in the ethnographic record outside of permanent villages and towns are relatively ephemeral, thus new Minor Causeways-Canals were created as settlements cycled around the forest islands and provide more evidence of occupation than the ephemeral settlements themselves.

LANDSCAPE MOVEMENT AS A MAP OF SOCIAL INTEGRATION AND ORGANIZATION

The causeways-canals of the BHC represent engineered networks for social interaction. Their linear patterning stands in sharp contrast to natural formations. Even the animal paths that wander between forest islands often follow or are determined by what humans created. The irregular paths, trails, and roads of modern everyday life that crisscross the occupied areas around the town of Baures and surrounding forest islands stand in sharp contrast to the highly ordered precolumbian landscape. Although the informal would have been easier to create and maintain, the precolumbian peoples apparently preferred more orderly, formal circulation and structure. The number and patterning of Minor Causeways-Canals show a strong desire of individual agents to directly connect with neighbors and a rich sphere of social interaction.

Major Causeways-Canals, characterized by their impressive number, length, width, volume of earth, and straightness, were a visible form of monumentality and a means to show community labor, pride, and aesthetics. Construction of these overengineered, larger, and more elegant features may have been driven by healthy competition between communities. In the ethnographic and historical record for Amazonia, the social, political, economic, and ritual organization of complex and non-complex societies is based on dynamic and delicate balancing of alliance, competitive feasting, labor reciprocity, trade, host-guest asymmetry, raiding, and warfare (e.g., DeBoer 1986, 2001; Heckenberger 2005; Lathrap 1970; McEwan, Barreto, and Neves 2001). The Jesuit Father Eder ([1703] 1985) complained about the Baure use of causeways for visiting and drinking with friends, an activity that he considered wasteful and unproductive.

All activities rely on physical connections linking people face to face across the landscape. The vast network of causeways and canals probably facilitated and solidified these social processes. Many Major Causeways-Canals lead to or radiate from ring ditches on the larger forest islands, suggesting integrated design and the special ritual function of social gatherings. By directing the eye to the distant horizon on a near flat landscape or convergence on key forest islands, Major Causeways-Canals provide a powerful phenomenological experience even today (Figure 10.9). Major Causeways-Canals may have been elegant, wide tree-lined avenues when in use, further emphasizing a sense of monumentality and order. Equally impressive are three clearly

10.9 Reconstruction of use of Major Causeways-Canals in the Baures region. (Artwork by Daniel Brinkmeier)

artificial canals that traverse narrow sections of long forest islands, which would eliminate the need for hours of canoe portage or circumnavigation. Some of these features required considerable labor due to the volume of soil and rock excavated (Erickson, Winkler, and Candler 1997).

The density, patterning, and type of trail, path, road, and water networks may reflect the social organization, demography, and complexity of these societies. Based on their number, design, and context in the San Martin Forest Island Complex, Minor Causeways-Canals probably were constructed, used, and maintained by individual extended families or small groups of families in hamlets dispersed over adjacent forest islands (Figure 10.10). Each provided personal, direct physical connection to kin, neighbors, and friends. We can predict households and hamlets stretching along the edges of forest islands overlooking the open savanna. Fewer in number and more impressive in scale of construction, the Major Causeways-Canals connect many of the same places, but are strategically placed to efficiently connect all large forest islands with single or parallel routes.

I am convinced that the tangled mass of Minor Causeways-Canals was organized bottom-up by families, hamlets, lineages, and communities rather than imposed top-down from a central political authority. But does a single causeway-canal between two adjacent forest islands represent the work of

10.10 Reconstruction of the landscape of movement of the Baures Hydraulic Complex. (Artwork by Clark Erickson)

a single household, a community, or multiple communities? If an independent community occupied each forest island, did neighboring communities collaborate on the construction and maintenance of causeways and canals? We have documented rare cases of straight Major Causeways-Canals with a slight sharp angle midway between forest islands, which may have been the result of two collaborating communities building their own half of a shared project. Some paired, parallel Major Causeways-Canals between forest islands may also represent the work of two interacting communities.

If polities beyond groups of communities existed, nested spatial patterns of interaction would be expected. Patrick Brett (2007) applied Network Analysis (e.g., Jenkins 2001) to the patterning of causeways and canals of the BHC. The analysis determines the centrality, spatial integration, hierarchy, flow, and accessibility through consideration of nodes and connections. The Degree of Centrality, which measures "centrality" of nodes on forest islands based on number of associated individual causeways-canals, highlighted eight important nodes. The high Degree of Centrality suggests that these locations are centers of population and social, political, and economic hierarchy. Although the most important node was expected to be located in the center of the BHC, the Degree of Centrality defines the central location as a node in the San Martin Forest Island Complex. Surprisingly, forest island size was not associated with Degree of Centrality. Other indices of Betweenness Centrality (which measures control of movement) and Closeness Centrality (which takes into consideration distance) delineate a connecting "spine" of important forest islands running northeast to southwest through the center of the BHC. Brett's analysis suggests a weakly hierarchical organization.

Another basic assumption is that the presence and density of causeways and canals map degrees of human interaction within a social network and their absence marks disjunctures, boundaries of territories, and buffer zones. Forest islands near rivers on the east and west edges of the BHC have few or no causeways-canals, thus may be the frontier of an integrated region of social interaction. Because of deep flooding and year-round water in the rivers, causeways-canals were not needed or too difficult to build. Few causeways and canals are found outside of the BHC despite similar environments. The Network Analysis and GIS suggest an interacting, bounded regional society with a diverse, densely settled population with highly structured circulation and movement.

Ethnographic analogy suggests that households and hamlets were capable of building and maintaining the Minor Causeways-Canals and that villages, lineages, and communities could have created the Major Causeways-Canals as public works. In 1994, the indigenous community of Cairo near the town of Baures built a straight causeway measuring 1 km to connect two forest islands in a few weeks (Figure 10.11). Although the road connected two forest islands of individual communities, the road was entirely built by the "end of the line" community to improve pedestrian and oxcart access to the town of Baures. A second causeway of 0.5 km was constructed between the town plaza and port on the Negro River. These grass-roots efforts by the community were also a symbol of pride and empowerment (Erickson, Winkler, and Candler 1997; Erickson 2001).

Based on our raised field experiments, profiles of earthworks, and the GIS, an estimate of labor for the 476 linear km of Major Causeway-Canals in the BHC is 713,864 m³ of earth moved or 1,427,727 person-hours or 285,545 person-days. The construction of the 93.491 linear km of the Minor Causeway-Canals of the San Martin Forest Island Complex sample required movement of 9,349 m³ of earth that represents 18,698.2 person-hours or 3,740 person-days. The average labor for a single Minor Causeway-Canal is 22 person-days (based on 170 Minor Causeway-Canals). A minimal unit of a family of 5 could construct a single feature in 4.4 days or two families as predicted here could do the work in 2.2 days.

Based on energetics, spatial organization and patterning, and scale, the Minor Causeways-Canals of the Baures region are a local phenomenon created through the agency of those that inhabited these locales. In the case of the Major Causeways-Canals, the overall organization was more complex and weakly hierarchically organized, but individual Major Causeways-Canals were within the capacity of communities. Based on these characteristics, the Major Causeways-Canals were created and served to integrate society at a larger scale than the more local Minor Causeways-Canals. The political organization of the Baure during the late precolumbian and early Colonial periods has often been described as a chiefdom or possibly an alliance of chiefdoms (Block 1994; Denevan 1966; Métraux 1942; Steward and Faron 1959; and others). By attributing the Minor and possibly Major Causeways-Canals to communities and smaller organizations, I do not imply that the features necessarily exist outside of chiefdoms, states, and empires. Communities and their works appear, thrive, and fail within the context of hierarchical states, globalism, failed states, and other forms of complex society.

10.11 A 1-km Major Causeway-Canal built by the community of Cairo in 1994.

CONCLUSION

The precolumbian causeways-canals provided basic transportation and communication, but also may have served as land tenure boundaries, water management, ideological statements about order, pride, and aesthetics, and stages for ritual events and processions for households, communities, and polities. In a society with no stone pyramids, palaces, temples, or cities, monumentality was expressed in grand avenues and canals, far beyond what was necessary for daily life in terms of number, density, redundancy, width, engineering, and complexity. These characteristics in turn imply multigenerational organization of human labor and energy to build and maintain these local, regional, and interregional scale structures.

As the result of the structures of everyday life, the causeways-canals of the BHC embody formal characteristics, rules, or grammar: shape, length, width, source and destination, environmental context, and straightness. As products of agency, certain variations in individual earthworks and groups of earthworks are expected. The Major Causeways-Canals were sufficient in size to permit two-way traffic, ideal for moving groups of humans at the community and intercommunity levels of organization and possibly extending to regional scale organizations. In contrast, the Minor Causeway-Canals were limited to one-way movement and more suitable for individual or small group movement between hamlets or individual households. The straightness and basic form imply a shared concept of a "proper" earthwork.

Landscapes of movement are key elements of the social reproduction of community and formation of cultural landscapes through the recursive historical relationship between agency and structure. Although treated synchronically in this chapter, the causeways-canals have a complex temporal dimension. Once created through human agency of repetitive movement or formal design and construction, causeways-canals begin to structure future movement within the cultural landscape. Placement of new causeways-canals had to consider previously established features that may have been used contemporaneously or been abandoned, thus invoking memory. The high density and numbers of Minor causeway-canals at the local level in the San Martin Forest Island Complex suggest that these features were created, used, and abandoned at a high rate, possibly during an individual's or household's lifetime. The lack of intersection or crossing of Minor and Major Causeways-Canals indicates that the builders of new features respected the existence of the older features. In some cases, a clear palimpsest of Minor Causeways-Canals is embedded on the landscape as a series of superimposed features. Select Minor Causeways-Canals probably became Major Causeways-Canals over time as needs and destinations of travel changed. In turn, these features channeled movement of increasingly larger groups of interacting peoples and expanded the spatial scale of interconnected movement at the subregional and regional level.

Trails, paths, and roads are the connective tissue for the threads of activities that constitute the practice of everyday life. In the case of formal engineered roads, the implications of agency and structure of movement extend into the social, political, economic, ideological, and symbolic spheres. Even ephemeral movement activity of individuals and small groups is sometimes physically registered in the topography and vegetation patterning of the cultural landscape. From the local level to the regional level, the more formal means of movement are engineered and embedded into the landscape in highly visible and more permanent ways. As patterned physical features, the agency and structure of movement is amenable to archaeological investigation. Archaeologists traditionally focused on significant places or sites and their interrelationships. An archaeology of movement combined with a landscape approach and practice theory provides an exciting new perspective to understand past peoples' lives. As a product of the dynamic interrelationship between agency and structure, trails, paths, and roads are active rather than passive cultural objects.

Acknowledgments

Fieldwork in the Baures region was conducted in 1995 and 1996 under permit from the Bolivian government to Clark Erickson and Wilma Winkler (Agro-Archaeological Project of the Beni). I thank Wilma Winkler, Alexei Vranich, Freddy Bruckner, Oscar Saavedra, Conrad Bruckner, Edwin Bruckner, Anita Bruckner, Oscar Ferrier Toledo, Hans Schlink, Kenneth Lee, Ricardo Bottega, Rodolfo Pinto Parada, and John Walker for their valuable help. Three guides, Osmar Cuellar, Jesus Zapata, and Eduardo Esero, accompanied me during fieldwork in 1996. Satellite imagery was provided by the Global Land Cover Facility and aerial photographs and topographic maps were purchased from the Military Geographic Institute and the Air Force of Bolivia. Patrick Brett helped created the GIS. Jason Ur, James Snead, and a reviewer provided useful comments.

NOTES

1. Eder wrote in Latin. The 1888 and 1985 translations are Latin to Spanish by Armentia and Barnadas respectively. The 1973–1981 translation is from Latin to Hungarian to English by Bogler and Bognar. I have combined the best of each translation and added my own editing for clarity based on my knowledge of the causeways, canals, and local environment.

2. Burned wood from the base of the causeway was radiocarbon dated to 335 years BP (before present) ±20 (OS-17293) or an uncalibrated calendar date of AD 1615 (between AD 1595 and 1635). The corrected date at 68.2% confidence is AD 1490 (0.26) AD 1530; AD 1560 (0.74) AD 1630.

11

Precolumbian Causeways and Canals as Landesque Capital

CLARK L. ERICKSON AND JOHN H. WALKER

The study of past and contemporary trails, paths, and roads is relevant to political economy, history, sociology, urban planning, folklore, development, and anthropology. These features are material expressions of both patterned human movement through everyday repetitive activities and the physical structures that channel human activities through their division of space into place, territory, boundary, access, and orientation (Barrett 1999a, 1999b; Chadwick 2002; Snead 2002; Tilley 1993, 2004). Trails, paths, and roads are simultaneously expressions of agency, practice, and structure (Erickson, Chapter 10, this volume; Ingold 1993). Landscape is a useful concept for understanding the role of these features in everyday lives, a framework within which archaeology provides a unique perspective. Examination of trails, paths, and roads as physical landscape features and formal built environment provides insights about economic infrastructure, social interaction, social organization, engineering, worldview, and indigenous knowledge that are often unavailable to ethnographers and historians. As subtle and sometimes imposing landscape features, trails, paths, and roads recursively structure and reflect ongoing daily and special activities and document change and discontinuity when interpreted as palimpsests.

In this chapter, we show how roads are a central element of the precolumbian agrarian and residential landscape in the savannas of the Llanos de Mojos of the Bolivian Amazon. In this case, formal raised roads or causeways with associated canals provided efficient means of movement and connection between settlements, fields, and resources across the landscape. In addition to their obvious transportation and communication functions, these earthworks played a key role in water management, topographic transformation, and engineering of the environment at a regional scale.

In contrast to the Western obsession to drain what are considered marginal wetlands for agriculture, farmers in the Bolivian Amazon may have intentionally expanded wetlands and wetland productivity through earthwork construction, which impedes, rather than enhances, drainage (Erickson 1980, 2006b). The precolumbian farmers did not use causeways as dikes to prevent inundation of fields and settlements, but rather to expand and enhance inundation for agricultural production. At the same time, impounding water with well-placed causeways and the creation of canals improved and extended the season of transportation by canoe across the landscape. The grid-like structure also permanently marked land tenure in a highly visible manner. As a vast investment of labor, innovation, and engineering resulting in permanent land improvement by generations of precolumbian peoples, causeways and canals became important landesque capital. This engineered landscape continues to structure the lives of contemporary peoples and the environment in subtle and direct ways.

THE CONCEPT OF LANDESQUE CAPITAL

Agricultural landscapes are patterned built environments, a large-scale accumulation or palimpsest created by generations of inhabitants who have imposed their structures on the land (e.g., Denevan 2001; Doolittle 2000; Whitmore and Turner 2001). These landscapes are places where people lived their everyday lives, working, traveling, and farming. These same landscapes contain and express elements of the non-routine ritual, sacred, aesthetic, and political realms. An essential attribute of cultural landscape features is their recursive nature; they are both models of and models for society (Erickson, Chapter 10, this volume). In all cases, nature was transformed in the process of production through labor, society, and history. This transformation can result in land improvements and/or degradation over time (Erickson 2006a, 2008; Kirch 2005; Redman et al. 2004). Under good management, the improvements on the land accumulate through the efforts of generations of inhabitants, each exploiting and adding to the permanent infrastructure (e.g., canals, terraces, and raised fields) and enhanced soils.

As noted by William Doolittle (1984), substantial landscape accumulation, often at monumental and regional scale, can be made either over short periods with heavy labor investments or through a long-term accretion process. Accumulation can be coordinated or simply the result of piecemeal improvements. Many impressive cultural landscapes are created, used, and maintained by small farming communities over hundreds of generations (Denevan 2001; Erickson 2006b; Walker 2004). Harold Brookfield (2001; Blaikie and Brookfield 1987) proposed the term *landesque capital* or *landscape capital* to describe an important element of this phenomenon. Brookfield (2001:55) defines the landesque capital concept as certain innovations that create enduring fixed capital in the land beyond a single crop or cropping cycle. The innovations can be skills, technology, and labor that are directed towards improving infrastructure and enhancing soils on existing fields or new land that was previously unusable (ibid. 55). Current farmers benefit from permanent landesque capital created by generations of previous occupants. Once created, landesque capital is inherited, used, and maintained by later generations (ibid. 216). These farmers can increase the landesque capital or simply maintain it (ibid. 216). Over time, highly productive, sustainable anthropogenic landscapes are formed.[1]

The landesque capital of complex, patterned, and highly evolved anthropogenic landscapes is amenable to archaeological and historical ecological investigation as a physical record of human activities over the short and long term (Balée and Erickson 2006b; Fisher 2005, 2007; Kirch 1994). Trails, paths, and roads are important categories of landesque capital, although rarely discussed as such. In this chapter, we explore the use of formal roads, specifically causeways and canals, as landesque capital to facilitate movement and channel people and water across the landscape at the local and regional scale.

THE BOLIVIAN AMAZON

The Bolivian Amazon lies between the Andes Mountains to the west and the highlands of southwestern Brazil to the east and the Pantanal and Chaco regions to the southeast. The region is drained by the Madeira River, which flows into the Amazon River some 1500 km to the north. The Llanos de

Mojos (or Llanos de Moxos; Plains of Mojos) is a seasonally flooded tropical savanna located in the Department of the Beni within the Bolivian Amazon (Figure 11.1).

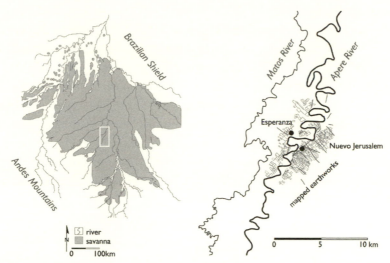

11.1 The Llanos de Mojos (gray) and the Middle Apere landscape of the Bolivian Amazon.

The Llanos de Mojos is a relatively flat landscape, with elevations varying by a few meters. Large, active, sediment-laden rivers with headwaters in the Andes Mountains, such as the Beni, Mamoré, and Madre de Dios, meander across the landscape within defined floodplains. In contrast, smaller tributaries such as the Apere River are more stable in their course and have low, forested levees slightly higher than the surrounding savanna. The climate is warm and humid, with sharp seasonality. The wet season peaks between December and March and the inundation produced by the heavy seasonal rains, as well as rising river levels downstream, threatens crop agriculture and ranching. In some years, half of the landscape is underwater. During the dry season from June to September, water becomes scarce and modern farming and ranching are difficult. The environment is a mosaic of forests, savannas, and wetlands, all subject to a strong seasonal cycle of rainfall and inundation.

Today, cattle ranching dominates the cultural landscape. Ranchers move their herds across long distances, from areas near permanent wetlands in the dry season to high refuges during the wet season. Although rarely farmed, ranchers regularly burn the savannas to encourage new grass and keep the forest at bay. (The importance of burning to savanna ecology is illustrated by the encroachment of forest on savanna between 1975 and 2001 as ranching activity declined.) The savanna, wetland, and forest mosaic are rich in fauna and flora. The rivers, lakes, swamps, and seasonally inundated savannas are full of fish, caimans, and river turtles. Major game animals include deer, peccary, capybara, tapir, paca, armadillo, and agouti.

Ranchers, native peoples, and colonists establish gardens, orchards, and slash-and-burn fields within the better-drained gallery forests and forest islands. Key crops today are manioc, maize, sweet potato, squash, New World taro, rice, and tropical fruit trees. Most communities and ranches are in gallery forests and forest islands. The modern situation contrasts sharply with the precolumbian strategies of intensive agriculture on the savannas.

PRECOLUMBIAN CAUSEWAYS AND CANALS IN THE BOLIVIAN AMAZON

The Bolivian Amazon is a highly patterned cultural landscape of earthworks and settlements. Earthworks include settlement mounds, raised fields, causeways, canals, reservoirs, and fish weirs (Denevan 1966, 1991, 2001; Erickson 1996, 2000a, 2000b, 2006a; Erickson and Balée 2006; Walker 2004). Roads, in this case raised earthen causeways with associated canals, are common landscape features that crisscross the savannas, wetlands, and forests of the region (CEAM 2003; Denevan 1966, 1991, 2001; Erickson 2000c, 2001, and Chapter 10, this volume; Lee 1995; Michel 1993; Nordenskiöld 1916; Pinto Parada 1987). Because of the intentionality, design, monumentality, and engineering used in their construction, causeways and canals are classified as formal *roads* rather than informal trails or paths to highlight the intentionality, design, linearity, monumentality, and engineering that were used in their creation.

Causeways are flanked by canals on one or both sides where earth was removed to raise the road platform (Figure 11.2). Although badly eroded by cattle ranching and farming activities, causeways are visible from the air as dark straight lines of trees and bushes that stand out against the grasses of the savanna (Figure 11.3). Canals are marked by aquatic vegetation and standing water during the wet season and darker vegetation and soils during

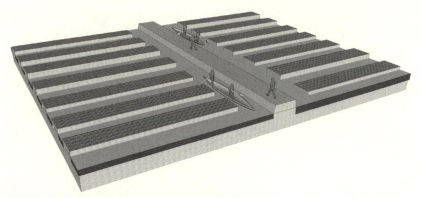

11.2 Detail of an engineered landscape in the Bolivian Amazon. Causeways are flanked by canals on one or both sides where earth was removed to form the road platform. Raised field platforms and canals fill the landscape on both sides of the causeway. (Artwork by Clark Erickson)

the dry season. Causeways range in elevation from 0.2 to 2 m and in width from 1 to 20 m. Most causeways are straight over lengths ranging from tens of meters to kilometers. Causeways are generally found in seasonally inundated areas of poor drainage, but are rarely found in permanent wetlands, deeply flooded zones, or well-drained gallery forest and forest islands. Causeways connect archaeological settlements, raised fields, resources, rivers, wetlands, and other causeways, forming physical networks of local and regional scale.

CAUSEWAYS AND CANALS AS ENGINEERED HYDRAULIC WORKS

Most of the seasonal inundation of the Bolivian Amazon is what is termed "benign flooding" (Siemens 1996:133). In these hydraulic regimes, overflowing rivers with sources in the Andes and within the region, local rainfall, runoff, rising water tables, and backup of drainage in the lower reaches of river systems gently cover much of the flat landscape with a sheet of water. In the savannas and low-lying forests, this inundation generally ranges from a few centimeters to several meters deep. Although relatively shallow, the mass of water at the height of the rainy season is millions of cubic meters (Hanagarth 1993; Langstroth 1996).

The "wetland margin," the surface affected by the rise and fall of the

11.3 Precolumbian causeways (white lines), associated raised field blocks (gray polygons), gallery forest, and levees (black forested areas) on the savanna near the Jerusalem and Esperanza ranches, Middle Apere River (computer-generated oblique perspective of an aerial photograph layered over a digital elevation model).

floodwaters (Siemens 1996), is vast and heterogeneous in a flat landscape such as the Bolivian Amazon. In Amazonian studies, the classic distinction between floodplain and upland (*várzea* and *terra firme*) (Lathrap 1970) does not apply because most of the landscape is inundated to some degree at various times. The highest ground is often adjacent to the rivers themselves—the linear levee formations of sediments dumped by the slowing of flow velocity during hundreds of years of inundation. These geomorphological features support gallery forests and are exploited using slash and burn, agroforestry, and gardening. The *bajios* (back swamps or wetlands) between rivers are generally the lowest elevations and often hold water year round. The savannas, wetlands, and forests are crosscut by abandoned river channels, meander scars, and their associated levees. The larger levees support forest islands and gallery forest. Other prominent features include shallow "oriented lakes" (both open and choked with vegetation) and other permanent wetlands (CEAM 2003; Denevan 1966; Hanagarth 1993; Plafker 1963).

To many modern inhabitants, government institutions, and nongovernment agencies, the seasonal cycles of inundation are limitations to growth and development of the region. In contrast, the precolumbian farmers of the Bolivian Amazon were attracted to this dynamic landscape and took advantage of the seasonal cycles of inundation. The inhabitants practiced a form of passive recessional floodwater agriculture: enhancing and exaggerating its effect through massive transformation of the landscape. In contrast to traditional irrigators in arid and temperate environments, they exploited the natural cycles of water using simple earthworks to channel and manage water at a regional scale. In other settings of benign flooding such as the Southwest United States and Mali, farmers use check dams and dikes to retain moisture in soils that are planted after floodwater and run-off recede (Brookfield 2001; Doolittle 1984). In contrast, the precolumbian farmers in the Bolivian Amazon planted their crops *during* the period of inundation, taking advantage of the water management provided by a variety of earthworks including causeways, canals, and raised fields.

Our hypothesis that causeways and canals were used to manage inundations and enhance wetlands comes from numerous observations of *unintentional* pooling of water behind modern raised causeways in the Bolivian Amazon. In 1979, a massive lake was formed to the south of the newly constructed raised road between San Borja and San Ignacio. In 1985, the raised road between Trinidad and Puerto Almacén blocked the floodwaters and created a huge body of water that washed over and destroyed the road surface, which made it impassable for many weeks (Figure 11.4). In both cases, engineers determined that the road construction crew failed to install the required number of drains in the raised road.[2]

During the wet season in the Bolivian Amazon, causeways only a meter in height that link areas of higher ground can impound significant amounts of water with minimal effort (Figures 11.5, 11.6). A single square kilometer of raised fields and canals can control 250,000 m^3 of water during a flood of 0.5 m and retain it long after the floods recede (Erickson 2003c, 2006a). Grids of causeways and canals also significantly enhance water control capacity. In such cases, the canals of raised fields and associated causeways function as micro-catchment basins connected to a network of canals, streams, rivers, and other water bodies. For the precolumbian peoples who built them, these earthworks would have significantly extended growing seasons and reduced agricultural risk. The presence of aquatic fauna and flora would have been an additional benefit, both for subsistence and because recycled organic material enhanced production on the raised fields.

11.4 Modern raised road between the city of Trinidad and Puerto Almacén unintentionally impounding a large lake (right) in 1985.

The tens of thousands of kilometers of linear terrestrial-aquatic interface created by construction of causeways and canals, and raised field platforms and canals has the potential to significantly raise agricultural productivity, biomass, and biodiversity at the local and regional scales (Erickson 2006a, 2008).

THE MIDDLE APERE RIVER LANDSCAPE

Precolumbian causeways and canals in the Bolivian Amazon are found along the tributaries of the Mamoré River, which crosses the region south to north, and in the northeastern part of the region, around the modern town of Baures (Erickson, Chapter 10, this volume). Some of the most impressive causeways, canals, and raised fields are found on the Middle Apere River (Figure 11.7). Although flat and featureless to the untrained eye, the Middle Apere River region has considerable ecological and topographical heterogeneity. The local savanna is broad and open, and forests are generally confined to galleries along the rivers. Causeways, canals, raised fields, settlement mounds, and occupation sites cover an area larger than 60 km^2

Prehispanic Hydraulic Systems in the Llanos de Moxos

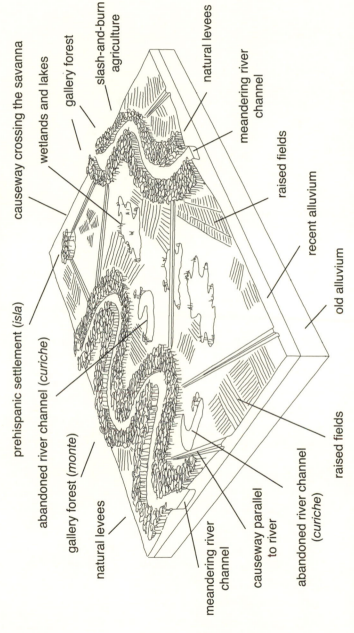

causeway crossing the savanna

wetlands and lakes

gallery forest

slash-and-burn agriculture

natural levees

meandering river channel

raised fields

recent alluvium

old alluvium

raised fields

abandoned river channel (*curiche*)

causeway parallel to river

meandering river channel

natural levees

gallery forest (*monte*)

abandoned river channel (*curiche*)

prehispanic settlement (*isla*)

11.5 Reconstruction of causeways, canals, and raised fields between adjacent rivers in the Bolivian Amazon. (Artwork by Clark Erickson)

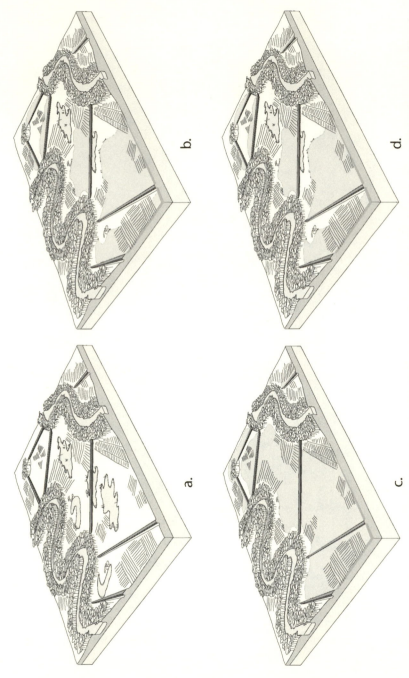

11.6 Reconstruction of causeways, canals, and raised fields between adjacent rivers in the Bolivian Amazon: (a) dry season, (b) early wet season, (c) late wet season, and (d) early dry season. (Artwork by Clark Erickson)

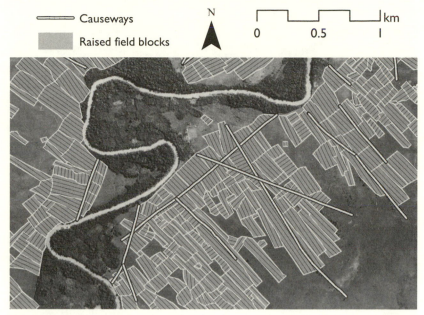

11.7 Precolumbian causeways (wide white lines) and raised field blocks (thin white lines) overlaid on an aerial photograph.

along both sides of the river. Raised fields extend nearly continuously on the levee backslope from the river channel to the edge of permanent wetlands, a distance of 3 km. Numerous long causeways crisscross the area of raised fields. Here, we compare a model of the natural flow of water on the landscape based on general geomorphology and hydrology to a model of the anthropogenic flow of water after transformation by the construction of earthworks (causeways, canals, and raised fields). Precolumbian farmers of the Bolivian Amazon superimposed their anthropogenic, cultural landscape as a complex dynamic palimpsest on nature.

Methods

In our case study, the indigenous knowledge of engineering is embedded in the physical structure of the landscape. Our approach is to do "reverse engineering" using mapping, survey, excavations, and modeling to determine the structure, function, and meaning from the highly patterned archaeological remains. Causeways were mapped using digitized aerial photographs, which were georeferenced using GPS points and landmarks visible on LANDSAT ETM images. Causeways and blocks of raised fields were digitized on-screen. A digital elevation model (DEM) is based on shuttle-borne radar data (SRTM). The SRTM DEM is unsuitable for comparing the ground elevations of forested and non-forested areas, because the radar records the tops of trees rather than the surface of the earth. However, for comparisons across non-forested savanna where most earthworks are located, the data are useful.

The DEM was used to create two models of water flows. The Natural Landscape Model (Figure 11.8) was based on the original SRTM DEM, processed to "fill in" basins created through flaws in the data.[3] This model simulates the flow of water over the landscape without taking into account the effect of causeways. The Modified Landscape Model (Figure 11.9) is based on the same processed SRTM DEM. In this model, the elevations of pixels crossed by the digitized causeways were raised by 1 m to simulate original causeway elevations, which are too small in scale to be recognized in the 90 m pixel DEM. Comparison of the two models shows the difference between a hypothetical natural landscape and an imposed anthropogenic landscape. The differences between these two models represent the hydraulic effects of causeways. Note that the study site only includes one of two adjacent river levees.

Analysis and Interpretation

Figures 11.5, 11.6, and 11.10 show the river levee and river levee back-slope in relation to the river channel and bajios. The hypothetical movement of water from rainfall, overbank flooding, and bajio flooding is presented in Figure 11.10 to illustrate the discussion below. In the Natural Landscape Model (Figure 11.8), floodwater movement across the savanna is primarily determined by the local river levee backslope that directs flow towards the southeast rather than the overall regional slope of the landscape towards the north-northeast. The change in elevation is approximately 1 m per 1 km down the local river levee backslope and 1 m per 10 km over the course of the Apere River and overall regional slope. As a result, overbank floodwater first drains away from the Apere River to the southeast and later drains to the north-northeast along the bajios between the rivers. Although flow dynamics are complex, the first determinant of the floodwater movement is down the river levee backslopes and the secondary determinant is the overall regional slope.

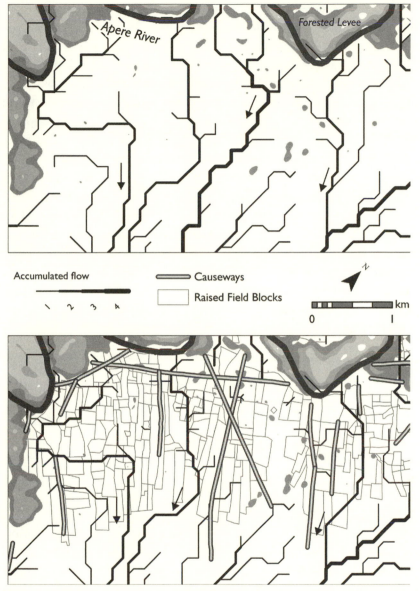

11.8 The Model of Natural Landscape. The Model shows how water moves down the levee backslopes and away from the Apere River. Progressively lighter shades of gray represent the accumulation of moving water.

11.9 The Model of Modified Landscape. The Model shows how causeways alter the flow of water down the levee backslopes and away from the Apere River. Progressively lighter shades of gray represent the accumulation of moving water with overlay of causeways (black lines) and raised field blocks (light gray).

Other drainage characteristics can be inferred from the local topography. During local rainfall, most runoff flows down the levee backslopes perpendicular to the river to the bajios rather than entering the river. When the rivers crest, overflow also moves down the levee backslope perpendicular to the river. Later, as the entire drainage becomes saturated, water backs up in the bajios, river channel, and seasonal rivers from downstream. At this time, rising regional floodwaters can creep up the levee backslope from the bajios.

When precolumbian causeways are added to the DEM and the hydrological analysis is run a second time to create the Modified Landscape Model, the anthropogenic impact on local drainage is clear (Figure 11.9). The causeways that are parallel and close to the river channel may block some rainfall runoff from draining into the river or may have helped distribute water for more even flow down the levee backslope, but their effect is minimal on hydrology at the height of the inundations. These causeways may have functioned to protect the upper levee backslope gardens and settlements from floodwater from the river, but their height (less than 1 m) suggests their impact on flooding was relatively insignificant.

Causeways that are perpendicular to the river divert and isolate some of the flow of water down the backslope, but do not impede the general flow of water or impound large bodies of water due to their low elevation, small cross-section, and downslope orientation. These causeways were not meant to block large volumes of water from riverbank overflow. Instead, they probably channeled, organized, and stored rainwater runoff in the beginning of and during the wet season, and the rising waters in the wetlands between the rivers at the end of the wet season. Most of the year, water soaks into the soil rather than running off due to the relatively flat slope and low water table. Instead of wholesale diversion of overbank flow from the river onto the levee backslope, the primary hydrological function of the causeways may have been to create local catchment areas where local rainfall and floodwater were harvested for agriculture and the period of canoe access to wetlands during the dry season was extended. Throughout the year, access to the wetlands for fishing, hunting, and collection of aquatic resources was improved through causeway construction and impounding of water. The resulting expansion of seasonal wetlands on the levee backslopes also improved nutrient capture and production within the blocks of causeways.

The raised fields between the causeways also had hydraulic functions. Individual raised fields are organized in bundles or blocks averaging 3.2 ha, oriented roughly to the intercardinal directions. The alternating orientations of raised field blocks produce a checkerboard pattern, although the blocks vary in size and in shape from squares to long rectangles. Some exceptions to these orientations are found on the levee backslopes of abandoned river channels on the larger present-day Apere River levee backslope and within the wide, sweeping meanders of the Apere River. Similar to the causeways, most raised field blocks are oriented either perpendicular to the river course or to the direction of local slope.

These orientations and the checkerboard pattern are intentional. Because the individual raised fields and raised field blocks have multiple orientations, the overall intent was to drain and retain water (Figure 11.10). Many raised field canals have no outlets and raised field blocks are encircled by low earthen bunds (which also functioned as raised field platforms and as a means of pedestrian circulation through the raised fields). The overall effect of these features was the creation of micro water-catchment basins.

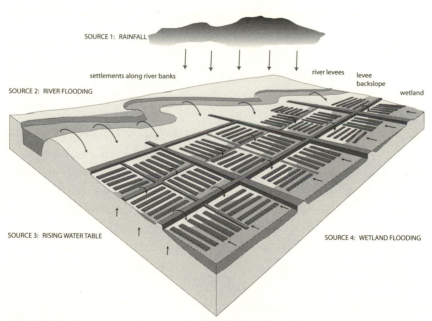

11.10 Reconstruction of water movement across the engineered landscape of the Middle Apere River. (Artwork by Clark Erickson)

When optimal water levels within raised field blocks were reached, excess water would drain over the bunds into lower-lying raised field blocks further down slope or into the larger canals along perpendicular causeways into the bajios. These catchments provided drainage, water control, traps for sediment and nutrients, and aquatic routes for canoe traffic.

Thus, through building individual raised fields, raised field blocks, bunds, canals, and causeways, precolumbian farmers created a sophisticated integrated system of water management. Because the runoff from each block of raised fields affects neighboring blocks, farmers would have had to cooperate at the local level. In addition, the grid or checkerboard pattern of field blocks, some surrounded by clear bunds, probably marks land tenure and reflects the size and organization of the different groups responsible for their construction, use, and maintenance (Walker 2004). In turn, these blocks are combined in higher-level units covering square kilometers bounded by causeways and canals. In contexts where landesque capital is highly developed and agriculture is intensive, formal marking of family and community land holdings is expected and often necessary. Causeways provide a highly visible marker of land tenure.

When local topography and associated raised fields are considered, causeways appear to function to create, expand, and manage wetlands at a local and regional structure. In addition, these water management systems enhanced the productivity of economic resources of natural wetlands. The expansion of wetlands through earthworks provided habitats for fish, the main source of protein for precolumbian Amazonian peoples. Finally, by slowing and changing the flows of sediment-rich water, causeways could have increased the accumulation of sediment and resulted in enhanced soil fertility.

The orientations, positions, and patterning of most causeways and raised field blocks show clear integration. Associated causeways and field blocks have the same orientations (with a few exceptions) and causeways rarely divide individual blocks. The analysis suggests that most causeways and raised fields were designed, built, and maintained as locally integrated farming systems. In most cases, parallel and perpendicular causeways are oriented with the general orientations of the raised field blocks within them. The integration suggests that the causeways and raised fields were created at the same time or gradually co-evolved as generations of farmers learned how to engineer the local hydrology and invested in permanent landesque capital.

On a flat, seasonally inundated landscape, the construction of earthworks such as causeways, canals, and raised fields will affect local and regional hydrology, regardless of intent. Because normal annual inundation
during the wet season and drying out of the landscape in the dry season are
substantial processes in scale and intensity, causeways, canals, and raised
fields could not completely control water. However, we have shown that
the imposition of causeways, canals, and raised fields on the landscape significantly altered the benign flooding in positive ways and improved human
circulation on the landscape for foot and canoe traffic. The combination
of raised fields, canals, and causeways enhanced natural wetlands and ar-
tificially expanded wetlands over large areas. The engineering features
also captured early rains and impounded water well into the dry season
when most of the savanna dried out. The builders of these raised fields
and causeways were familiar with the syncopated rhythm of the river, rain,
and seasons. Farmers used earthworks to create a structured anthropogenic
landscape and appropriated those rhythms and the local topography to enhance farming, hunting, and fishing, complementing their other functions
as transportation and communication between settlements and people and
resources.

CAUSEWAYS AND CANALS AS MODES OF TRANSPORTATION AND COMMUNICATION

The hydraulic model explains the presence and organization of many causeways and canals, but not all. As stressed above, the causeways and canals
that best fit the hydraulic model also were used for the circulation of farmers and goods between settlements, their fields, and the resources of the
bajio, river, and forest. Although the river provided the most accessible year-
round means of transportation and communication for canoe-using communities living on the levee, straight causeways and canals parallel to the
rivers were more direct routes than following the meandering river, reduc-
ing travel time. Although most settlement was dispersed along the highest
river levee, the causeways and canals permitted farmers to live anywhere on
the landscape and still maintain social connections. Farmers dispersed over
the landscape could also use the web of causeways and canals to commute
to fields and share labor with neighbors in times of need.

   In three areas, causeways and canals radiate from common points that are either on or near archaeological sites high on the river levee. For example, seven causeways-canals radiate from the Providencia Mound, a small settlement or burial mound overlooking a vast complex of raised fields (Figures 11.3 and 11.7). These causeways bisect individual raised field blocks and "go against the grain" of the overall grid, suggesting that these were built after the raised fields were established (Figure 11.7). These causeways clearly prioritized pedestrian and canoe traffic between settlements (or settlements and resources) over hydraulic functions (Figure 11.2). Although created primarily to move people and goods across the landscape, radial causeways and canals also had intentional effects on hydrology by facilitating distribution of floodwaters over the upper backslope for more even and slower flow through the raised fields. In addition, the footprints of radial patterns of causeways probably mapped individual community territories and social networks (similar to those of the Baures Hydraulic Complex, Erickson, Chapter 10, this volume). In summary, the need for efficient transportation and communication trumped the hydraulic function in the above cases.

CONCLUSIONS

The precolumbian peoples of the Middle Apere River created a formal landscape of movement through the construction of earthworks that improved, channeled, and controlled human and water circulation. Although far from seamless, this integration of settlements, transportation, communication, fields, land tenure, resource enhancement, and water management is a clear example of accumulated landesque capital. As landesque capital, successive generations inherited a rich infrastructure imposed on the landscape. They were highly visible statements of the organization of labor by the community, and the ties between that community and the land. The people who created and maintained this landesque capital invested their labor and probably considered these improvements as aesthetic components of an orderly cultural landscape and highly visible ties to their lands and communities.

The remarkable preservation of the landscape and lack of overlay by other land-use strategies until the Colonial and Modern periods is further evidence of precolumbian landesque capital. The engineered landscape was used over a considerable period. Estimated labor for construction of the causeways and raised fields of the 65 km² Middle Apere Complex is 28,716 person-days and 638,500 person-days respectively (based on movement at a rate of 2.5 m^3 per person per 5-hour day; Appendix 2). No earthworks discussed here required large groups of workers to build any specific feature.

Determining whether these landscapes were built through accretion or were constructed all at once depends on other evidence. The overall design of the Middle Apere River cultural landscape was laid out from the beginning, including the orientation and the spacing of raised fields and causeways. Once established, the structure imposed on the landscape was maintained and fine-tuned as needed by later generations. Based on the repetitive, formal patterns of earthworks, we argue that most of the cultural landscape was intentionally designed rather than the unintentional result of long-term farming and settlement.

The Bolivian Amazon provides a valuable comparative case for other wetland-focused complex cultures in the Americas, including the savanna cultures of South America, the Aztecs and the Maya of Mesoamerica, and the Mississippians of North America. In these cultures, wetland environments were sought out rather than avoided. This case study shows that the concept of landesque capital can be understood through the archaeological record. The archaeological study of landesque capital also contributes to an understanding of precolumbian indigenous knowledge. This case shows how multigenerational local knowledge conserved, enhanced, and managed water, aquatic resources, and soils; facilitated and determined human movement and settlement; and ordered society through the engineering of the landscape. Archaeology is uniquely positioned to study the local and regional histories of particular landscapes and show how its inhabitants were able to sustain resources and populations over centuries and millennia through the creation of landesque capital.

Acknowledgments

The authors thank Wilma Winkler, project co-investigator, Marcello Canuto, Dante Angelo, Georgina Bocchietti, and Jaime Bocchietti who participated in the fieldwork of 1994. Freddy Arce provided overflights. Isora de Gutierrez, the owner of the Esperanza Ranch, and Gilberto Gutierrez, administrator of the Jerusalem Ranch, were gracious hosts. Members of the Community of Chawaya helped excavate and map causeways and raised fields. Aerial photographs and topographic maps were provided by the National Institute of Geography in La Paz. Global Land Cover Facility, Department of Geography (University of Maryland) and the USGS provided Landsat TM, Landsat ETM, DEM, and ASTER imagery. A National Science Foundation Grant (BSC-9212339) funded fieldwork and laboratory analysis. Oswaldo Rivera of the National Institute of Archaeology and the Ministry of Culture granted permits.

NOTES

1. Brookfield and colleagues originally used the landesque capital to explain land degradation whereby neglect of maintenance of infrastructure results in decline of agricultural productivity and environmental quality. In contrast, many contemporary studies including Brookfield (2001) emphasize the positive implications of the concept, as we do in this chapter.

2. Kenneth Lee (1979, 1995) proposed that earthworks of the Bolivian Amazon were used as temporary water enclosures for sustained agricultural production. Fields would be flooded for a period of years for the cultivation of water hyacinth (*tarope*) and other aquatic flora and fauna, which would later be incorporated into the soil as a green manure when the fields were drained. Enhancement of soils and resources through water management in integrated complexes of raised fields, causeways, canals, and lakes is documented archaeologically (CEAM 2003; Erickson 1980, 2000a, 2000c, 2008 for the Bolivian Amazon; Erickson 1980, 1993, 1996, 2006a; Flores and Paz 1987; Lennon 1982, 1983; Smith, Denevan, and Hamilton 1968:361 for the Andes) and experimentally (CEAM 2003; C. Pérez 1995; T. Pérez 1996; Saveedra 2006; Stab and Arce 2002).

3. The appropriateness of this approach is confirmed by the USGS Hydrosheds project, which is carrying out the same procedure using SRTM around the world (http://hydrosheds.cr.usgs.gov/).

12

Routes through the Landscape: A Comparative Approach

TIMOTHY EARLE

Landscapes are cultural artifacts, involving movement both real and imagined. Human groups build landscapes by everyday use and ceremonial activities, and *this volume* examines routes of movement in various New World cases from North America (Southwest, Mojave, and Missouri River basin), Central America (lowland Maya and two from Costa Rica), and South America (two from lowland Bolivia), and in one Old World case (northern Mesopotamia). We focus on the routes established by repeated movement and improved by markings and various facilities. The chapters provide diverse and rich operational models for investigating movement that include logistical movement for subsistence, social networks, ceremonial routes, and monumental expressions of ideology.

In this chapter, I take an explicitly comparative approach to understand landscapes of movement cross-culturally. Because the diverse case studies presented in this volume vary in form, socio-political organization, context, scale, function, technology, labor invested, and theoretical framework, I construct a working typology and cultural evolutionary model to explain this variation. The model assumes a continuum of societies and their associated modes of movement from simple to complex, local to interregional, and expedient to monumental. Although the differing scales of political organization in which they occur explain most variation in paths, trails, and roads, notable exceptions are found. Factors such as topography and hydrology, subsistence intensity, mobility and technology, and alternate sources of power also play a role. While the model predicts the presence of certain types of movement, we must also account for the absence of expected traits.

How can we understand the dramatic differences in movement documented by the diverse cases in this volume? What shaped the similar and different ways that routes of movement were made and used? The conference participants identified several important variables for comparison: the amount of construction, technology of transport, characteristics of terrain, ownership, function, form, scale, and meaning. Each participant described his or her case according to these variables, and these summaries are included in Appendix 2.

Routes of movement are ubiquitous, almost elemental to human existence, but contrasts begin to emerge from case to case. To find patterns, I took the case summaries and coded them according to political scale, types of routes, technology of transport, construction investment, subsistence intensity, the most important route functions, and major barriers to movement (Appendix 1). Using a working typology of routes (paths, trails, and roads), I examined their distribution and function according to the scales of political integration. Trails and paths are universal, providing routes for general movement both regional and local, but their specific character is highly variable according to terrain, technology, and subsistence. Hunter-gatherers, for example, have extensive seasonal movements for changing food resources, but their choice of canoes, horses, or foot affects the ways and modifications of the routes used. Formal roads are restricted to complex societies, and prior to modern democratic states, they were constructed as part of power strategies involving processional ceremonies, military domination, and information flow, and administration. Formal roads were, however, not universal to all or even most states and chiefdoms; extensive road construction suggests variation in social complexity. The rich variation in routes and their uses illustrated by this conference suggests important differences in how societies are organized that offers a productive direction for future research.

ROUTES AND FUNCTIONS OF MOVEMENT

At the beginning of our discussions, we agreed not to categorize routes of movement into types, because variation would certainly be continuous and multidimensional. Because they are not inherent or natural, such typologies obscure the diverse and contingent ways that human societies operate. I violate that agreement here and develop a working typology of paths, trails, and roads as a means to code the continuous variation represented (Table 12.1). Although some participants reject this working typology, I feel that the exercise is critical for sensitive comparative analysis. Routes of movement fall broadly along spectra representing differences in use, physical marking, and construction. These types represent a range of options that express elements of spatial scale (local and short distance vs. regional and long distance), numbers of travelers, amount of construction, projected permanency, and formality of routes. Most routes can have multiple functions including subsistence, trade, socializing, war, and ceremony.

Table 12.1 Heuristic Typology of Routes of Movement

ROUTES	SPATIAL EXTENT	TIMING	VOLUME	CONSTRUCTION	PRIMARY FUNCTIONS
Paths	local	every day	low	low	logistic
Trails	regional and long distance	seasonal and periodic	medium	low	logistic and ceremonial
Roads	local, regional, long distance	daily, seasonal, and periodic	high	high	ceremonial and military

Paths are local trodden ways, unmodified and unmarked except in difficult terrain as up cliff faces or across wet spots, or where built as streets through dense settlements or as public routes through agricultural facilities. They provide the routes of general movement between houses, fields, and other destinations (Snead, Chapter 3, this volume). Although often difficult to describe archaeologically, paths existed in all societies, serving the daily rounds of individuals to farm, to collect firewood and other necessities, to visit friends and neighbors, and to attend to personal rituals at household and community shrines. The functions of paths are essentially individual; they are made by individuals for personal movement. As patterns of household activities change, so will paths. Paths can be quite stable when constrained by specific landscape characteristics, but they should be considered no more permanent than the patterns of household movements. People usually improve paths only in minor ways, clearing vegetation as they walk along, removing a stone likely to trip the walker, placing steppingstones or brush across wet places, making openings across fences, and providing handholds up a cliff face.

Archaeologically, the recognition of paths is difficult because of their ephemeral nature. Openings in a wall or steps up a terrace may identify waypoints on paths, but paths are by definition without much physical modification or permanence. Many potential archaeological signatures would seem likely, and systematic work on paths could include intensive micro-sampling to describe patterns in soil chemistry (Robin 2002, 2006), micro-artifacts (Hodder and Cessford 2004), and the micro-morphology of compacted soils. In plowed fields, paths are largely unrecognizable.

Trails are regional and long-distance routes marked by repeated use, by signs such as blazes, cairns, and petroglyphs, and on maps. Because they involve movement by people often through unfamiliar foreign lands, trails must have those markings to aid direction. In their search for routes of least effort across broad terrain, animals clear early trails. After appropriation by humans, continued animal use helps to keep them open. The importance of trails to individuals depends on the extent of mobility in a society, being especially significant for nomadic groups of hunter-gatherers, pastoralists, or mixed economies. Some minimal improvements are made at steep or muddy spots. As endpoints of trail networks, entrance gates can be significant constructions on trails, limiting access of outsiders to a village, especially when warfare is prevalent. The nature and extent of trails reflect the particular constraints of a region's topography, periodic movement, and land tenure practices.

The functions of trails are essentially the same as for paths, but at greater distances. They are characteristically used for trade between resource-differentiated regions, and for seasonal movements, inter-group ceremonies, and sacred journeys. Trail use is both individual and group oriented, linking different local groups and separated resource areas. As individuals move greater distances from their home bases, their intimate knowledge of a route decreases and so marks are increasingly important. Because of their more extensive knowledge, frequent travelers can treat distant routes more like local paths, using their personal knowledge to find short cuts, alternative routes, and desirable diversions, such as a good place to rest.

The ceremonial uses of trails are well described in our case studies. For example, the O'odham song journeys describe a landscape of sacred journeys to obtain spiritual powers (Darling, Chapter 4, this volume), the Mandan/Hidatsa travel along their trails to the spiritually charged mountains (Zedeño, Hollenback, and Grinnell, Chapter 6, this volume), and the Hopi follow the Salt Lake trail for group ceremonies (Ferguson, Berlin, and Kuwanwisiwma, Chapter 2, this volume). As groups increase in size, the importance of ceremonies and their connection to trails may also increase (Earle 1991). As illustrated by the berms and petroglyphs at the approaches to pueblos in the Southwest (Snead, Chapter 3, this volume), marking entrances to villages can designate social and ceremonial transitions.

With historical documentation, trails are accessible for detailed study, but the lack of construction makes them difficult to document archaeologically. Trails are by definition marked, but the media used (stone, wood, or songs) determines the ability to recognize them. Use can create recognizable patterns, as entrenching with repeated passage or a linear spread of ceramics (probably to carry water) found along the trails of the western deserts (Darling, Chapter 4, this volume; Ferguson, Berlin, and Kuwanwisiwma, Chapter 2, this volume; Snead, Chapter 3, this volume). In Costa Rica, trails probably existed in both the regions described, but they were identified only in the Arenal, where runoff from frequent rains on its slopes eroded trenches along the routes connecting villages and cemeteries (Sheets, Chapter 8, this volume). Although plowing destroys trail patterns created by use, routine aerial photographic analysis and regional mapping often recognize the linear character of trails (Ferguson, Berlin, and Kuwanwisiwma, Chapter 2, this volume). Water-based movement, however, can be identified by site locations along streams and on islands accessible only by watercraft.

Roads are regional and sometimes long-distance routes built by chiefdoms and states. Roads have major capital improvements that include bridges, culverts, causeways, and pavements that facilitate and formalize movement. The amount of labor invested in roads can be quite substantial. In the two Bolivian cases, labor in road construction ranged from about 14,000 person-days for the causeways of the Middle Apere River complex (Erickson and Walker, Chapter 11, this volume) to 286,000 person-days for those of the Baures Hydraulic Complex (Erickson, Chapter 10, this volume) or, for the Maya, from 9,000 person-days for Sacbe T at the Xunantunich site to 93,000 person-days for Mendez Causeway at the Tikal site (Keller, Chapter 7, this volume). In these cases, however, the investment in roads is but a fraction of the broader investment in agricultural landscapes in Bolivia and monuments among the Maya. The capital improvements to roads are still striking and make them permanent, all-weather routes. They typically demonstrate some regional planning by a central authority or other social agents. Their construction makes them unambiguous, and their formal design directs the person on them. The straight white Maya causeways stood out brilliantly in the tropic green of day and black of night. As discussed later, however, some states and chiefdoms did not construct roads (Ur, Chapter 9, this volume), and that negative evidence is important to consider.

Roads have new functions, although they can serve family and social functions typical of the other routes. All roads considered by the conference are found in complex societies where roads radiate out from centers as in the chiefdoms of Costa Rica (Sheets, Chapter 8, this volume) and of lowland Bolivian (Erickson and Walker, Chapter 11, this volume; Erickson, Chapter 10, this volume), and the more complex Maya states. However, these roads do not appear to be constructed to facilitate economic systems; the largely local or low-volume movement of goods can be handled by trails or watercraft transport. Rather, roads are constructed to formalize routes of ceremonial movement, often only on a regional scale surrounding a ceremonial center. Erickson and Walker (Chapter 11, this volume) describe the causeways and canals of lowland Bolivia as connections and divisions in the landscape, essentially a social and political topography of relationships. The road networks surrounding the Chaco Canyon Great Houses provided a social map across the landscape of identity and connections (Snead, Chapter 3, this volume). In the Inka and Roman empires, roads were built to support the long-distance, logistical movement of armies under all weather conditions, in addition to moving goods and people.

Because of their built facilities and infrastructure, roads are relatively easy to document archaeologically. The linear form of roads can be recognized on aerial photographs and their facilities described and mapped on survey. What is required is a systematic regional approach as exemplified by Hyslop's (1984) study of Inka roads. Dating of roads can be difficult and requires identifying palimpsest, but excavations that target radiocarbon samples, documenting specific building styles and technologies, recognizing changing transport technology as with the introduction of carts, and analyzing spatial coherence can resolve many problems. In our conference, roads were described archaeologically for several chiefdoms and states, where their function and form was quite variable.

Three patterns exist in the evidence from our cases. First, all cases have both paths and trails, and few apparent changes are evident with the development of larger-scale societies. Small-scale societies have equally as elaborate networks of trails as do more complex societies. In all cases, the paths and trails provide for general-purpose movement involving subsistence, trade, socializing, warfare, and ritual journeys, and variation reflects the specific importance, terrain, and technology of travel.

Second, as the scale of political integration increases, so does the amount of labor investment in route construction (Table 12.2). Trails and pathways with lower labor investment are found in all societies, but formal roads, involving medium and large investment, are limited to chiefdoms and states. The most developed road systems are found in states like the Inka empire, but at least equally important, many chiefdoms and states, like the northern Mesopotamian example (Ur, Chapter 9, this volume) appear not to have constructed roads, and their absence is significant.

Table 12.2 Political Scale and Labor Investment

LABOR	FAMILY LEVEL	LOCAL GROUPS	CHIEFDOMS	STATES
Low	Mojave	O'odham, Hopi, Pajarito, Mandan, Arenal		Northern Mesopotamia
High			Cutris, Apere, Baures, Chaco Canyon	Maya
Very High				Inka

Third, the primary functions of routes of movement vary to some degree with the scale of political integration, a rough measure of social complexity (Johnson and Earle 2000). In family-level groups (tens of people), the main function of routes was logistical, everyday movement for subsistence, although trading and social and ritual activities were certainly important. With the formation of local groups (hundreds of people), logistical movements were still primary, but, as ceremonial activities became increasing important to the group, ceremonial treks and processions were frequently practiced (Ferguson, Berlin, and Kuwanwisiwma, Chapter 2, this volume). Additionally, warfare involved inter-group movement, as suggested by the phrase "going on the war path" (Zedeño, Hollenback, and Grinnell, Chapter 6, this volume). Ceremonial and military functions, however, became primary with the building of roads by chiefdoms with numbers in the low to mid thousands and states with populations of fifty thousand and above. The primary justification for most regional roads in chiefdoms appears to be ceremonial, while the Inka and Roman roads appear to have functioned militarily as a means to dominate expansive empires.

FACTORS DETERMINING THE NATURE OF ROUTES

Scales of political integration and their functions probably explain much cross-cultural variation in routes developed by humans. The primary conclusion of my earlier article on roads was that, as larger-scale political systems developed, new functions of integration were added and that these added functions changed the character of the routes of movement (Earle 1991). The development of routes, I argued, involves a progressive addition of paths for logistical local movement, trails for longer-distance movement often involving ceremonies, and roads developed by chiefdoms and states largely for ceremonial and military purposes. Although the basic logic still seems valid, the analysis of the cases from the Penn Museum Conference shows that other factors affect variation in routes that crosscut this laddered development. A consideration of these factors beyond an evolutionary typology provides a richer understanding of the potential options in human routes. Factors of particular importance appear to be topography and hydrology, subsistence intensity, mobility and technology, and alternative sources of power.

Topography and Hydrology

Natural topography is crucial. Reasonably, moderate and extreme barriers channel movement and result in more heavily used and developed routes of travel (Table 12.3). In cases with moderate barriers, movement was quite obviously with the grain of the topography down routes of least effort, although the technology of transport radically affected costs and thus routes chosen. Trails along ridges, for example, are low cost for those on foot, but much less so for carts. The Mandan traversed the open, grass-covered plains, following established routes along the rivers that were difficult to cross with their travois trains, which etched their repeated routes into the prairie sod (Zedeño, Hollenback, and Grinnell, Chapter 6, this volume). At particularly rough points of travel along trails, low-cost improvements were quickly built. Channeling of movement created particular routes of repeated use and changes in the technology created a palimpsest of routes braided through a landscape (Ferguson, Berlin, and Kuwanwisiwma, Chapter 2, this volume). On the Pajarito Plateau (Snead, Chapter 3, this volume), villages were placed defensively so that access was often up a steep rock face; simple stairs, steps, hand-and-toe holds, and ladders were built to ease access. Short stairs were often chiseled out on slopes of the major trails in the Southwest. Often, marking was required when routes were not clearly visible and distant travelers could lose their way. Through forests, trails were probably marked by blazes and bent trees, but these would not be visible archaeologically. In arid environments, marking was particularly important. Across the parched Mojave and Sonoran deserts where individuals and small groups traveled long distances through areas with limited water supplies, stone cairns, petroglyphs, and significant natural features marked routes linking permanent water sources, and these routes were memorized through elaborate song cycles (Fowler, Chapter 5, this volume; Darling, Chapter 4, this volume). Most local and regional movement by paths and trails would have been largely unimproved with braided and intersecting opportunistic routes.

Table 12.3 Topographic Barriers to Movement

TOPOGRAPHIC BARRIERS	CASES
Extreme	Apere, Baures, Inka
Moderate	Mojave, O'odham, Hopi, Pajarito, Mandan, Maya
Minor	Arenal, Cutris, Chaco Canyon, Northern Mesopotamia

In areas with more extreme barriers to movement, such as inundated landscapes, paths and trails could be constructed. In the Neolithic, for example, wooden walkways were built across the marshy fens of England to improve paths around the communities of local groups (Coles and Coles 1986). In the seasonally inundated lowlands of Bolivia, families visiting each other and going to their fields built pathways and canals into the locally engineered agricultural field systems to allow for movement (Erickson, Chapter 10, this volume; Erickson and Walker, Chapter 11, this volume). On the other extreme, where water routes existed, as in the American Northeast or Amazonia, river systems and lakes guided movement by canoe without the need for marking or improving the routes.

In conclusion, topographic conditions determine to some degree the amount that routes, both local and regional, were marked and improved. With more extreme barriers, movement was more routinized and improvements likely. Although the amount of improvement appears to increase with more complex societies, such factors as topography complicate evolutionary trends.

Subsistence Intensity, Mobility, and Technology

Under environmental conditions where improvements to routes were sensible, the factors determining improvements appear to have been subsistence intensity, mobility, and the technology of movement. As population densities grew and subsistence intensification increased, long-range mobility for individuals and groups apparently decreased, as territorial divisions between more densely packed local groups limited movement. At the same time, however, an increase in the total numbers of people moving to trade and socialize would have increased, resulting in remarkably little change in the observed pattern of paths and trails. Trail systems and technologies of movement were as well developed in low-density as in high-density societies, prior to the construction by states of roads and harbors. The technologies of transport considered by the conference included walking, riding animals dragging frames and carts, and water crafts. Particular technologies affect overall mobility and the need to improve routes of travel in contrasting ways (Table 12.4). Thus canoes or horse-drawn frames result in the use of very different types of routes for seasonal movement.

Table 12.4 Technology of Transport and Amount of Landscape Modification

LANDSCAPE MODIFICATION	TECHNOLOGY OF TRANSPORT
None	canoes on open water
Little	walking
Some	horses (travois), litters, canoe canals

Low-density populations were typically all mobile, maintaining seasonal rounds to exploit changing food availability, to trade, and to visit with dispersed relatives. Movement was extensive, with long-distance movement on foot but also with special technologies that aided transport. The Mojave were low-density, nomadic foragers, who traveled on foot (often running) across a broad and open landscape with well-marked trails (Fowler, Chapter

5, this volume). These trails allowed movement through the year to make use of seasonal, dispersed resources, to visit camp to camp, and to gather for periodic ceremonies. The O'odham were low-density horticulturalists, who created similar trails across the Sonoran Desert to join with other communities, to visit hunting lands, to fight, and to collect stone and other special resources found only in specific locations (Darling, Chapter 4, this volume). O'odham carrying baskets aided the movement of foods and other goods across substantial distances. The Mandan were fairly low density horticulturalists settled along rivers of the Plains, and their historical adoption of horses probably increased significantly their seasonal mobility. They used a shared network of trails along the major rivers, as they moved seasonally to hunt, to trade at special rendezvous places, to raid horses from neighboring groups, and to gather for ceremony (Zedeño, Hollenback, and Grinnell, Chapter 6, this volume). Their use of travois frames aided the transport of substantial household goods across the open prairies and thus made mobile seasonal settlements possible. In most circumstances, the Mandan avoided crossing rivers except at natural fords, but when necessary they used small skin bullboats for such passage. Although not covered in the session's papers, we discussed the extensive use of watercraft through the northeastern woods of North America. Where streams, lakes, and the sea interlaced a landscape, long-distance movement was often by canoe, permitting high mobility with little route modification.

Populations of moderate density may have more restricted movements, but increased population density meant that movement along trails was substantial, and broad web-like networks connected many communities and other destinations. The pueblo groups in the Southwest had extensive systems of trails that mapped out daily movements, intercommunity visiting, and special ceremonial journeys to shrines. For example, hundreds of kilometers were traveled ceremonially on the Salt Trail from the three mesas to Zuni Salt Lake (Ferguson, Berlin, and Kuwanwisiwma, Chapter 2, this volume). On open, friable stone surfaces, the routes were clearly worn, and at specific awkward locations, travelers improved trails with simple changes, like carving a few steps or clearing stones (Snead, Chapter 3, this volume). In the Arenal area of Costa Rica, the repeated movement of people between local villages and their cemeteries wore down trails that became deeply trenched by erosion (Sheets, Chapter 8, this volume). Changing technology of movement has resulted in some alteration to trails in traditional societies. For North America, Zedeño and colleagues (Chapter 6, this volume) stressed that, with the adoption of horses, trails had to be less steep and improved to lessen the chance of injury. Throughout the Southwest, the adoption of burros and then mechanized vehicles for travel required different slopes and surfaces, and thus groups relocated routes and improved particular spots (Ferguson, Berlin, and Kuwanwisi-wma, Chapter 2, this volume).

High-density populations often constructed engineered landscapes with new property relationships that strongly limited movement. In lowland Bolivia, the local farmers built massive raised-field complexes with flood control devices (Erickson, Chapter 10, this volume; Erickson and Walker, Chapter 11, this volume), and within these facilities, they built paths to allow daily, low-cost movement through the fields. As another example of an engineered landscape with built paths, Hawaiian irrigation complexes incorporated earthen bunds that both impounded water for the taro fields and created paths through the fields to individual farmer's holdings (Earle 1978). In such situations, paths and trails could encourage significant building of routes that became heavily used and channeled along linear public spaces. The construction of urban streets illustrates this process, and the same logic may apply to the agricultural fields surrounding early cities in northern Mesopotamia. Here each town or city was surrounded by deeply entrenched, radiating routes (Ur, Chapter 9, this volume). These road-like features were not constructed, except perhaps for some embankment defining their edges along owned fields.

The main conclusion is that agricultural intensification increased the engineering of landscapes and the owned division of space. Property rights thus resulted in barriers to movement, resulting in the highly routinized movement also seen with topographic barriers. In the extremes, paths can take on many of the characteristics of constructed roadways, although we believe them to have been created by families without hierarchical direction. The technology of transport further affected to some degree the routes developed, and the contrast between water- and land-based technologies was probably most important.

Alternative Sources of Power

The emergence of chiefdoms and states is based on the ability to control three power sources: ideological, military, and economic (Earle 1997), and these complex societies appear often to have invested considerable labor in the construction of roads as part of these power strategies (Table 12.5). The most widespread use of roads in early complex societies appears to have been ideological. Especially among chiefdoms, constructed roads appear to have functioned primarily for ceremonial occasions that would have legitimized central authority. They were associated with political centers, where the roads formalized radial and circular patterns of movement to materialize the regional social order (DeMarrais, Castillo, and Earle 1996). In lowland Bolivia, roads were part of ceremonial complexes that may have supported the local chiefdoms, in addition to community identification and unity (Erickson, Chapter 10, this volume; Erickson and Walker, Chapter 11, this volume). From ceremonial centers built on higher ground, broad causeways radiated to connect smaller islands in the seasonally inundated savanna of the Baures Hydraulic Complex. These causeways required substantial labor investments to form a processional stage for ceremonies that probably mapped the political system. At centers of the Cutris chiefdom in Costa Rica, leaders apparently organized the construction of roads that averaged 9 km long and ranged from 6 m wide and 2 m deep over most of their length to 40 m wide and 5 m deep for the last kilometer. These roads were strong statements, permanently altering the landscape as ceremonial stages of regional movement (Sheets, Chapter 8, this volume). In the American Southwest, most societies were relatively egalitarian and the routes of movement, although used ceremonially, were minimally formalized (Snead, Chapter 3, this volume; Ferguson, Berlin, and Kuwanwisiwma, Chapter 2, this volume). More complex societies such as chiefdoms, however, did emerge in two contexts: the Chaco Canyon phenomenon in northern New Mexico and the Hohokam of southern Arizona. Roads similar to those of the Cutris chiefdom have been described for the Chaco Canyon chiefdoms. Although less integrated than originally thought, the roads surely defined repeated routes for ceremonial events focused on the Great Houses (Vivian 1997a, 1997b).

Table 12.5 Power Functions of Roads

POWER FUNCTIONS	CHIEFDOMS	STATES
Ceremonial	Cutris, Apere, Baures, Chaco Canyon	Maya
Military		Inka and perhaps Maya
Economic	None	Northern Mesopotamia

Ceremonial use of roads is also recorded for some states. Around most Maya ceremonial/political centers, radiating causeways defined ceremonial directions of movement. The Mendez Causeway at the site of Tikal was 50 m wide, and the smaller roads at the site of Xunantunich were still up to 19 m wide, constructed in a single planned event (Keller, Chapter 7, this volume). The incline of the ramps on these routes of movement suggests that key people were carried on litters. Hyslop (1984) suggests that a primary significance of the Inka road system was to provide an ideological map of the empire in which all regions were interconnected. Such roads as those of the Cutris chiefdom or the Maya states were major capital investments to the landscape. Given that all transport was based on foot or litter, the width and scale of such routes were to impress; no economic or military use could justify widths greater than a few meters.

Not all chiefdoms or states, however, marked the landscape monumentally with ceremonial roads. Our consideration of the ceremonial roads of Chaco Canyon must be compared to those of the equally or more complex Hohokam chiefdoms. Despite extensive regional fieldwork involving aerial photography, no evidence exists that the Hohokam built major roads. Although they constructed an engineered landscape of irrigation and central settlements requiring considerable organization and labor, roads were not important. The Hohokam most certainly had important ceremonial events, but ceremonial processions were apparently not significant. The specific spatial layout of a complex society may result in different use of ceremonial movement and the development of associated road systems. Roads may be developed in the chiefdoms and states in which population is more spread out, such that structural integration must be realized. Roads can be seen as constructed by chiefs and kings in elaborate schemes of legitimization; but chiefdoms need not construct roads, because the particular strategies of power used are themselves highly variable and opportunistic.

The military represents an alternative source of power, especially with the establishment of states. Despite extensive information on warfare in chiefdoms, little evidence exists that roads were built as a means to develop military control. Warfare was still quite small scale, and warriors could move along the regular network of trails not unlike the Mandan used theirs. The use of chariots in Bronze Age Mycenaean city-states may have required the building of some roads (Jansen 2001). States, however, clearly developed roads as a means to move troops. I wonder whether the infrequent long causeways between major Maya centers may have served to guarantee military domination. Probably the best-known example of the importance of military roads was the Roman Empire, where an extensive, integrated, and all-weather system was built to allow the rapid deployment of troops. For the Inka Empire, the roads often required massive labor investments, with terraced and paved routes a meter or two in width, suspension bridges across mountain gorges, and causeways across wet lands (Hyslop 1984). The road system was integrated for large stretches, providing ease of movement for administrators and commanders and for military forces to quell rebellion. The contemporary Aztec Empire was quite different. In the Basin of Mexico, the Aztec constructed wide stone causeways as part of their engineered landscapes for intensive wetland farming, but outside the Basin, no major road system was constructed, despite the fact that the Empire depended on its military's ability to suppress rebellious regions. The Inka-Aztec contrast, like the Chaco-Hohokam contrast, suggests that significant variation existed for the institutionalization of complex societies, and that the nature of movement may be one of the most important factors to consider.

The third major source of power is economic, but roads probably were *not* built for economic integration prior to the establishment of mercantile states. As long as transport was primarily by foot, horses, or watercraft, goods could be moved without the major improvements associated with roads. Simply stated, few economies of scale existed for moving goods that would justify major capital investments. Where possible, goods would be moved more cheaply by water, and these natural routes required little alteration prior to the increased scale of shipping in the industrial age. Among the northern Mesopotamian city-states, radiating road-like trails provided most movement through the highly intensified landscapes, and people moved regionally or long distances from town to town (Ur, Chapter 9, this volume). For the Aztec, for example, Hassig (1991) reminds us that simple trails allowed individuals carrying burdens to pass each other, and such trails were really all that was needed to move substantial amounts of goods. The use of beasts of burden in caravans served long-distance Asian traders and the Inka state. Caravans created a need to select routes with less slope than possible for walking, but major improvements required for economic exchange were limited to occasional bridges and some harbor facilities. The economy as a source of power simply did not require the development of roads prior to the much higher volumes of trade associated with integrated markets.

As a working hypothesis, roads probably served no necessary function in political economies of emergent complex societies.

My main conclusion is that roads were built by some chiefdoms and states largely as strategies to concentrate power. Chiefdoms that built roads used them primarily for ceremonial occasions that presumably materialized the political order. Some states also used roads ceremonially, but large states and empires could also develop roads largely for military uses. Many chiefdoms and states, however, did not build roads, and we can presume that alternative sources of power were relied on.

CONCLUSION

In an early publication, I suggested that routes of movement could be understood in an evolutionary framework (Earle 1991:14–15), and this seems still to be true. Paths and trails characterize all societies, but formal roads with substantial labor investment in construction characterize only chiefdoms and states. Roads are special routes, augmenting paths and trails that served normal functions of subsistence, trade, and social visiting. As I suggested then, the developments of roads were not justified on economic grounds, because the movement of goods was relatively small scale and would involve only the individual person or small group who could walk single file on a simple trail. Rather, roads were constructed under the guidance of a ruling segment to serve political purposes such as legitimating ceremonies and military movements.

Although my 1991 model captured some key variation that was supported by the cases discussed at the present seminar, it failed to account for the substantial variation presented in this volume. Another problem with the original model is that it predicted only the *presence* of paths, trails, and roads, but not their absence. Why for example are roads important in many chiefdoms and states, but absent in others? Roads are not a trait that can identify a level of complexity, but rather appear to reflect specific sources of power in complex societies. Since paths and trails, and not roads, served to move most goods, chiefdoms and states that emphasized economic sources of power need not construct roads. The contrast between the Chaco Canyon and Hohokam chiefdoms in terms of the development of roads similarly illustrates that power strategies apparently emphasized roads in one situation but not another; exchange was extensive in Hohokam society, although roads were not. Roads were advanced in the Inka Empire, which was dependent on military and ideological sources of power, but in the Aztec empire, dependent on long-distance tribute and local markets, roads were much less developed. Political factors determined the types of routes developed, complicated by environmental conditions, intensification, property rights, and transport technology. Although what we think of as roads appear always to be built by complex political systems, individual families and local groups improve routes of movement under specific conditions, including the selection of locations for defense and the construction of engineered landscapes.

Paths, trails, and roads are the physical imprint of repeated economic and sociopolitical interaction and a material model for proper order (Earle 1991:10). Routes capture the different ways that movement is significant and becomes etched in the landscape. Examination of variation in routes of movement shows the alternative ways that societies operate and change under contrasting sociopolitical and environmental conditions. The simplest lessons from the conference discussions are that routes of movement are significant, that routine methods should be developed to describe and analyze them, and that the analysis of variation in routes offers great insight into the essence of human societies and their evolution.

Appendix 1

Coding of the Cases of Paths, Trails, and Roads Discussed in the Conference "Landscapes of Movement: Trails, Paths, and Roads in Anthropological Perspective"

TIMOTHY EARLE

I coded the descriptions of the landscapes of movement for each case in the volume, augmented by Chaco (Vivian 1997a, 1997b) and Inka (Hyslop 1984) roads. Variables include political scale, types of routes, technology of transport, construction investment, subsistence intensity, route functions, and barriers to movement.

Political scale ranges from family-level societies with polities in the tens, local groups in the hundreds, chiefdoms in the low and mid-thousands, to states above 50,000 subjects (Johnson and Earle 2000).

Types of routes are paths, trails, and roads as described in each chapter and defined in Chapter 12. Since paths are assumed universal but are hard to recognize archaeologically, I do not include them here. Trails can also be assumed to exist in all societies.

Technology of transport includes situations with no modification (canoes on open water), little modification (walking), and some modification (horses with travois, ramps for litters, and canoe canals).

Construction investment is measured by labor invested in route facilities within a political region and ranges from low, representing tens of person-days (stair steps, simple bridges, and the like), to high, representing thousands of person-days (canoe paths), to very high, representing millions of person-days (stone causeways, earthen causeways, and canals).

Subsistence intensity is ranked as low (hunting and gathering), medium (horticulture), and high (permanent agriculture).

Route functions are subjective categories based on those most emphasized in each chapter, including logistical, trade, ceremonial, social, and military.

Barriers to movement are described as extreme (inundation, broken topography), moderate (mountains, rivers, and deserts), and low (rolling uplands).

Family-level Groups (polity sizes in the tens)

Mojave (Fowler, Chapter 5): trails; technology, foot; construction, low; subsistence intensity, low; most important function, logistical; barriers, water availability.

Local Groups (polity sizes in the hundreds)

O'odham (Darling, Chapter 4): trails; technology, foot; construction, low; subsistence intensity, low to moderate; most important function, logistical; barriers, water availability.

Pajarito Plateau (Snead, Chapter 3): trails; technology, foot; construction, low; subsistence intensity, low to moderate; most important functions, logistical and ceremonial; barriers, broken terrain.

Hopi (Ferguson, Berlin, and Kuwanwisiwma, Chapter 2): trails; technology, foot and, historically, burros; construction, low; subsistence intensity, low to moderate; most important functions, logistical and ceremonial; barriers, water availability and broken terrain.

Mandan and Hidatsa (Zedeño, Hollenback, and Grinnell, Chapter 6): trails; technology, foot, horse with travois, and small skin boats; construction, low; subsistence intensity, low to moderate; most important functions, logistical, trade, and ceremonial; barriers, rivers.

Arenal (Sheets, Chapter 8): trails; technology, foot; construction, low; subsistence intensity, low; most important function, ceremonial; barriers, none.

Chiefdoms (polity sizes in the low and mid-thousands)

Cutris Chiefdom (Sheets, Chapter 8): roads; technology, foot; construction, medium; subsistence intensity, medium; most important function, ceremonial; barriers, none.

Baures Hydraulic Complex (Erickson, Chapter 10): paths, trails, and roads; technology, foot and canoe; construction, high; subsistence intensity, high; most important functions, logistical, social, and ceremonial; barriers, inundated environment.

Apere River Complex (Erickson and Walker, Chapter 11): paths, trails, and roads; technology, foot and canoe; construction, high; subsistence intensity, high; most important functions, logistical and ceremonial; barriers, inundated environment.

Chaco Canyon (Vivian 1997a, 1997b; Snead, Chapter 3): roads; technology, foot; construction, medium; subsistence intensity, medium; most important function, ceremonial; barriers, water availability.

States (polity sizes above 50,000)

Northern Mesopotamia (Ur, Chapter 9): paths; technology, foot and animal carts; construction, low; subsistence intensity, high; most important function, logistical; barriers, property rights.

Maya (Xunantunich; Keller, Chapter 7): roads; technology, foot and litters; construction, medium; subsistence intensity, high; most important function, ceremonial; barriers, none.

Inka (Hyslop 1984): roads; technology, foot, litters, and llama caravans; construction, high; subsistence intensity, high; most important function, military; barriers, broken terrain and rivers.

Appendix 2

Comparative Variables for Trails, Paths, and Roads

In the course of the conference, the participants agreed to key variables defining landscapes of movement in their individual studies for comparative purposes. The variables are:

1. Amount of construction/over what time
2. Technology of movement
3. Characteristics of terrain
4. Points/places of access (terminal points, resources, facilities, shrines)
5. Ownership/access/stewardship
6. Functions
7. Form/network organization
8. Scale
9. Meaning

The responses of the authors are provided below in chapter order.

HOPI (ARIZONA/NEW MEXICO)
T. J. Ferguson, G. Lennis Berlin, and Leigh J. Kuwanwisiwma

Amount of construction/over what time

Hopi trails are generally unconstructed linear features. They are formed by use rather than engineered construction projects. There may be some clearing of rocks out of a pathway, but the traces we find archaeologically appear to have been worn into the earth by virtue of walking or traveling along a route. The period of trail formation is difficult to determine archaeologically but entails centuries, probably 500 to 1000 years.

Technology of movement

Hopi trails started out as pedestrian paths. After the adoption of livestock in the 17th century, Hopis started using burros to travel the Salt Trails to the Grand Canyon and Zuni Salt Lake. This led to some minor changes in routes as trails and roads for pack animals and wheeled vehicles needed increasingly wider tracks with more gradual gradients and curves to avoid breaks in topographical features. In the 19th and early 20th centuries, wagons were used on some portions of the Salt Trails between villages. In the 20th century, cars and trucks were used as modes of transportation on some portions of the Salt Trails, as well as other segments in the regional trail network. Use of motorized vehicles creates primitive, unconstructed "two-track" roads (i.e., linear features with a track for right and left wheels). Eventually many trails were incorporated into improved dirt roads, paved highways, and interstate highways.

Characteristics of terrain

Hopi trails are situated on the Colorado Plateau of the Southwestern United States. Topography includes mesas, buttes, and valley floors. Trails primarily follow the drainages of valley floors but in places they run over mesa tops and through hilly sections. Vegetation is primarily desert scrubland and pinyon-juniper woodland, although some trails run through Ponderosa pine forest. The desert terrain is relatively dry and generally sparsely vegetated but during the rainy season mud bogs can create impediments to travel. Avoiding muddy sections is one process by which parallel tracks are created in trail systems.

Points/places of access

Hopi trails originate in villages on the tops of the Hopi Mesas. The destinations of trails include shrines and resource collection areas (one and the same in the case of salt sources), as well as the villages and settlements of other tribes with whom the Hopis traded or bartered. Some trails lead to mountain tops where there are shrines and resources. Water is essential for spiritual and physical well-being (for both people and livestock), so Hopi trails generally run by or near springs. Hopi trails are associated with numerous shrines and offering places along their route, used for ritual deposits and prayers during journeys. The Hopi Salt Trail to the Grand Canyon has one shrine containing thousands of petroglyphs pecked as a ritual activity by individuals visiting the Tutuveni shrine. Trails are also marked with markers (cairns, distinctive rocks) used to sight the route.

Ownership/access/stewardship

Many trails were multi-functional. Segments of the Salt Trail to the Grand Canyon were widely used for travel between villages (e.g., Oravyi and Munqapi). Other, more outlying segments of the Salt Trail were used primarily during religious pilgrimages. The Hopis maintain spiritual stewardship over their trails, and this spiritual component to trails becomes increasingly important as trails fall out of active use. Ownership of trails in terms of property rights and exclusive land tenure has evolved over time. In the ancient past, many trails were used by multiple social and ethnic groups. For instance, the trails between Hopi and Havasupai, and Hopi and Zuni, were used by both tribes connected to them. Interestingly, the Hopi-Zuni trail is called the Zuni Trail at Hopi, and the Hopi Trail at Zuni, reflecting the ultimate destination. A similar situation pertains to the Havasupai-Hopi trail connecting the Hopi villages with the Havasupai villages in Cataract Canyon. Today, one of the principal reasons why pedestrian trails fall out of use is that they run across jurisdictions where Hopi has been excluded. As land went from the public domain into private ownership, the construction of fences made it difficult to continue to use many pedestrian trails and pack trails.

Functions

The primary functions of Hopi trails were utilitarian (access and transport of resources, trading expeditions) and ritual (access to shrines and sacred areas).

Form/network organization

The network organization of the Hopi trail system was an irregular, web-like grid shaped by topography and multiple destinations. Many trails had spurs that connected one trail with other trails leading to other destinations. For instance, the Hopi trail to the Zuni Salt Lake had several different routes that could be followed to go directly to the lake, to travel to Zuni Pueblo during a journey to or from the lake, or to go to other shrine locations downstream of the lake.

Scale

The scale of the Hopi trail system is regional in scope. The straight-line distance from Third Mesa to the Salt Mine in the Grand Canyon is 112 km; from First Mesa to the Zuni Salt Lake is 220 km; from the Grand Canyon to Zuni Salt Lake is 336 km. The actual length of the trails is longer due to curving segments. Shorter trail segments exist between the Hopi villages and nearby sites (farms, sheep camps, wood hauling areas) but these are not included in our study.

Meaning

The most ancient trails are said to have been established by spiritual beings to connect Hopi villages with religious shrines and places of cultural importance. For example, the Hopi Salt Trail to the Grand Canyon is said to have been established by the Pöqangwnatupkom (Twin Brothers) when Salt Woman moved from the Hopi Mesas to Öngtupqa (Salt Canyon). After this trail was established, generations of Hopi men used the route during pilgrimages to collect salt and conduct rituals in the Grand Canyon (Bartlett 1940).

Trails embody spiritual values that complement their physical imprint on the ground. The cultural importance of trails is related to the ritual activities and shrines associated with them. Hopi depictions of trails provide cognitive maps that visualize the landmarks encountered during travel and the ritual activities undertaken during the journey (see Figure 2.1).

Trails are important to the Hopi people because they have religious associations. Regional trails are like umbilical cords that spiritually link Hopi villages with outlying shrines and sacred features on the landscape. The trails are revered because they physically connect the Hopi people with these shrines and the deities they are associated with, such as the Pöqangwnatupkom (Twin Brothers) and Öng.wùuti (Salt Woman). Closer to home, within the Hopi villages, trails and pathways connect plazas and kivas to other places where ritual activities are conducted. The sacredness of religious pilgrimages and ceremonial routes is constant, even though the ritual use of these trails may be periodic. Some trails located near the villages are used daily for prosaic activities, yet these pathways always retain their religious significance, even though this significance may only be visible to the public when it is in ritual use.

Trails have cultural significance because they were historically used by Hopi ancestors. Many are associated with the ancient routes followed by clans when they migrated to the Hopi Mesas. Therefore, trails, like other ancestral sites, are considered to be monuments on the land that warrant preservation so these "footprints" can be used to teach young Hopi people about their cultural heritage.

Many trails lead to ancestral villages that connect past and present Hopi use of the landscape. Artifact scatters are often found along trail networks, as are temporary shelters, camps, and resting areas. *Tutuveni* (petroglyphs) are also frequently found in association with trails. Many of these petroglyphs have semiotic functions marking the past use of an area by Hopi clans.

ANCESTRAL PUEBLO (PAJARITO PLATEAU)
James E. Snead

Amount of construction/over what time

The Pajarito trails are largely produced by foot traffic alone. The narrow width and straight profile of some of these erosional features are probably indications of intentional modification, but this has not been demonstrated. Some constructed features, such as hand-and-toe holds, steps, stairs, and berms, are associated with trails in particular instances. In relatively rare cases cairns, trail markers (usually petroglyphs), and walls perpendicular to the trail route are also present. Since significant portions of these trails would have run across mesa tops or valley bottoms where they cannot currently be recognized and where we have no evidence of associated features, the overall level of formality was low.

The time investment in the construction of features along the Pajarito trails is difficult to estimate. Most hand-and-toe holds could probably have been pecked out over the course of a few hours; steps would have taken a few days; stairs, several days/weeks depending on scale and size of work crew. The fact that several stairs have been repeatedly reconstructed adds to the labor investment calculation.

Technology of movement

Movement along the Pajarito trails was entirely by individuals walking on foot in file. No draft animals were employed nor is there evidence of multiple individuals traveling parallel except possibly in the case of some of the major stairs. Burdens would have been carried by individuals either in baskets or on backs. Running is another possible option, given the cultural role of running in Pueblo society, but this cannot be demonstrated archaeologically.

Characteristics of terrain

The terrain of the Pajarito Plateau consists of relatively flat, steep-sided potreros or mesas separated by valleys and canyons of variable width and depth. Much of the travel "with" the grain of the land ran along the tops of the potreros, descending into the canyons only when necessary. Travel "across" the grain of the land climbed up and down the canyon sides. Since many canyons were bounded by sheer cliffs, movement was channeled toward passable topography, although in some cases notably steep slopes were climbed via stairs or (apparently) ladders. Otherwise the environment consisted of open woodland and grassland that presented few barriers to movement.

Points/places of access

Local Pajarito trails connect various elements of the local community together, such as residences, storage areas, and fields. Intermediate-scale trails run to outlying areas of these communities, such as shrines. The long-distance Pajarito trails typically link different environmental zones. During some time periods regional trails also connected communities with each other. Restricted points of access were rare and are typically associated with the late precolumbian era, when particular entry points into community centers were designated.

Ownership/access/stewardship

There is little direct evidence for ownership of the Pajarito trails. In some cases, however, the presence of petroglyph "trail markers" has been taken as identifying owners of nearby fields or facilities, and the "gateway trails" associated with community houses also appear to denote local identity, perhaps related to the trails themselves. Ethnographically, trails have names that usually pertain to their destinations rather than anything suggesting ownership. The construction of guard pueblos at some of the major trail junctions in the late precolumbian period seems to have been an attempt to monitor or even block traffic along the trails. Ethnohistorical sources suggest that at least one of these guard pueblos was inhabited by "trail keepers" whose responsibilities were undefined. Maintenance of the trails, where required, was probably the responsibility of adjacent communities.

Functions

The Pajarito trails served to move individuals and small groups across the landscape. At the local scale people conducted their daily routines; intermediate-scale trails provided access to places that were relatively nearby but visited only occasionally; the regional trails provided access to more remote areas for hunting, procurement of resources such as tool stone or other raw commodities, or provided pathways along which people carried goods as items of trade or exchange. Visits to relatives or allies would also have been conducted along the regional pathways, and it is also presumed that the same trails carried war bands in times of conflict.

Form/network organization

Local-level trails on the Pajarito are redundant in character, reflecting opportunistic patterns of use. Mid-scale trails were constructed as needed and thus conform to no clear pattern. The regional trails typically reflect the logic of terrain and are found where topography allows travel. This network can be visualized as a "ladder" with a single post: one major north-south route traversing the different potreros, each of which is also crossed by a perpendicular trail running east-west. The initial Ancestral Pueblo communities were placed along these paths. In late precolumbian times the network shifted in response to a reorganization of the settlement, with the original trails remaining in use but linked to the new communities by new feeder paths.

Scale

Local-level Pajarito trails represent dense, redundant networks surrounding the community houses. In Tsankawi, the only systematically documented case, the total length of the many trails running along the mesa close to the community house is nearly 8 km. The idiosyncrasy of the subregional trails makes it difficult to estimate their scale. Total length of the major regional trails on the Pajarito Plateau cannot yet be calculated, but distances in the hundreds of kilometers are likely.

Meaning

Trail-related ethnography in the Eastern Pueblos is limited. The general interest that modern Pueblo people have concerning trails, however, is a sign of their cultural importance. I have argued that as long-term trail use inscribed these features into the landscape they were invested with meaning in association with the broader landscape. To a certain extent this meaning could be created and manipulated with associated features, stairs, etc., but memory must also have been a critical element.

O'ODHAM TRAILS (SOUTHERN ARIZONA)
J. Andrew Darling

Amount of construction/over what time

Trails are the product of continuous foot travel across preexisting game trails, natural corridors between resource areas (such as water sources), or along established routes of travel. Most trails are created through repeated usage. In most cases trails consist of linear tracks worn into the desert pavement. Over time rocks and debris are gradually pushed to the side creating informal low berms. Trails generally range between 30 and 50 cm wide with occasional tracks paralleling the main trail. In some instances evidence for the casual clearance of stones and debris by travelers has been noted. Geographic and environmental considerations also determine the location and appearance of trails. In the O'odham-Hohokam region of the arid Southwest, there is a great deal of continuity in trail use from prehistoric to historic periods. Unusually good preservation of trails in stable desert pavement means that numerous trail segments are preserved, producing criss-crossing arrangements or numerous parallel tracks following a similar route.

Technology of movement

Trails in the arid Southwest are generally footpaths. During the early contact period, explorers and trappers relied upon the preexisting Native American infrastructure, trails, and guides in order to access unexplored territory. In effect the preexisting system was expropriated and eventually adapted to the European technological requirements for wagons and livestock. I have not studied the issue of the technology of movement extensively, although the Yumans and the Pimans were well known for their carrying baskets and such devices are portrayed on Hohokam pottery as well. Ceramics found along trails appear more often to be jars or ollas suggesting that water was often carried. One account of travel among the Yumans mentions numerous burnt-out torches along trails suggesting that travel at night through the desert was not uncommon, particularly during hot summers.

I propose that trail infrastructure includes certain aspects of O'odham song culture, which generally features journeys as a major component, that serve to generate and maintain a shared sense of geography or cognitive space, not only identifying places but the geographic relationships between them. This constitutes a form of geographic information processing, which will determine how people make decisions about routes and trail practice.

Characteristics of terrain

O'odham trails are situated in an arid desert environment below the Mogollon Rim, roughly between 1000 and 5000 ft above sea level in Arizona, Sonora, Nevada, and California, characterized by strips of riverine vegetation, desert scrub, and stands of saguaro in the uplands. Trails tend to crosscut river courses by crossing through mountain passes. Travelers must thus carry water, but trails also link up water sources such as streams and tanks. Many trails run across or perpendicular to biotic or environmental zones as they pass from lowland valley to foothills to mountain passes and back.

Points/places of access

Trails, particularly as can be gathered from the Oriole Songs and verified on the ground, link up sacred mountains, rock art sites, and trail shrines. Songs are about the facilities (places), not about the trails themselves. Other trails do exist that appear to be oriented more towards interconnecting settlements or accessing resource zones. Long-distance journeys for warfare also seem to follow routes similar to ceremonial journeys expressed in songs and may generally bypass settlements. Terminal points are not apparent since in the songs, the journey seems to reflect the cycle or passage of the sun and moon. Secular journeys however may connect several trail segments. Any cross-country trail could be used in general at any time for different functions and it is the purpose of the trip that influenced what the itinerary would be and how decisions about travel were made.

Ownership/access/stewardship

Trails do not seem to be owned but routes of travel reflect regional and cultural differences. The Akimel O'odham (River or Northern Pima) may have had their own route for the sacred Salt Journey to the Sonoran Coast that differed from the Salt Journey undertaken by the Tohono O'odham (Papago). Similarly, trails through the Santan Mountains were also used by Apaches on raids against Pima settlements in the Gila River Valley.

Functions

O'odham trail functions were diverse. Functions such as warfare, sacred journeys, and resource acquisition would be best suited to certain trails or itineraries and not others. I suggest that travelers referenced where they were going with the body of geographic knowledge encoded in song culture and stories.

Form/network organization

Trail networks appear to be structured by the location of water resources, settlements, and mountain passes at which trails tend to converge in a somewhat dendritic fashion. Some trails used for warfare or long journeys may bypass settlements rather than access each nearest settlement on the way.

Scale

Trail networks in the arid Southwest are regional in scale and appear to crosscut ethnic and linguistic boundaries separating the Pima and the Yuma. Song journeys suggest that travel up to 450–500 km was not unusual. Oriole Song details seem to indicate that people are most familiar with places closest to home so there are more songs about these locations, but as the traveler in the mythic journey gets farther away, distance between places (and individual songs about each place or step in the journey) increases. In general, however, distance does not seem to play a part in the order or spacing of places described in a song journey.

Meaning

Meaning is best informed by the ways in which repeated secular activities like song performances provide specific and often repeated details of geography which relate the spiritual and natural worlds to trail networks that can be found on the ground. If a song series were sung in an improper order the meaning of the song would be undermined. In fact, it is the general O'odham practice that when a group of singers make a mistake, they must go back to the beginning and start over. Since it may take several hours to sing an entire song series, this could have important implications. On an actual journey, however, such an error would be tantamount to making a wrong turn, which in the arid Southwest could be fatal.

Another aspect is that most songs originate with singers as dreams and many of these songs are attributed to spiritual birds. For this reason the perspective of the journey as told in the songs is often from the bird's-eye view. I think this is important to understanding how cross-domain mappings occur and geographic or cognitive sensibilities crucial to orientation in space are perceived. Songs are not the only source of this information but they play an important role.

Finally, journeys in O'odham society are significant as avenues for obtaining or expanding spiritual power. Sacred or ceremonial journeys are undertaken for this reason. Since spiritual journeys often take place in the form of dreams later enacted on the ground, spatial sense or cognitive geography is further emphasized in the negotiation of landscape.

MOJAVE DESERT
Catherine S. Fowler

Amount of construction/over what time

The Mojave Desert trails probably required minimal construction, but were worn down through a long period of use. The main trails may go back several thousand years. They are marked by heavily patinated petroglyphs and associated with sherd scatters over 1000 years old. In some cases desert gravels have been cleared, forming slight berms to each side. A few trails on rocky slopes show some rock removal or other movement, and at least a couple have several steps cut into the rock. Trail markers (cairns, petroglyphs, etc.) and trail features (end points at some lidded tinajas) would have taken various amounts of labor, from an afternoon to a day or two;

but most cairns, at least, were probably built up over time by purposefully hauling river cobbles upslope.

Technology of movement

The trails originally were intended for foot travel. Some likely began as animal trails, especially bighorn sheep trails, but foot trails are broader than the somewhat V-shaped sheep trails. Differences in difficulty of some trails depend on whether they were intended for hunters traveling alone or accompanied by a family with children and old people, and what burdens are being carried. I have seen well-laden women do beautifully on ascents up steep trails.

Characteristics of terrain

The landscape crossed by these trails is heterogeneous: desert sand in some cases, mountains reaching 3,000 ft or so, and rocky desert gravel in other areas. The most visible trails are in the rocky desert gravel. Because this area is extremely dry, these tracks ultimately lead to water.

Points/places of access

Based on the maps drawn for Kelly and Laird and by consultants, most trails are somewhat braided. They are fairly straight across low desert country and lead directly up slopes; but some intersect at various points and "shortcuts" exist. Kelly felt that trails followed certain contours in the desert mountains and often followed washes. Some trails ended at desert springs, tinajas, and other water sources. Most trails across the Mojave ended at the Colorado River, although they obviously extended into the heart of the Southwest, Great Basin, and California. Mountain sheep, deer, pine nuts, turquoise, crystals, salt, shell beads, and other trade items were to be found at the far ends. Shrines in the form of rock cairns are the primary markers, along with petroglyphs. The functions of numerous cross intaglios and geoglyphs of various ages are largely unknown.

Ownership/access/stewardship

As far as can be determined, many people used the trails, including Mojave, Chemehuevi, Southern Paiute, Yumans, and more distant travelers from California and the Southwest. We do not know that trails and their access were regulated in any way. Individuals do speak of dreaming the journeys that give them the right to hunt in certain locations or territories, but the use was not exclusive. Stewardship may have been an element of a general Southern Paiute ethic, involving cleaning out tinajas or other water sources, cutting overgrown willows, and picking up debris.

Functions

Trails functioned to enhance general travel, communication, trade networks, and movement of camps. Most trails led to water and subsistence and trade resources.

Form/network organization

These trails appear to have grown informally through time rather than by planning. On the other hand, someone had to figure out where the water was; the easiest ways were to traverse mountain ranges and then pass that information down to following generations.

Scale

The scale of these trails is very human, and largely individual. Groups that moved on them would have been small. The only parallel tracks reported are some distance apart, as if one individual might be trailing another but at a safe distance. We record no close parallel tracks similar to the Pajarito trails.

Meaning

The meanings of trails are both physical and spiritual. Some trails have no physical manifestation but represent mental (spiritual) journeys that cover broad tracts of land and are meant to be sung. Points along the way are "real," but not necessarily the tracks. The Salt Song, Mountain Sheep Song, and Deer Song chart a man's (and sometimes a woman's) hunting territory, but also tell of great mythic journeys of spirits in forming the earth and locating resources. This meaning has remained more important than the actual trails today, although there is a perception that physical features do exist and that all zones through which the spiritual journey may once have gone must be protected.

NORTHERN PLAINS
Maria Nieves Zedeño, Kacy Hollenback, and Calvin Grinnell

NOTE: Trail = on the ground evidence, Route = direction followed (mode and distance discussed under technology and scale, respectively).

Amount of construction/over what time

I have not yet found information on construction of these trails. However, from my ethnographic experiences I know that potential mountain routes are (a) spotted by the traveler, (b) scouted and tested by foot and horse; (c) mapped out "mentally"; and (d) improved with tools for future use. Trails are maintained ad hoc, for instance, by cutting of overgrown vegetation or removing/adding rocks and timber for crossings. This is particularly true of horse trails, which are carefully aligned and maintained so as not to place the animal at risk. Trails in public lands (e.g., treaty rights lands) are treated in this way, regardless of regulations. Travel and trail maintenance in hunting grounds are so significant that the tribes generally oppose the use of ATVs (even though tribal members use them, too) in public lands and consult to develop MOAs on public travel across the grounds.

No construction or improvement is mentioned in the literature on older trails, but mention of "old Indian trails" suggests indirectly that they were used often enough to leave material imprint.

Technology of movement

In the northern Plains individuals traveled by foot and, since ca. the 17th century, by horse, although even then some foot travel was undertaken for a short distance or through strategy. Travois trains were used to carry loads over long distances. They typically consisted of a large animal skin (elk, most likely) stretched over four poles in a trapezoidal shape. The narrow end of the long poles attached to a harness for dogs or horses. Travois trails left parallel ruts, narrow and deep.

Travois trains followed well-known routes across open terrain, clear of the forest and foothills, but paralleled closely natural features. For example, the N-S Old North Trail ran parallel to, and "at a uniform distance" from, the Rocky Mountain Front (McClintock 1910:434–37). Similarly, the travois trail that ran E-W from the Front to the mouth of the Yellowstone River followed the contours of the Missouri River. The end portion of a travois trail to this rendezvous can be seen at Fort Union Trading Post. These routes were so commonly used by dog and horse travois as well as riders that they resembled the old wagon roads.

By contrast, trails across forested or mountainous terrain were used by small groups of people or individuals traveling by foot or by horse, and who sought shelter and seclusion. These trails were basically narrow footpaths often just wide enough for one person or horse, particularly along cliff sides.

Tribes that lived along the Missouri River, notably the Mandan, used bullboats in combination with other modes of transportation. The size and shape of a bullboat (circular wooden frame covered with a single buffalo hide) did not lend itself to true river navigation; rather, it was used for river crossing and for floating goods downstream. In the old days the bullboat was thought to be a woman's craft, and women used it to gather wood and other resources along the riverine trail network. The bullboat was also used by warriors, probably carried along for river crossings.

Plains people welcomed technological improvements in transportation (other than the horse), which makes sense given the geographical breadth of their subsistence systems and social and political networks. For example, "buggies" or wagons were readily adopted, as well as keelboats. Steamboats and the railroad, in particular, were also readily adopted, perhaps because in numerous instances railways (e.g., the Northern Pacific) followed familiar routes. Trains were marvelous and free of charge (a government grace), and allowed people to broaden horizons and accomplish impossible tasks. Runners, for example, used the railroads as often as they could.

Characteristics of terrain

The area stretching roughly from the Red River of the North to the Rocky Mountain Front and from the north bank of the Missouri River to the Bighorn Mountains in Montana and the Cannonball River in Dakota is characterized by end moraines and glacial tills which are in turn deeply cut by water/snow action. The upper Missouri River trench (with its spectacular "breaks") and the canyon of the Little Missouri River in the Badlands are extreme examples in point. Away from the main river systems, the area exhibits characteristic rolling prairie topography with spring-fed and runoff coulees. To the extreme northwest (northwest Montana, east of the Rockies), cliffs and flatlands were shaped by ancient inland seas. Conspicuous landforms such as buttes are scattered across the prairie.

Spread across the region traversed by the trails discussed in Chapter 6 were important mountain ranges, including the Turtle Mountains on the Canadian-North Dakota border (hardly a mountain but historic travelers and explorers such as La Verendrye and Thompson used them as navigational landmarks, and so did the Indians), the Killdeer Mountains in north-central North Dakota, the Little Rockies in northeast Montana, the Bear Paws in north-central Montana, and the Sweetgrass Hills in northwest Montana. These mountain ranges, which are conveniently located along some of the most important travel routes, provided a wealth of resources, including large and small game, bird feathers, minerals such as pigments and clays, flint and other stones, and useful plants. They, too, were religious destination points in their own right and had associated origin myths.

Points/places of access

See "Functions" section below.

Ownership/access/stewardship

From maps and narratives one can infer that parallel trails along major routes were owned at the tribal/ethnic group level. Segments of macro trails to the confines of knowledge probably were owned, or at least temporarily controlled, by those whose territory they crossed. I have no subgroup information on trail ownership or stewardship, except that the lower Missouri River tribes (Omaha, etc.) had trail chiefs, who determined the direction of and ordered the work on trails.

Functions

I would differentiate between trails to central places and trails to the "confines" of people's knowledge of the world, at least in the case of the semi-sedentary Mandan and Hidatsa. Trails to central places are centripetal; trails to the confines are thoroughfares. Trails to central places carried people and goods to major trading centers, which in turn may or may not have been population centers. Central places could be classified by form, function, and historical trajectory in great detail. In the Mandan case, villages were both central places and population centers. Trading rendezvous were central places where nobody lived. Some of the sacred buttes and mountains where spirits lived and where special resources were collected were also central places, as were those mentioned in the myths. Their role as destination place or stopping place depended on the purpose of the journey. For example, warriors would stop at a particular butte on their way to a specific mission; in contrast, bundle groups would travel to the same butte specifically to fulfill a ceremonial obligation.

The mouth of the Yellowstone was a special case, a rendezvous place without a population center but also a territorial boundary marker for a number of tribes. Its vicinity is loaded with sacred places (e.g., mythical and real eagle trapping lodges; buffalo shrines, sacred paint quarries, etc.). This central place was not only a destination but also a stopping place on the road to the Mandan villages. Hence the need to discuss places connected by a trail sequentially (as in direction of movement and order of activities) as well as hierarchically (Zedeño and Stoffle 2003).

So, the trails that followed the Missouri River from the Rocky Mountain Front to the Mandan villages had stopping places and central places in their own right, between origin and final destination. Each place probably had a trail or network of trails of its own, depending on its intrinsic qualities as well as its relations to other places.

Shrines and areas of resource collection were common along major trails, either in the immediate vicinity or a short distance away. Many of the most important shrines are located along the Missouri River.

Trails to the confines of knowledge are those major arteries that took people to places far beyond the familiar environment shared by neighboring friends and enemies. These were few and far between, but travel across the plains in all directions is characteristic of prehistoric and historic interaction, and had multifarious functions: trading, raiding, warfare, adoption, slave-capture, intermarriage, resource collection, vision questing, scouting.

I think this pattern repeated at the microregional level, where travel to the confines of familiar territories (own, and friendly neighbors), as in the case of vision-questing war parties, served both a literal war/scouting function and a highly ritualized social function. Eagle trapping, for instance, coincided with both riverine trails and wintering camps (Bowers 1948), and hunting along riverine grounds also conforms to the main pattern. Travel to one's territorial confines was also done ceremonially by those individuals who had to place offerings at the boundary-marking buttes where spirits lived and where sacred bundles originated.

Form/network organization

Trail networks across the plains, which for the most (known) part paralleled streams and mountain chains, took the shape of a long main axis with shorter segments developed on either side at intervals roughly corresponding to tributaries. This pattern likely repeated along major travel routes (e.g., Red River of the North, Missouri River, Yellowstone River, and

Powder River), which were, in turn, connected by portages (at least in theory, since they were not navigated) between headwaters of tributaries.

Networks from trails that paralleled the N-S mountain ranges and major
topographic features also exhibited this pattern, where river routes running
perpendicularly to the trail would connect people to the forested hilltops or
to the open prairie and buttes.

No doubt, minor trails developed as people needed to cut across the terrain perpendicularly to parallel trails or to portage; these trails were sighted
as the crow flies, and they pointed in the general direction of accessible
climbs and river crossings.

Scale

Trails on the Plains fall into basic scales: the macrogeographical and the
microgeographical. (a) Macrogeographical: as indicated by the development
of prehistoric trade of precious items by the Adena and then the Hopewell,
long-distance movement through the region has early origins. My thought
is that this pattern of movement continued, in all or part, until the demise
of the fur trade (ca. 1850s). This resilience in the face of profound change
also speaks for the character and condition of travel 500 mi across the plains
(800 km as the crow flies; even more from the Mandan villages to the three
forks).

Travel at this scale implies that trails crossed territories of various tribes,
and thus they doubled as thoroughfares in peace time or major war paths. In
the late 1900s, when the buffalo were retreating toward the Rockies, hunting parties from as far as Pembina or Winnipeg (Red River Cree-Ojibwa)
would follow the macro trails into Montana. So did the Mandan and Hidatsa, who in the summer hunts would travel up to 200 mi with women
and children to quarter meat and dress the robes that then would be floated
downriver in bullboats (Zedeño et al. 2006a, 2006b).

(b) Microgeographical: travel within the confines of the territory represents a critical scale of movement. Much of this travel involved intimate
interaction with places and resources, at an intensity and depth that macro
travel seldom reached. In the case of warfare, young males seeking political
and social standing through visions of war would undertake journeys to
the confines of the homeland and perhaps ventured outside the territorial
boundaries until they reached their goals. Hunting also was accomplished
at this scale. Microgeographical travel was also characterized by scouting

new routes as much as following known ones; however, the consistent naming of landmarks along the micro war paths indicates to me that certain
routes were strictly observed, and that the trails that logically developed
were also followed frequently.

Meaning

As discussed in detail in Chapter 6, movement across the landscape
through time played a crucial role in identity formation at various levels,
from individual to national. In the Mandan case, one can see layers of meaning, each corresponding to a historical era: the migration from the Mississippi River (migration route/trail markers); the fabled time of Mandan
wealth (pre-smallpox of 1781) (taking over macrogeographical trading control), the time of consolidation and pressure from advancing enemy Sioux
and European colonization (travel restricted to familiar and friendly territory), and the time of accommodation to the American nation-state (travel
forbidden then, now modern roads).

Each of these historical layers of movement had, in turn, its own spatial
realm, as well as its own system of relations with other people, resources,
and places. The trail maps to an extent capture these spatial, historical, relational dimensions, but one must add narrative and oral tradition to gain
a deeper and broader sense of trails as signifiers of the evolution of movement and identity formation.

MAYA LOWLANDS
Angela Keller

Amount of construction/over what time

Where they have been excavated, Maya roads appear to have been built
as single construction events. Following Eliot Abrams' (1994) energetics
studies at Copan, I have estimated the amount of labor necessary to construct Sacbe I at Xunantunich, Belize. Sacbe I is a plastered masonry road
285 m long, 19 m wide, and roughly 0.5 m high, and it might have required
just over 9,300 person-days to construct. This is the equivalent of roughly
90 to 150 people working over a 2 to 3 month period (the dry-season building season suggested by Abrams).

According to Justine Shaw's (2001:265) review of lowland Maya causeways,
the average Maya road was somewhat longer than Sacbe I, at approximately

400 m. Extrapolating from my Sacbe I labor estimate, a typical Maya road might have required 13,000 person-days to construct. As a further example, the impressive Mendez Causeway at Tikal (ca. 50 m wide and 1,000 m long) is roughly ten times larger than Xunantunich's Sacbe I. The Mendez Causeway may represent 93,000 person-days of labor; or 930 to 1,550 people working over a 2 to 3 month period. It is also possible that roads of this magnitude were completed by smaller groups of workers over multiple building seasons.

Technology of movement

Foot traffic was the exclusive form of movement along Maya roads. This includes not only individuals, but some litter-carrying of elites and ritual objects. Movement of goods and heavier items was accomplished by individuals using packs.

Characteristics of terrain

The terrain of the Maya lowlands is undulating with low hills typically less than 200 m AMSL. Mean annual rainfall varies from 500 mm in the north to 3,000 mm in the south. Vegetation is generally dense sub-tropical rainforest, trending to drier scrub forest in the northern Yucatan Peninsula. The central and southern lowlands (Chiapas, Guatemala, Honduras, and Belize) are marked by several major rivers and their tributaries, whereas the northern lowlands contain many natural water-filled sinkholes (cenotes) and small lakes, but no surface rivers.

Points/places of access

All documented roads are connected to civic centers, either directly or indirectly as part of a larger network of roads. Roads connect a variety of features and groups to architectural cores. At the termini, or "ends," of these roads are spatially discrete ceremonial or civic spaces, isolated pyramidal structures (often associated with stone monuments), elite residential groups, cenotes, and distinct civic centers (typically smaller than the central or primate site).

Ownership/access/stewardship

The largest, stone-built roads were most likely owned and managed by the ruling elite of the centers to which they were attached. These stone roads are generally accessible only from the spaces they connect. While an able-bodied person might be able to climb onto a road at any point, formal access features (e.g., ramps, stairs, side terraces) were rare. This suggests that access to the roads was controlled (to some degree) in the centers and termini.

In Classic period imagery, only rulers and their retinue are depicted in processions, arguably along the roads. The great width of many of the roads, though, suggests that they were designed to accommodate large, possibly mixed-status crowds. Colonial period texts describe travelers, merchants, emissaries, warriors, and spies using roads (though not necessarily stone roads), as well as kings and their retainers.

Functions

There is no consensus on the function of Maya roads. Reasonable arguments have been made for ritual, social, political, economic, military, and administrative functions. I tend to believe that all of these, to some degree, are correct. Over their use-lives Maya roads likely hosted a variety of activities from procession to trade.

Nevertheless, the lack of integration of road systems one-to-another and the lack of roads along major trade routes suggests that Maya roads were not built primarily to facilitate trade. The grand scale and fine construction of these roads far surpass the utilitarian needs of foot traffic for commerce or other purposes.

Further, the intimate association of roads with centers, and the lack of an integrated network of roads across the lowlands, suggests that these center-focused road networks were designed as separate entities by distinct polities. Longer, intersite roads may reflect the consolidation of previously independent centers into larger polities.

Form/network organization

Maya road networks have been described as having linear, radial, dendritic, and cruciform arrangements. Radial arrangements (including the more-complicated dendritic, and more-formal cruciform patterns) seem to be the norm across the lowlands. Linear systems, like that of Sayil, Mexico, are less common, but notable in the southeastern Petén and the Yucatan Peninsula. These linear systems seem to be more common in areas with broken, hilly terrain where civic architecture is clustered on several adjacent hilltops.

One of the oddest road systems is that of Tikal, which has a unique triangular circuit pattern. The Tikal roads and their arrangement may be related to the construction and consecration of Twin Pyramid Complexes, which are also all but unknown outside of the site of Tikal.

Scale

Most Maya road systems extend only a few hundred meters around the architectural cores to which they are connected. Nevertheless, at several sites (e.g., Caracol, Chichen Itza, Cobá, Calakmul) complex and extensive road systems existed. Caracol's vast road network encompasses roughly 88 km^2 (or 8,800 ha; Chase and Chase 2001) of densely occupied and terraced terrain. The longest known road, connecting Cobá to Yaxuná, extends 100 km across the Yucatan Peninsula.

Meaning

The meaning of Maya roads is far from certain. From my own work with linguistic, ethnographic, ethnohistorical, and archaeological materials, I believe that Maya roads were primarily statements of power. My feeling is that many of the archaeologically recorded roads, particularly the larger masonry roads attached to major centers, were intimately associated with the power and the person of the local ruler. These were the king's (or queen's) roads, the *noh ch'ibal behob,* reflecting the flow and extent of divine power. I also suspect that Maya roads were designed to support commemorative rites entailing procession, and particularly calendrical rites.

COSTA RICA
Payson Sheets

[Variables arranged by site / region; El Arenal (Northwestern Costa Rica: AD 5000–1000) and Cutris (Eastern Costa Rica, AD 500–1000)]

Amount of construction/over what time

Arenal

Arenal paths were the product of erosion caused by foot traffic, and thus reflect no formal construction.

Cutris

The Cutris roads show considerable construction. The longest two roads average 9 km in length, and for all but the last kilometer average about 6 m wide and 2 m deep, with ditches and berms on both sides. In the last kilometer, the roads widen to 35 and 40 m, and deepen to perhaps 5 m or more below the surrounding ground surface, with high berms. The degree of maintenance necessary is unknown, but probably considerable given the mean precipitation of ca. 300 mm annually.

Secondary ring-roads are also present, with each segment connecting to the larger radial main roads. They average 600 m long, about 5 m wide, and 2 m deep. A zig-zag road to the south connects two main roads with length, depth, and width about the same as the other ring roads.

Technology of movement
Arenal
Movement on the Arenal paths was on foot and single file, occasionally traversed by people carrying heavy rocks for cemetery construction, the dead and their offerings for burial, and abundant food and drink for feasting at cemeteries.
Cutris
Movement occurred on foot and represents group processions rather than single-file traffic.

Characteristics of terrain
Arenal
The Arenal landscape is hilly with gently rolling topography that varies in elevation from 400 to 1000 m with some steep slopes (40°) where steep paths go up and down.
Cutris
The terrain of Cutris is gently sloping (approximately 1°, toward the North).

Points/places of access
Arenal
The ends of the Arenal paths are primarily villages and cemeteries, but may include sources of stone for construction and springs. Shrines of a sort are found along Silencio Phase paths, where stone repositories were developed inside the obtuse angle bend of the path near the cemetery. One feature had a large monolith with incised designs or a petroglyph. This same path had a right-angle spur that allowed some of the traffic to

access the top of a local hill, perhaps to view the cemetery from a couple
kilometers away.

Cutris

In the Cutris center, radial roads connect to small towns of perhaps a
few hundred people located at the ends of each road. Ring roads connect
the main radial roads at 200 to 600 m from where the radial roads begin at
the site center.

Ownership/access/stewardship

Arenal

In the Arenal case, we found strong association of a particular village
with its cemetery and thus the path that links them, so communities must
have had a strong sense of ownership of that path as well as the activities
that took place along it.

Cutris

In the Cutris case, a chief in this ranked society probably owned the
roads and ring roads because of his labor control for its construction, use,
and maintenance.

Functions

Arenal

We propose single file processions to and from the Arenal cemetery for
burial and feasting at time of interment and repeated afterward. Ethnographic cases mention spirits of deceased needing guidance to get to cemetery and the entrenched paths would help that.

Cutris

Processions from the towns at the ends of the radial roads into the
chiefly center of Cutris probably symbolized the authority of the chief, in
addition to honoring the deceased and connecting with the spirits of the deceased. We also have some evidence of chiefs being buried in Cutris center.
A defensive function of ring roads is also possible.

Form/network organization

Arenal

In the Arenal case, linear segments of straight path connected individual
villages with the cemetery.

Cutris

The form of movement is formal with the Cutris Chiefdom in center, radial roads connecting to town located 6 to 9 km away, and ring roads a few hundred meters from the site center.

Scale

Arenal

The Arenal narrow paths range from 200 m to over 10 km in length. The original width of path was about 0.25 m, but erosion-caused entrenching has expanded the width of paths to 4–6 m or more and depth to 7 m.

Cutris

In the Cutris case, the main radial roads extend 6–9 km from the chiefly center, possibly defining a territory.

Meaning

Arenal

Although the formation of the Arenal paths occurred through use and erosion, the continuity of travel along these routes over generations despite inefficiency implies that this form of movement had acquired particular meaning.

Cutris

Roads of the Cutris center are expressions of differential power, as the chief needs to organize labor for construction, use, and maintenance of the large radiating roads and connecting ring roads. In addition to their monumentality, the deceased chiefs (according to other excavated chiefdom-level sites in Costa Rica) were buried in the site center and accessed by the living chief. Thus, roads provided access to the powerful spirit benefiting the living chief, his household, and the public at large.

NORTHERN MESOPOTAMIA (EARLY BRONZE AGE)
Jason Ur

Amount of construction/over what time

Paths/roadways as non-constructed features were created over 400–500 years through continuous passage of human, animal, and wheeled traffic (Ur 2003; Van Liere and Lauffray 1954–55; Wilkinson 1993). This movement ultimately resulted in paths up to 100 m wide and 2 m deep. To some extent, these are still forming, since there is some channel surface runoff, which erodes them yet further.

Technology of movement

These pathways hosted an uncertain combination of human foot traffic, animal feet (sheep, goats, donkeys, cattle, in probable descending order of frequency), and animal-drawn wheeled vehicles (not known archaeologically but textually [Sallaberger 1996] and through images on cylinder seals [Jans and Bretschneider 1998]). The majority of the disturbances which created these features probably came from animal feet, rather than human feet.

Characteristics of terrain

Deep alluvial soils characterize the region, once highly productive for agriculture (Courty 1994; Wilkinson 2000). Today seasonal and perennial drainages are downcut into the plain. Although by no means flat, the terrain superficially appears to be isometric; certainly there were few natural topographic impediments to movement. By EBA, the plain was probably already largely a human creation in terms of vegetation, probably given over entirely to either cereal cultivation or wild grasses. This geography was highly amenable to track formation by compaction and wind and water erosion.

Points/places of access

At most EBA sites, roadways originate at a vague point near the mound; at the largest (urban) sites, they appear to originate at possible gate locations, which today survive as gullies in the mound edge (Brak and Hamoukar) or gaps in the site's outer wall (Beydar and Leilan). Assuming that they were used for field access, the "offramps" would have been any point along the road that gave access to the intended field (assuming the traveler had rights of access). For movement of humans and animals out to the pastures beyond the cultivated zone, the terminal point was the interface between the farthest cultivation and the uncultivated or pasture zone beyond it. There are also examples of roadways which run continuously from settlement to settlement. In this alluvial environment, no evidence survives for any roadside shrines or other facilities along the route.

Ownership/access/stewardship

I suspect that these roadways formed because of patterns of ownership, but the ownership was of the fields to either side of the roadway. In this sense, the roadway itself was unowned, neutral space where it was safe to walk and to move animals and goods. There is no evidence that any sort of maintenance was performed on the roadways.

Functions

At the most mundane level, the roadways functioned to move human and animal traffic to and from the central settlement to its surrounding fields, the pasture beyond them, and to other neighboring settlements beyond that. The primary reasons for this movement were related to the subsistence economy: cereal agriculture and sheep and goat pastoralism. These roadways moved wheeled traffic to and from the fields (carrying manure to the fields for fertilizer, and carrying the harvested cereals back to the settlement), but probably also goods between neighboring settlements and across regions. In the latter cases, these goods were probably primarily high-value luxury goods or manufactured items (metals and metal objects, textiles, etc.) but at the very local level, bulk staples might have also been moved (although the economic mechanisms for this trade are debated). Under extreme conditions, bulk cereals might have been moved further, but this was highly un-economic. Textual references suggest that political elites moved along these roads in donkey cart entourages in the process of cementing their status through face-to-face visits with local elites. All of the excavated urban sites have revealed shrines or temple households, so there remains the possibility of pilgrimage traffic, but we have no idea of the extent to which non-members of the temple households would have participated in rituals, if at all.

Form/network organization

Two scale-dependent spatial patterns are visible. At the local level, the most common pattern is one of radiating roadways from the central settlement, with roadways often bifurcating at a distance from the settlement. Often these radiating roadways faded out at or near the boundary between cultivation and pasture beyond it. Almost all settlements of the EBA have such radiating systems, from the largest (e.g., Tell Brak) to small 1-ha villages. At the regional scale, these local radiating patterns were interconnected, allowing movement across entire regions by means of settlement-to-settlement traffic. No major "superhighways" existed that bypassed small sites to carry traffic directly between larger centers.

Scale

The roadways themselves might be called "monumental" (up to 100 m wide and 2 m deep) as long as this is understood to be the unintended result of generations of traffic, rather than any sort of "materialization." The largest of the radial networks extend out to a radius of 5 km but most are around 3 km; thus the cultivated catchments are between 30 km^2 and 80 km^2. The scale of the entire network is immense; more than 1,700 km of roadways have been documented via CORONA satellite photographs (Ur 2003) with many more kilometers not yet mapped. The entire Upper Khabur basin was crisscrossed with sites and interconnecting roadways; the basin itself is 200 km EW and about 100 km NS, but the roadways spill over into the plains to the west and to the east, where they continue another 100 km to Nineveh (modern Mosul). Although impossible to prove the contemporaneity of all roadways, most of the EBA-articulated features probably were used simultaneously.

Meaning

Meaning is the most difficult aspect of EBA roadways. As non-constructed features which formed over several centuries, roadways were not the material manifestation of, or symbolic of, any particular worldview or understanding of the cosmos (as in Mayan sacbeob), nor did they serve to project political or military power (as in the Inka and Roman roads). As in the Arenal case (Chapter 8, this volume), they may have ultimately been assigned meaning, but it is difficult to say what that would have been, given the proto-historic time period. As a product of a resilient pattern of land ownership, they may have come to be associated with unequal control over land, but this is pure speculation.

BOLIVIAN AMAZON (CAUSEWAYS-CANALS)
Clark L. Erickson

Amount of construction/over what time

The Major Causeways-Canals (Major CC) and Minor Causeways-Canals (Minor CC) of the Baures Hydraulic Complex (BHC) are tentatively mapped; thus, construction and maintenance labor of the features is estimated. Major CC are created by removing earth from adjacent canals to create a raised platform using digging sticks, shovels, baskets, and cloth.

Based on ethnographic analogy of construction of modern causeways and canals and experimental raised fields in the Bolivian Amazon, a single person can move 1 m³ per hour or 5 m³ per day (5 hour day). Major CC vary in cross-section and length; thus, estimates of earth moved and labor costs in construction of individual CC are difficult. The Major CC total 475.909 linear km. If we assume that the causeways of Major CC are 4 m wide and 1 m tall, a total of 1,903,636 m³ of earth was moved or a total of 1,903,636 person-hours or 380,727 person-days of labor were invested for the BHC.

The construction and maintenance costs of Minor CC or canoe paths of the San Martin Forest Island Complex are much lower than Major CC discussed above. Canoe paths required little effort, since poling or paddling a large dugout canoe repeatedly in the same location will produce a channel in the savanna. The straight trajectory of the Minor CC up to 2 km indicates more planning, design, and construction than today's informal canoe paths but still much less than the Major CC. The Minor CC total 93.491 linear km. If we assume a channel of 50 cm wide and 30 cm deep, a total of 14,023.65 m³ of earth was moved for the creation of the Minor CC of the San Martin Hydraulic Complex, representing 14,023.65 person-hours or 2,805 person-days. The average labor for a single Minor CC is 16.5 person-days. A family of five could construct a single feature in a little over 3 days. Maintenance involves periodic removal of vegetation and sediments, although regular use keeps the channel free.

Due to their straightness, most Major CC were created in a single episode, although earthworks may have been enlarged through periodic maintenance and reconstruction.

A single corrected radiocarbon date from the base of a causeway in the BHC of 1615 BP probably indicates protohistoric construction and use. Pottery from ring-ditch sites and settlements suggests that the majority of the earthworks are late prehistoric in date and were used for 300–500 years.

Technology of movement

The widths of Major CC suggest that they were constructed for two-way traffic (heavily loaded canoes and human porters). Minor CC are smaller and shorter. In some cases, Minor CC are simply shallow depressions with little raised platform. Many Major CC were wider and taller than necessary to avoid floods and move bi-directional pedestrian and canoe traffic. Many Major and Minor CC are parallel and redundant.

Characteristics of terrain

The landscape consists of forest, savanna, wetlands, and earthworks. The forest occurs along rivers as gallery forest and in forest islands. Forest islands in the Baures region are natural formations. Savanna and wetlands are predominant. Because of the flat terrain, large areas of the savannas are inundated during the wet season. Forest islands tend to remain dry.

Earthworks such as causeways, canals, fish weirs, ponds, reservoirs, and ring-ditch sites alter the character and drainage of the BHC, in addition to providing enhanced resources, transportation, communication, and settlement locations.

Points/places of access

Individual Major and Minor CC generally begin and end on forest islands. Forest islands were locations of settlements, gardens, fields, agroforestry, and hunting. Most large forest islands have one or more ring-ditch sites which are interpreted as settlements, cemeteries, forts, central places, and temples. Most multiple Minor CC connect forest islands in close proximity. In many areas, causeways and canals overlap with fish weirs and enhance fish availability through water management.

Most Major and Minor CC rarely cross or intersect. When this happens, one usually bisects the other suggesting sequential construction and use. Individual causeways and canals are part of a larger integrated network within the BHC over 550 km^2.

Ownership/access/stewardship

Minor CC (canoe paths) were built, maintained, and owned by pairs of individual families or multiple families living in hamlets on separate forest islands (although used by a larger spectrum of society). They represent the agency of individuals and small social groups by their scale, construction, location, destinations, numbers, and density. The features document repetitive movement. Although simple to construct, the straightness of the features indicates intentionality, planning, and design.

The Major CC represent a larger social realm of interaction, access, and ownership. Long, wide Major CC between adjacent forest islands probably were constructed and used by paired communities on separate forest islands.

Functions

The functions of the Major CC were transportation, communication, water management, and symbols of community pride. The Minor CC were smaller versions primarily used for local transportation and communication. Networks of causeways, canals, and natural waterways provided a means to move bulk staples and people and create local and regional interaction.

Form/network organization

The Baure are recognized as having urban-scale settlements, regional organization, powerful leaders, temples, forts, and large populations, and the term chiefdom has been applied to this society.

The network of Major CC of the BHC are regional (550 km²). Using Major CC, an individual could traverse the entire BHC. Individual Major CC are organized locally between adjacent forest islands. Most forest islands are connected to their neighbors by Major and Minor CC (1 to 7.5 km). A few larger forest islands, assumed to be population and possibly political centers, have multiple radial Major CC, suggesting a weak hierarchy of center vs. hinterland. Major CC appear to be organized at the multicommunity level.

Most Minor CC are local in organization. All are straight. Because the majority of Minor CC connect nearby forest islands, the organization is beyond the individual. The density and number of Minor CC of the San Martin Forest Island Complex suggest interacting households or hamlets. Collectively, each forest island represented a community.

Scale

Major CC are found throughout the Bolivian Amazon and linked vast regions. The Major CC of the BHC cover an area of 550 km². The surrounding area has few causeways and canals. The San Martin Forest Island Complex of 3–4 km² represents a small-scale landscape. Eleven Major CC connect forest islands of the complex and beyond over 4.6 km. The main cluster of 168 Minor CC over 3 km² represents a local landscape. The boundary of this particular study area is culturally, rather than arbitrarily defined by the patterning, direction, and presence-absence of the Minor CC. This complex of Minor CC represents the scale of interacting families living in hamlets, multiple families or lineages, and/or communities.

Meaning

Based on the intent, design, scale, and over construction, the Major and Minor CC were public symbols of identity and pride. Some Major CC were probably a form of monumentality where large stone architecture was unknown. On the flat, open landscape, perfectly straight, long, wide elevated avenues, crossing which appear to reach the horizon, created an impressive experience for travelers. The obsession with straightness in the built environment also shows a concern with microcosm, axis mundi, and sacred alignments.

The Major and Minor CC mark who was connected socially and who was not, creating a map of organization and interaction.

BOLIVIAN AMAZON (EARTHWORKS)
Clark L. Erickson and John H. Walker

Amount of construction/over what time

Precolumbian earthworks, including causeways, canals, raised fields, settlement mounds, fish weirs, and other structures are found throughout the Bolivian Amazon. We focus on an arbitrarily defined area of causeways, canals, and raised fields along the Middle Apere River of 12.77 km². The landscape of causeways, canals, and raised fields on the Middle Apere River is tightly integrated (23.93 linear km of causeways and 12.77 km² of raised fields). Raised fields with wavelengths of 5 m and platforms raised 0.5 m required movement of 125,000 m³ of earth per km², or a total of 1,596,250 m³ of earth.

Raised field experiments showed that farmers can move 0.5 m² per person-hour. Using a 5-hour work-day, 6000 person-hours or 1200 person-days are required to built a 3-m-wide, 1-m-tall, and 1-km-long causeway. Thus, the measured causeways on the Middle Apere River required 143,580 person-hours or 28,716 person-days to construct. The raised fields required 3,192,500 person-hours, or 638,500 person-days to construct.

Radiocarbon dates show earthworks were constructed and maintained as landesque capital for more than 2,000 years. The landscape was built through accumulation of effort and infrastructure over this time. The organization of labor was within the capabilities of small communities. The integrated landscape probably involved collaboration between hamlets and communities. Although capable of managing large quantities of water, increasing crop production, and lowering risk, the precolumbian engineering was relatively simple.

Technology of movement

Causeways and canals had hydraulic and land-tenure functions for raised field agriculture. Some causeways and canals connect settlements, fields, rivers, and wetlands, suggesting that year-round transportation and communication were the primary functions. Canals would have extended the use of canoes into the dry season. One person can move a ton or more by canoe.

Although the technology was simple (moving earth from adjacent canals to create the raised road), most earthworks are long and straight implying intention and pride.

Characteristics of terrain

Relevant characteristics of the terrain include topography, hydrology, slope, and vegetation. The Bolivian Amazon is a low plain crossed by many rivers. These rivers deposit their sediments on forested levees, which gently slope (levee backslope) towards the low-lying wetlands between rivers. Microtopography determines which areas of the landscape are inundated or dry.

Most settlements and modern fields are located on the highest levees. Causeways, canals, and raised fields are generally found on the levee backslope where seasonal inundation occurs. The anthropogenic topography created by causeways and canals could manage water for raised fields and transportation by canoe and provide dry walking surfaces.

Points/places of access

The regularly spaced causeways and canals were oriented parallel or perpendicular to the course of the river. Some causeways and canals have settlements and mounds as terminal points; others connect a settlement with the river, wetlands, and raised fields. Some parallel to the river were shortcuts bypassing large meanders. The raised fields are integrated into the network of causeways and canals suggesting hydraulic and transportation functions.

Ownership/access/stewardship

The issue of ownership, access, and stewardship is central to our argument of causeways and canals as landscape capital. This landscape represents the accumulation of many small investments of labor and engineering over millennia. The patterned raised-field blocks and easily accessed causeways and canals create an orderly structured landscape. The patterning suggests land tenure and labor organization, key to accumulated landesque capital. Experimental raised fields and causeways show that earthworks can be created at the local level. As accumulated and inherited landesque capital, the earthworks benefited successive generations of farmers as a valuable resource.

Functions

The causeways and canals served for transportation, communication, organization of the landscape, and water management. Hydraulically, the causeways organized capture, flow, and drainage of water on the levee backslopes. In the early wet season, causeways and canals channeled and impeded rainwater that moved down the levee backslope and managed rising water from the wetlands below. In the late wet season and early dry season, causeways and canals held water.

Form/network organization

The causeways are 0.5–1 m tall, 2–4 m wide, and length ranges from 276 m to 2.5 km. They are built of earth from adjacent canals. The network integrated the river, settlements, wetlands, and raised fields. Eleven causeways are parallel to the general course of the Apere River and 16 causeways are perpendicular to the river, crossing the backslopes. Both types allowed transportation and communication along the river (in both the dry season and the wet season) and between the river and intervening wetlands, in addition to the hydraulic functions.

Scale

Our study area (65 km²) represents a medium scale of landscape. The boundaries are artificial because the features discussed extend many kilometers across the regional landscape. Causeways and canals range in length from 276 to 2,508 m, providing a minimal measurement of social interaction scale. Because local causeways and canals intersect up and down the river, in addition to canoe traffic in the river and wetlands, the potential social interaction sphere is much larger.

The causeways oriented parallel and perpendicular to the river define units of 100 to 300 ha which we interpret as land tenure, possibly at the lineage or community level. These causeways contain tens of individual blocks of parallel raised fields (0.2–38.9 ha or an average of 3.23 ha), possibly the work of individual families.

Meaning

We argue that the causeways and canals had multiple meanings as landesque capital. The first meaning was social as boundaries of land tenure, production, and community organization. What they connect and did not connect were expressions of territory and place. The second meaning of patterned landscape was a physical representation of family, lineage, and community identity, organization, and pride. The precolumbian landscape features were overconstructed in the sense that much of the structure is beyond what would be necessary, which implies design, aesthetics, and pride. A fourth meaning is the value of the landscapes for contemporary inhabitants. Local ranchers and native peoples are proud of the precolumbian design and engineering of these landscapes.

References Cited

Abel, A. H., ed. 1939. *Tabeau's Narrative of Loisel's Expedition to the Upper Missouri*. Norman, OK: University of Oklahoma Press.

—— 1997. *Chardon's Journal at Ft. Clark, 1834–1839*. Lincoln, NE: University of Nebraska Press.

Abercrombie, Thomas. 1998. *Pathways of Memory and Power*. Madison, WI: University of Wisconsin Press.

Abizaid, Christian. 2005. An Anthropogenic Meander Cutoff along the Ucayali River, Peruvian Amazon. *The Geographical Review* 95(1): 122–35.

Adams, Colin, and Ray Laurence, eds. 2001. *Travel and Geography in the Roman Empire*. London: Routledge.

Adams, Kim, Garry Cantley, Richard W. Effland, Jr., and Barbara Macnider. 1989. An Archaeological Assessment of a Portion of the Santan Mountains, Pinal County, Arizona. *Cultural Resource Report 60*. Tempe, AZ: Archaeological Consulting Services.

Adams, Kim, Ann Valdo Howard, and Barbara S. Macnider. 1989. Archaeological Data Recovery for the Santan Mountains Land Exchange. *Cultural Resource Report 61a*. Tempe, AZ: Archaeological Consulting Services.

Adams, R. M. 2001. Complexity in Archaic States. *Journal of Anthropological Archaeology* 20:345–60.

Addison, William. 1980. *The Old Roads of England*. London: B. T. Batsford.

Agnew, John A. 1989. The Devaluation of Place in Social Science. In *The Power of Place: Bringing Together Geographical and Sociological Imaginations*, ed. John A. Agnew and James S. Duncan, pp. 9–29. Boston, MA: Unwin Hyman.

Ahler, S. A. 1988. *Summary and Conclusions. Archeological Mitigations at Taylor Bluff Village (32ME366), Knife River Indian Villages National Historic Site*. Grand Forks, ND: Department of Anthropology, University of North Dakota.

Ahler, S. A., ed. 2003. *Archaeology at Menoken Village, a Fortified Late Plains Woodland Community in Central North Dakota.* Flagstaff, AZ: Paleocultural Research Group.

Ahler, S. A., and T. D. Thiessen. 1991. *People of the Willows: The Prehistory and Early History of the Hidatsa Indians.* Grand Forks, ND: University of North Dakota Press.

Ahlstrom, Richard V. N. 2003. *Archaeological Investigations in Clark County Wetlands Park: The 170A Pipeline Project.* Archaeological Report No. 01-27. Las Vegas, NV: HRA.

Akkermans, P. M. M. G., and G. Schwartz. 2003. *The Archaeology of Syria: From Complex Hunter-Gatherers to Early Urban Societies (ca. 16,000–300 BC).* Cambridge: Cambridge University Press.

Altamirano, Diego Francisco. 1891 [ca. 1710]. Historia de la Misión de Mojos. In *Documentos históricos de Bolivia: Historia de la Misión de los Mojos,* redactado por Manuel V. Ballivian. La Paz: Imprenta El Comercio.

Ambrosino, James N., Traci Ardren, and Travis W. Stanton. 2003. The History of Warfare at Yaxuná. In *Ancient Mesoamerican Warfare,* ed. M. Kathryn Brown and Travis W. Stanton, pp. 109–23. Walnut Creek, CA: Altamira Press.

Amodio, Emanuele, Rodrigo Navarrete, and Ana Cristina Rodriguez. 1997. *El Camino de los Españoles: Aproximaciones históricas y arqueológicas al Camino Real Caracas– La Guaira en la época colonial.* Caracas: Instituto del Patrimonio Cultural.

Andrews Heath de Z., Dorothy. 1980. *Vocabulario de Mayathan, Mayan Dictionary: Maya-English, English-Maya.* Merida: Self-published.

Anonymous. 1743 [ca. 1703]. Some Account of the Country Inhabited by the Moxos. Extract of a Spanish Relation Containing the Life and Death of Father Cipriano Barace of the Society of Jesus, Founder of the Mission of Moxos in Peru. In *Travels of the Jesuits into Various Parts of the World,* ed. John Lockman, vol. 2, pp. 437–68. London: John Noon.

Anschuetz, Kurt L., Richard H. Wilshusen, and Cherie Scheick. 2001. An Archaeology of Landscapes: Perspectives and Directions. *Journal of Archaeological Research* 9(2): 157–211.

Apple, Russell. 1965. *Trails: From Steppingstones to Kerbstones.* Bernice P. Bishop Museum Special Publication 53. Honolulu: Bernice P. Bishop Museum.

Arce Z., Julio. 1993. *Evaluación y comparación de rendimientos de cuatro cultivos en tres anchuras de camellones (campos elevados) en la Estación Biológica del Beni (Prov. Ballivián, Dpto. Beni).* Tésis de licenciatura. Bolivia: Universidad Técnica del Beni, Trinidad, Beni.

Archi, A. 1998. The Regional State of Nagar According to the Texts of Ebla. In *About Subartu: Studies Devoted to Upper Mesopotamia, Subartu 4, 2,* ed. M. Lebeau, pp. 1–15. Turnhout: Brepols.

Arnold, Dean, and Kenneth A. Prettol. 1989. Aboriginal Earthworks near the Mouth of the Beni, Bolivia. *Journal of Field Archaeology* 15:457–65.

Ashmore, Wendy. 2002. Decisions and Dispositions: Socializing Spatial Archaeology. *American Anthropologist* 104(4): 1172–83.

—— 2003. Social Archaeologies of Landscape. In *A Companion to Social Archaeology*, ed. L. Meskell and R. Preucel, pp. 255–71. Oxford: Blackwell.

—— 2004. Ancient Maya Landscapes. In *Continuities and Changes in Maya Archaeology: Perspectives at the Millennium*, ed. Charles W. Golden and Greg
Borgstede, pp. 97–112. London: Routledge.

Ashmore, Wendy, and A. Bernard Knapp, eds. 1999. *Archaeologies of Landscape:
Contemporary Perspectives*. Oxford: Blackwell.

Aston, Michael, and Trevor Rowley. 1974. *Landscape Archaeology*. Newton Abbot,
Devon: David & Charles.

Atkin, Tony, and Joseph Rykwert, eds. 2005. *Structure and Meaning in Human
Settlements*. Philadelphia, PA: University of Pennsylvania Museum of Archaeology and Anthropology.

Aveni, Anthony. 2000. *The Mystery of the Nasca Lines*. Austin, TX: University of
Texas Press.

Aveni, Anthony F., and Helaine Silverman. 1991. Between the Lines: Reading
the Nazca Markings as Rituals Writ Large. *The Sciences* 31(4): 36–42.

Ayres, Harral. 1940. *The Great Trail of New England*. Boston: Meador.

Bahr, Donald. 1986. Pima Swallow Songs. *Cultural Anthropology* 1(2): 171–87.

Bahr, Donald, J. Giff, and M. Havier. 1979. Piman Songs on Hunting. *Ethnomusicology* 23(2): 245–96.

Bahr, Donald, J. Gregorio, D. Lopez, and A. Alvarez. 1974. *Piman Shamanism
and Staying Sickness*. Tucson, AZ: University of Arizona Press.

Bahr, Donald, and J. Haefer. 1978. Song in Piman Curing. *Ethnomusicology* 22(1):
89–122.

Bahr, Donald, Lloyd Paul, and Vincent Joseph. 1997. *Ants and Orioles, Showing
the Art of Pima Poetry*. Salt Lake City, UT: University of Utah Press.

Bahr, Donald, J. Smith, W. S. Allison, and J. Hayden. 1994. *The Short Swift Time
of Gods on Earth*. Berkeley, CA: University of California Press.

Bakker, J. A. 1976. On the Possibility of Reconstructing Roads from the TRB Period.
Berichten van de Rijksdienst voor het Oudheidkundig Bodenmonderzoek 26:63–91.

Balée, William, and Clark Erickson, eds. 2006. *Time and Complexity in Historical
Ecology: Studies from the Neotropical Lowlands*. New York: Columbia University Press.

Barker, Graeme, and Tom Rasmussen. 1998. *The Etruscans*. London: Blackwell.

Barrera Vásquez, Alfredo, ed. 1995. *Diccionario Maya: Maya-Español, Español-
Maya*. 3rd ed. México, DF: Editorial Porrúa, S.A.

Barrett, John C. 1994. *Fragments from Antiquity: An Archaeology of Social Life in
Britain, 2900–1200 BC*. Oxford: Blackwell.

—— 1999a. The Mythical Landscapes of the British Iron Age. In *Archaeologies
of Landscape: Contemporary Perspectives*, ed. Wendy Ashmore and A. Bernard
Knapp, pp. 253–65. Oxford: Blackwell.

—— 1999b. Chronologies of Landscape. In *The Archaeology and Anthropology of Landscape,* ed. P. J. Ucko and R. Layton, pp. 21–30. London: Routledge.

—— 2001. Agency, the Duality of Structure and the Problem of the Archaeological Record. In *Archaeological Theory Today,* ed. I. Hodder, pp. 141–64. Malden, MA: Blackwell.

Barrett, John C., Richard Bradley, and Martin Green, eds. 1990. *Landscape, Monuments, and Society: The Prehistory of Cranborne Chase.* Cambridge: Cambridge University Press.

Bartlett, Katherine. 1940. How Don Pedro de Tovar Discovered the Hopi and Don Garcia Lopez de Cardenas Saw the Grand Canyon, with Notes upon Their Probable Route. *Plateau* 12:37–45.

Basso, Keith H. 1996a. Wisdom Sits in Places: Notes on a Western Apache Landscape. In *Senses of Place,* ed. Steven Feld and Keith H. Basso, pp. 53–90. Santa Fe, NM: School of American Research Press.

—— 1996b. *Wisdom Sits in Places.* Albuquerque, NM: University of New Mexico Press.

Bauer, Brian. 1998. *The Sacred Landscape of the Inca: The Cusco Ceque System.* Austin, TX: University of Texas Press.

Bauer, Brian S., and David S. P. Dearborn. 1995. *Astronomy and Empire in the Ancient Andes: The Cultural Origins of Inca Sky Watching.* Austin, TX: University of Texas Press.

Beaglehole, Ernest. 1937. *Notes on Hopi Economic Life.* Yale University Publications in Anthropology. New Haven, CT: Yale University Press.

Beardsley, Felicia. 2006. Archaeological Investigations in Tofol, Kosrae, Eastern Micronesia. Research report submitted to the National Park Service.

Beck, Coleen M. 1979. Ancient Roads on the North Coast of Peru. Ph.D. dissertation. University of California, Berkeley.

—— 1991. Cross-cutting Relationships: The Relative Dating of Ancient Roads on the North Coast of Peru. In *Ancient Road Networks and Settlement Hierarchies in the New World,* ed. Charles Trombold, pp. 66–79. Cambridge: Cambridge University Press.

Becker, Kenneth M., and Jeffrey H. Altschul. 2008. Path Finding: The Archaeology of Trails and Trail Systems. In *Fragile Patterns. The Archaeology of the Western Papaguería,* ed. Jeffrey H. Altschul and Adrianne G. Rankin, pp. 419–46. Tucson, AZ: SRI Press.

Becker-Donner, Etta. 1956. Archaeologiche Funde am Mittleren Guaporé (Brazilien). *Archiv für Völkerkunde* 11:202–49.

Beckwith, Martha. 1938. *Mandan-Hidatsa Myths and Ceremonies.* Memoirs of the American Folklore Society 32. New York: American Folklore Society.

Bell, J. 1992. On Capturing Agency in Theories about Prehistory. In *Representations in Archaeology,* ed. J. C. Gardin and C. S. Peebles, pp. 30–55. Bloomington, IN: Indiana University Press.

Bell, Tyler, and Gary Lock. 2000. Topographic and Cultural Influences on

Walking the Ridgeway in Later Prehistoric Times. In *Beyond the Map: Archaeology and Spatial Technologies,* ed. Gary Lock, pp. 85–100. Amsterdam: IOS Press.

Bell, Tyler, Andrew Wilson, and Andrew Wickham. 2002. Tracking the Samnites: Landscape and Communications Routes in the Sangro Valley, Italy. *American Journal of Archaeology* 106(2): 69–86.

Belloc, Hilaire. 1911. *The Old Road.* London: Constable & Co.

Ben-David, Chaim. 2002. The Zoar Ascent—A Newly Discovered Roman Road Connecting Zoar-Safi and the Moabite Plateau. In *Limes XVIII: Proceedings of the XVIIIth International Congress of Roman Frontier Studies Held in Amman, Jordan,* ed. Philip Freeman, Julian Bennett, Zbigniew T. Fiema, and Birgittan Hoffman, pp. 103–12. BAR International Series 1084(II). Oxford.

Benavides Castillo, Antonio. 1981. *Los Caminos de Cobá y sus Implicaciones Sociales (Proyecto Coba).* Coleccion Científica Arqueología, Centro Regional Sureste. México DF: Instituto Nacional de Antropología e Historia.

Bender, Barbara, ed. 1993. *Landscape: Politics and Perspectives.* Providence, RI: Berg.

—— 2001. Landscapes On-the-Move. *Journal of Social Archaeology* 1(1): 75–89.

Bender, Barbara, and Margot Winer, eds. 2001. *Contested Landscapes: Movement, Exile, and Place.* Oxford: Berg.

Bengtsson, L., and S. Avilés. 2000. Proyecto Contactos prehistóricos entre los Andes y la Amazonía: Informe de la primera fase de trabajo de campo en Bolivia. La Paz: Göterborgs Universitet, Unidad Nacional de Arqueología.

Berlin, G. Lennis, T. J. Ferguson, and E. Richard Hart. 1993. Photointerpretation of Native American Trails in the Zuni Salt Lake Region of New Mexico and Arizona. In *Traditional Cultural Properties of Four Tribes: The Fence Lake Mine Project,* Vol. 1, ed. E. Richard Hart and T. J. Ferguson, pp. 1–103. Seattle, WA: Institute of the North American West.

Bernardini, Wesley. 2005. *Hopi Oral Tradition and the Archaeology of Identity.* Tucson, AZ: University of Arizona Press.

—— 2007. *Hopi History in Stone: The Tutuveni Petroglyph Site.* Arizona State Museum Archaeological Series 200. Tucson, AZ.

Bevington, Gary. 1995. *Maya for Travelers and Students: A Guide to Language and Culture in Yucatán.* Austin, TX: University of Texas Press.

Bey, George J., III, Craig A. Hanson, and William M. Ringle. 1997. Classic to Post Classic Ek Balam, Yucatan: Architectural and Ceramic Evidence for Defining the Transition. *Latin American Antiquity* 8(3): 237–54.

Biga, M. G. 1998. The Marriage of Eblaite Princess Tagrish-Damu with a Son of Nagar's King. In *About Subartu: Studies Devoted to Upper Mesopotamia, Subartu 4, 2,* ed. M. Lebeau, pp. 17–39. Turnhout: Brepols.

Bintliff, John. 2004. Time, Structure, and Agency: The Annales, Emergent Complexity, and Archaeology. In *A Companion to Archaeology,* ed. John Bintliff, pp. 174–94. Oxford: Blackwell.

Bintliff, J. L., and A. M. Snodgrass. 1988. Off-Site Pottery Distributions: A Regional and Interregional Perspective. *Current Anthropology* 29:506–13.

Birmingham, J. M. 1961. The Overland Route across Anatolia in the Eighth and Seventh Centuries B.C. *Anatolian Studies* 11:185–95.

Bischoff, Matt C. 2005. Life in the Past Lane: The Route 66 Experience. *Technical Series 86*. Tucson, AZ: Statistical Research.

Blaikie, P., and Harold Brookfield. 1987. *Land Degradation and Society*. New York: Methuen.

Blakely, Jeffrey A., and James A. Sauer. 1985. The Road to Wadi al-Jubah: Archaeology on the Ancient Spice Route in Yemen. *Expedition* 27(1): 2–9.

Blakeslee, Donald J., and Robert Blasing. 1988. Indian Trails in the Central Plains. *Plains Anthropologist* 33:17–25.

Block, David. 1994. *Mission Culture in the Upper Amazon: A Native Tradition, Jesuit Enterprise and Secular Policy in Moxos, 1660–1880*. Lincoln, NE: University of Nebraska Press.

Boas, Franz. 1934. *Geographical Names of the Kwakiutl*. New York: Columbia University Press.

Boglar, L., and A. Bognar. 1973–81. F. X. Eder's Description of Peruvian Missions from the 18th Century. *Acta Ethnographica* (Budapest) 22(1–2): 1–49; 30(1–2): 111–41, 379–406. Budapest: Akadémiai Kiadó.

Bolles, David, and William J. Folan. 2001. An Analysis of Roads Listed in Colonial Dictionaries and Their Relevance to Pre-Hispanic Linear Features in the Yucatan Peninsula. *Ancient Mesoamerica* 12:299–314.

Borgo, David. 2004. The Play of Meaning and the Meaning of Play in Jazz. *Journal of Conciousness Studies* 11(3–4): 174–90.

Borstad, Karen A. 2000. Ancient Roads in the Madaba Plains of Transjordan: Research from a Geographic Perspective. Ph.D. dissertation. University of Arizona, Tucson.

Boserup, E. 1965. *The Conditions of Agricultural Growth: The Economics of Agrarian Change under Population Pressure*. Chicago, IL: Aldine.

Botero Páez, Sofia, Norberto Vélez Escobar, and Lucas Mateo Guingue Valencia. 2000. Ubicación de la ruta seguida por los conquistadores Robledo y Núñez Pedroso en el descubrimiento de los valles de Aburrá y Ríonegro, Antioquia, Colombia. In *Caminos Precolombinos: las Vías, los Ingenieros y los Viajeros*, ed. Leonor Herrera and Marianne Cardale de Schrimpff, pp. 195–217. Bogotá: Instituto Colombiano de Antropología y Historia.

Bourdieu, Pierre. 1977. *Outline of a Theory of Practice*. Cambridge: Cambridge University Press.

Bowers, Alfred W. 1948. *A History of the Mandan and Hidatsa*. Chicago, IL: University of Chicago Press.

—— 1950. *Mandan Social and Ceremonial Organization*. Chicago, IL: University of Chicago Press.

—— 1963. *Hidatsa Social and Ceremonial Organization*. Washington, DC: USGPO.

Bowman, I. 1924. *Desert Trails of the Atacama*. New York: American Geographic Society.

Bozzoli de Wille, Maria. 1975. Birth and Death in the Belief System of the Bribri Indians of Costa Rica. Ph.D. dissertation, Anthropology. University of Georgia, Athens.

Bradley, Richard. 2000. *An Archaeology of Natural Places*. London: Routledge.

Brett, Patrick. 2007. A GIS and Network Model of the Pre-Columbian Hydraulic Complex of Baures. Master's thesis, Anthropology. University of Pennsylvania, Philadelphia.

Brew, J. O. 1950. The Highway and the Anthropologist. In *Highways in Our National Life*, ed. Jean Labatut and Wheaton J. Lane, pp. 3–9. Princeton, NJ: Princeton University Press.

Briant, Pierre. 1996. *Histoire de l'Empire Perse*. Paris: Fayard.

Briones, Luis, Lautaro Nuñez, and Vivien G. Standen. 2005. Geoglifos y Tráfico Prehispánico de Caravanas de Llamas en el Desierto de Atacama (Norte De Chile). *Chungará* 37(2): 195–223.

Britt, Claude. 1973. An Old Navajo Trail with Associated Petroglyph Trail Markers, Canyon de Chelly, Arizona. *Plateau* 46 (1): 6–11.

Brody, Hugh. 1981. *Maps and Dreams: Indians and the British Columbia Frontier*. Vancouver, BC: Douglas & McIntyre.

Brookfield, Harold. 2001. *Exploring Agrodiversity*. New York: Columbia University Press.

Brown, Cecil. 1983. Where Do Cardinal Directions Come From? *Anthropological Linguistics* 25(2): 121–61.

Brück, Joanna. 1998. In the Footsteps of the Ancestors: A Review of Christopher Tilley's *A Phenomenology of Landscape: Places, Paths, and Monuments*. *Archaeological Review from Cambridge* 15(1): 23–36.

Bruguier, B. 2000. Les ponts en pierre du Cambodge ancien: Aménagement ou controle du territoire? *Bulletin de l'École Française d'Extrême-Orient* 87:529–51.

Brumfiel, E. M. 1992. Distinguished Lecture in Archeology: Breaking and Entering the Ecosystem—Gender, Class, and Faction Steal the Show. *American Anthropologist* 94:551–67.

Brumfiel, E. M., and J. W. Fox, eds. 1994. *Factional Competition and Political Development in the New World*. Cambridge: Cambridge University Press.

Burrus, Ernest J. 1971. *Kino and Manje, Explorers of Sonora and Arizona*. Jesuit Historical Institute. St. Louis, MO: St. Louis University.

Bustillos Carrillo, Antonio. 1964. *El Sacbé de los Mayas*. Mexico, DF: Costa-Amic.

Bynum, M. R. 1995. Studies in the Topography of Southern Corinthia. Ph.D. dissertation, Classics. University of California, Berkeley.

Calandra, Horacio Adolfo, and Susana Alicia Salceda. 2004. Bolivian Amazonia: Archaeology of the Llanos de Mojos. *Acta Amazónica* 34(2): 155–63.

Campbell, Matthew. 2006. Memory and Monumentality in the Raratongan Landscape. *Antiquity* 80:102–17.

Campbell, T. N., and William T. Field. 1968. Identification of Comanche Raiding Trails in Trans-Pecos Texas. *West Texas Historical Association Year Book* 44:128–44.

Canouts, Veletta, Jennifer Allison-Ray, and John C. Ravesloot. 2002. The Huhugam Heritage Center: Interpreting the Archaeological Landscape. *Visible Archaeology on the Gila River Indian Reservation.* PMIP Report 21. Sacaton, AZ: Cultural Resource Management Program, Gila River Indian Community.

Capedri, Silvio. 2003. Trachytes Used for Paving Roman Roads in the Po Plain: Characterization by Petrographic and Chemical Parameters and Provenance of Flagstones. *Journal of Archaeological Science* 30(4): 491–509.

Cardale de Schrimpff, Marianne. 1996. *Caminos Prehispanicos en Calima.* Bogotá: Fundación de Investigaciones Arqueológicas Nacionales Banco de la República Asociación Pro-Calima.

—— 2000a. Caminos al paisaje del pasado: reflexiones sobre los caminos precolombinos en Colombia. In *Caminos Precolombinos: las Vías, los Ingenieros y los Viajeros,* ed. Leonor Herrera and Marianne Cardale de Schrimpff, pp. 43–85. Bogotá: Instituto Colombiano de Antropología y Historia.

—— 2000b. Caminos precolombinos de las Cordilleras de Colombia: balance y propuestas para el futuro. In *Caminos Precolombinos: las Vías, los Ingenieros y los Viajeros,* ed. Leonor Herrera and Marianne Cardale de Schrimpff, pp. 269–99. Bogotá: Instituto Colombiano de Antropología y Historia.

Caroll, Alex K., M. Nieves Zedeño, and Richard W. Stoffle. 2004. Landscapes of the Ghost Dance: A Cartography of Numic Ritual. *Journal of Archaeological Method and Theory* 11(2): 127–56.

Carrasco V., Ramón. 1993. Formación Sociopolítica en el Puuc: El Sacbe Uxmal-Nohpat-Kabah. In *Perspectivas Antropológicas en el Mundo Maya,* ed. Josefa Iglesias Ponce de León and Francesc Ligorred Perramon, pp. 199–212. Publication No. 2. Madrid: Sociedad Española de Estudios Mayas.

Carson, James Taylor. 2002. Ethnogeography and the Native American Past. *Ethnohistory* 49(4): 769–88.

Carsten, J., and S. Hugh-Jones. 1995. *About the House: Lévi-Strauss and Beyond.* New York: Cambridge University Press.

Carvajal, Gaspar de. 1988 [1541–42]. Discovery of the Orellana River. In *The Discovery of the Amazon According to the Account of Friar Gaspar de Carvajal and Other Documents,* ed. J. Toribio Medina, pp. 167–235. New York: American Geographical Society.

Casanova, Frank E. 1967. Trails to Supai in Cataract Canyon. *Plateau* 39(3): 124–30.

Casebier, Dennis G. 1972. *Carleton's Pah-Ute Campaign.* Narco, CA: Dennis G. Casebier.

Casey, Edward S. 1996. How to Get from Space to Place in a Fairly Short Stretch of Time. In *Senses of Place,* ed. Steven Feld and Keith H. Basso, pp. 13–52. Santa Fe, NM: School of American Research Press.

Casparie, W. A. 1987. Bog Trackways in the Netherlands. *Palaeohistoria* 29: 35–65.

Castillo, Joseph del. 1906 [1676]. *Relación de la provincia de Mojos.* Redactado por M. V. Ballivian, Documentos para la Historia Geográfica de Bolivia, Serie Primera, Epoca Colonial. Tomo I, *Las Provincias de Mojos y Chiquitos,* pp. 294–395. La Paz: J. M. Gamarra.

Castillo Farreras, Victor M. 1969. Caminos del Mundo Nahuatl. *Estudios de Cultura Nahuatl* 8:175–87.

Castro, Victoria, Varinia Varela, Carlos Aldunate, and Edgardo Araneda. 2004. Principios Orientadores y Metodología para el Estudio del Qhapaqñan en Atacama: Desde El Portezuelo del Inka hasta Río Grande. *Chungará* 36(2): 463–81.

Catlin, George. 1965 [1834]. *Letters and Notes on the Manners, Customs, and Condition of the North American Indians.* Minneapolis, MN: Ross and Haines.

Caylor, Herta B. 1976. Brief Note on the Maps. Appendix A in *The Chemehuevis,* by Carobeth Laird, pp. 263–76. Banning, CA: Malki Museum Press.

CEAM, ed. 2003. *Moxos: una limnocultura; cultura y medio natural en la Amazonia Boliviana.* Barcelona: Centre d'Etudis Amazonics.

Chadwick, Adrian, ed. 2004. *Stories from the Landscape: Archaeologies of Inhabitation.* Oxford: Archaeopress.

Chakrabarti, Dilip K. 2005. *The Archaeology of the Deccan Routes: The Ancient Routes from the Ganga Plain to the Deccan.* Delhi: Munshiram Manoharlal.

Charles, M. 1998. Fodder from Dung: The Recognition and Interpretation of Dung-Derived Plant Material from Archaeological Sites. *Environmental Archaeology* 1:111–22.

Charles, M., and A. Bogaard. 2001. Third-Millennium BC Charred Plant Remains from Tell Brak. In *Excavations at Tell Brak.* Vol. 2: *Nagar in the Third Millennium BC,* ed. D. Oates, J. Oates, and H. McDonald, pp. 301–26. Cambridge: McDonald Institute for Archaeological Research and the British School of Archaeology in Iraq.

Charlton, Thomas H. 1991. The Influence and Legacy of Teotihuacan on Regional Routes and Urban Planning. In *Ancient Road Networks and Settlement Hierarchies in the New World,* ed. Charles Trombold, pp. 186–97. Cambridge: Cambridge University Press.

Chase, Arlen F., and Diane Z. Chase. 1987. *Glimmers of a Forgotten Realm: Maya Archaeology at Caracol, Belize.* Orlando, FL: University of Central Florida Press.

—— 1996. The Causeways of Caracol. *Belize Today* 10(3/4): 31–32.

—— 2001. Ancient Maya Causeways and Site Organization at Caracol, Belize. *Ancient Mesoamerica* 12:273–81.

Cheetham, David. 2004. The Role of "Terminus Groups" in Lowland Maya

Site Planning: An Example from Cahal Pech. In *The Ancient Maya of the Belize Valley: Half a Century of Archaeological Research,* ed. James F. Garber, pp. 125–48. Gainesville, FL: University Press of Florida.

Chevalier, Raymond. 1976. *Roman Roads.* Berkeley, CA: University of California Press.

Chisholm, M. 1962. *Rural Settlement and Land Use: An Essay in Location.* London: Hutchinson.

Clarkson, Persis. 1990. The Archaeology of the Nazca Pampa, Peru: Environmental and Cultural Parameters. In *The Lines of Nazca,* ed. A. Aveni, pp. 115–72. Memoirs of the American Philosophical Society 183. Philadelphia: American Philosophical Society.

Clarkson, Persis B., and Luis Briones. 2001. Geoglifos, senderos y etnoarqueologia de caravanas en el desierto chileno. *Boletin del Museo Chileno de Arte Precolombino* 8:35–45.

Cobos, Rafael, and Terance L. Winemiller. 2001. The Late and Terminal Classic-period Causeway Systems of Chichen Itza, Yucatan, Mexico. *Ancient Mesoamerica* 12:283–91.

Coe, Michael D. 1965. A Model of Ancient Community Structure in the Maya Lowlands. *Southwest Journal of Anthropology* 21(2): 97–114.

—— 2003. *Angkor and the Khmer Civilization.* London: Thames & Hudson.

Coe, William R. 1988. *Tikal: A Handbook of the Ancient Maya Ruins.* 2nd ed., with revisions by Carlos Rudy Larios V. Guatemala: Centro Impresor Piedra Santa. First published 1967 by University of Pennsylvania Museum of Archaeology and Anthropology, Philadelphia.

Coello Rodríguez, Antonio. 2000. El camino inca en el distrito de San Damián, provincia de Huarochirí, Perú. In *Caminos Precolombinos: las Vías, los Ingenieros y los Viajeros,* ed. Leonor Herrera and Marianne Cardale de Schrimpff, pp. 167–93. Bogotá: Instituto Colombiano de Antropología y Historia.

Coggins, Clemency C. 1980. The Shape of Time: Some Political Implications of a Four-part Figure. *American Antiquity* 45:729–39.

—— 1988. Classic Maya Metaphors of Death and Life. *RES* 16:64–84.

Coleman, Simon, and John Eade. 2004. Introduction: Reframing Pilgrimage. In *Reframing Pilgrimage, Cultures in Motion,* ed. Simon Coleman and John Eade, pp. 1–25. London: Routledge.

Coleman, Simon, and John Elsner. 1994. The Pilgrim's Progress: Art, Architecture, and Ritual Movement at Sinai. *World Archaeology* 26(1): 73–89.

Coles, Bryony, and John Coles. 1986. *Sweet Track to Glastonbury: The Somerset Levels in Prehistory.* London: Thames & Hudson.

Colton, Harold S. 1941. Prehistoric Trade in the Southwest. *Scientific Monthly* 52(4): 308–19.

—— 1964. Principal Hopi Trails. *Plateau* 36:91–94.

Colton, Mary Russell, and Harold S. Colton. 1931. Petroglyphs, the Record of a Great Adventure. *American Anthropologist* 33(1): 32–37.

Comfort, Anthony, Catherine Abadie-Reynal, and Rifat Ergeç. 2000. Crossing the Euphrates in Antiquity: Zeugma Seen from Space. *Anatolian Studies* 50:99–126.

Comfort, Anthony, and Rifat Ergeç. 2001. Following the Euphrates in Antiquity: North-South Routes around Zeugma. *Anatolian Studies* 51:19–49.

Cordell, Linda S., David E. Doyel, and Keith W. Kintigh. 1994. Processes of Aggregation in the Prehistoric Southwest. In *Themes in Southwest Prehistory,* ed. George J. Gumerman, pp. 109–33. Santa Fe, NM: School of American Research Press.

Courty, M. A. 1994. Le cadre paléographique des occupations humaines dans le bassin du Haut-Khabur (Syrie du Nord-Est). Premiers Résultats. *Paléorient* 20:21–59.

Craine, Eugene R., and Reginald C. Reidorp, eds. and trans. 1979. *The Codex Pérez and the Book of Chilam Balam of Maní.* Norman, OK: University of Oklahoma Press.

Crawford, O. G. S. 1953. *Archaeology in the Field.* London: Phoenix House.

Crown, Patricia L., and W. H. Wills. 2003. Modifying Pottery and Kivas at Chaco: Pentimento, Restoration, or Renewal? *American Antiquity* 68(3): 511–32.

Crumley, Carole L. 1987. A Dialectical Critique of Hierarchy. In *Power Relations and State Formation,* ed. T. C. Patterson and C. W. Gailey, pp. 155–69. Washington, DC: American Anthropological Association.

—— 1995. Heterarchy and the Analysis of Complex Societies. In *Heterarchy and the Analysis of Complex Societies,* ed. Robert M. Ehrenreich, Carole L. Crumley, and Janet E. Levy, pp. 1–5. Archeological Papers of the American Anthropological Association 6. Washington, DC: American Anthropological Association.

Crumley, Carole L., and William H. Marquardt, eds. 1987. *Regional Dynamics: Burgundian Landscapes in Historical Perspective.* San Diego, CA: Academic Press.

D'Altroy, T. N., and T. K. Earle. 1985. Staple Finance, Wealth Finance, and Storage in the Inka Political Economy. *Current Anthropology* 26:187–206.

Darling, J. Andrew, and B. Sunday Eiselt. 2003. Trails Research in the Gila Bend. In "Trails, Rock Features and Homesteading in the Gila Bend Area; A Report on the State Route 85, Gila Bend to Buckeye, Archaeological Project," ed. John C. Czarzasty, Kathleen Peterson, and Glen E. Rice. Anthropological Field Studies 43. Draft on file in Office of Cultural Resource Management, Department of Anthropology, Arizona State University, Tempe, AZ.

Darling, J. Andrew, and Barnaby V. Lewis. 2007. Songscapes and Calendar Sticks. In *The Hohokam Millennium,* ed. Paul Fish and Suzanne Fish, pp. 130–39. Santa Fe, NM: School of American Research Press.

Darling, J. Andrew, John C. Ravesloot, and Michael R. Waters. 2004. Village Drift and Riverine Settlement: Modeling Akimel O'odham Land Use. *American Anthropologist* 106(2): 282–95.

Darling, Patrick J. 1984. *Archaeology and History in Southern Nigeria: The Ancient Linear Earthworks of Benin and Ishan.* Cambridge Monographs in African Archaeology 11. BAR International Series 215. Oxford: BAR.

Darnell, John C. 2002. The Narrow Doors of the Desert: Ancient Egyptian Roads in the Theban Western Desert. In *Inscribed Landscapes: Marking and Making Place,* ed. Bruno David and Meredith Wilson, pp. 104–21. Honolulu, HI: University of Hawai'i Press.

Darnell, John C., and Deborah Darnell. 2002. Caravan Tracks of the Almat Tal. In *Theban Road Survey in the Egyptian Western Desert 1.* Oriental Institute Publications 119. Chicago, IL.

Darvill, Timothy. 1999. Traditions of Landscape Archaeology in Britain: Issues of Time and Scale. In *One Land, Many Landscapes: Papers from a Session Held at the European Association of Archaeologists Fifth Annual Meeting in Bournemouth 1999,* ed. Timothy Darvill and Martin Gojda, pp. 33–45. BAR International Series 987. Oxford: BAR.

David, Bruno, and Meredith Wilson, eds. 2002. *Inscribed Landscapes: Marking and Making Place.* Honolulu, HI: University of Hawai'i Press.

Davies, Hugh. 2002. *Roads in Roman Britain.* Stroud: Tempus.

Davis, James T. 1961. *Trade Routes and Economic Exchange among the Indians of California.* University of California Archaeological Survey Reports 54. Ramona, CA.

Dearman, J. Andrew. 1997. Roads and Settlements in Moab. *Biblical Archaeologist* 60(4): 205–13.

DeBoer, Warren. 1986. Pillage and Production in the Amazon: A View through the Conibo of the Ucayali Basin, Eastern Peru. *World Archaeology* 18(2): 231–46.

—— 2001. The Big Drink: Feast and Forum in the Upper Amazon. In *Feasting in the Archaeological Record,* ed. Michael Dietler and Brian Hayden, pp. 215–40. Washington, DC: Smithsonian Institution Press.

Della Portella, Ivana, ed. 2004. *The Appian Way.* Verona: Arsenale Editrice.

De Marrais, Elizabeth, Luis Jaime Castillo, and Timothy Earle. 1996. Ideology, Materialization, and Power Strategies. *Current Anthropology* 37(1): 15–32.

Denevan, William M. 1966. *The Aboriginal Cultural Geography of the Llanos de Mojos of Bolivia.* Berkeley, CA: University of California Press.

—— 1991. Prehistoric Roads and Causeways in Lowland Tropical America. In *Ancient Road Networks and Settlement Hierarchies in the New World,* ed. Charles Trombold, pp. 230–42. Cambridge: Cambridge University Press.

—— 1992. Stone vs. Metal Axes: The Ambiguity of Shifting Cultivation in Prehistoric Amazonia. *Journal of the Steward Anthropological Society* 20(1–2): 153–65.

—— 2001. *Cultivated Landscapes of Native Amazonia and the Andes.* Oxford: Oxford University Press.

—— 2006. Pre-European Forest Cultivation in Amazonia. In *Time and Complexity* in *Historical Ecology: Studies from the Neotropical Lowlands,* ed. William Balée and Clark Erickson, pp. 153–64. New York: Columbia University Press.

Descola, Philippe. 1994. *The Society of Nature: A Native Ecology in Amazonia.* Cambridge: Cambridge University Press.

Devereux, George. 1961. *Mohave Ethnopsychiatry: The Psychic Disturbances of an Indian Tribe.* Washington, DC: Smithsonian Institution Press.

Dienhart, John M. 1989. *The Mayan Languages: A Comparative Vocabulary* 1–3. Odense: Odense University Press.

Dierks, Klaus. 1992. *Namibian Roads in History: From the 13th century till Today.* Frankfurt am Main: Johann Wolfgang Goethe-Universität.

Dietler, M. 2003. Clearing the Table: Some Concluding Reflections on Commensal Politics and Imperial States. In *The Archaeology and Politics of Food and Feasting in Early States and Empires,* ed. T. L. Bray, pp. 271–82. New York: Kluwer.

Dietler, M., and B. Hayden, eds. 2001. *Feasts: Archaeological and Ethnographic Perspectives on Food, Politics, and Power.* Washington, DC: Smithsonian Institution Press.

Dillon, Brian. 1984. Island Building and Villages of the Dead: Living Archaeology in the Comarca de San Blas, Panama. *Journal of New World Archaeology* 6(2): 49–65.

Dittert, Alfred E., and Ward Alan Minge. 1993. An Ethnohistoric Account of the Traditional Cultural Properties Identified by the Acoma Tribe in and adjacent to the SRP Fence Lake Mine Project Area. In *Traditional Cultural Properties of Four Tribes: The Fence Lake Mine Project,* by E. Richard Hart and T. J. Ferguson, pp. 1–59. Seattle, WA: Institute of the North American West.

Dobres, Marcia-Anne, and John E. Robb. 2005. "Doing" Agency: Introductory Remarks on Methodology. *Journal of Archaeological Method and Theory* 12:159–66.

Dobres, Marcia-Anne, and John E. Robb, eds. 2000. *Agency in Archaeology.* London: Routledge.

Doolittle, William E. 1984. Agricultural Change as an Incremental Process. *Annals of the Association of American Geographers* 74(1): 124–37.

—— 2000. *Cultivated Landscapes of Native North America.* Oxford: Oxford University Press.

Dornan, Jennifer L. 2002. Agency and Archaeology: Past, Present, and Future Directions. *Journal of Archaeological Method and Theory* 9:303–29.

Dorsey, David A. 1991. *The Roads and Highways of Ancient Israel.* Baltimore, MD: Johns Hopkins University Press.

Dougherty, Bernardo, and Horacio Calandra. 1981. Nota preliminar sobre investigaciones arqueológicas en los Llanos de Moxos, Departamento del Beni, Republica de Bolivia. *Revista del Museo de la Plata, Sección Arqueológica* 53:87–106.

—— 1983. Archaeological Research in Northeastern Beni, Bolivia. *National Geographic Society Research Reports* 21:129–36.

—— 1984. Prehispanic Human Settlement in the Llanos de Mojos, Bolivia. In *Quaternary of South America and Antarctic Peninsula*, vol. 2, ed. Jorge Rabassa, pp. 163–99. Rotterdam: A. D. Balkema.

Dowdle, Jason. 1987. Road Networks and Exchange Systems in the Aeduan Civitas, 300 B.C.–A.D. 300. In *Regional Dynamics: Burgundian Landscapes in Historical Perspective*, ed. Carole L. Crumley and William H. Marquardt, pp. 265–94. San Diego: Academic Press.

Duke, Darren. 2006. *Archaeological Reconnaissance of Sloan Canyon*. Sacramento, CA: Far Western Archaeological Consultants.

Dunnell, Robert C. 1992. The Notion Site. In *Space, Time, and Archaeological Landscapes*, ed. Jacqueline Rossignol and LuAnn Wandsnider, pp. 21–41. New York: Plenum.

Dunsany, Lord. 1954. The Return. In *The Sword of Welleran and Other Tales of Enchantment*. New York: Devin-Adair Co.

Earle, Timothy. 1991. Paths and Roads in Evolutionary Perspective. In *Ancient Road Networks and Settlement Hierarchies in the New World*, ed. Charles D. Trombold, pp. 10–16. Cambridge: Cambridge University Press.

Eder, Ferencz Xaver (Francisco Javier). 1985 [1772]. *Breve descripción de las reducciones de Mojos*. Historia Boliviana. Cochabamba: Traducción y edición de. Josep M. Barnadas.

—— 1888 [1791]. *Descripción de la Provincia de los Mojos en el Reino del Perú*, trad. Nicolás Armentia. La Paz: Imprenta El Siglo Industrial.

Edmonson, Munro S. 1982. *The Ancient Future of the Itza: The Book of Chilam Balam of Tizimin*. Austin, TX: University of Texas Press.

—— 1986. *Heaven Born Merida and Its Destiny: The Book of Chilam Balam of Chumayel*. Austin, TX: University of Texas Press.

—— 1997. *Quiché Dramas and Divinatory Calendars*. Middle American Research Institute Publication 66. New Orleans, LA: Tulane University.

Eidem, J., I. Finkel, and M. Bonechi. 2001. The Third Millennium Inscriptions. In *Excavations at Tell Brak*. Vol. 2, *Nagar in the Third Millennium BC*, by D. Oates, J. Oates, and H. McDonald, pp. 99–120. Cambridge: McDonald Institute for Archaeological Research and the British School of Archaeology in Iraq.

Eiseman, Fred B., Jr. 1959. The Hopi Salt Trail. *Plateau* 32(2): 25–32.

—— 1961. Discovery of the Hopi Salt Cave. *Spout* (November): 2–7.

Ellis, Florence H. 1961. The Hopi, Their History and Use of Lands. Defendant's Exhibit E-500, Indian Claims Commission Docket 229. Published in 1974 by Garland.

Equiluz, Diego de. 1884 [1696]. *Historia de la Misión de Mojos*. Lima: Imprenta del Universo.

Erickson, Clark L. 1980. Sistemas agrícolas prehispánicos en los Llanos de Mojos. *América Indígena* 40(4): 731–55.

—— 1988. Raised Field Agriculture in the Lake Titicaca Basin: Putting Ancient Andean Agriculture Back to Work. *Expedition* 30(3): 8–16.

—— 1993. The Social Organization of Prehispanic Raised Field Agriculture in the Lake Titicaca Basin. In *Economic Aspects of Water Management in the Prehispanic New World,* ed. Vernon Scarborough and Barry Isaac, pp. 369–426. Research in Economic Anthropology Supplement 7. Greenwich, CT: JAI.

—— 1995. Archaeological Perspectives on Ancient Landscapes of the Llanos de Mojos in the Bolivian Amazon. In *Archaeology in the American Tropics: Current Analytical Methods and Applications,* ed. Peter Stahl, pp. 66–95. Cambridge: Cambridge University Press.

—— 1996. *Investigación arqueológica del sistema agrícola de los camellones en la cuenca del lago Titicaca del Perú.* La Paz, Bolivia: Centro de Información para el Desarrollo y Programa Interinstitucional de Waru Waru (PIWA).

—— 2000a. An Artificial Landscape-Scale Fishery in the Bolivian Amazon. *Nature* 408:190–93.

—— 2000b. Lomas de ocupación en los Llanos de Moxos. In *La Arqueología de las Tierras Bajas,* ed. Alicia Durán Coirolo and Roberto Bracco Boksar, pp. 207–26. Montevideo: Comisión Nacional de Arqueología, Ministerio de Educación y Cultura.

—— 2000c. Los caminos prehispánicos de la Amazonia boliviana. In *Caminos Precolombinos: las Vías, los Ingenieros y los Viajeros,* ed. Leonor Herrera and Marianne Cardale de Schrimpff, pp. 15–42. Bogotá: Instituto Colombiano de Antropología e Historia.

—— 2001. Pre-Columbian Roads of the Amazon. *Expedition* 43(2): 21–30.

—— 2002. Large Moated Settlements: A Late Precolumbian Phenomenon in the Amazon. Paper presented at the 2nd Annual Meeting of The Society for the Anthropology of Lowland South America (SALSA). Annapolis, MD: St. Johns College.

—— 2006a. The Domesticated Landscapes of the Bolivian Amazon. In *Time and Complexity in Historical Ecology: Studies from the Neotropical Lowlands,* ed. William Balée and Clark Erickson, pp. 235–78. New York: Columbia University Press.

—— 2006b. Intensification, Political Economy, and the Farming Community: In Defense of a Bottom-Up Perspective of the Past. In *Agricultural Practices and Strategies,* ed. Charles Stanish and Joyce Marcus, pp. 336–63. Los Angeles, CA: Cotsen Archaeological Institute, UCLA.

—— 2008. Amazonia: The Historical Ecology of a Domesticated Landscape. In *Handbook of South American Archaeology,* ed. Helaine Silverman and William Isbell, pp. 157–83. New York: Springer.

Erickson, Clark L., and William Balée. 2006. The Historical Ecology of a Complex Landscape in Bolivia. In *Time and Complexity in Historical Ecology: Studies in the Neotropical Lowlands,* ed. William Balée and Clark Erickson, pp. 187–234. New York: Columbia University Press.

Erickson, Clark L., Wilma Winkler, and Kay Candler. 1997. Informe sobre las investigaciones arqueológicas en Baures en 1996. Manuscript. Philadelphia, PA, and La Paz: University of Pennsylvania and el Instituto Nacional de Arqueología.

Erickson, Clark, Wilma Winkler, Alexei Vranich, John Walker, and Dante Angelo. 1995. Informe preliminar sobre investigaciones arqueológicas en Baures, Departamento del Beni, Bolivia. Parte I y Parte II. Manuscript. Philadelphia, PA, and La Paz: University of Pennsylvania and el Instituto Nacional de Arqueología.

Espinoza Reyes, Ricardo. 2002. *La gran ruta inca, el capaqñan: The Great Inca route, the Capaqñan*. Lima: Petroleos del Perú.

Evans, Christopher. 1999. Cognitive Maps and Narrative Trails: Fieldwork with the Tamu-mai (Gurung) of Nepal. In *The Archaeology and Anthropology of Landscape*, ed. Peter J. Ucko and Robert Layton, pp. 439–57. London: Routledge.

Ewers, John C. 1968. *Indian Life on the Upper Missouri*. Norman, OK: University of Oklahoma Press.

—— 1980. *The Horse in Blackfoot Indian Culture with Comparative Material from Other Western Tribes*. Reprint, Bureau of American Ethnology Bulletin 159. Washington, DC: Smithsonian Institution Press, 1955.

Ezell, Paul H. 1961. *The Hispanic Acculturation of the Gila River Pimas*. American Anthropological Association Memoir 90. Menasha, WI.

——1963. *The Maricopas. An Identification from Documentary Sources*. University of Arizona Anthropological Papers 6. Tucson, AZ: University of Arizona Press.

Fabian, Stephen. 1992. *Space-Time of the Bororo of Brazil*. Gainesville, FL: University Press of Florida.

Falola, Toyin. 1991. The Yoruba Caravan System of the Nineteenth Century. *International Journal of African Historical Studies* 24(1): 111–32.

Farmer, Malcolm F. 1935. The Mohave Trade Route. *The Masterkey* 9(4): 154–57.

Farriss, Nancy M. 1987. Remembering the Future, Anticipating the Past: History, Time, and Cosmology among the Maya of Yucatan. *Comparative Studies in Society and History* 29(3): 566–93.

Feld, Steven, and Keith Basso, eds. 1996. *Senses of Place*. Santa Fe, NM: School of American Research Press.

Fenwick, Helen. 2004. Ancient Roads and GPS Survey: Modeling the Amarna Plain. *Antiquity* 78(302): 880–85.

Ferguson, T. J. 1998. *Öngtupqa niqw Pisisvayu (Salt Canyon and the Colorado River), the Hopi People and the Grand Canyon*. Kykotsmovi, AZ: Hopi Cultural Preservation Office, The Hopi Tribe.

Ferguson, T. J., Roger Anyon, and G. Lennis Berlin. 1999. By Foot, Burro, and Wagon: Historic Routes of Travel through the Zuni Indian Reservation:

The Hawikku-Hopi Trail, Zuni Salt Trails, and Beale Wagon Road. Manuscript on file with Zuni Heritage and Historic Preservation Office. Zuni, NM: Pueblo of Zuni.

Ferguson, T. J., G. Lennis Berlin, and E. Richard Hart. 1995. *Hopi and Zuni Trails and Traditional Cultural Properties in and near the Interstate, Dead Wash, and Kelsey Housing Clusters on Chambers-Sanders Trust Lands, Apache County, Arizona.* Zuni Heritage and Historic Preservation Office Report 484. Zuni, NM: Pueblo of Zuni.

Ferguson, T. J., and E. Richard Hart. 1985. *A Zuni Atlas.* Norman, OK: University of Oklahoma Press.

Ferguson, T. J., and Eric Polingyouma. 1993. *Sio Önga*, An Ethnohistory of Hopi Use of the Zuni Salt Lake. In *Traditional Cultural Properties of Four Tribes: The Fence Lake Mine Project,* by E. Richard Hart and T. J. Ferguson, pp. 1–103. Seattle, WA: Institute of the North American West.

Ferreira Priegue, Elisa. 1988. Los Caminos Medievales de Galicia. *Boletin Avriense,* Anexo 9. Ourense: Museo Arqueoloxico Provincial.

Fewkes, Jesse Walter. 1900. Tusayan Migration Traditions. In *19th Annual Report of the Bureau of American Ethnology for the Years 1897–1898,* part 2, pp. 573–634. Washington, DC: USGPO.

—— 1906. Hopi Shrines near the East Mesa, Arizona. *American Anthropologist* 8:346–75.

Fischer, Moshe, Benjamin Isaac, and Israel Roll. 1996. *Roman Roads in Judea II.* BAR International Series 618. Oxford: BAR.

Fisher, Charles L. 1999. *Archaeology of the Colonial Road at the John Ellison House, Knox's Headquarters State Historic Site, Vails Gate, Town of New Windsor, Orange County, New York.* Waterford: New York State Office of Parks, Recreation and Historic Preservation, Bureau of Historic Sites.

Fisher, Christopher. 2005. Abandoning the Garden: Demographic and Landscape Change in the Lake Pátzcuaro Basin, Mexico. *American Anthropologist* 107(1): 87–95

—— 2007. Agricultural Intensification in the Lake Pátzcuaro Basin: Landesque Capital as Statecraft. In *Seeking a Richer Harvest: The Archaeology of Subsistence Intensification, Innovation, and Change,* ed. T. Thurston and C. Fisher, pp. 91–106. Studies in Human Ecology and Adaptation 3. New York: Springer.

Fleming, Andrew. 1988. *The Dartmoor Reaves.* London: B. T. Batsford.

—— 1998. *Swaledale: Valley of the Wild River.* Edinburgh: Edinburgh University Press.

—— 1999. Phenomenology and the Megaliths of Wales: A Dreaming too far? *Oxford Journal of Archaeology* 18(2): 119–26.

Flores, Jorge, and Percy Paz. 1987. Cultivation in the Qocha of the South Andean Puna. In *Arid Land Use Strategies and Risk Management in the Andes,* ed. David L. Browman, pp. 271–96. Boulder, CO: Westview.

Fogagnolo, Stefania, and Massimiliano Valenti. 2005. *Via Severiana.* Stato, Italy: Istituto Poligrafico e Zecca Dello.

Folan, William J. 1991. Sacbes of the Northern Maya. In *Ancient Road Networks and Settlement Hierarchies in the New World,* ed. Charles D. Trombold, pp. 222–29. Cambridge: Cambridge University Press.

Folan, William J., Jacinto May Hau, Joyce Marcus, W. Frank Miller, and Raymundo González Heredia. 2001. Los Caminos de Calakmul, Campeche. *Ancient Mesoamerica* 12:293–98.

Folan, William J., Ellen R. Kintz, and Laraine A. Fletcher. 1983. *Coba: A Classic Maya Metropolis.* New York: Academic.

Fonseca, Oscar. 1981. Guayabo de Turrialba and Its Significance. In *Between Continents, Between Seas,* ed. Suzanne Abel-Vidor, pp. 104–11. New York: Abrams.

Foucault, Michel. 1986. Of Other Spaces. *Diacritics* 16(1): 22–27.

Fowler, Andrew P., and John R. Stein. 2001. The Anasazi Great House in Space, Time, and Paradigm. In *Anasazi Regional Organization and the Chaco System,* ed. David E. Doyel, pp. 101–22. Maxwell Museum of Anthropology, Anthropological Papers 5. Albuquerque, NM.

Fowler, M. J. F. 2004. Archaeology through the Keyhole: The Serendipity Effect of Aerial Reconnaissance Revisited. *Interdisciplinary Science Reviews* 29:118–34.

Fowler, Peter J. 1998. Moving through the Landscape. In *The Archaeology of Landscape,* ed. P. Everson and T. Williamson, pp. 25–41. Manchester: Manchester University Press.

—— 2000. *Landscape Plotted and Pieced: Landscape History and Local Archaeology in Fyfield and Overton, Wiltshire.* London: Society of Antiquaries of London.

Fox, John W. 1994. Political Cosmology among the Quiché Maya. In *Factional Competition and Political Development in the New World,* ed. Elizabeth M. Brumfiel and John W. Fox, pp. 158–70. Cambridge: Cambridge University Press.

Frachetti, Michael. 2006. Digital Archaeology and the Scalar Structure of Pastoralist Landscapes: Modeling Mobile Societies of Prehistoric Central Asia. In *Digital Archaeology: Bridging Method and Theory,* ed. T. Evans and P. Daly, pp. 128–47. London: Routledge.

—— 2008. Variability and Dynamic Landscapes of Mobile Pastoralism in Ethnography and Prehistory. In *Archaeology of Mobility: Old and New World Nomadism,* ed. H. Barnard and W. Wendrich, pp. 366–96. Cotsen Institute of Archaeology Monographs 4. Los Angeles, CA: Cotsen Institute of Archaeology, UCLA.

Fredricksen, M. W., and J. B. Ward-Perkins. 1957. The Ancient Road Systems of the Central and Northern Ager Faliscus. *Papers of the British School in Rome* 25:67–208.

Freidel, David A., and Jeremy A. Sabloff. 1984. *Cozumel: Late Maya Settlement Patterns.* New York: Academic.

Freidel, David A., Linda Schele, and Joy Parker. 1993. *Maya Cosmos: Three Thousand Years on the Shaman's Path*. New York: William Morrow.

French, David. 1981. *Roman Roads in Asia Minor*. BAR International Series 392. Oxford: BAR.

—— 1996. Roman Roads. In *Oxford Companion to Archaeology*, ed. Brian Fagan, pp. 612–14. Oxford: Oxford University Press.

—— 1998. Pre- and Early Roman Roads of Asia Minor: The Persian Road. *Iran* 36:15–44.

Gabriel, Kathryn. 1991. *Roads to the Center Place. A Cultural Atlas of Chaco Canyon and the Anasazi*. Boulder, CO: Johnson Books.

Galliazo, Vittoria, ed. 2002. *Via Claudia Augusta: Un'Arteria alle Origini dell'Europa: Ipotesi, Problemi, Prospettive*. Regione del Veneto: Comune di Feltre.

Garson, Adam. 1980. Prehistory, Settlement and Food Production in the Savanna Region of La Calzada de Paez, Venezuela. Ph.D. dissertation, Anthropology. Yale University, New Haven, CT.

Garstang, John. 1943. Hittite Military Roads in Asia Minor: A Study in Imperial Strategy. *American Journal of Archaeology*, 2nd ser., 47:35–62.

Gates, Jennifer E. 2005a. Traveling the Desert Edge: The Ptolemaic Roadways and Regional Economy of Egypt's Eastern Desert in the Fourth through First Centuries BCE. Ph.D. dissertation. University of Michigan, Ann Arbor, MI.

—— 2005b. Hidden Passage: Graeco-Roman Roads in Egypt's Eastern Desert. In *Space and Spatial Analysis in Archaeology*, ed. Elizabeth C. Robertson, Jeffrey D. Seibert, Deepika C. Fernandez, and Marc U. Zender, pp. 315–22. Calgary, AB: University of Calgary Press.

Gelb, I. J. 1979. Household and Family in Early Mesopotamia. In *State and Temple Economy in the Ancient Near East*, vol. 1, ed. E. Lipinski, pp. 1–98. Leuven: Departement Oriëntalistiek, Katholieke Universiteit.

Gelo, Daniel J. 2000. Comanche Land and Ever Has Been: A Native Geography of the Nineteenth-Century Comancheria. *Southwestern Historical Quarterly* 53(3): 273–308.

Genotte, Jean-François. 2001. The Mapa De Otumba. *Ancient Mesoamerica* 12(1): 127–47.

Gibson, Erin. 2007. The Archaeology of Movement in a Mediterranean Landscape. *Journal of Mediterranean Archaeology* 20(1): 61–87.

Giddens, Anthony. 1984. *The Constitution of Society: Outline of the Theory of Structuration*. Cambridge: Polity Press.

Gillespie, S. D. 2000. Rethinking Ancient Maya Social Organization: Replacing "Lineage" with "House." *American Anthropologist* 102:467–84.

Glaskin, Katie. 2005. Innovation and Ancestral Revelation: The Case of Dreams. *Journal of the Royal Anthropological Institute*, n.s., 11:297–314.

Glowczewski, Barbara. 2000. *Dream Trackers: Yapa Art and Knowledge of the Australian Desert*. CD-ROM. Paris: UNESCO.

Golledge, Reginald G. 2003. Human Wayfinding and Cognitive Maps. In *Colonization of Unfamiliar Landscapes. The Archaeology of Adaptation,* ed. Marcy Rockman and James Steele, pp. 25–43. London: Routledge.

Gómez, Oswaldo. 1996. Calzadas Mayas: Un Estudio desde el Sureste de Petén. In *IX Simposio de Investigaciones Arqueológicas en Guatemala, 1995,* ed. Juan Pedro Laporte and Héctor L. Escobedo, pp. 135–51. Guatemala City: Museo Nacional de Arqueología y Etnología.

Goodale, Jane C. 2003. Tiwi Island Dreams. In *Dream Travelers. Sleep Experiences and Culture in the Western Pacific,* ed. Roger Ivar Lohmann, pp. 149–67. New York: Palgrave Macmillan.

Gorenflo, L. J., and Thomas L. Bell. 1991. Network Analysis and the Study of Past Regional Organization. In *Ancient Road Networks and Settlement Hierarchies in the New World,* ed. Charles D. Trombold, pp. 80–98. Cambridge: Cambridge University Press.

Gorenstein, Shirley, and Helen Perlstein Pollard. 1991. Xanhari: Protohistoric Tarascan Routes. In *Ancient Road Networks and Settlement Hierarchies in the New World,* ed. Charles Trombold, pp. 169–85. Cambridge: Cambridge University Press.

Graf, David F. 1994. The Persian Royal Road System. In *Continuity and Change: Proceedings of the Last Achaemenid History Workshop,* ed. Heleen Sancisi-Weerdenburg, Amélie Kuhrt, and Margaret Cool Root, pp. 167–89. Leiden: Nederlands Instituut Voor Het Nabije Oosten.

—— 1995. The Via Nova Traiana in Arabia Petraea. In *The Roman and Byzantine Near East: Recent Archaeological Research,* ed. John Humphrey, pp. 241–67. Journal of Roman Archaeology Supplementary Series 14.

—— 1997. The Via Militaris in Arabia. *Dumbarton Oaks Papers* 51:271–81.

Graham, Shawn. 2006. Networks, Agent-Based Models, and the Antonine Itinerary: Implications for Roman Archaeology. *Journal of Mediterranean Archaeology* 19(1): 45–64.

Greene, K. 1986. *The Archaeology of the Roman Economy.* Berkeley, CA: University of California Press.

Grégoire, J. P., and J. Renger. 1988. Die Interdependenz der wirtschaftlichen und gesellschaftlich-politischen Strukturen von Ebla. In *Wirtschaft und Gesellschaft von Ebla,* ed. H. Waetzoldt and H. Hauptmann, pp. 211–24. Heidelberg: Heidelberger Orientverlag.

Grimm, Thaddeus C. 1985. Time-Depth Analysis of Fifteen Siouan Languages. *Siouan and Caddoan Linguistics* 5:12–27.

Grinnell, Calvin. 2004. Come See Our River: The Mandan-Hidatsa-Arikara Homeland. Paper presented at Lewis and Clark Symposium, Many Voices. Bismarck, ND.

Groot de Mahecha, Ana María. 2000. Sal, caminos y mercaderes: el caso de los muiscas en el siglo XVI. In *Caminos Precolombinos: las Vías, los Ingenieros y los Viajeros,* ed. Leonor Herrera and Marianne Cardale de Schrimpff, pp. 243–66. Bogotá: Instituto Colombiano de Antropología y Historia.

Guest, John S. 2005. *The Ancient Road: From Aleppo to Baghdad in the Days of the Ottoman Empire.* New York: Columbia University Press.

Gutiérrez Osinaga, Daniel J. 2005. Avances en la Arqueología de Caminos Precolombinos en Bolivia Tramo: Paria-Tapacarí (Sitios asociados y características formales de construcción del camino). *Arqueobolivia Nuevos Aportes* 3:93–114.

Gutiérrez Osinaga, Daniel J., and C. Jaimes. 2000. Patrón y Variabilidad de Construcción del camino Precolombino del Choro. In *Memorias de la XIV Reunión Anual de Etnología: Aportes Indígenas Estados y Democracias*, vol. 1, pp. 233–38. La Paz: Museo Nacional de Etnografía y Folklore.

Hamalainen, Pekka. 2003. The Rise and Fall of Plains Indian Horse Cultures. *The Journal of American History* 90:833–62.

Hanagarth, Werner. 1993. *Acerca de la geoecología de las sabanas del Beni en el noroeste de Bolivia.* La Paz: Instituto de Ecología.

Hanke, Wanda. 1957. Einige funde im Beni Gebiet, Ostbolivien. *Archiv für Völkerkunde* (Wien) 12:136–43.

Hanks, William F. 1990. *Referential Practice: Language and Lived Space among the Maya.* Chicago, IL: University of Chicago Press.

Hansen, Richard D. 1991. The Road to Nakbe. *Natural History* 5(91): 8–14.

Harner, Michael J. 1957. Potsherds and the Tentative Dating of the San Gorgonio–Big Maria Trail. *University of California Archaeological Survey Reports* 37:35–37.

Harrington, John P. 1916. The Ethnogeography of the Tewa Indians. *Bureau of American Ethnology, Annual Report 29 1907–1908.* Washington, DC: USGPO.

Harris, John F., and Stephen K. Stearns. 1992. *Understanding Maya Inscriptions: A Hieroglyphic Handbook.* Philadelphia, PA: University of Pennsylvania Museum of Archaeology and Anthropology.

Harris, Trevor. 2000. Session 2 Discussion: Moving GIS: Exploring Movement within Prehistoric Cultural Landscapes Using GIS. In *Beyond the Map: Archaeology and Spatial Technologies,* ed. Gary Lock, pp. 116–123. Amsterdam: IOS Press.

Hart, E. Richard, and Andrew L. Othole. 1993. The Zuni Salt Lake Area: Potential Impacts to Zuni Traditional Cultural Properties. In *Traditional Cultural Properties of Four Tribes: The Fence Lake Mine Project,* vol. 1, ed. E. Richard Hart and T. J. Ferguson, pp. 1–185. Seattle, WA: Institute of the North American West.

Hartmann, Gayle H., and William K. Hartmann. 1979. Prehistoric Trail Systems and Related Features on the Slopes of Tumamoc Hill. *Kiva* 45:39–69.

Hassig, Ross. 1985. *Trade, Tribute, and Transportation: The Sixteenth-Century Political Economy of the Valley of Mexico.* Norman: University of Oklahoma Press.

—— 1991. Roads, Routes, and Ties that Bind. In *Ancient Road Networks and Settlement Hierarchies in the New World,* ed. Charles D. Trombold, pp. 17–27. Cambridge: Cambridge University Press.

Haury, Emil W. 1976. *The Hohokam, Desert Farmers and Craftsmen: Excavations at Snaketown, 1964–1965.* Tucson, AZ: University of Arizona Press.

Hawkins, G. S. 1969. *Ancient Lines in the Peruvian Desert.* Cambridge, MA: Smithsonian Astrophysical Observatory.

—— 1974. Prehistoric Desert Markings in Peru. *National Geographic Society Research Reports, 1967 Projects* 15:117–44.

Hayden, J. D. 1967. A Summary Prehistory and History of the Sierra Pinacate, Sonora. *American Antiquity* 32(3): 335–44.

Heckenberger, Michael J. 2005. *The Ecology of Power: Culture, Place, and Personhood in the Southern Amazon, A.D. 1000–2000.* New York: Routledge.

—— 2008. Amazonian Mosaics: Identity, Interaction, and Integration in the Tropical Forest. In *Handbook of South American Archaeology,* ed. Helaine Silverman and William Isbell, pp. 941–61. New York: Springer.

Heckenberger, Michael, A. Kuikuro, U. Kuikuro, J. Russell, M. Schmidt, C. Fausto, and B. Franchetto. 2003. Amazonia 1492: Pristine Forest or Cultural Parkland? *Science* 301:1710–13.

Heckenberger, Michael, J. Russell, C. Fausto, J. Toney, M. Schmidt, E. Pereira, B. Franchetto, and A. Kuikuro. 2007. Pre-Columbian Urbanism, Anthropogenic Landscapes, and the Future of the Amazon. *Science* 321(5893): 1214–17.

Heizer, Robert F. 1941. Aboriginal Trade between the Southwest and California. *Masterkey* 15(5): 185–88.

—— 1978. Trade and Trails. In *Handbook of North American Indians.* Vol. 8, *California,* ed. Robert F. Heizer, pp. 690–93. Washington, DC: Smithsonian Institution.

Helms, Mary W. 1988. *Ulysses Sail.* Princeton, NJ: Princeton University Press.

Hendrickson, M. 2007. Arteries of Empire: An Operational Study of Transport and Communication. In "Angkorian Southeast Asia (9th to 15th centuries CE)." Ph.D. dissertation. University of Sydney.

—— 2008. New Evidence of Brown Glazed Stoneware Kilns along the East Road from Angkor. *Bulletin of the Indo-Pacific Prehistory Association* 28:52–56.

Herrera, Leonor, and Marianne Cardale de Schrimpff, eds. 2000. *Caminos Precolombinos: las Vías, los Ingenieros y los Viajeros.* Bogotá: Instituto Colombiano de Antropología e Historia.

Hester, J., P. Hobler, and J. Russell. 1970. New Evidence of Early Roads in Nubia. *American Journal of Archaeology* 74: 385–89.

Hewett, Edgar Lee. 1904. Archaeology of Pajarito Park, New Mexico. *American Anthropologist* 6:629–59.

Hiebert, Fredrik T. 1999. On the Track of the Ancient Silk Road. *Expedition* 41(3): 37–41.

Hillier, Bill, and Julienne Hanson. 1984. *The Social Logic of Space.* Cambridge: Cambridge University Press.

Hindes, Margaret G. 1959. A Report on Indian Sites and Trails, Huntington

Lake Region, California. Paper on California Archaeology 70. *Annual Reports of the University of California Archaeological Survey* 48. Berkeley.

Hindle, B. P. 1993. *Roads, Tracks and Their Interpretation.* London: Batsford.

—— 1998. *Medieval Roads and Tracks.* Princes Risborough: Shire.

Hirsch, Eric, and Michael O'Hanlon, eds. 1995. *The Anthropology of Landscape: Perspectives on Place and Space.* Oxford: Clarendon Press.

Hirth, Kenneth. 1991. Roads, Thoroughfares and Avenues of Power at Xochicalco, Mexico. In *Ancient Road Networks and Settlement Hierarchies in the New World,* ed. Charles Trombold, pp. 211–21. Cambridge: Cambridge University Press.

Hobsbawm, Eric. 1983. Introduction: Inventing Traditions. In *The Invention of Tradition,* ed. Eric Hobsbawm and Terence Ranger, pp. 1–14. Cambridge: Cambridge University Press.

Hocquenghem, Anne-Marie. 1994. Los espanoles en los caminos del extremo norte del Peru en 1532. *Bulletin de l'Institut Français de l'Études Andines* 23(1): 1–67.

Hodder, I., and C. Cessford. 2004. Daily Practice and Social Memory at Çatalhöyük. *American Antiquity* 69(1): 17–40.

Hodder, Ian, and Robert Preucel. 1996. *Contemporary Archaeology in Theory.* Cambridge, MA: Blackwell.

Hoffman, Eva. 1989. *Lost in Translation: A New Life in a New Language.* New York: Dutton.

Hoopes, John. 1994. Ceramic Analysis and Culture History in the Arenal Region. In *Archaeology, Volcanism, and Remote Sensing in the Arenal Region, Costa Rica,* ed. P. Sheets and B. McKee, pp. 158–210. Austin, TX: University of Texas Press.

Hoopes, John, and Mark Chenault. 1994. Excavations at Sitio Bolivar: A Late Formative Village in the Arenal Basin. In *Archaeology, Volcanism, and Remote Sensing in the Arenal Region, Costa Rica,* ed. P. Sheets and B. McKee, pp. 87–105. Austin, TX: University of Texas Press.

Hough, Walter. 1906. Sacred Springs in the Southwest. *Records of the Past* 5(6): 164–69.

Houston, Stephen D., David Stuart, and Karl A. Taube. 1989. Folk Classification of Classic Maya Pottery. *American Anthropologist* 91(3): 720–26.

—— 2006. *The Memory of Bones: Body, Being, and Experience among the Classic Maya.* Austin, TX: University of Texas Press.

Howard, Richard M. 1959. Comments on the Indian's Water Supply at Gran Quivira National Monument. *El Palacio* 85(3): 85–91.

Hunn, Eugene. 1994. Place-Names, Population Density, and the Magic Number 500. *Current Anthropology* 35(1): 81–85.

Hurst, Winston, Owen Severance, and Dale Davidson. 1993. Uncle Albert's Ancient Roads. *Blue Mountain Shadows* 12 (Summer): 2–9.

Hyslop, John. 1984. *The Inka Road System.* New York: Academic.

—— 1990. *Inca Settlement Planning.* Austin: University of Texas Press.

—— 1991. Observations about Research on Prehistoric Roads in South America. In *Ancient Road Networks and Settlement Hierarchies in the New World,* ed. Charles D. Trombold, pp. 28–33. Cambridge: Cambridge University Press.

—— 1992. *Qhapaqñan. El sistema vial incaico.* Instituto Andino de Estudios Arqueológicos. Lima: Epígrafe, S.A.

Hyslop, John, and Mario Rivera. 1984. An Expedition on the Inca Road in the Atacama Desert. *Archaeology* 37:33–39.

Im, Sokrithy. 2004. Angkorian Communication Routes and Associated Structures. *Udaya* 5:39–81.

Ingold, Tim. 1993. The Temporality of the Landscape. *World Archaeology* 25(2): 152–74.

—— 2000. *The Perception of the Environment: Essays in Livelihood, Dwelling, and Skill.* London: Routledge.

Inomata, Takeshi, and Lawrence Coben, eds. 2006. *Archaeology of Performance: Theaters of Power, Community, and Politics.* Lanhan, MD: Altamira.

Irvin, Michael, and Craig Cooper. 2006. *Crossroads of the Continent: Early Trade in Kansas.* Topeka, KS: KAM Contributors.

Isaac, Benjamin, and Israel Roll. 1982. *Roman Roads in Judaea, I: The Legio-Scythopolis Road.* BAR International Series 141. Oxford: BAR.

Isbell, William H., and Alexei Vranich. 2004. Experiencing the Cities of Wari and Tiwanaku. In *Andean Archaeology,* ed. Helaine Silverman, pp. 167–82. Oxford: Blackwell.

Ismail, F., W. Sallaberger, P. Talon, and K. Van Lerberghe. 1996. *Administrative Documents from Tell Beydar (Seasons 1993–1995). Subartu 2.* Turnhout: Brepols.

Ives, Ronald L. 1946. Ancient Trails in the Dugway Area, Utah. *The Masterkey* 20(4): 113–24.

Jackson, Robert B. 2002. *At Empire's Edge: Exploring Rome's Egyptian Frontier.* New Haven, CT: Yale University Press.

Jager, Sake W. 1985. A Prehistoric Route and Ancient Cart-Tracks in the Gemeente of Anloo (Province of Drenthe). *Palaeohistoria* 27:185–202.

Jans, G., and J. Bretschneider. 1998. Wagon and Chariot Representations in the Early Dynastic Glyptic: They Came to Tell Beydar with Wagon and Equid. In *About Subartu: Studies Devoted to Upper Mesopotamia, Subartu 4, 2,* ed. M. Lebeau, pp. 155–94. Turnhout: Brepols.

Jansen, Anton G. 2001. *A Study of the Remains of Mycenaean Roads and Stations of Bronze-Age Greece.* Lewiston, NY: Edwin Mellen Press.

Jenkins, David. 2001. A Network Analysis of Inka Roads, Administrative Centers, and Storage Facilities. *Ethnohistory* 48:655–87.

Jenkinson, Clay S. 2003. *A Vast and Open Plain—The Writings of the Lewis and Clark Expedition in North Dakota, 1804–1806.* Bismarck, ND: State Historical Society of North Dakota.

Jett, Stephen C. 1994. Cairn Trail Shrines in Middle and South America. *Conference of Latin American Geographers Yearbook* 20:1–8.

—— 2001. *Navajo Placenames and Trails of the Canyon de Chelly System, Arizona.* New York: Peter Lang.

Johnson, Allen W., and Timothy Earle. 2000. *The Evolution of Human Societies: From Foraging Group to Agrarian State.* 2nd ed. Stanford, CA: Stanford University Press.

Johnson, F. J., and P. H. Johnson. 1957. An Indian Trail Complex of the Central Colorado Desert: A Preliminary Survey. *University of California Archaeological Survey Reports* 37:22–34.

Johnson, Matthew. 2007. *Ideas of Landscape.* Malden, MA: Blackwell.

Johnston, Robert. 1999. An Empty Path? Processions, Memories and the Dorset Cursus. In *Pathways and Ceremonies: The Cursus Monuments of Britain and Ireland,* ed. A. Barclay and J. Harding, pp. 39–48. Oxford: Oxbow.

Joyce, R. A., and S. D. Gillespie, eds. 2000. *Beyond Kinship: Social and Material Reproduction in House Societies.* Philadelphia, PA: University of Pennsylvania Press.

Joyce, Rosemary, and Jeanne Lopiparo. 2005. Postscript: Doing Agency in Archaeology. *Journal of Archaeological Method and Theory* 12(4): 365–74.

Kahane, Anne, Leslie Murray Threipland, and John Ward-Perkins. 1968. The Ager Veientanus, North and East of Rome. *Papers of the British School in Rome* 36:1–218.

Kantner, John. 1997. Ancient Roads, Modern Mapping: Evaluating Chaco Anasazi Roadways Using GIS Technology. *Expedition* 39(3): 49–62.

Kapches, M. 1992. Back to the Beaten Paths. *Archaeological Newsletter, Royal Ontario Museum* 47:1–4.

Karns, Harry J. 1954. *Unknown Arizona and Sonora 1693–1721.* English Translation of Captain Juan Mateo Manje, Luz de Tierra Incógnita. Tucson, AZ: Arizona Silhouettes.

Kaschko, Michael W. 1973. Functional Analysis of the Trail System of the Lapakahi Area. In *Lapakahi, Hawai'i: Archaeological Studies,* ed. H. D. Tuggle and P. B. Griffin, pp. 127–44. Asian and Pacific Archaeological Series 5. Manoa, HI: Social Science Research Institute, University of Hawai'i.

Keller, Angela H. 2006. Roads to the Center: The Design, Use, and Meaning of the Roads of Xunantunich, Belize. Ph.D. dissertation, Anthropology. University of Pennsylvania, Philadelphia.

Kelly, Isabel T. 1932–34. Southern Paiute Field Notes. Copies in possession of C. S. Fowler, University of Nevada, Reno (notebooks cited by year, number, and pages).

Kelly, Robert L. 1992. Mobility/Sedentism: Concepts, Archaeological Measures, and Effects. *Annual Review of Anthropology* 21:43–66.

Kelly, Robert, and L. Todd. 1988. Coming into the Country: Early Paleoindian Hunting and Mobility. *American Antiquity* 53:231–44.

Kelm, Heinz. 1953. Archologische Fundstucke aus ostbolivien. *Baessler-Archiv neue folge* 11:65–92.

Kendall, Ann. 2000. Una red de caminos prehispánicos: rutas de comercio en el distrito de Ollantaytambo, Cuzco, Perú. In *Caminos Precolombinos: las Vías, los Ingenieros y los Viajeros,* ed. Leonor Herrera and Marianne Cardale de Schrimpff, pp. 221–241. Bogotá: Instituto Colombiano de Antropología y Historia.

Kennedy, David L. 1982. *Archaeological Explorations on the Roman Frontier in North-east Jordan: The Roman and Byzantine Military Installations and Road Network on the Ground and from the Air.* BAR International Series 134. Oxford: BAR.

—— 1997. Roman Roads and Routes in North-East Jordan. *Levant* 29:71–93.

Kennedy, David L., and Derrick Riley. 1990. *Rome's Desert Frontier from the Air.* London: Batsford.

Killion, T. W. 1992. Residential Ethnoarchaeology and Ancient Site Structure: Contemporary Farming and Prehistoric Settlement Agriculture at Matacapan, Veracuz, Mexico. In *Gardens of Prehistory: The Archaeology of Settlement Agriculture in Greater Mesoamerica,* ed. T. W. Killion, pp. 119–49. Tuscaloosa, AL: University of Alabama Press.

Kinahan, J. 1986. The Archaeological Structure of Pastoral Production in the Central Namib Desert. *South African Archaeological Society,* Goodwin Series, 5:78.

Kincaid, Chris, ed. 1983. *Chaco Roads Project Phase I: A Reappraisal of Prehistoric Roads in the San Juan Basin.* Albuquerque, NM: Department of the Interior, Bureau of Land Management.

Kino, E. F. 1948. *Kino's Historical Memoir of Pimeria Alta,* ed. Herbert Eugene Bolton. Berkeley, CA: University of California Press.

Kirch, Patrick V. 1992. *Anahulu: The Anthropology of History in the Kingdom of Hawaii.* Vol. 2, *The Archaeology of History.* Chicago, IL: University of Chicago Press.

—— 1994. *The Wet and the Dry: Irrigation and Agricultural Intensification in Polynesia.* Chicago, IL: University of Chicago Press.

—— 2005. Archaeology and Global Change: The Holocene Record. *Annual Review of Environment and Resources* 30:409–40.

Kloner, Amos, and Chaim Ben-David. 2003. Mesillot on the Arnon: An Iron Age (pre-Roman) Road in Moab. *Bulletin of the American Schools of Oriental Research* 330:65–81.

Kohler, Timothy A., and George J. Gumerman, eds. 2000. *Dynamics in Human and Primate Societies.* New York: Oxford University Press.

Konrad, Herman W. 1991. Pilgrimage as Cyclical Process: The Unending Pilgrimage of the Holy Cross of the Quintana Roo Maya. In *Pilgrimage in Latin America,* ed. Alan Morinis, pp. 123–37. Westport, CT: Greenwood.

Koskinen, Aarne A. 1963. On the Symbolism of "The Path" in Polynesian Thinking. In *Linking of Symbols: Polynesian Patterns 1,* by Aarne A. Koskinen, pp. 58–70. Publications of the Finnish Society for Missionary Research 10. Helsinki: Finnish Society for Missionary Research.

Kosok, Paul. 1965. *Life, Land and Water in Ancient Peru*. New York: Long Island University.

Kozak, David L., and David I. Lopez. 1999. *Devil Sickness and Devil Songs*. Washington, DC: Smithsonian Institution Press.

Kracke, Waud. 2003. Beyond the Mythologies: A Shape of Dreaming. In *Dream Travelers. Sleep Experiences and Culture in the Western Pacific,* ed. Roger Ivar Lohmann, pp. 211–35. New York: Palgrave Macmillan.

Kroeber, Alfred L. 1925. *Handbook of the Indians of California*. Bureau of American Ethnology Bulletin 78. Washington, DC: USGPO.

―――― 1948. *Seven Mohave Myths*. Anthropological Records 11, no. 1. Berkeley, CA: University of California Press.

―――― 1951. *A Mohave Historical Epic*. Anthropological Records 11, no. 2. Berkeley, CA: University of California Press.

Kurjack, Edward B., and E. Wyllys Andrews, V. 1976. Early Boundary Maintenance in Northwest Yucatan, Mexico. *American Antiquity* 41:318–25.

Kurjack, Edward B., and Silvia Garza T. 1981. Pre-Columbian Community Form and Distribution in the Northern Maya Area. In *Lowland Maya Settlement Patterns,* ed. Wendy Ashmore, pp. 287–309. Albuquerque, NM: University of New Mexico Press.

Kuwanwisiwma, Leigh J., and T. J. Ferguson. 2004. Ang Kuktota—Hopi Ancestral Sites and Cultural Landscapes. *Expedition* 46(2): 242–49.

Laird, Carobeth. 1976. *The Chemehuevis*. Banning, CA: Malki Museum Press.

Lakoff, George, and Mark Johnson. 1980. *Metaphors We Live By*. Chicago, IL: University of Chicago Press.

―――― 1999. *Philosphy in the Flesh. The Embodied Mind and Its Challenge to Western Thought*. New York: Basic.

LaMotta, Vincent. 2004. The Archaeology of Itinerant Land Use in the Western Papagueria: The Theoretical, Historical, and Ethnoarchaeological Perspectives. Report prepared for Statistical Research Inc., Tucson, AZ.

Langstroth, Robert. 1996. Forest Islands in an Amazonian Savanna of Northeastern Bolivia. Ph.D. dissertation, Geography. University of Wisconsin, Madison.

Lansing, J. S. 2003. Complex Adaptive Systems. *Annual Review of Anthropology* 32:183–204.

Lathrap, Donald. 1970. *The Upper Amazon*. London: Thames & Hudson.

Laurence, Ray. 1999. *The Roads of Roman Italy: Mobility and Cultural Change*. New York: Routledge.

Lavery, John. 1990. Some Aspects of Mycenaean Topography. *Bulletin of the Institute of Classical Studies* 37:165–71.

―――― 1995. Some "New" Mycenaean Roads at Mycenae. *Bulletin of the Institute of Classical Studies* 40:264–65.

Lawrence, D. S., and S. M. Low. 1990. The Built Environment and Spatial Form. *Annual Review of Anthropology* 19:453–505.

Lebeau, M. 1997. La situation géographique, la topographie et les périodes d'occupation de Tell Beydar. In *Tell Beydar, Three Seasons of Excavations (1992–1994): A Preliminary Report, Subartu 3*, ed. M. Lebeau and A. Suleiman, pp. 7–19. Turnhout: Brepols.

Lee, Georgia. 2002. Wahi Pana: Legendary Places on Hawai'i Island. In *Inscribed Landscapes: Marking and Making Place*, ed. Bruno David and Meredith Wilson, pp. 79–92. Honolulu: University of Hawai'i Press.

Lee, Kenneth. 1979. 7,000 años de historia del hombre de Mojos: agricultura en pampas estériles: informe preliminar. *Universidad Beni*, pp. 23–26. Trinidad: Universidad Técnica del Beni.

—— 1995. Complejo Hidráulico de las llanuras de Baures (Area a ser protegida), Provincia Itenez, Departamento del Beni, República de Bolivia. Manuscript, presentado a CORDEBENI, Trinidad.

Lefebvre, Henri. 1991. *The Production of Space*. Oxford: Blackwell.

Lehmer, Donald J. 1971. *Introduction to Middle Missouri Archaeology*. Washington, DC: National Park Service.

Lehmer, D. J., and Stephen C. Levinson. 1996. Language and Space. *Annual Reviews in Anthropology* 25:353–82.

Lehner, M. 2000a. Absolutism and Reciprocity in Ancient Egypt. In *The Breakout: The Origins of Civilization*, ed. M. Lamberg-Karlovsky, pp. 69–97. Peabody Museum Monograph 9. Cambridge, MA: Peabody Museum of Harvard University.

—— 2000b. The Fractal House of Pharaoh: Ancient Egypt as a Complex Adaptive System, a Trial Formulation. In *Dynamics in Human and Primate Societies*, ed. T. A. Kohler and G. J. Gumerman, pp. 275–353. Oxford: Oxford University Press.

Lekson, Steve. 1999. *The Chaco Meridian: Centers of Political Power in the Ancient Southwest*. Walnut Creek, CA: AltaMira.

Lekson, Stephen H., John R. Stein, Thomas C. Windes, and W. James Judge. 1988. The Chaco Canyon Community. *Scientific American* 259(1): 100–109.

Lennon, Thomas J. 1982. Raised Fields of Lake Titicaca, Peru: A Pre-Hispanic Water Management System. Ph.D. dissertation, Anthropology. University of Colorado, Boulder.

—— 1983. Pattern Analysis in Prehistoric Raised Fields of Lake Titicaca, Peru. In *Drained Field Agriculture in Central and South America*, ed. J. Darch, pp. 183–200. BAR, International Series 189. Oxford: BAR.

Lepper, B. T. 1995. Tracking Ohio's Great Hopewell Road. *Archaeology* 48(6): 52–56.

—— 1996. The Newark Earthworks and the Geometric Enclosures of the Scioto Valley: Connections and Conjectures. In *A View from the Core: A Synthesis of Ohio Hopewell Archaeology*, ed. P. J. Pacheco, pp. 224–41. Columbus, OH: Ohio Archaeological Council.

Lewis, N. N. 1987. *Nomads and Settlers in Syria and Jordan, 1800–1980.* Cambridge: Cambridge University Press.

Lewis, Pierce. 1996. Landscapes of Mobility. In *The National Road,* ed. Karl Raitz, pp. 3–44. Baltimore, MD: Johns Hopkins University Press.

Libby, Orin G. 1908. Typical Villages of the Mandans, Arikara and Hidatsa in the Missouri River Valley, North Dakota. *Collections of the State Historical Society of North Dakota* 2:498–508.

Lipo, Carl P., and Terry L. Hunt. 2005. Mapping Prehistoric Statue Roads on Easter Island. *Antiquity* 79(303): 158–68.

Lippi, Ronald. 2000. Caminos antiguos en el Pichincha occidental, Ecuador. In *Caminos precolombinos: las Vías, los Ingenieros y los Viajeros,* ed. Leonor Herrera and Marianne Cardale de Schrimpff, pp. 117–35. Bogotá: Instituto Colombiano de Antropología y Historia.

Livingston, Dewey. 1992. History of the Painted Desert Inn, Petrified Forest National Park, Arizona. Part of Package 199, Historic Structure Report, National Park Service, Denver Service Center. Petrified Forest National Park, AZ. Manuscript on file.

Lizarazu, Juan de. 1906 [1638]. Informaciones hechas por Don Juan de Lizarazú sobre el descubrimiento de los Mojos. In *Juicio de límites entre el Perú y Bolivia* 9, pp. 124–216. Madrid: Imprenta de los Hijos de M. G. Hernández.

Llobera, Marcos. 1996. Exploring the Topography of Mind: GIS, Social Space, and Archaeology. *Antiquity* 70:612–22.

—— 2000. Understanding Movement: A Pilot Model towards the Sociology of Movement. In *Beyond the Map: Archaeology and Spatial Technologies,* ed. Gary Lock, pp 65–84. Amsterdam: IOS.

Lloyd, J. William. 1911. *Aw-aw-tam Indian Nights.* Westfield, NJ: Lloyd Group.

Loendorf, Lawrence L., and Joan L. Brownell. 1980. The Bad Pass Trail. *Archaeology in Montana* 21(3): 11–102.

Lohmann, Roger Ivar. 2004. Review of "Dream Trackers: Yapa Art and Knowledge of the Australian Desert." *Anthropology of Conciousness* 15(2): 69–70.

Lolos, George J. 1998. Studies in the Topography of Sikyonia. Ph.D. dissertation, Classics. University of California, Berkeley.

Lolos, Yannis. 2003. Greek Roads: A Commentary on the Ancient Terms. *Glotta* 79:137–74.

Loud, Llewellyn L. 1918. *Ethnogeography and Archaeology of the Wiyot Territory.* University of California Publications in American Archaeology and Ethnology 14, no. 3. Berkeley: University of California Press.

Low, Setha, and Denise Lawrence-Zúñiga, eds. 2003. *The Anthropology of Space and Place.* Malden, MA: Routledge.

Lowenthal, David. 1975. Past Time, Present Place: Landscape and Memory. *The Geographical Review* 65:1–36.

Lowie, Robert. 1948. The Tropical Forest: An Introduction. In *Handbook of South American Indians.* Vol. 3, *Tropical Forest Tribes,* ed. Julian Steward, pp.

1–56. Smithsonian Institution, Bureau of American Ethnology Bulletin 143. Washington, DC: USGPO.

Lumholtz, Carl. 1912. *New Trails in Mexico*. New York: Scribner's.

Lynch, Thomas F. 1993. The Identification of Inca Posts and Roads from Catarpe to Rio Frío, Chile. In *Provincial Inca: Archaeological and Ethnohistorical Assessment of the Impact of the Inca State*, ed. Michael A. Malpass, pp. 117–44. Iowa City: University of Iowa Press.

—— 1996. Inka Roads in the Atacama: Effects of Later Use by Mounted Travellers. *Dialogo Andino* 14/15:187–204. Arica.

Lyons, Patrick. 2003. *Ancestral Hopi Migrations*. Tucson, AZ: University of Arizona Press.

MacDonald, Burton. 1988. *The Wadi el Hasa Archaeological Survey 1979–1983, West-Central Jordan*. Waterloo, ON: Wilfrid Laurier University Press.

—— 1996. The Route of the Via Nova Traiana Immediately South of the Wadi al Hasa. *Palestine Exploration Quarterly* 128:12–15.

Madry, Scott. 1987. Sensing in a Temperate Regional Archaeological Survey in France. In *Regional Dynamics: Burgundian Landscapes in Historical Perspective*, ed. Carole L. Crumley and William H. Marquardt, pp. 173–235. San Diego: Academic Press.

Madry, Scott, and Carole Crumley. 1990. An Application of Remote Sensing and GIS in a Regional Archaeological Survey. In *Interpreting Space: GIS and Archaeology*, ed. K. Allen, S. Green, and E. Zubrow, pp. 364–81. London: Taylor & Francis.

Madry, Scott, and Lynn Rakos. 1996. Line-of-Sight and Cost Surface Analysis for Regional Research in the Arroux River Valley. In *New Methods, Old Problems: Geographic Information Systems in Modern Archaeological Research*, ed. H. D. G. Maschner, pp. 104–26. Center for Archaeological Investigations, Occasional Paper No. 23. Carbondale, IL.

Maldonado Cárdenas, Rubén. 1995. Los Sistemas de Caminos del Norte de Yucatán. In *Seis Ensayos Sobre Antiguos Patrones de Asentamiento en el Área Maya*, ed. Ernesto Vargas Pacheco, pp. 68–92. México, DF: Universidad Nacional Autónoma de México, Instituto de Investigaciones Antropológicas.

Mallery, Garrick. 1881. *Sign Language among North American Indians, Compared with That among Other Peoples and Deaf-mutes*. First Annual Report of the Bureau of American Ethnology, Smithsonian Institution. Washington, DC: USGPO.

Malouf, Carling I. 1962. The Old Indian Trail. *Archaeology in Montana* (4)1: 9–11.

—— 1980. On the Trail of the Indian. *Archaeology in Montana* 21(3): 1–9.

Malpas, Jeff. 1998. Finding Place: Spatiality, Locality, and Subjectivity. In *Philosophy and Geography III: Philosophies of Place*, ed. Andrew Ligh and Jonathan M. Smith, pp. 21–43. Lanham, MD: Rowman & Littlefield.

Mandelbaum, David G., ed. 1958. Language and Environment (1933). *Selected Writings of Edward Sapir in Language, Culture and Personality*. Berkeley, CA: University of California Press.

Manson, Joni L. 1998. Trans-Mississippi Trade and Travel: The Buffalo Plains and Beyond. *Plains Anthropologist* 43(166): 385–400.

Marbán, Pedro. 1889 [ca. 1676]. Relación de la Provincia de la Virgen de Mojos. *Boletin de la Sociedad Geográfica de La Paz* 1(2): 120–61.

Marchand, Jeannette. 2002. Well-built Kleonai: A History of the Peloponnesian City Based on a Survey of the Visible Remains and a Study of the Literary and Epigraphic Sources. Ph.D. dissertation. University of California, Berkeley.

Margary, Ivan D. 1967. *Roman Roads in Britain*. London: John Baker.

Marshall, Michael P. 1991. El Camino Real de Tierra Adentro: An Archaeological Investigation. Report on file, New Mexico Historic Preservation Division. Santa Fe.

—— 1997. The Chacoan Roads: A Cosmological Interpretation. In *Anasazi Architecture and American Design*, ed. Baker H. Morrow and V. B. Price, pp. 62–74. Albuquerque, NM: University of New Mexico Press.

Martin, Simon. 2001. Court and Realm: Architectural Signatures in the Classic Maya Southern Lowlands. In *Royal Courts of the Ancient Maya 1: Theory, Comparison, and Synthesis*, ed. Takeshi Inomata and Stephen D. Houston, pp. 168–94. Boulder, CO: Westview.

Mathews, Jennifer P., and James F. Garber. 2004. Models of Cosmic Order: Physical Expression of Sacred Space among the Ancient Maya. *Ancient Mesoamerica* 15:49–59.

Mathien, Frances Joan. 1991. Political, Economic, and Demographic Implications of the Chaco Road Network. In *Ancient Road Networks and Settlement Hierarchies in the New World*, ed. Charles Trombold, pp. 99–110. Cambridge: Cambridge University Press.

Matthews, D. M. 1997. *The Early Glyptic of Tell Brak*. Fribourg: University Press of Fribourg.

Matthews, Keith J. 2002. The Creation of Landscapes on the Edge of Empire: Roads and the Landscape in Northwest Britannia. In *Via Claudia Augusta: Un'Arteria alle Origini dell'Europa: Ipotesi, Problemi, Prospettive*, Vittoria Galliazzo, pp. 397–416. Congresso internazionale "Via Claudia Augusta," 1999, Feltre, Italy. Feltre: Comune di Feltre.

Matthews, Washington. 1877. *Ethnography and Philology of the Hidatsa Indians*. Miscellaneous Publications 7, U.S. Geological and Geographical Survey of the Rocky Mountain Region. Washington, DC: USGPO.

McClintock, Walter. 1910. *The Old North Trail*. London: Macmillan.

McEwan, Colin, Cristina Barreto, and Eduardo Neves, eds. 2001. *Unknown Amazon: Culture in Nature in Ancient Brazil*. London: British Museum.

McEwan, Gordon. 1987. *The Middle Horizon in the Valley of Cuzco, Peru: The Impact of the Wari Occupation of the Lucre Basin*. BAR International Series 372. Oxford: BAR.

McGuire, Randall H., and Michael B. Schiffer, eds. 1982. *Hohokam and Patayan. Prehistory of Southwestern Arizona*. New York: Academic.

McKee, Brian, Tom Sever, and Payson Sheets. 1994. Prehistoric Footpaths in Costa Rica: Remote Sensing and Field Verification. In *Archaeology, Volcanism, and Remote Sensing in the Arenal Region, Costa Rica,* ed. P. Sheets and B. McKee, pp. 142–57. Austin, TX: University of Texas Press.

McLeod, M. D. 1981. *The Asante.* London: British Museum Publications.

Mejia Xesspe, T. 1939. Acueductos y Caminos Antiguos de la Hoya del Rio Grande de Nasca. *International Congress of Americanists.* Lima 1:559–69.

Mendenhall, Walter C. 1909. *Some Desert Watering Places in Southeastern California and Southwestern Nevada.* U.S. Department of the Interior, Water Supply Paper 224. Washington, DC: U.S. Geological Survey.

Mercer, Jean Ann. 1993. Fence Lake Coal Mine Project: Potential Impacts to Traditional Cultural Properties of the Ramah Navajo. In *Traditional Cultural Properties of Four Tribes: The Fence Lake Mine Project,* vol. 2, ed. E. Richard Hart and T. J. Ferguson, pp. 1–33. Seattle, WA: Institute of the North American West.

Metraux, Alfred. 1942. *The Native Tribes of Eastern Bolivia and Western Matto Grosso.* Smithsonian Institution, Bureau of American Ethnology Bulletin 134. Washington, DC: USGPO.

Meyer, Roy Willard. 1977. *The Village Indians of the Upper Missouri: The Mandans, Hidatsas, and Arikaras.* Lincoln, NE: University of Nebraska Press.

Michaelis, Helen. 1981. Willowsprings: A Hopi Petroglyph Site. *Journal of New World Archaeology* 4:1–23.

Michel, Marcos. 1993. Prospección Arqueológica de San Ignacio de Moxos, Provincia Moxos, Departamento del Beni, Bolivia. Thesis, Facultad de Ciencias Sociales, Carrera de Arqueología. Universidad Mayor de San Andrés, La Paz.

Miller, Heather M. L. 2006. Comparing Landscapes of Transportation: Riverine-Oriented and Land-Oriented in the Indus Civilization and the Mughal Empire. In *Space and Spatial Analysis in Archaeology,* ed. Elizabeth C. Robertson, Jeffrey D. Seibert, Deepika C. Fernandez, and Marc U. Zender, pp. 281–91. Calgary, AB: University of Calgary Press.

Miller, Jay. 1983. Basin Religion and Theology: A Comparative Study of Power (Puha). *Journal of California and Great Basin Anthropology* 5(1–2): 66–86.

Miller, N. F. 1984. The Use of Dung as Fuel: An Ethnographic Example and an Archaeological Application. *Paléorient* 10:71–79.

Mills, Peter R. 2002. Social Integration and the Ala Loa: Reconsidering the Significance of Trails in Hawaiian Exchange. *Asian Perspectives* 41(1): 148–66.

Moore, Jerry D. 2005. *Cultural Landscapes in the Ancient Andes: Archaeologies of Place.* Gainesville, FL: University Press of Florida.

Moorey, P. R. S. 2001. Clay Models and Overland Mobility in Syria, c. 2350–1800 BC. In *Beiträge zur Vorderasiatischen Archäologie Winfried Orthmann Gewidmet,* ed. J. W. Meyer, M. Novák, and A. Pruß, pp. 344–51. Frankfurt am Main: Johann Wolfgang Goethe-Universität.

Moreno de Ángel, Pilar, and Jorge Orlando Melo Gonzalez, eds. 1995. *Caminos Reales de Colombia*. Bogotá: Fondo Fen.

Morinis, Alan. 1992. Introduction: The Territory of the Anthropology of Pilgrimage. In *Sacred Journeys: The Anthropology of Pilgrimage*, ed. Alan Morinis, pp. 1–28. Westport, CT: Greenwood.

Morrison, K. D. 1994. The Intensification of Production: Archaeological Approaches. *Journal of Archaeological Method and Theory* 1:111–59.

Morrison, Tony. 1978. *Pathways to the Gods: The Mystery of the Andean Lines*. New York: Harper & Row.

Morriss, Richard K. 2005. *Roads: Archaeology and Architecture*. Stroud: Tempus.

Motsinger, Thomas N. 1998. Hohokam Roads at Snaketown, Arizona. *Journal of Field Archaeology* 25(1): 89–96.

Murillo Herrera, Mauricio. 2002. Análisis crítico de las investigaciones en el sitio Guayabo (UCR-43), de Turrialba y las repercusiones sociales con relación al manejo de sus recursos culturales. Documento inédito. Trabajo Final de Graduación para optar por el grado de Licenciado en Antropología con énfasis en Arquelogía. Escuela de Antropología y Sociología, Universidad de Costa Rica.

Myer, William E. 1929. *Indian Trails of the Southeast*. Forty-second Annual Report of the Bureau of American Ethnology, pp. 727–857. Washington, DC: USGPO.

Myers, Andrew J. 1997. An Examination of Late Prehistoric McFate Trail Locations. *Pennsylvania Archaeologist* 67(1): 45–53.

Myers, Fred R. 1986. *Pintupi Country, Pintupi Self: Sentiment, Place, and Politics among Western Desert Aborigines*. Washington, DC: Smithsonian Institution Press.

—— 1991. Representing Culture: The Production of Discourse(s) for Aboriginal Acrylic Paintings. *Cultural Anthropology* 6(1): 26–62.

—— 2000. Ways of Placemaking. In *Culture, Landscape, and the Environment: The Linacre Lectures 1997*, ed. Kate Flint and Howard Morphy, pp. 72–110. Oxford: Oxford University Press.

Mylonas, G. E. 1966. *Mycenae and the Golden Age*. Princeton, NJ: Princeton University Press.

Nabokov, Peter. 1981. *Indian Running*. Santa Fe, NM: Ancient City Press.

Ng, Olivia, and Paul R. Cackler. 2006. The Life and Times of a British Logging Road in Belize. In *Space and Spatial Analysis in Archaeology*, ed. Elizabeth C. Robertson, Jeffrey D. Seibert, Deepika C. Fernandez, and Marc U. Zender, pp. 293–300. Calgary: University of Calgary Press.

Nimuendajú, Curt. 1939. *The Apinayé*. Anthropological Series 8. Washington, DC: Catholic University of America.

—— 1946. *The Eastern Timbira*. University of California Publications in American Archaeology and Ethnology 41. Berkeley, CA: University of California Press.

Nordenskiöld, Erland. 1916. Die Anpassung der Indianer an die Verhältnisse in den überschwemmungsgebieten in Südamerika [La adaptación de los indios a la situación de los territorios inundados de Sudamérica]. *Ymer* 36:138–55.

—— 1918. Palisades and Noxious Gases among the South American Indians. *Ymer* 38:220–43.

—— 2001 [1924]. *Exploraciones y aventuras en sudamerica.* Pueblos Indigenas de las Tierras Bajas de Bolivia no. 18. La Paz: Apoyo para el Campesino Indígena del Oriente Boliviano.

—— 2003. *Indios y Blancos en el Noreste de Bolivia.* La Paz: Apoyo para el Campesino-Indígena del Oriente Boliviano.

Oates, J. 2001. Equid Figurines and "Chariot" Models. In *Excavations at Tell Brak.* Vol. 2, *Nagar in the Third Millennium BC,* ed. D. Oates, J. Oates, and H. McDonald, pp. 279–93. Cambridge: McDonald Institute for Archaeological Research and the British School of Archaeology in Iraq.

Obenauf, Margaret S. 1991. Photointerpretations of Chacoan Roads. In *Ancient Road Networks and Settlement Hierarchies in the New World,* ed. Charles D. Trombold, pp. 34–41. Cambridge: Cambridge University Press.

Offield, T. W. 1975. Line-Grating Diffraction in Image Analysis: Enhanced Detection of Linear Structures in ERTS Images, Colorado Front Range. *Modern Geology* 5:101–7.

O'Hanlon, Michael, and Linda Frankland. 2003. Co-present Landscapes: Routes and Rootedness as Sources of Identity in Highlands New Guinea. In *Landscape, Memory and History,* ed. P. J. Stewart and A. Strathern, pp. 166–88. London: Pluto.

Orbigny, Alcide Dessalines d'. 2002. *Viaje a la América meridional: Brasil, República del Uruguay, República Argentina, la Patagonia, República de Chile, República de Bolivia, República del Perú: realizado de 1826 a 1833.* La Paz: Instituto Francés de Estudios Andinos.

Orr, Heather S. 2001. Procession Rituals and Shrine Sites: The Politics of Sacred Space in the Late Formative Valley of Oaxaca. In *Landscape and Power in Ancient Mesoamerica,* ed. Rex Koontz, Kathryn Reese-Taylor, and Annabeth Headrick, pp. 55–80. Boulder, CO: Westview.

Ortiz, Alfonso 1969. *The Tewa World: Space, Time, Being, and Becoming in a Pueblo Society.* Chicago, IL: University of Chicago Press.

—— 1979. San Juan Pueblo. In *Handbook of North American Indians.* Vol. 9, *Southwest,* ed. Alfonso Ortiz, pp. 278–95. Washington, DC: Smithsonian Institution Press.

Oyuela Caycedo, Augusto. 1990. Las Redes de Caminos Prehispánicas en la Sierra Nevada de Santa Marta. In *Ingeniería Prehispánica,* pp. 47–72. Bogotá: Instituto Colombiano de Antropología and Fondo Eléctrico Nacional (FEN).

Palmer, Gabrielle G., ed. 1993. *El Camino Real de Tierra Adentro.* NM: Bureau of Land Management, New Mexico State Office.

Parmentier, Richard J. 1987. *The Sacred Remains: Myth, History, and Polity in Belau*. Chicago, IL: University of Chicago Press.

Pärssinen, Martti, and Antti Korpisaari, eds. 2003. Western Amazonia. In *Amazônia Ocidental. Multidisciplinary Studies on Ancient Expansionistic Movements, Fortifications and Sedentary Life*. Renvall Institute 14. Helsinki: University of Helsinki Press.

Pásztor, Emília, Curt Roslund, Britt-Mari Näsström, and Heather Robertson. 2000. The Sun and the Rosaring Ceremonial Road. *European Journal of Archaeology* 3(1): 57–67.

Pattison, Natalie B. 1985. Rock Stairways of Chaco Canyon. In *Prehistory and History of the Southwest: Collected Papers in Honor of Alden Hayes*, ed. Nancy Fox, pp. 63–71. Papers of the New Mexico Archaeological Society 11. Albuquerque.

Pattison, Natalie B., and L. D. Potter. 1977. *Prehistoric and Historic Steps and Trails of Glenn Canyon–Lake Powell*. Lake Powell Research Project Bulletin 45. Los Angeles, CA: University of California, Los Angeles.

Pérez, Celia A. 1995. Niveles de fertilizantes orgánica con tarope (Eichhornia azurea [Sw.] Kunth) en el cultivo de maíz en campos elevados en la Estación Biológica del Beni. Thesis, Agronomy. Universidad Técnica del Beni, Trinidad, Bolivia.

Pérez, Teresa A. 1996. Evaluación de los fertilizantes orgánicos en yuca (Manihot esculenta Cr.) en campos elevados de la Estación Biológica del Beni. Thesis, Agronomy. Universidad Técnica del Beni, Trinidad, Bolivia.

Pfälzner, P. 2001. *Haus und Haushalt: Wohnformen des dritten Jahrtausends vor Christus in Nordmespotamien. Damaszener Forschungen* 9. Mainz: Philipp von Zabern.

Pigniolo, Andrew R., Jackson Underwood, and James H. Cleland. 1997. *Where Trails Cross: Cultural Resources Inventory and Evaluation for the Imperial Project, Imperial County, California*. San Diego, CA: KEA Environmental.

Pikoulas, Yannis A. 1999. The Road-Network of Arkadia. In *Defining Ancient Arkadia*, ed. Thomas Heine Nielsen and James Roy, pp. 248–319. Acts of the Copenhagen Polis Center 6. Copenhagen.

Pinto Parada, Rodolfo. 1987. *Pueblo de Leyenda*. Trinidad: Editorial El Tiempo de Bolivia.

Pires de Campos, Antonio. 1862. Breve noticia que dá o Capitão Antonio Pires de Campos, do gentio barbaro que há na derrota viagem das minas do Cuyabá e seu reconcavo . . . até o dia 20 maio de 1723. *Revista Trimensal do Instituto Histórico e Geográfico Brasileiro* (Rio de Janeiro) 25:437–58.

Pitezel, Todd A. 2007. Surveying Cerro de Moctezuma, Chihuahua, Mexico. *Kiva* 72(3): 353–69.

Plafker, George. 1963. Observations on Archaeological Remains in Northeastern Bolivia. *American Antiquity* 28:372–78.

Plog, Fred. 1990. Some Thoughts on Full-Coverage Surveys. In *The Archaeology* of Regions: A Case for Full-Coverage Survey, ed. Suzanne K. Fish and Stephen A. Kowalewski, pp. 243–48. Washington: Smithsonian Institution Press.

Pohn, H. A. 1970. *Analysis of Images and Photographs by a Ronchi Grating.* Report PB197-101. Springfield, VA: U.S. Department of Commerce, NTIC.

Poidebard, A. 1934. *La Trace de Rome dans le Désert de Syrie. Bibliothéque Archéologique et Historique 18.* Paris: Librairie Orientaliste Paul Geuthner.

Pollock, Susan. 2003. Feasts, Funerals, and Fast Food in Early Mesopotamian States. In *The Archaeology and Politics of Food and Feasting in Early States and Empires,* ed. T. L. Bray, pp. 17–38. New York: Kluwer.

Poole, Deborah A. 1991. Rituals of Movement, Rites of Transformation: Pilgrimage and Dance in the Highlands of Cuzco, Peru. In *Pilgrimage in Latin America,* ed. N. Ross Crumrine and Alan Morinis, pp. 307–38. Westport, CT: Greenwood.

Posey, Darrell. 1983. Indigenous Ecological Knowledge and Development of the Amazon. In *Dilemma of Amazonian Development,* ed. Emilio Moran, pp. 225–57. Boulder, CO: Westview.

Potter, James M. 2004. The Creation of Person, the Creation of Place: Hunting Landscapes in the American Southwest. *American Antiquity* 69(2): 322–38.

Potter, Timothy W. 1979. *The Changing Landscape of South Etruria.* New York: St. Martin's Press.

Powers, Robert P., and Janet D. Orcutt. 1999a. Summary and Conclusion. In *The Bandelier Archaeological Survey, Intermountain Cultural Resources Management, Professional Paper 57,* ed. Robert P. Powers and Janet D. Orcutt, pp. 551–89. Santa Fe, NM: Intermountain Region, National Park Service.

———, eds. 1999b. *The Bandelier Archaeological Survey. Intermountain Cultural Resources Management, Professional Paper 57.* Santa Fe, NM: Intermountain Region, National Park Service.

Price-Williams, Douglass, and Rosslyn Gaines. 1994. The Dreamtime and Dreams of Northern Australian Aboriginal Artists. *Ethos* 22(3): 373–88.

Pritchett, W. Kendrick. 1980. *Studies in Ancient Greek Topography, Part III (Roads).* Berkeley, CA: University of California Press..

Prümers, Heiko. 2006. Improntas de esteras en cerámica prehispánica del sitio Bella Vista (Depto. Beni, Bolivia). In *Actas III Jornadas Internacionales sobre Textiles Precolombinos,* ed. V. Solanilla Demestre, pp. 207–12. Barcelona: Departament d'Art de la Universitat Autònoma de Barcelona, Institut Català Iberoamericana.

Prümers, Heiko, C. Carla Jaimes Betancourt, and Roberto Plaza Martínez. 2006. Algunas tumbas prehispánicas de Bella Vista, Prov. Iténez, Bolivia. In *Zeitschrift für Archäologie Außereuropäischer Kulturen* (Wiesbaden) 1:251–84.

Purser, Margaret. 1988. All Roads Lead to Winnemucca: Local Road Systems and Community Material Culture in Nineteenth-Century Nevada. *Perspectives in Vernacular Architecture* 3:120–34.

Quartermaine, Jamie, Barrie Trinder, and Rick Turner. 2003. *Thomas Telford's*

Holyhead Road: The A5 in North Wales. Council for British Archaeology, Research Report 135. York.

Raffino, R. 1982. *Los Inkas del Kollasuyu.* Buenos Aires: Ramos Americana.

—— 1993. *Inca: Arqueología, historia y urbanismo del altiplano andino.* Buenos Aires: Editoríal Corregidor.

Raffles, Hugh, and Antoinette WinklerPrins. 2003. Further Reflections on Amazonian Environmental History: Transformations of Rivers and Streams. *Latin American Research Review* 38(3): 165–87.

Raftery, Barry. 1990. *Trackways through Time: Archaeological Investigations on Irish Bog Roads, 1985–1989.* Rush, Co. Dublin: Headline.

Raitz, Karl, ed. 1996. *The National Road.* Baltimore, MD: Johns Hopkins University Press.

Rappaport, Joanne. 1985. History, Myth, and the Dynamics of Territorial Maintenance in Tierradentro, Colombia. *American Ethnologist* 12:27–45.

Rea, Amadeo. 1997. *At the Desert's Green Edge.* Tucson, AZ: University of Arizona Press.

Redfield, Robert, and Alfonso Villa Rojas. 1934. *Chan Kom: A Maya Village.* Carnegie Institution of Washington Publication 448. Washington, DC. Facsimile reprint. Chicago, IL: University of Chicago Press, 1990.

Redman, Charles L., Stephen R. James, Paul Fish, and J. Daniel Rogers, eds. 2004. *The Archaeology of Global Change: The Impact of Humans on Their Environment.* Washington, DC: Smithsonian Institution Press.

Reents-Budet, Dorie, ed. 1994. *Painting the Maya Universe: Royal Ceramics of the Classic Period.* Durham, NC: Duke University Press.

Reid, Dawn M. 1995. Inter- and Intra-site Sacbeob of the Naranjal Area. In *The View from Yalahau: 1993 Archaeological Investigations in Northern Quintana Roo, Mexico,* ed. Scott L. Fedick and Karl A. Taube, pp. 121–28. Latin American Studies Program Field Report Series No. 2. Riverside, CA: Latin American Studies Program, University of California.

Reina Aoyama, Leticia. 1998. Las rutas de Oaxaca. *Dimensión Antropológica* 5(12): 49–76.

Reister, Jurgen. 1981. *Arqueología y Arte Rupestre en el Oriente Boliviano.* La Paz: Editorial Amigos del Libro.

Renger, J. M. 1995. Institutional, Communal, and Individual Ownership or Possession of Arable Land in Ancient Mesopotamia from the End of the Fourth to the End of the First Millennium BC. *Chicago-Kent Law Review* 71:269–319.

Restall, Matthew. 1998. *Maya Conquistador.* Boston, MA: Beacon.

Ringle, William M. 1999. Pre-Classic Cityscapes: Ritual Politics among the Early Lowland Maya. In *Social Patterns in Pre-Classic Mesoamerica,* ed. David C. Grove and Rosemary A. Joyce, pp. 183–224. Washington, DC: Dumbarton Oaks Research Library and Collection.

Rival, Laura M. 2002. *Trekking through History: The Huaorani of Amazonian Ecuador.* New York: Columbia University Press.

Robertson, Benjamin P. 1983. Other New World Roads and Trails. In *Chaco Roads Project, Phase I; A Reappraisal of Prehistoric Roads in the San Juan Basin,* ed. C. Kincaid, pp. 2-1–2-7. Albuquerque, NM: U.S. Department of the Interior, Bureau of Land Management, Albuquerque District Office.

Robin, Cynthia. 2002. Outside of Houses: The Practices of Everyday Life at Chan Noohol, Belize. *Journal of Social Archaeology* 2(2): 245–67.

—— 2006. Gender, Farming, and Long-Term Change: Maya Historical and Archaeological Perspectives. *Current Anthropology* 47(3): 409–33.

Rockman, Marcy. 2003. Knowledge and Learning in the Archaeology of Colonization. In *Colonization of Unfamiliar Landscapes: The Archaeology of Adaptation,* ed. M. Rockman and J. Steele, pp. 3–24. London: Routledge.

Rodman, Margaret C. 1992. Empowering Place: Multilocality and Multivocality. *American Anthropologist* 94(3): 640–56.

Roe, Frank G. 1955. *The Indian and the Horse.* Norman, OK: University of Oklahoma Press.

Rogers, Malcolm. 1941. Aboriginal Culture Relations between Southern California and the Southwest. *San Diego Museum Bulletins* 5(3): 1–6.

—— 1966. *Ancient Hunters of the Far West.* San Diego, CA: Copley Press.

Roll, Israel. 2002. Crossing the Rift Valley: The Connecting Arteries between the Road Networks of Judaea/Palestina and Arabia. In *Limes XVIII: Proceedings of the XVIIIth International Congress of Roman Frontier Studies Held in Amman, Jordan,* ed. Philip Freeman, Julian Bennett, Zbigniew T. Fiema, and Birgittan Hoffman, pp. 215–30. BAR International Series 1084(II). Oxford: BAR.

Roney, John R. 1992. Prehistoric Roads and Regional Integration in the Chacoan System. In *Anasazi Regional Organization and the Chaco System,* ed. David E. Doyel, pp. 123–31. Anthropological Papers 5. Albuquerque, NM: Maxwell Museum of Anthropology.

Ross, C. S., R. L. Smith, and R. A. Bailey. 1961. Outline of the Geology of the Jemez Mountains, New Mexico. In *Guidebook of the Albuquerque Country,* ed. S. A. Northrop, pp. 139–43. Socorro, NM: New Mexico Geological Society.

Roth, George E. 1976. Incorporation and Changes in Ethnic Structure: The Chemehuevi Indians. Ph.D. dissertation, Anthropology. Northwestern University, Evanston, IL.

Roys, Ralph L. 1965. *Ritual of the Bacabs.* Norman, OK: University of Oklahoma Press.

Russell, Frank. 1975 [1908]. *The Pima Indians.* Tucson, AZ: University of Arizona Press.

Saavedra, Oscar. 2006. Sistema prehispánico de camellones en la amazonia boliviana. In *Camellones y abarrados: Contexto social, usos, y retos del pasado y del presente,* ed. Francisco Valdez, pp. 295–314. Quito: Ediciones Abya-Yala.

Sahlins, Marshall. 1992. *Anahulu: The Anthropology of History in the Kingdom of Hawaii 1, Historical Ethnography.* Chicago, IL: University of Chicago Press.

Sallaberger, W. 1996. Grain Accounts: Personnel Lists and Expenditure Documents. In *Administrative Documents from Tell Beydar (Season 1993–1995)*, *Subartu 2*, ed. F. Ismail, W. Sallaberger, P. Talon, and K. Van Lerberghe, pp. 89–106. Turnhout: Brepols.

Sallaberger, W., and J. A. Ur. 2004. Tell Beydar/Nabada in Its Regional Setting. In *Third Millennium Cuneiform Texts from Tell Beydar (Seasons 1996–2002)*, *Subartu 12*, ed. L. Milano, W. Sallaberger, P. Talon, and K. Van Lerberghe, pp. 51–71. Turnhout: Brepols.

Sample, L. L. 1950. *Trade and Trails in Aboriginal California*. University of California Archaeological Survey Reports 8. Berkeley.

Sanhueza Tohá, Cecilia. 2004. Medir, Amojonar, Repartir: Territorialidades y Prácticas Demarcatorias en el Camino Incaico de Atacama (II Región, Chile). *Chugara* 36(2): 483–89.

Santley, Robert S. 1991. The Structure of the Aztec Transport Network. In *Ancient Road Networks and Settlement Hierarchies in the New World*, ed. Charles D. Trombold, pp. 198–210. Cambridge: Cambridge University Press.

Savage, Stephen H., Kurt Zamora, and Donald R. Keller. 2002. Archaeology in Jordan, 2001 Season. *American Journal of Archaeology* 106(3): 435–58.

Saville, Marshall H. 1930. Ancient Causeways of Yucatan. *Museum of the American Indian, Heye Foundation. Indian Notes and Monographs* 7:89–99.

—— 1935. The Ancient Maya Causeways of Yucatan. *Antiquity* 9(33): 67–73.

Scarre, Chris. 1996. Roads and Tracks. In *Oxford Companion to Archaeology*, ed. Brian Fagan, pp. 381–82. Oxford: Oxford University Press.

Schiffer, Michael B. 1999. *The Material Life of Human Beings: Artifacts, Behavior, and Communication*. London: Routledge.

Schlereth, Thomas J. 1997. *Reading the Road: U.S. 40 and the American Landscape*. Rev. ed. Knoxville, TN: University of Tennessee Press.

Schloen, J. D. 2001. *The House of the Father as Fact and Symbol: Patrimonialism in Ugarit and the Ancient Near East*. Studies in the Archaeology and History of the Levant 2. Winona Lake, IN: Eisenbrauns.

Schreiber, Katharina. 1984. Prehistoric Roads in the Carhuarazo Valley, Peru. In *Current Archaeological Projects in the Central Andes: Some Approaches and Results*, ed. Ann Kendall, pp. 75–94. BAR International Series. Oxford: BAR.

—— 1991. The Association between Roads and Polities: Evidence for a Wari Road System in Peru. In *Ancient Road Networks and Settlement Hierarchies in the New World*, ed. Charles Trombold, pp. 243–52. Cambridge: Cambridge University Press.

—— 1992. *Wari Imperialism in Middle Horizon Peru*. Anthropological Papers of the University of Michigan 87. Ann Arbor: Museum of Anthropology, University of Michigan.

Schreiber, Stephen D. 1997. Engineering Feats of the Anasazi: Buildings, Roads, and Dams. In *Anasazi Architecture and American Design*, ed. Baker H. Morrow and V. B. Price, pp. 77–87. Albuquerque, NM: University of New Mexico Press.

Schroeder, A. H. 1961. An Archaeological Survey of the Painted Rocks Reservoir, Western Arizona. *The Kiva* 27(1): 1–28.

Sever, Thomas, and David Wagner. 1991. Analysis of Prehistoric Roadways in Chaco Canyon Using Remotely Sensed Digital Data. In *Ancient Road Networks and Settlement Hierarchies in the New World*, ed. Charles Trombold, pp. 42–52. Cambridge: Cambridge University Press.

Severance, Owen. 1999. Prehistoric Roads in Southeastern Utah. In *La Frontera: Papers in Honor of Patrick H. Beckett*, ed. Meliha S. Duran and David T. Kirkpatrick, pp. 185–95. Papers of the Archaeological Society of New Mexico 25. Alburquerque.

Sevin, Veli. 1988. The Oldest Highway: Between the Regions of Van and Elazio in Eastern Anatolia. *Antiquity* 62:547–51.

Sharer, Robert J. 1992. The Preclassic Origin of Lowland Maya States. In *New Theories on the Ancient Maya*, ed. Elin C. Danien and Robert J. Sharer, pp. 131–36. Philadelphia, PA: University of Pennsylvania Museum of Archaeology and Anthropology.

—— 1994. *The Ancient Maya.* 5th ed. Stanford, CA: Stanford University Press.

Shaw, Justine M. 2001. Maya Sacbeob: Form and Function. *Ancient Mesoamerica* 12:261–72.

—— 2008. *White Roads of the Yucatan: Changing Social Landscapes of the Yucatec Maya.* Tucson, AZ: University of Arizona Press.

Sheets, Payson. 1994. Summary and Conclusions. In *Archaeology, Volcanism, and Remote Sensing in the Arenal Region, Costa Rica*, ed. P. Sheets and B. McKee, pp. 312–25. Austin, TX: University of Texas Press.

Sheets, Payson, and Brian McKee, eds. 1994. *Archaeology, Volcanism, and Remote Sensing in the Arenal Region, Costa Rica.* Austin, TX: University of Texas Press.

Sheets, Payson, and Thomas L. Sever. 1991. Prehistoric Footpaths in Costa Rica: Transportation and Communication in a Tropical Rainforest. In *Ancient Road Networks and Settlement Hierarchies in the New World*, ed. Charles D. Trombold, pp. 53–65. Cambridge: Cambridge University Press.

Sheridan, Thomas E. 2006. *Landscapes of Fraud. Mission Tumacácori, the Baca Float, and the Betrayal of the O'odham.* Tucson, AZ: University of Arizona Press.

Sidebotham, Steven E., and Ronald E. Zitterkopf. 1995. Routes Through the Eastern Desert of Egypt. *Expedition* 37(2): 39–52.

Sidebotham, Steven E., Ronald E. Zitterkopf, and John A. Riley. 1991. Survey of the 'Abu Sha'ar-Nile Road. *American Journal of Archaeology* 95(4): 571–622.

Siemens, Alfred. 1996. Benign Flooding on Tropical Lowland Floodplains. In *The Managed Mosaic: Ancient Maya Agriculture and Resource Use*, ed. Scott Fedick, pp. 132–42. Salt Lake City, UT: University of Utah Press.

Silverman, Helaine, and William Isbell, eds. 2008. *Handbook of South American Archaeology.* New York: Springer.

Simmons, Leo W., ed. 1942. *Sun Chief, the Autobiography of a Hopi Indian.* New Haven, CT: Yale University Press.

Simmons, Marc. 2001. *Following the Santa Fe Trail: A Guide for Modern Travelers.* Santa Fe, NM: Ancient City Press.

Skinner, Alanson. 1920. Notes on the Bribri of Costa Rica. *Indian Notes and Monographs* 6(3). New York: Museum of the American Indian, Heye Foundation.

Smith, Adam T. 2001. The Limitations of Doxa: Agency and Subjectivity from an Archaeological Point of View. *Journal of Social Archaeology* 1(2): 155–71.

Smith, Claire, and Heather Burke. 2007. *Digging It Up Down Under. A Practical Guide to Doing Archaeology in Australia.* New York: Springer.

Smith, Clifford T., W. M. Denevan, and R. Hamilton. 1968. Ancient Ridged Fields in the Region of Lake Titicaca. *Geographical Review* 134:353–67.

Smith, Nigel J. H. 1999. *The Amazon River Forest: A Natural History of Plants, Animals, and People.* New York: Oxford University Press.

Smith, Watson. 1952. *Kiva Mural Decorations at Awatovi and Kawaika-A.* Papers of the Peabody Museum of American Archaeology and Ethnology, Harvard University, 37. Cambridge, MA.

Snarskis, Michael. 1981. The Archaeology of Costa Rica. In *Between Continents, Between Seas,* ed. Suzanne Abel-Vidor, pp. 15–84. New York: Abrams.

Snead, James E. 2001. Pajarito Trails Project, Final Report of the 1999 Season, II: Fieldwork in Otowi and Sandia Canyons. Report submitted to the Office of Environment, Safety, and Health (ESH-20). Los Alamos, NM: Los Alamos National Laboratory.

—— 2002. Ancestral Pueblo Trails and the Cultural Landscape of the Pajarito Plateau, New Mexico. *Antiquity* 76:756–65.

—— 2005. Ancient Trails of the Pajarito Plateau. In *The Peopling of Bandelier,* ed. Robert P. Powers, pp. 79–85. Santa Fe, NM: School of American Research Press.

—— 2008. *Ancestral Landscapes of the Pueblo World.* Tucson, AZ: University of Arizona Press.

Snead, James, Winifred Creamer, and Tineke Van Zandt. 2004. 'Ruins of Our Forefathers': Large Sites and Site Clusters in the Northern Rio Grande. In *The Pueblo IV Period in the American Southwest,* ed. Charles Adams and Andrew Duff, pp. 26–34. Tucson: University of Arizona Press.

Snead, James, and Robert Preucel. 1999. The Ideology of Settlement: Ancestral Keres Landscapes in the Northern Rio Grande. In *Archaeologies of Landscape: Contemporary Perspectives,* ed. W. Ashmore and A. Bernard Knapp, pp. 169–200. Oxford: Blackwell.

Snygg, John, and Tom Windes. 1998. Long, Wide Roads and Great Kiva Roofs. *Kiva* 64(1): 7–25.

Sofaer, Anna, Michael Marshall, and Rolf Sinclair. 1989. The Great North Road: A Cosmographic Expression of the Chaco Culture of New Mexico. In *World*

Archaeoastronomy, ed. Anthony Aveni, pp. 365–76. Cambridge: Cambridge University Press.

Soja, Edward. 1989. *Postmodern Geographies. The Reassertion of Space in Critical Social Theory.* London: Verso.

Solnit, Rebecca. 2000. *Wanderlust. A History of Walking.* New York: Penguin.

Spencer, Baldwin, and F. J. Gillen. 1968. *The Native Tribes of Central Australia.* New York: Dover.

Spencer, Charles. 1994. Factional Ascendance, Dimensions of Leadership, and the Development of Centralized Authority. In *Factional Competition and Political Development in the New World,* ed. Elizabeth Brumfiel and John Fox, pp. 31–43. Cambridge: Cambridge University Press.

Spencer, Charles, Elsa Redmond, and Maria Rinaldi. 1994. Drained Fields at La Tigra, Venezuelan Llanos: A Regional Perspective. *Latin American Antiquity* 5:119–43.

Spicer, Edward, and Rosamond B. Spicer. 1992. The Nations of a State. *Boundary 2* 19(3): 26–48. Special issue, *1492–1992: American Indian Persistence and Resurgence.*

Staccioli, Romolo Augusto. 2004. *The Roads of the Romans.* Los Angeles, CA: Getty.

Stahl, Peter W., and James A. Zeidler. 1990. Differential Bone–Refuse Accumulation in the Food-Preparation and Traffic Areas on an Early Ecuadorian House Floor. *Latin American Antiquity* 1:150–69.

Stanley, John M. 1992. The Great Maharashtrian Pilgrimage: Pandharpur and Alandi. In *Sacred Journeys: The Anthropology of Pilgrimage,* ed. Alan Morinis, pp. 65–87. Westport, CT: Greenwood.

Stanton, Travis W., and Traci Arden. 1997. Urban Design and Internal Causeways at Yaxuna. Paper presented at 62nd Annual Meeting of Society for American Archaeology, Nashville, TN.

Stanton, Travis W., and David A. Freidel. 2005. Placing the Centre, Centring the Place: The Influence of Formative Sacbeob in Classic Site Design at Yaxuná, Yucatán. *Cambridge Archaeological Journal* 15(2): 225–49.

Steele, C., H. McDonald, R. Matthews, and J. Black. 2003. Impact of Empire. Later Third-Millennium Investigations: The Late Early Dynastic and Akkadian Periods. In *Excavations at Tell Brak.* Vol. 4, *Exploring an Upper Mesopotamian Regional Centre, 1994–1996,* ed. R. Matthews, pp. 193–269. Cambridge: McDonald Institute and British School of Archaeology in Iraq.

Steen, Charlie R. 1977. *Pajarito Plateau Archaeological Survey and Excavations.* Los Alamos, NM: Los Alamos Scientific Laboratory.

Stehberg, Rubén. 2001. Los caminos Inka en Chile. In *Tras la Huella del Inka en Chile,* ed. C. Aldunate del Solar and L. Cornejo B., pp. 92–103. Museo Chileno de Arte Precolombino.

Stehberg, Rubén, and Ángel Cabeza. 1991. Sistema vial Incaica en el Chile Semi-arido. *Comechingonia* 9(2): 153–216.

Stehberg, Rubén, and Nazareno Carvajal. 1986. Road System of the Incas in the Southern Part of Their Tawantinsuyu Empire. *National Geographic Research* 4(1): 74–97.

Stehberg, Rubén, Nazareno Carvajal, and Roxana Seguel. 1986. El Tambo Conchuca y su Relación con la Ruta de Penetración Inka al Centro de Chile. *Comechingonia* 4 (Special Number: El Imperio Inka): 13–42.

Stehberg, Rubén, H. Niemeyer, and C. Coros. 1999. Investigaciones de la red vial inkaica en el sector de Salto del Soldado (Valle de Aconcagua, Chile Central). *Actas del XIII Congreso Nacional de Arqueología Argentina.* La Plata.

Stein, G. J. 1998. Heterogeneity, Power, and Political Economy: Some Current Research Issues in the Archaeology of Old World Complex Societies. *Journal of Archaeological Research* 6:1–44.

—— 2004. Structural Parameters and Sociocultural Factors in the Economic Organization of North Mesopotamian Urbanism in the Third Millennium BC. In *Archaeological Perspectives on Political Economies,* ed. G. M. Feinman and L. M. Nicholas, pp. 61–78. Salt Lake City, UT: University of Utah Press.

Stein, John R. 1983. Road Corridor Descriptions. In *Chaco Roads Project Phase I,* ed. C. Kincaid, pp. 8-1–8-15. Albuquerque, NM: Bureau of Land Management, New Mexico State Office.

Stein, John R., and Peter J. McKenna. 1988. *An Archaeological Reconnaissance of a Late Bonito Phase Occupation near Aztec Ruins National Monument, New Mexico.* Santa Fe: Southwest Cultural Resources Center, National Park Service.

Stephen, A. M. 1936. *Hopi Journal of Alexander M. Stephen,* ed. Elsie Clews Parsons. New York: Columbia University Press.

Sterner, Judith A. 2003. *The Ways of the Mandara Mountains: A Comparative Regional Approach.* Cologne: Rüdiger Köppe Verlag.

Steward, Julian, and Louis Faron. 1959. *Native Peoples of South America.* New York: McGraw-Hill.

Stewart, Kathleen C. 1996. An Occupied Place. In *Senses of Place,* ed. Steven Feld and Keith H. Basso, pp. 137–66. Santa Fe, NM: School of American Research Press.

Stewart, Kenneth M. 1983. Mohave. In *Handbook of North American Indians.* Vol. 10, *Southwest,* ed. Alfonso Ortiz, pp. 55–70. Washington, DC: Smithsonian Institution Press.

Stone, E. C., and P. Zimansky. 2004. *The Anatomy of a Mesopotamian City: Survey and Soundings at Mashkan-shapir.* Winona Lake, IN: Eisenbrauns.

Stothert-Stockman, Karen. 1967. *Pre-Colonial Highways of Bolivia. Part 1: The La Paz-Yungas Route Via Palca.* La Paz: Academia Nacional de Ciencias de Bolivia.

Strassberg, Richard. 1994. Introduction: The Rise of Chinese Travel Writing. In *Inscribed Landscapes: Travel Writing in Imperial China,* ed. Richard Strassberg, pp.1–56. Berkeley: University of California Press.

Strobel, A. 1997. Ancient Roads in the Roman District of South Peraea: Routes of Communication in the Eastern Area of the Dead Sea. In *Studies in the His-*

tory and Archaeology of Jordan 6, ed. G. Bisheh, M. Zaghloul, and I. Kehrberg, pp. 271–80. Amman: Department of Antiquities.

Strube, Erdmann, Leon. 1963. *Vialidad Imperial de los Incas*. Instituto de Estudios Americanistas 33. Cordoba: Universidad Nacional de Cordoba.

Stuart, David. 1998. The Fire Enters His House: Architecture and Ritual in Classic Maya Texts. In *Function and Meaning in Classic Maya Architecture*, ed. Stephen D. Houston, pp. 373–426. Washington, DC: Dumbarton Oaks Research Library and Collection.

—— 2006. *The Inscribed Markers of the Coba-Yaxuna Causeway and the Glyph for Sakbih*. *Mesoweb*, <http://www.mesoweb.com/stuart/notes/Sacbe.pdf>, accessed February 22, 2009.

Swanson, Steven. 2003. Documenting Prehistoric Communication Networks: A Case Study in the Paquime Polity. *American Antiquity* 68(4): 753–67.

Tal, Oren. 2005. Some Remarks on the Coastal Plain of Palestine under Achaemenid Rule—An Archaeological Synopsis. In *L'Archéologie de l'Empire Achéménide: Novelles Recherches*, ed. Pierre Briant and Rémy Boucharlat, pp. 71–96. Paris: Éditions de Boccard.

Taylor, C. C. 1979. *Roads and Tracks of Britain*. London: Dent.

Taylor, Walter W. 1954. An Analysis of Some Salt Samples from the Southwest. *Plateau* 27(2): 1–7.

Tedlock, Barbara. 1992. *Time and the Highland Maya*. 2nd ed. Albuquerque, NM: University of New Mexico Press.

Tedlock, Dennis. 1996. *Popol Vuh: The Definitive Edition of the Mayan Book of the Dawn of Life and the Glories of Gods and Kings*. Rev. ed. New York: Simon and Schuster.

—— 2003. *Rabinal Achi: A Mayan Drama of War and Sacrifice*. New York: Oxford University Press.

Thiessen, Thomas D. 1993. *Early Explorations and the Fur Trade at Knife River. The Phase I Archeological Research Program for the Knife River Indian Villages National Historic Site, Part II: Ethnohistorical Studies*. Lincoln, NE: National Park Service Midwest Archeological Center.

Thiessen, T. D., W. R. Wood, and A. W. Jones. 1979. The Sitting Rabbit 1907 Map of the Missouri River in North Dakota. *Plains Anthropologist* 24(84) pt. 1:145–67.

Thomas, Christopher, and James Rackham, eds. 1996. Bramcote Green, Bermondsey: A Bronze Age Trackway and Palaeo-Environmental Sequence. *Proceedings of the Prehistoric Society* 61:221–53.

Thomas, Julian. 1993. The Politics of Vision and the Archaeologies of Landscape. In *Landscape: Politics and Perspectives*, ed. Barbara Bender, pp. 19–48. Providence, RI: Berg.

—— 1996. *Time, Culture and Identity: An Interpretive Archaeology*. London: Routledge.

Thompson, J. Eric S. 1930. The Causeways of the Cobá District, Eastern Yucatan. *Proceedings from the 23rd International Congress of Americanists*, pp. 181–84. New York: Science Press.

—— 1934. Sky Bearers, Colors and Directions in Maya and Mexican Religion. Contributions to American Archaeology 10. In *Contributions to American Anthropology and History* 2(5–12): 211–42. Washington, DC: Carnegie Institution of Washington.

—— 1962. *A Catalog of Maya Hieroglyphs*. Norman, OK: University of Oklahoma Press.

Thwaites, R. G., ed. 1906. *Early Western Travels 1748–1846: Part II of Maximilian, Prince of Wied's, Travels in the Interior of North America, 1832–1834*. Cleveland, OH: Arthur H. Clark.

Tilley, Christopher. 1994. *A Phenomenology of Landscape: Places, Paths and Monuments*. Oxford: Berg.

—— 2004. *The Materiality of Stone: Explorations in Landscape Phenomenology*. Oxford: Berg.

Timperley, Harold W., and Edith Brill. 1965. *Ancient Trackways of Wessex*. London: Phoenix House.

Titiev, Mischa. 1937. A Hopi Salt Expedition. *American Anthropologist* 39(2): 244–58.

—— 1972. *The Hopi Indians of Old Oraibi: Change and Continuity*. Ann Arbor, MI: University of Michigan Press.

Tonkinson, Robert. 2003. Ambrymese Dreams and the Mardu Dreaming. In *Dream Travelers. Sleep Experiences and Culture in the Western Pacific*, ed. Roger Ivar Lohmann, pp. 87–105. New York: Palgrave Macmillan.

Toom, D. L. 1992. Early Village Formation in the Middle Missouri Subarea of the Plains. *Research in Economic Anthropology Supplement* 6:131–91.

—— 1996. Archeology of the Middle Missouri. In *Archeological and Bioarcheological Resources of the Northern Plains: A Volume in the Central and Northern Plains Archeological Overview*, ed. G. C. Frison and R. C. Mainfort, pp. 56–76. Arkansas Archeological Survey Research Series No. 47. Fayetteville, AR: Arkansas Archeological Survey.

Toren, Christina. 1999. *Mind, Materiality, and History: Explorations in Fijian Ethnography*. London: Routledge.

Tozzer, Alfred M., ed. and trans. 1941. *Landa's Relacion de las Cosas de Yucatán: A Translation (annotated with appendices)*. Papers of the Peabody Museum of American Archaeology and Ethnology, Harvard University, 18. Cambridge, MA.

Trigger, Bruce. 1990. Monumental Architecture: A Thermodynamic Explanation of Symbolic Behavior. *World Archaeology* 22(2): 119–31.

Trombold, Charles D. 1991a. An Introduction to the Study of Ancient New World Road Networks. In *Ancient Road Networks and Settlement Hierarchies in the New World*, ed. Charles D. Trombold, pp. 1–16. Cambridge: Cambridge University Press.

—— 1991b. Causeways in the Context of Strategic Planning in the La Quemada Region, Zacatecas, Mexico. In *Ancient Road Networks and Settlement Hierarchies in the New World*, ed. Charles Trombold, pp. 145–68. Cambridge: Cambridge University Press.

——, ed. 1991c. *Ancient Road Networks and Settlement Hierarchies in the New World*. Cambridge: Cambridge University Press.

Tsoar, H., and Y. Yekutieli. 1992. Geomorphological Identification of Ancient Roads and Paths on the Loess of the Northern Negev. *Israel Journal of Earth Sciences* 41:209–16.

Tucker, Sara J. 1942. *Indian Villages of the Illinois Country*. Scientific Papers 2(1) of the Illinois State Museum. Springfield, IL.

Turner, Victor. 1974. *Dramas, Fields, and Metaphors: Symbolic Action in Human Society*. Ithaca, NY: Cornell University Press.

Tyrrell, J. B., ed. 1916. *David Thompson's Narrative of His Explorations in Western America 1784–1812*. Toronto, ON: Champlain Society.

Ubbeloedde Doering, Heinrich. 1966. *On the Royal Highways of the Inca*. Chur, Switzerland: Platt Publishing.

Ucko, Peter J., and Robert Layton, eds. 1999. *The Archaeology and Anthropology of Landscape: Shaping Your Landscape*. London: Routledge.

Underhill, Ruth M. 1946. *Papago Indian Religion*. New York: Columbia University Press.

UNESCO. 2004. *The Chinese Silk Road as World Cultural Heritage Route: A Systematic Approach towards Identification and Nomination*. Paris: UNESCO World Heritage Centre.

Upton, Dell. 1990. Imagining the Early Virginia Landscape. In *Earth Patterns: Essays in Landscape Archaeology*, ed. William M. Kelso and Rachel Most, pp. 71–88. Charlottesville, VA: University Press of Virginia.

Ur, Jason A. 2002a. Settlement and Landscape in Northern Mesopotamia: The Tell Hamoukar Survey 2000–2001. *Akkadica* 123:57–88.

—— 2002b. Surface Collection and Offsite Studies at Tell Hamoukar, 1999. *Iraq* 64:15–44.

—— 2003. CORONA Satellite Photography and Ancient Road Networks: A Northern Mesopotamian Case Study. *Antiquity* 77(295): 102–15.

—— 2004. Urbanism and Society in the Third Millennium Upper Khabur Basin. Ph.D. dissertation, Near Eastern Languages and Civilizations. Oriental Institute of the University of Chicago.

Ur, Jason A., and C. Colantoni. In press. The Cycle of Production, Preparation, and Consumption in a Northern Mesopotamian City. In *Inside Ancient Kitchens: New Directions in the Study of Daily Meals and Feasts*, ed. E. Klarich. Boulder, CO: University Press of Colorado.

Urry, John. 2000. *Sociology beyond Societies. Mobilities for the Twenty-first Century*. London: Routledge.

Valenzuela R., Daniela. 2004. Paisaje, Senderos y Arte Rupestre de Quesala, Puna de Atacama. *Chungará* 36(Supl): 673–86.

van der Leeuw, S., and J. McGlade. 1997. Structural Change and Bifurcation in Urban Evolution: A Non-Linear Dynamical Perspective. In *Time, Process and Structured Transformation in Archaeology*, ed. S. van der Leeuw and J. McGlade, pp. 331–72. London: Routledge.

Van Dyke, Ruth M. 2003. Memory and the Construction of Chacoan Society. In *Archaeologies of Memory*, ed. Ruth M. Van Dyke and Susan E. Alcock, pp. 180–200. London: Blackwell.

—— 2008. *The Chaco Experienc: Landscape and Ideology at the Center Place.* Santa Fe, NM: School of Advanced Research Press.

Vanhove, Doris. 1996. *Roman Marble Quarries in Southern Euboea and the Associated Road Systems.* Leiden: Brill.

Van Lerberghe, K. 1996. The Livestock. In *Administrative Documents from Tell Beydar (Season 1993–1995), Subartu 2*, ed. F. Ismail, W. Sallaberger, P. Talon, and K. Van Lerberghe, pp. 107–17. Turnhout: Brepols.

Van Liere, W. J. 1963. Capitals and Citadels of Bronze–Iron Age Syria and Their Relationship to Land and Water. *Les annales archéologiques de Syrie* 13:109–22.

Van Liere, W. J., and J. Lauffray. 1954–55. Nouvelle Prospection Archéologique dans la Haute Jezieh Syrienne. *Les Annales Archéologiques de Syrie* 4–5:129–48.

Vansina, Jan. 1985. *Oral Tradition as History.* Madison, WI: University of Wisconsin Press.

Vazquez, Ricardo, Juan Vicente Guerrero, and Julio Cesar Sanchez. 2003. Cutris: Descripcion, cronologia, y afiliacion de un Centro Arquitectonico con Caminos Monumentales en la Llanura de San Carlos, Costa Rica. *Vinculos* 28(1–2): 149–74.

Vermeulen, Frank, and Mark Antrop, eds. 2001. *Ancient Lines in the Landscape: A Geo-archaeological Study of Protohistoric and Roman Roads and Field Systems in Northwestern Gaul.* Bulletin antieke beschaving, supplement 7. Leuven: Beschaving, Peeters.

Vidal, Silvia, and Alberta Zucchi. 2000. Los Caminos del Kuwai: Evidencias del Conocimiento Geopolítico, de las Expansiones y Migraciones de los Grupos Arawakos. In *Caminos Precolombinos: las Vías, los Ingenieros y los Viajeros*, ed. Leonor Herrera and Marianne Cardale de Schrimpff, pp. 87–113. Bogotá: Instituto Colombiano de Antropología y Historia.

Villa Rojas, Alfonso. 1934. The Yaxuna-Coba Causeway. *Contributions to American Anthropology and History* 9:187–208.

Vint, James M. 1999. Ceramic Artifacts. In *The Bandelier Archaeological Survey, Intermountain Cultural Resources Management, Professional Paper 57*, ed. Robert P. Powers and Janet D. Orcutt, pp. 389–467. Santa Fe, NM: National Park Service, Intermountain Region.

Vivian, R. Gwinn. 1997a. Chacoan Roads: Morphology. *Kiva* 63(1): 7–34.

—— 1997b. Chacoan Roads: Function. *Kiva* 63(1): 35–68.

Vogel, Virgil J. 1986. *Indian Names in Michigan.* Ann Arbor, MI: University of Michigan Press.

Vogt, Evon Z. 1970. *The Zinacantecos of Mexico: A Modern Maya Way of Life.* New York: Harcourt Brace Jovanovich.

—— 1976. *Tortillas for the Gods: A Symbolic Analysis of Zinacanteco Rituals.* Cambridge, MA: Harvard University Press.

Von Hagen, Victor Wolfgang. 1979. *The Royal Road of the Inca.* London: Gordon and Cremonesi.

Von Werlof, Jay. 1987. *Spirits of the Earth: A Study of Earthen Art in the North American Deserts.* Vol. I, *The North Desert.* El Centro, CA: Imperial Valley College Museum.

—— 1988. Trails in Eastern San Diego County and Imperial County: An Interim Report. *Pacific Coast Archaeological Society Quarterly* 24(1): 51–75.

—— 2004. *That They May Know and Remember.* Vol. 2, *Spirits of the Earth.* Ocatillo, CA: Imperial Valley College Desert Museum.

Vranich, Alexei. 1996. Complejo hidráulico prehispánico de Baures: Informe sobre Baures. Manuscript on file, Proyecto Agro-Arqueológico del Beni, CORDEBENI, and Instituto Nacional de Arqueología de Bolivia, La Paz.

Walker, John H. 2004. *Agricultural Change in the Bolivian Amazon.* Latin American Archaeology Reports. Pittsburgh, PA: University of Pittsburgh.

Wallace, Dwight T. 1991. The Chincha Roads: Economics and Symbolism. In *Ancient Road Networks and Settlement Hierarchies in the New World,* ed. Charles Trombold, pp. 253–63. Cambridge: Cambridge University Press.

Walsh, Michael R. 1998. Lines in the Sand: Competition and Stone Selection on the Pajarito Plateau, New Mexico. *American Antiquity* 63(4): 573–93.

Walter, Damian. 2001. The Medium of the Message: Shamanism as Localized Practice in the Nepal Himalayas. In *The Archaeology of Shamanism,* ed. Neil S. Price, pp. 105–19. London: Routledge.

Warhus, Mark. 1997. *Another America.* New York: St. Martin's.

Waterman, T. T. 1920. Yurok Geography. *University of California Publications in American Archaeology and Ethnology* 16(5): 177–314.

Waters, Michael R. 1982. Appendix H. Ceramic Data from Lowland Patayan Sites. In *Hohokam and Patayan. Prehistory of Southwestern Arizona,* ed. R. H. McGuire and M. B. Schiffer, pp. 571–80. New York: Academic.

Wedel, Mildred Mott. 1971. J.-B. Benard, Sieur de la Harpe: Visitor to the Wichitas in 1719. *Great Plains Journal* 10(2): 7–70.

Weiner, James F. 1991. *The Empty Place: Poetry, Space, and Being among the Foi of Papua New Guinea.* Bloomington: Indiana University Press.

Weiss, H. 1997. Late Third Millennium Abrupt Climate Change and Social Collapse in West Asia and Egypt. In *Third Millennium BC Climate Change and Old World Collapse,* ed. H. N. Dalfes, G. Kukla, and H. Weiss, pp. 711–23. NATO ASI Series vol. I 49. Berlin: Springer.

—— 2000. Causality and Chance: Late Third Millennium Collapse in Southwest Asia. In *La Djéziré et l'Euphrate Syriens de la protohistoire à la fin du IIe millénaire av. J.-C.: Tendances dans l'interprétation historique des donnés nouvelles, Subartu 7*, ed. O. Rouault and M. Wäfler, pp. 207–17. Turnhout: Brepols.

Weiss, H., and M. A. Courty. 1993. The Genesis and Collapse of the Akkadian Empire: The Accidental Refraction of Historical Law. In *Akkad: The First World Empire*, ed. M. Liverani, pp. 131–55. History of the Ancient Near East Studies 5. Padova: Sargon.

Weiss, H., M. A. Courty, W. Wetterstrom, F. Guichard, L. Senior, R. Meadow, and A. Curnow. 1993. The Genesis and Collapse of Third Millennium North Mesopotamian Civilization. *Science* 261:995–1004.

Whitmore, Thomas M., and B. L. Turner II. 2001. *Cultivated Landscapes of Middle America on the Eve of Conquest*. New York: Oxford University Press.

Widell, M. 2004. Some Observations on the Administration, Agriculture and Animal Management of Tell Beydar. *Ugarit-Forschungen* 35:717–33.

Wiedemann, Torsten, Marc Antrop, and Frank Vermeulen. 2001. Analysis of the Roman Road System around Cassel and Application of a GIS-Model in Sandy Flanders. In *Ancient Lines in the Landscape: A Geo-Archaeological Study of Protohistoric and Roman Roads and Field Systems in Northwestern Gaul*, ed. Frank Vermeulen and Marc Antrop, pp. 83–96. Leuven: Bulletin Antieke Beschaving.

Wierzbicka, Anna. 1997. *Understanding Cultures through Their Key Words*. Oxford: Oxford University Press.

Wilkinson, Tony J. 1982. The Definition of Ancient Manured Zones by Means of Extensive Sherd-Sampling Techniques. *Journal of Field Archaeology* 9:323–33.

—— 1993. Linear Hollows in the Jazira, Upper Mesopotamia. *Antiquity* 67:548–62.

—— 1994. The Structure and Dynamics of Dry-Farming States in Upper Mesopotamia. *Current Anthropology* 35:483–520.

—— 2000. Archaeological Survey of the Tell Beydar Region, Syria, 1997: A Preliminary Report. In *Tell Beydar: Environmental and Technical Studies, Subartu 6*, ed. K. Van Lerberghe and G. Voet, pp. 1–37. Turnhout: Brepols.

—— 2003. *Archaeological Landscapes of the Near East*. Tucson, AZ: University of Arizona Press.

Wilkinson, T. J., J. H. Christiansen, J. A. Ur, M. Widell, and M. Altaweel. 2007a. Urbanization within a Dynamic Environment: Modeling Bronze Age Communities in Upper Mesopotamia. *American Anthropologist* 109:52–68.

Wilkinson, T. J., M. Gibson, J. Christiansen, M. Widell, D. Schloen, N. Kouchoukos, C. Woods, J. C. Sanders, K.-L. Simunich, M. Altaweel, J. A. Ur, and C. Hritz. 2007b. Modeling Settlement Systems in a Dynamic Environment: Case Studies from Mesopotamia. In *The Model-Based Archaeology of Socionatural Systems*, ed. T. A. Kohler and S. van der Leeuw, pp. 175–208. Santa Fe, NM: School of American Research.

Wilkinson, Tony J., and D. J. Tucker. 1995. *Settlement Development in the North Jazira, Iraq.* Warminster: Aris & Phillips.

Will, G. F., and T. C. Hecker. 1944. Upper Missouri River Valley Aboriginal Culture in North Dakota. *North Dakota Historical Quarterly* 11(1–2): 5–126.

Williamson, T. 1998. Questions of Preservation and Destruction. In *The Archaeology of Landscape: Studies Presented to Christopher Taylor,* ed. P. Everson and T. Williamson, pp. 1–24. Manchester: Manchester University Press.

Wilson, D. R. 1982. *Air Photo Interpretation for Archaeologists.* New York: St. Martin's.

Wilson, G. L. 1928. *Hidatsa Eagle Trapping.* Anthropological Papers of the American Museum of Natural History 30 (pt. 4). New York.

Wilson, Meredith, and Bruno David. 2002. Introduction. In *Inscribed Landscapes: Marking and Making Place,* ed. Bruno David and Meredith Wilson, pp. 1–9. Honolulu: University of Hawai'i Press.

Windes, Thomas C. 1991. The Prehistoric Road Network at Pueblo Alto, Chaco Canyon, New Mexico. In *Ancient Road Networks and Settlement Hierarchies in the New World,* ed. Charles D. Trombold, pp. 111–31. Cambridge: Cambridge University Press.

Winslowe, John R. (pseud. Gladwell Richardson). 1969. Ancient Salt Trails. *True West* (August): 26–29, 42.

Witcher, Robert. 1998. Roman Roads: Phenomenological Perspectives on Roads in the Landscape. In *TRAC 97: Proceedings of the Seventh Annual Theoretical Roman Archaeology Conference,* ed. Colin Forcey, John Hawthorne, and Robert Witcher, pp. 60–70. Oxford: Oxbow Books.

Wood, W. R. 1972. Contrastive Features of Native North American Trade Systems. In *For the Chief,* ed. F. W. Voget and R. L. Stephenson, pp. 153–69. University of Oregon Anthropological Papers 4. Eugene, OR.

—— 1993. Hidatsa Origins and Relationships. In *The Phase I Archeological Research Program for the Knife River Indian Villages National Historic Site, Part II: Ethnohistorical Studies,* ed. T. D. Thiessen, pp. 11–28. Lincoln, NE: National Park Service Midwest Archeological Center.

——, ed. 1980. *The Explorations of the La Verendryes in the Northern Plains, 1738–43.* Lincoln, NE: University of Nebraska Press.

Wood, W. R., and T. D. Thiessen, eds. 1985. *Early Fur Trade on the Northern Plains: Canadian Traders among the Mandan and Hidatsa Indians, 1738–1818.* Norman, OK: University of Oklahoma Press.

Wright, Henry T. 2003. Archaeological Survey in the Eastern Desert Conducted by the University of Michigan and the University of Asiut: Interim Report. In *Excavations at Coptos (Qift) in Upper Egypt 1987–1992,* pp. 225–32. *Journal of Roman Archaeology* Supplementary Series no. 53.

Wust, I., and C. Barreto. 1999. The Ring Villages of Central Brazil: A Challenge for Amazonian Archaeology. *Latin American Antiquity* 10(1): 1–21.

Wylie, Alison. 1985. The Reaction Against Analogy. In *Advances in Archaeo-*

logical Method and Theory 8, ed. Michael B. Schiffer, pp. 63–111. New York: Academic.

Yoffee, N. 2005. *Myths of the Archaic State: Evolution of the Earliest Cities, States, and Civilizations.* Cambridge: Cambridge University Press.

Young, J. H. 1956. Greek Roads in South Attica. *Antiquity* 30(118): 94–97.

Zedeño, Maria Nieves. 1997. Landscape, Land Use, and the History of Territory Formation: An Example from the Puebloan Southwest. *Journal of Archaeological Method and Theory* 4:67–103.

—— 2000. On What People Make of Places—A Behavioral Cartography. In *Social Theory in Archaeology,* ed. M. B. Schiffer, pp. 97–111. Salt Lake City, UT: University of Utah Press.

Zedeño, Maria Nieves, Fletcher Chmara-Huff, Alex Carroll, and Rebecca Toupal. 2006. *Red Spring to Cane Spring: Landscapes of Movement along the Greater Belted Range.* Tucson, AZ: Bureau of Applied Research in Anthropology, University of Arizona.

Zedeño, M. N., K. Hollenback, C. Basaldú, V. Fletcher, and S. Miller. 2006. *Cultural Affiliation and Ethnographic Assessment of Three National Park Units, North Dakota.* Tucson, AZ: Bureau of Applied Research in Anthropology, University of Arizona.

Zedeño, Maria Nieves, Samrat Miller, Kacy Hollenback, and John Murray. 2007. *Blackfeet Sacred Site Protection along the Birch Creek Watershed, Lewis and Clark National Forest, Montana.* Tucson, AZ: Bureau of Applied Research in Anthropology, University of Arizona.

Zedeño, Maria Nieves, and Richard W. Stoffle. 2003. Tracking the Role of Pathways in the Evolution of a Human Landscape: The St. Croix Riverway in Ethnohistorical Perspective. In *Colonization of Unfamiliar Landscapes: The Archaeology of Adaptation,* ed. Marcy Rockman and James Steele, pp. 59–80. London: Routledge.

Contributors

James E. Snead, Ph.D.
Assoc. Prof., Dept. of Sociology and
    Anthropology
George Mason University
4400 University Drive – MS 3G5
Fairfax, VA 22030

Clark L. Erickson, Ph.D.
Assoc. Prof., Dept. of Anthropology
(Assoc. Curator, American Section,
    Penn Museum)
University of Pennsylvania
3260 South Street
Philadelphia, PA 19104-6324

J. Andrew Darling, Ph.D.
Coordinator, Cultural Resource
    Management Program
Gila River Indian Community
P.O. Box 2140
Sacaton, AZ 85247

G. Lennis Berlin, Ph.D.
Dept. of Geography and Public
    Planning
Southwest Forest Science Complex
    (Bldg. 82), Rm. 119
P.O. Box 15016
Flagstaff, AZ 86011-5016

Timothy Earle, Ph.D.
Dept. of Anthropology
Northwestern University
1810 Hinman Ave.
Evanston, IL 60208

T. J. Ferguson, Ph.D.
Anthropological Research, LLC
5000 W. Placita de los Vientos
Tucson, AZ 85745

Catherine S. Fowler, Ph.D.
Dept. of Anthropology (096)
Univ. of Nevada, Reno
Reno, NV 89557

Calvin Grinnell, Resource
    Specialist
Cultural Preservation Office
Mandan Hidatsa Arikara Nation
404 Frontage Road
New Town, ND 58763

Kacy Hollenback
Doctoral Student
Dept. of Anthropology
Haury Bldg. #30
University of Arizona
Tucson, AZ 85711

Angela H. Keller, Ph.D.
Dept. of Anthropology
University of California, Riverside
1334 Watkins Hall
900 University Avenue
Riverside, California 92521-0418

Leigh J. Kuwanwisiwma
Hopi Cultural Preservation Office
P.O. Box 12378
Kykolsmovi, AZ 86039

Payson Sheets, Ph.D.
Dept. of Anthropology
University of Colorado, Boulder
1350 Pleasant St.
Hale Sciences 350/233
Boulder, CO 80309-0233

Jason Alik Ur, Ph.D.
Dept. of Anthropology
Harvard University
Peabody Museum
11 Divinity Ave.
Cambridge, MA 02138

John H. Walker, Ph.D.
Dept. of Anthropology
University of Central Florida
4000 Central Florida Blvd.
Orlando, FL 32816-1360

Maria Nieves Zedeño, Ph. D.
Anthropology Bldg. #30
University of Arizona
Tucson, AZ 85711